Critical Issues on Changing Dynamics in Employee Relations and Workforce Diversity

Radha Yadav
Dayananda Sagar University, India

Priyanka Panday
Doon Business School, India

Naman Sharma
Indian Institute of Foreign Trade, India

A volume in the Advances in Human Resources Management and Organizational Development (AHRMOD) Book Series

IGI Global
PUBLISHER of TIMELY KNOWLEDGE

Published in the United States of America by
IGI Global
Business Science Reference (an imprint of IGI Global)
701 E. Chocolate Avenue
Hershey PA, USA 17033
Tel: 717-533-8845
Fax: 717-533-8661
E-mail: cust@igi-global.com
Web site: http://www.igi-global.com

Library of Congress Cataloging-in-Publication Data

Names: Yadav, Radha, 1988- editor. | Panday, Priyanka, 1989- editor. | Sharma, Naman, 1986- editor.
Title: Critical issues on changing dynamics in employee relations and workforce diversity / Radha Yadav, Priyanka Panday, and Naman Sharma, editors.
Description: Hershey : Business Science Reference, 2020. | Includes bibliographical references and index. | Summary: "This book addresses the challenges and issues pertaining to the changing dynamics of employee relations and provides additional support to better deal with critical issues related to people management"-- Provided by publisher.
Identifiers: LCCN 2019054344 (print) | LCCN 2019054345 (ebook) | ISBN 9781799835158 (hardcover) | ISBN 9781799835165 (paperback) | ISBN 9781799835172 (ebook)
Subjects: LCSH: Industrial relations. | Diversity in the workplace. | Personnel management.
Classification: LCC HD6971 .C845 2020 (print) | LCC HD6971 (ebook) | DDC 658.3--dc23
LC record available at https://lccn.loc.gov/2019054344
LC ebook record available at https://lccn.loc.gov/2019054345

This book is published in the IGI Global book series Advances in Human Resources Management and Organizational Development (AHRMOD) (ISSN: 2327-3372; eISSN: 2327-3380)

British Cataloguing in Publication Data
A Cataloguing in Publication record for this book is available from the British Library.

For electronic access to this publication, please contact: eresources@igi-global.com.

Advances in Human Resources Management and Organizational Development (AHRMOD) Book Series

ISSN:2327-3372
EISSN:2327-3380

Editor-in-Chief: Patricia Ordóñez de Pablos, Universidad de Oviedo, Spain

MISSION

A solid foundation is essential to the development and success of any organization and can be accomplished through the effective and careful management of an organization's human capital. Research in human resources management and organizational development is necessary in providing business leaders with the tools and methodologies which will assist in the development and maintenance of their organizational structure.

The **Advances in Human Resources Management and Organizational Development (AHRMOD) Book Series** aims to publish the latest research on all aspects of human resources as well as the latest methodologies, tools, and theories regarding organizational development and sustainability. The **AHRMOD Book Series** intends to provide business professionals, managers, researchers, and students with the necessary resources to effectively develop and implement organizational strategies.

COVERAGE

- Skills Management
- Human Relations Movement
- Entrepreneurialism
- Executive Compensation
- Personnel Retention
- Compliance
- Job Enrichment
- Process Improvement
- Organizational Behavior
- Corporate Governance

IGI Global is currently accepting manuscripts for publication within this series. To submit a proposal for a volume in this series, please contact our Acquisition Editors at Acquisitions@igi-global.com or visit: http://www.igi-global.com/publish/.

The Advances in Human Resources Management and Organizational Development (AHRMOD) Book Series (ISSN 2327-3372) is published by IGI Global, 701 E. Chocolate Avenue, Hershey, PA 17033-1240, USA, www.igi-global.com. This series is composed of titles available for purchase individually; each title is edited to be contextually exclusive from any other title within the series. For pricing and ordering information please visit http://www.igi-global.com/book-series/advances-human-resources-management-organizational/73670. Postmaster: Send all address changes to above address.

Titles in this Series

For a list of additional titles in this series, please visit:
http://www.igi-global.com/book-series/advances-human-resources-management-organizational/73670

Future of Work, Work-Family Satisfaction, and Employee Well-Being in the Fourth Industrial Revolution
Ethel Ndidiamaka Abe (University of KwaZulu-Natal, South Africa)
Business Science Reference • © 2021 • 382pp • H/C (ISBN: 9781799833475) • US $215.00

Handbook of Research on Cyberbullying and Online Harassment in the Workplace
Leslie Ramos Salazar (West Texas A&M University, USA)
Business Science Reference • © 2021 • 717pp • H/C (ISBN: 9781799849124) • US $265.00

Integration and Application of Business Graduate and Business Leader Competency-Models
Donta S. Harper (University of Washington, USA)
Business Science Reference • © 2021 • 275pp • H/C (ISBN: 9781799865377) • US $195.00

Human Resource Management Practices for Promoting Sustainability
Sulaiman Olusegun Atiku (Naimbia University of Science and Technology, Namibia) and Tinuke Fapohunda (Lagos State University, Nigeria)
Business Science Reference • © 2021 • 326pp • H/C (ISBN: 9781799845225) • US $195.00

Effective Strategies for Communicating Insights in Business
Ross Jackson (Wittenberg University, USA) and Amanda Reboulet (Air Force Civilian Service, USA)
Business Science Reference • © 2021 • 330pp • H/C (ISBN: 9781799839644) • US $195.00

Anywhere Working and the Future of Work
Yvette Blount (Macquarie University, Australia) and Marianne Gloet (University of Melbourne, Australia)
Business Science Reference • © 2021 • 287pp • H/C (ISBN: 9781799841593) • US $195.00

For an entire list of titles in this series, please visit:
http://www.igi-global.com/book-series/advances-human-resources-management-organizational/73670

IGI Global
PUBLISHER of TIMELY KNOWLEDGE

701 East Chocolate Avenue, Hershey, PA 17033, USA
Tel: 717-533-8845 x100 • Fax: 717-533-8661
E-Mail: cust@igi-global.com • www.igi-global.com

Table of Contents

Detailed Table of Contents

are popular in the management area. In this perspective, ethics is one of the most significant issues in both business and social life. Enhancement of negative work outcomes triggers the efforts for the establishment of ethical climates. Increase of the workplace deviance of employees also influences the need of moderating variables in the relationship between ethical climates and deviance. This chapter mentions ethical climate, workplace deviance, and mindfulness. Moreover, relations between variables are discussed in reference to the literature.

Despite many challenges ahead, the state-owned enterprises' roadmap to establish several new forms of holdings are still progressing in Indonesia. Indonesia's government believes that holdings are the best answer to manage all of 143 remaining state-owned enterprises for ease of control, efficiency, effectiveness in operations, and as a driver to boost bigger profit as well. Based on evidence in the state-owned enterprise PT Semen Indonesia's holding, the holding is tending to ignore labor's welfare. Welfare attention has diverted, and unfortunately, only a few are discussing about labor and its rights, especially in justifying distributing annually bonuses. This chapter investigates that holdings' implementation in Indonesia is significantly contrary in terms of labor's views compared with the original theory to build strong corporations for developing better welfare for all parties.

In global scenario it is necessity for all the organizations to employ diversified workforces. Workforce diversity helps the organization in improving productivity and innovative performance. The workforce diversity and inclusion strategies are directly linked to innovative business; they encourage employees to have different perspectives and ideas which drive innovation. To deal with global challenges through innovative performance, organizations have robust programs and policies to recruit and retain diversified workforces. Through this chapter, the author addresses how workforce diversity is fostering innovation in contemporary organizations.

This study develops an integrative model in order to identify the underlying factors that drive employees to engage in social media at work for businesses. More specifically, the model explains the interplay between employment statuses, motivation, job satisfaction, and social activities for the purpose of analyzing the positive effects of social media use and the negative effects of social media overload on social media policy implementation. Nevertheless, the model proposes a research roadmap can be examined by utilizing a framework for the assessment of the use of social media at work, as a tool to improve business organizations. Finally, it concludes with the discussion of several open issues and cutting-edge challenges.

The advent of m-commerce has contributed significantly to the evolution of the digital media environment. Today, almost everything (i.e., the exchange of goods, services, payments, and access of information) is growing fast via electronic media. The purpose of this chapter is to find the relationship between the customers and employees engaged in the m-commerce world. For doing this, researchers did a systematic review of the literature and found that if the digital companies provide a good quality of services to their employees and customers, they both engaged in the m-commerce world. As the digital world has a two-way communication mode, companies should work upon different types of strategies (i.e., to provide a better platform to their current offerings and should incorporate the valuable customers and employee feedback for improving the image of their offerings). There are several techniques that help the companies to engage their customers like gamification and artificial intelligence.

Preface

In today's scenario, the concept of industrial relation, which was primarily responsible for following labor legislation and maintaining the compliance function, has been replaced by the "Employee Relation" concept. HR has widened its horizon and has conveyed the idea of becoming a "Business partner." Many organizations are struggling to change the HR processes and technologies. New thinking and new visions are required to achieve business success. All competitive business factors have become commoditized, and talent is the ultimate driving factor for business success. The introduction of the new economic policy in 1991 had a significant bearing on industrial relations. Coupled with liberalization, policies changed the way industries functioned in India. It forced the government, employers, and trade unions to align themselves to new realities. There is an ongoing transition in industrial relations on a global scale as well. The focus is gradually shifting from traditional industrial relations, characterized by conflict resolution, to employee relations management, characterized by collaborative partnerships between the employers and the employees. Employee Relations Management focuses on this ongoing transition from industrial relations to employee relations.

Chapter 1 describes the Strategies for Harnessing the Changing Nature of Human Resources with a Special Focus on Diversity. The world is witnessing a fourth industrial revolution characterized by an unpredictable environment in which disruptive technologies and trends change the way humans live and work. While organizations are grappling with the fast-paced external environment's challenges, the last decade has also witnessed the changing nature of human resources, posing difficulties for the future of work. Millennials are entering the current workforce with high levels of education, substantial career aspirations, and faster growth in the organization, resulting in high attrition rates. This chapter focuses on understanding employee relations' changing nature concerning employee diversity and its role in managing employee retention.

Chapter 2 discusses the Challenges and Opportunities in Managing Employee Relations in Multinational Firms. The multinational firm (MNCs) operating in various countries or institutional contexts face a unique form of employee relationship management challenges. The chapter identifies language differences in diverse cultural contexts, staffing mix in various foreign subsidiaries, work-life balance, power conflict between parent firm and subsidiary, and virtual team management as significant employee relation challenges MNCs. The chapter provides strategic leadership to these challenges to have competitive advantages and practical recommendations for the MNCs managers based on the existing literature. Finally, the chapter also offers various gaps in the literature to be explored by future researchers.

Chapter 3 explains employee relations as a Tool of Strategic Competitive Environment; Challenging and ever-changing market scenario made it difficult for organizations to be different and sustain in the market. While having innovative products, USP (Unique Selling Proposition), and the like are on one side of the competition, attracting and retaining employees has emerged to become one of the organizations' critical concerns. This chapter explains how employee relations help organizations retaining employees and gain a competitive edge. This strategy will further help understand how these changes will impact the work and how the management can overcome the aftereffects by maintaining good employee relations.

Chapter 4 explores the relationship between Ethical Climate, Workplace Deviant, and Mindfulness. Postmodern organizational approaches in the knowledge-based business environment play a significant role in gaining the importance of knowledge-based talents and skills. Moreover, corporate governance-related progress impacts the structures and implications of organizations. Enterprises must follow the rules required by the age and regard the innovations to maintain their assets and provide a competitive advantage. For that reason, human-related innovations and practices get popular day by day in the management area. An increase in employees' workplace deviance also influences the need for moderating variables in the relationship between ethical climates and deviance. In this chapter, it was mentioned about the moral environment, workplace deviance, and mindfulness.

Chapter 5 focuses on explaining the impact of Ignoring Commitment of Labor's Welfare. This study is an empirical study based on Indonesian State-owned Enterprise (SOE) having sparking concerns and attracting great public attention throughout Indonesia. Amidst uncertainty within laws and politics - worsen by many leaders' vested personal interest- establishing many holdings based on the PT Semen Indonesia (PTSI) holding is unavoidably triggering fierce disputes. Many mandatory tasks require adjustments, and the consequences are wasting time and expenses; even more, the organization is severely suffering, especially leadership issues.

Chapter 6 explores workforce diversity is a more disputable topic in today's global business environment. Managing workforce diversity is a significant task for organizations as it affects the organization's performance, productivity, and innovativeness. As the term workforce diversity is becoming a trend after the liberalization of markets, many researchers have studied this topic from various perspectives and disciplines. This chapter deals with the conceptual review of workforce diversity and innovation and emphasizes how diversity will foster an organization's innovation performance. Research indicates that innovation gives the seeds for monetary growth. Design in a company context is about remodeling thinking into a new process, product, or service to generate a competitive advantage. For that innovation to show up depends as much on collective difference as on combination ability. If people assume alike, then no matter how clever they are, they most possibly will get stuck at the identical regionally most advantageous solutions. Finding new and better solutions, innovating requires thinking differently. If you convey many extraordinary views to a problem, you end up with more effective, innovative solutions. Workplace diversity can make sure there is a giant pool of knowledge, skills, existence experience, perspectives, and expertise. That's why diversity powers innovation.

Chapter 7, from a research perspective, sets a broad agenda for future research. Social media has become one of the most dominant tools for marketing and networking for firms operating in the business system. However, reviewing and synthesizing the literature indicates a gap in the area of social media use behavior of firms in dealing with online networks to increase their performance. This chapter helps fill up this gap and find out the connection between intention and usage is amplified or diminished depending on the employee's status, motivation, and job satisfaction, consistent with the idea that goals and mentalities differ across business departments.

Chapter 8 explores the employees' Attitude and Perception of Electronic Monitoring Surveillance Affecting Employee Behavior. It shows a positive attitude that led to their positive perception and resulted in their positive work behavior. The other organization indicates that if they properly communicate their purpose of using any, the employees will hold the right attitude and perception towards EMS and improve work behavior.

Chapter 9 explains the Dynamics of Employee Relationships in a Digitalized Workplace and its impact on workplace culture. Today's workstations are connected environments ensuring instant access to other employees and anything that employees need for work; this goes beyond any communication barrier. As a result, it is changing employee experiences to better engaged, innovative, and efficient ones. The chapter also talks about the related implications of media richness theory, media synchronicity theory, and media multiplicity theory at the workplace with particular reference to the digitalized work environment and virtual reality. Further, the chapter discusses the challenges of cyberloafing and Phubbing as consequences of the digitalized workplace and how those affect performance and employee relations.

Chapter 10 describes the factors of Change, like an Organization and Its Work. In today's sphere, varied personnel is flattering the norm. No organization or association in this world of globalization would endure without the changes for upbringing;

Exploiting on the possible welfares of changes, organizations may achieve a modest benefit in inventiveness, modernization, worldwide thoughts, problem-solving, and flexibility.

Chapter 11 discusses the Change in Nature of an Organization and Its Work. It's obvious- deviations are entirely around us. As the situation is promptly fluctuating, in today's sphere of globalization, the structure, pattern, and work process are changing drastically, and working for an organization that is likely to be very different due to competitive pressures and technological breakthroughs. Now the organizational work is more focused on technical competence, Workforce diversity, teamwork, leadership, social-based skills, strategic planning, cross-culture training, and effective communication, which holds the keys to the organization's growth. As the work environment's nature continues to change, new trends have emerged at the individual, team, and organizational levels.

Chapter 12 talks about Motivations and Challenges of Female Truck Drivers in the UK. Distribution and freight transportation plays a significant role in developing a region, but the sector is usually a male-dominated one. Considering the shortage of drivers in some countries such as the UK and the lack of studies investigating the challenges female drivers face, it is crucial to identify motivations and challenges. Identifying challenges would help to promote the industry to more female drivers. Thus, the paper aims to discover the main reasons and challenges and find if females feel they are treated equally to males within this industry. Accordingly, a qualitative study is designed, and a total of 16 interviews have been conducted with female truck drivers in the UK.

Chapter 13 demonstrates the impact of motivation on the type of organization they work. This study focuses on the motivational structures of physicians belonging to private and public health and also outline a neuroimaging methodology which would prove useful to identify the neurocognitive motivational systems of hospital physicians with the proposes the design of several intrasubject laboratory experiments, using the functional neuroimaging technique Magnetic Resonance Imaging (FMRI).

The book presents the fundamentals of employee relations and contemporary issues and addresses the critical challenges for employees' effective management. Each chapter highlights employee relations, managing for creativity and innovation, attracting and retaining talent, managing sustainability, and identifying new directions for Employee relation. The text includes numerous pedagogical features such as extensively worked industrial analysis that provides a sound basis for teaching and students. It successfully reinforces the link between theory practice and critical thinking.

Acknowledgment

We are grateful to several people associated with this book project, including the authors, editorial board members, IGI-Global's editorial team and reviewers. This book would not have been possible without their kind support.

Most of all, we are indebted to all the contributors to this book. All chapters included in the book were found to be an essential component without which this book would have remained incomplete. We are also grateful to every one of our editorial board members and chapter reviewers for their meticulous efforts and precious time to help us improve the quality of the content included in the book. We also want to acknowledge that few selected authors also served as the reviewers for the book. We duly appreciate their extra efforts in improving the overall book quality.

In the end, we are forever grateful to our families for their patience and selfless support to us in the completion of this book on time.

Radha Yadav

Priyanka Panday

Naman Sharma

Chapter 1
Strategies for Harnessing the Changing Nature of Human Resources With a Special Focus on Diversity

Betty Sibil
https://orcid.org/0000-0001-5797-1017
Pillai Institute of Management Studies and Research, India

Celina Joy
Pillai Institute of Management Studies and Research, India

ABSTRACT

The world is witnessing a fourth industrial revolution characterized by an unpredictable environment in which disruptive technologies and trends are changing the way humans live and work. While organisations are grappling with the challenges of the fast-paced external environment, the last decade has also witnessed the changing nature of human resource posing difficulties for the future of work. Millennials are entering the current workforce with high levels of education, huge career aspirations, and seeking a faster pace of growth in the organization resulting in high attrition rates. Traditional policies and practices of employee relations which steered human resources in the past may be inadequate to meet the growing challenges of organizations in the 21st century. This chapter will be an attempt to gain a deeper understanding of the changing nature of employee relations with respect to employee diversity and how it can be used as an employee retention tool in the rapidly changing environment.

DOI: 10.4018/978-1-7998-3515-8.ch001

INTRODUCTION

The world is at the cusp of the fourth industrial revolution. Moving on from using water and steam in the first industrial revolution to using electric power and Information Technology in the second and third industrial revolution respectively, the fourth industrial revolution amalgamates various technologies such as artificial intelligence (AI), the internet of things (IoT), autonomous vehicles, 5G telephony, nanotechnology, robotics, and the like. Globalisation and intense competition have also added to the woes of industry. These disruptions have affected all the factors of production in business especially people and the future of work. Referring to the report released by the Global Commission on The Future of Work, at the centenary celebrations of ILO (International Labour Organisation) in April 2019, India's Deputy Permanent Representative to the UN Ambassador K Nagaraj Naidu said that the country needs a "human-centred agenda" for the future of work that strengthens the social contract by placing people and the work they do at the centre of economic and social policy and business practice.

The challenges in business due to mergers and acquisitions, take overs, amalgamations, insolvency, bankruptcy, liquidity crunch, fluctuating exchange rates, volatile stock markets, to name a few, are on the rise. While these disruptions affect the external environment in which organizations thrive, it also brings unprecedented chaos in the labour market adding unpredictability to the future of work, requiring people's opportunities and well-being to be localized and re-examined. Automation may also make some jobs redundant in the near future. India is at an advantage as it can reap its demographic advantage as more than 50 per cent of its population is below the age of 25 and more than 65% below the age of 35.

While these external factors affect business dramatically, there are many internal factors that can be harnessed to negate its spiralling effect. One such factor is Human Resources of an organization. Most of these external challenges can be mitigated to a certain extent by harnessing the workforce to rise up to the occasion and face these challenges. Another promising trend is the increasing workforce diversity in organisations. While diversity brings along increased creativity and productivity, it can be counterproductive if not managed in a humane manner. It is here that the role of Employee Relations comes to the fore. Employee relations can be defined as a company's efforts to manage relationships between employees and employers. Good employee relations aim to create policies and processes which treat all employees with fairness and consistency.

What is it that the organizations of the 21st century are making available to their employees? Is it an organization that is synonymous with learning and growth? Or is it a creative environment with freedom to experiment and explore? Is it facilities and flexibility or is it opportunities to work on issues that have a far reaching impact like social initiatives? Will workforce diversity be the game changer? This chapter will be an attempt to gain a deeper understanding of employee relations and its changing nature and how it can be used as an employee retention tool. It will try to throw light on an employee's expectations from his/her job. It will also try and identify the employee relation practices adopted by the new-age organizations in creating environments that are more inclusive and engaging.

BACKGROUND

Employee Relations is again in the limelight in view of the rapidly changing business environment and the changing nature of the workforce. Human resources are the only unique invaluable resource that can be utilized to mitigate the threats of the rapidly changing business environment. Creating and maintaining harmonious employee relations is one of the most effective ways to retain employees and has the potential to become a stabilizing factor to attain high productivity. Employee relations are a potent mechanism that is within the control of the management and can be used to create a conducive working environment. Good employee relations must focus on employee friendly creative workplaces. Fairness plays a big part in maintaining good employee relations.

Employees are intangible assets that possess unique qualities. These unique qualities have the potential to add value in an exponential manner if mobilised in the right direction. All other factors of production can be replicated but employees and their distinctive skill sets are difficult to duplicate. These skilled and motivated people are central to the operations of any company that wishes to flourish in the new age (Bartlett and Ghoshal, 2002). Today there is a surplus of capital chasing a scarce resource, talented people and the knowledge they possess. Talented people are the constraining force and hence a strategic resource (Bartlett and Ghoshal, 2002). There is a shift in the way talented people are being viewed. Organisations no longer view them as mere factors of production to be mobilised, but as a resourceful talent to be invested in. As investors of talent they are justified in expecting beneficial returns.

The essence of employee relations is to build strong relations between managers and employees based on trust, fairness and mutual respect. A good employee relations climate leads to a motivated workforce that help enhance the performance of the organization. Employees are valuable resources that help organizations in achieving goals (Daniel, 2003). Lower levels of job satisfaction in large firms may be due to weak management-employee relations. Improving management-employee relations will not only increase satisfaction but also increase productivity and reduce turnover (Tansel & Gazioglu, 2003)

This change in ideology of looking at employees, not as assets but as investors has led to a paradigm shift in the employee relations strategies that are adopted to engage and retain employees (Kaye, Beverly; Jordan-Evans, Sharon, 2003). The focus now needs to shift to employee retention strategies that are valued by employees rather than strategies that aim to reduce turnover in the organisation (Vos, Meganck, 2009). It therefore becomes imperative to identify aspects that employees value and design initiatives that engages them in a meaningful manner.

EMPLOYEE RELATIONS - ISSUES

The last decade has also witnessed the changing nature of human resource which has in turn created a lot of challenges for the future of work. Millennials are entering the current workforce with high levels of education, huge career aspirations and seeking a faster pace of growth in the organization. This has resulted in high attrition rates which are further compounded by global opportunities for work. All this has made employee retention a big challenge.

There have been multiple studies that indicate a relation between employee engagement and financial performance of organizations (Bates, 2004; Baumruk, 2004; Harter et al., 2002; Richman, 2006). There have also been studies that predict a strong positive correlation between the quality of work-life factors and reduced absenteeism and turnover, high goal commitment, and increased performance and productivity (Curry, 1986; Futrell and Parasuraman, 1984; Motowidlo, 1984). All these studies point to the fact that engaged employees can make a huge difference to organizations. Working environment is a major factor that predicts employee engagement and organizations must focus specifically to ascertain a great environment for employees to work. (Anitha J., 2014). A powerful and influential mechanism to guarantee such an environment would be through its employee relations programs. Change and innovation in employee relations practices, thus is important in a dynamic and competitive environment is essential so that an organization may gain competitive advantage (Gennard, Judge, 2005)

In their book on Employee Relations, authors John Gennard and Graham Judge have emphasised the importance of employee relations to all organizations and not just to organizations that deal with worker unions. With time the nature of employee relations has evolved to encompass all types of jobs and organizations be it unionised or non-unionised. The authors also focus attention on how environmental changes over the past few decades have led to substantial changes in the way employee relations strategies have evolved (Gennard & Judge, 2005). According to Gennard and Judge a deeper understanding of the corporate environment and its impact on employee relations can help employee relation managers-professionals in mitigating risks associated with the same.

DIVERSITY - ISSUES, CONTROVERSIES & PROBLEMS

Workforce Diversity - Perspective

Employee relations today can be described as the individual relation that each employee has with his/her employer (Lewis, P, Thornhill, A and Saunders, M 2003). This emphasises the uniqueness of the concept and the relationship and the fact that a blanket approach cannot be adopted to maintain positive relations with all stakeholders.

In recent times the corporate world has seen increased discussion and debates on diversity and its implications on minority employees at the workplace (Zanoni and Janssens, 2007). The publication of the Workforce 2000 Report can be described as a defining moment in propelling diversity related research. This report predicted massive changes in demography which would compel organizations to revisit and modify their hiring and other such important HR strategies. As per the report, by the year 2000 employee demographics would have undergone considerable change. Corporations across the world would have considered the report as a bellwether of major changes to come and would have initiated changes to deal with this demographic discord. In the subsequent time period multiple researchers have attempted to define diversity and create categories to gain a deeper understanding of the concept and to facilitate research.

As per (Daniels and Macdonald, 2005) broadly there are three types of diversity. Social category diversity, informational diversity and value diversity. Social diversity is the diversity relating to demographic characteristics like age, gender, race etc. Informational diversity is the diversity with respect to background such as education, knowledge, experience, etc. Value diversity is the diversity pertaining to the deeper level of differences of a psychological nature like attitude, personality etc. In Industrial-Organizational (I-O) Psychology diversity mean differences with respect to ethnicity, race, gender, sexual orientation, age, religion, social class, disability, nationality, etc.

The diversity of today's workforce accentuates the need to customise employee relations to satisfy the requirements of this diverse workforce. At the same time, the nature of human resources has also undergone a tremendous change. The corporate world is witnessing a scenario where it has to cope with the challenges of attracting, motivating and retaining employees spanning four distinct generations. Factors such as immigration and employee mobility have led to an increase in ethnic and religious diversity at the workplace. The gender representation in the workforce remains skewed but signs of normalization have set in which means that today there are more number of women in the workforce there by boosting gender diversity. Increased awareness about one's sexual orientation and the social phenomenon of coming out in the open about it also adds to the diversity existing in organizations. Organizations have identified the advantage of including differently abled people in the workforce thereby increasing ability-related diversity. This diversity gives organizations the much needed edge to be ahead of the competition, to be more creative and innovative, and to deal with change. As expected, diversity co-occurs with differences in principles, preference (likes and dislikes) and perspectives (point of view). And differences can lead to difficulties. Difficulties arising from having to deal with heterogeneous populations.

In such circumstances the organization yields substantial power in the manner in which it manages and revamps employee relations. As per Lin Grensing-Pophal today organizations are witnessing five generations at the workplace namely the Traditionalists, Baby Boomers, Generation X, Generation Y and Generation Z. With an increasingly diverse workforce at hand employee relations can be the mechanism to help inculcate a feeling of equal opportunities. This helps in promoting an internal environment that emphasizes on fairness and projects a similar positive signal to all internal and external stakeholders namely prospective employees, suppliers, customers etc. It will also thwart/eliminate any external threats of the organization being entangled in litigation pertaining to discriminatory policies. Employee relations thus plays a dual role of optimizing an opportunity and negating a threat.

Workforce Diversity - Problems and Controversies

There are multiple studies to prove that diversity management is complicated and may not be a straightforward activity. The dynamics related to diversity management have undercurrents that makes it difficult to assess and estimate the repercussions and implications of the various diversity related inclusive initiatives constituted at the workplace.

Even though all these factors lead to diversity, each one does not merit equal attention. Few of the factors lead to a more serious disadvantage to the group in a workplace scenario than the others. As per Hays-Thomas (2004) diversity would focus on groups that have systematically been victims of workplace discrimination and opperession due to them belonging to such a group. Diversity can be derived from differences between gender, ethnicity, function, nationality, language, ability, religion, lifestyle or tenure (Kosek and Lobel, 1995). Diversity can be referred to as the distribution of personal attributes among interdependent members of a work unit (Jackson, Joshi and Erhardt, 2003)

Diversity in the workplace can reduce lawsuits and enhance creativity at the workplace. It can also help in improving the brand image of the organization (Green et. al., 2012). Diversity of the workforce leads to multiple perspectives and creative solutions to problems and challenges. Research has given evidence of the fact that higher levels of diversity among senior management leads to higher organizational performance (Kravitz 2003). It was also predicted that gender diversity would have a positive impact on performance of an organization. Departures from a 50-50 ratio in gender diversity leads to a decrease in firm performance. Profitability is highest when female population is at a fifty percent level especially in firms that were a part of the services, retail or wholesale sector. Gender diversity is most beneficial in circumstances or situations where creative problem solving, decision making and solution finding is important. It is not very beneficial in situations where the work to be undertaken requires physical skills. The implications of the study is that gender diversity is most useful in department like marketing and human resources where the above mentioned skills sets like creative decision making are important and have a bearing on the performance of the organisation. Gender diversity is also important at the top management level where it is important to have the ability to work and make decisions in different environments. Nemeth (1986) in his study mentioned that heterogeneous groups with minority members were more effective in generating creative ideas than homogenous groups.

However, the issue of diversity and the various measures taken by organizations to create inclusive environments may have a controversial side to it, as it may be looked at with contempt by people who are not beneficiaries of the same. It may on the contrary do more harm in the form of resentment and non-responsiveness towards people who belong to these minority groups (Allison, 1999). In spite of their belief in equal opportunity policies, numerous organizations have practices that are not completely of an inclusive nature. Through such practices, knowingly or unknowingly, they seem to limit the opportunities/options that they make available to their important stakeholders like customers and employees. Also there is a tendency for people to treat affirmative action (AA), equal employment opportunities (EEO) and diversity management as synonyms. If diversity management is same as EEO and AA then the problems that plagued the latter will also be applicable to diversity management. This approach can be detrimental for diversity management (Cox Jr. and Beale, 1997)

Diversity management involves understanding the value of differences, combating discrimination and promoting inclusiveness (Green, et al 2008). Negative attitudes and behaviours are the predominant barriers to diversity. HR practices that may have traces of these behavioural patterns can be detrimental to diversity at the workplace. HR managers must try and devise mechanisms that are devoid of the above mentioned biases. Human beings prefer to work in groups that are homogenous and this can be one factor that hinders diversity in organizations (Kreitz 2007) There may be an argument that minorities benefit from diversity -inclusive practices and that they do not deserve the positions that they hold (Kalev, Dobbin and Kelly, 2007)

Some of the inclusive practices with respect to diversity management in earlier years was limited to targeted recruitment and training programs that were adopted as per the OFCCP's guidelines for affirmative action (AA). As per Kelly and Dobbin (1998) these were among the most aggressive efforts that employers made on behalf of women and minorities, but they were among the most likely to face legal and political challenges and backlash, and thus became candidates for deinstitutionalization. AA initiatives were many a times judged as being of a preferential nature and were misinterpreted as a quota system that gave rise to preferential selection (Oswick and Noon, 2014)

Diversity is a double-edged sword and has the capacity to positively or negatively impact an organization depending on the way it is managed. Organizations that engage in practices that are perceived as fair practices with respect to diversity, they stand to reap the benefits of their actions in the long run. Feelings of having equal access to opportunities and fair treatment also have a positive relation with the retention capacity of organizations (Chrobot-Mason and Aramovich, 2013). In the same study it was observed organizations where employees feel a strong sense of identity, will have reduced likelihood of employee turnover.

INCLUSIVE PRACTICES TO BOOST DIVERSITY

As per CIPD Report on 'Diversity Management that Works - An Evidence-based View' of October 2019, diversity and inclusiveness initiatives at the workplace must pay attention to the organizational context in which the organization operates i.e. the location, size, sector etc.

One of the more defining works on diversity is the Hudson Institute Report, Workforce 2000 (Johnson and Packer, 1987). This report stated that diversity in terms of representation of women and ethnic minorities in the workforce would experience accelerated growth in the coming years. It stated that by the year 2000 only 15% of new entrants to the US workforce would be US-born white males. Bearing this in mind several organizations have proactively adopted practices of an inclusive nature. Practices that are different from the prescriptive Equal Employment Opportunities (EEO) and Affirmative Action. There are clear differences between EEO, AA and diversity management practices (Kelly and Dobbin, 1998). Some other organizations have been ignorant and chosen to continue with age old practices which lack elements of inclusivity.

Inclusive practices must go beyond addressing prejudice and discrimination issues and strive to achieve mechanisms of being more inclusive by which both the individual and organization stands to gain. Individuals should be able to be themselves and not feel the need to put up a pretense at any point in time; and in that way be able to contribute fully towards organizational endeavours (Ferdman and Sagiv, 2012.

Inclusive forms of leadership is critical for leveraging the diversity that exists within the workforce. It is not just an inclusive environment that is useful but also leaders who embrace diversity can help organizations in leveraging the benefits of diversity (Nishii & Mayer, 2009). The implications of the study are that leaders play an important role in engaging with diverse workforces and the nature of their interactions with them can prove beneficial to the organization.

Numerous studies confirm that benefits of employee diversity do not happen automatically. (Jackson, Joshi and Erhardt, 2003). Action steps have to be out in place to derive benefits from the diversity that exists within the employee workforce. One of the initiatives to enhance diversity is to encourage employees to increase levels of self-awareness which will help them in unravelling their individual biases with respect to diversity. (Green et. al, 2012). Once there is an awareness and understanding of one's inner biases, employees will be able to better manage and tune their reactions and responses in a pro-diversity environment. An on-going training initiative to enlighten employees on diversity and its benefits to an organization can be instrumental in reducing deviant behaviours with respect to diversity.

Training seems to be one of the predominant mechanisms used by organizations to address diversity issues. Many organizations also organize team training with other diversity-related initiatives as a diversity-intervention (Jackson, Joshi and Erhardt, 2003). Managing diversity also requires fundamental changes in the policies, procedures and culture of the organization. Multiple mechanisms applied concurrently can facilitate in creating an organization that not just reduces diversity based conflicts but also enhances the value that may be extracted from having such a workforce. 'Learning about Groups' can be another initiative through which employees can be sensitised regarding differences that exist within employee groups. Employees can be made aware of the stereotypes they have developed in their minds which creates hassles while interacting and working in high-diversity groups. Behavioural changes and creation of positive emotions towards other group members can go a long way in creating a productive, diverse workforce.

Mono-cropping leads to loss of biodiversity similarly mono-managing leads to loss of human-diversity at the workplace (Kreitz 2007). One approach to manage all employees may not be the most effective way to manage diversity. The concept of 'foxhole' diversity as given by Goldsmith and Thomas, 2003 may be one of the approaches that organizations can adopt with respect to diversity. While recruiting and selecting candidates what matters most is their skill sets and attitude and not race, gender, ethnicity, education, sexual orientation or geographic origin. This kind of a requirements-driven mental conditioning can go a long way in establishing an environment that is conducive for diversity.

Another diversity inclusive practice is to create a specialised position to achieve specific goals of increased diversity and inclusion. If diversity efforts are everybody's responsibility but no one's primary responsibility, then there is a high likelihood that these goals may not receive the required amount of attention and importance. Institutionalization of the diversity process is important whereby all organizational members are enthused to contribute towards diversity goals (Kalev, Dobbin and Kelly, 2007). As per Pless and Maak (2004) the 'Principle of Recognition' serves as an ideology on which a diversity-inclusive initiative can be based. Organizations should balance the need for individuals to be recognised as a unique person different from the rest and as a human being similar to others with corresponding essential needs. The essence is to recognize differences while looking for a common bond. The feeling of being different but equal to others, being their true selves not only in private but at their workplaces make people confident and motivated to give their best. But this also requires them to have a feeling of solidarity in relation to other members of the organization (Pless and Maak, 2004). Networking programs specifically for minorities can be initiated by employees or HR managers. These may take the form of meetings or seminars and conferences where members can meet and share information and career advice. These networks may also help in advocating policy changes and framing new policies (Kalev, Dobbin and Kelly, 2007).

Also by taking cognizance of inadvertent stigmatization and discrimination due to religion, organizations play a key role in creating environments in which diversity can thrive. Organizations must create workplaces in which disclosure of hidden identities are encouraged leading to an inclusive work environment. If employees have the freedom to live their real selves at their workplaces then they will be motivated and more engaged in their jobs (Reeves, McKinney & Azam, 2012). Encouraging underrepresented minority (URM) students to embrace their identities is critical for inclusion. When stereotypes are prevalent students normally cope by "fragmenting" their identities which can be detrimental to diversity initiatives (Puritty et al., 2017)

CURRENT PERSPECTIVES - EMPLOYEE RELATIONS AND DIVERSITY

The concept of Employee Relations and Diversity has been often debated and discussed in the light of its benefits to an organisation. Creating and sustaining good employee relations and increasing workforce diversity raises the overall productivity, brings in creativity and reduces conflicts while boosting morale. Human Resources are the most important manageable asset for any business. However, the perceived threats of working with employees spanning four distinct generations along with the increasing diversity in the workforce can be very exacting.

Today's millennials are not driven by the idea of simply getting a job for some money in return. They are looking for a sense of purpose. They want to be part of the organisation that has a well-defined mission and vision. They look for organisations that have strong mission that will have a meaningful impact on society. This strong sense of purpose resonates with their mind set.

Unlike the earlier generations, today's millennials attach a significant values to learning and creating. They are drawn to organisations that allow them to create and constantly innovate and think out of the box. They tend to avoid organizations that work in silos and restrict creative freedom while reprimanding failures.

The current generation also prefer lateral reporting structures with easier access to the senior management. They are constantly seeking to engage and be part of the decision making process. Some organizations have adhered to these factors and allow interns to also be a part of their internal working committees.

Flexibility is another aspect that can build strong employee relations. A rising trend among the millennials is the importance given to work life balance and pursuing further education or multiple hobbies outside of work. Flexibility in terms of timings, locations, work from home facilities etc. will not only attract workforce diversity, maintain gender balance but also result in higher engagement levels at work.

Another highlight of the current generation is that they like to engage with organisations that have a strong commitment to saving the environment whether it is using environment friendly equipment or using processes that generate less waste. They are conscious of the environmental impact of business.

Another interesting aspect of the current workforce is the level of diversity in organisations. Workforce diversity brings a lot of positives to the dynamics of the organisation. Diverse workforces always lend themselves to satisfied employee populations. Companies are gearing themselves more than ever to ensure D &I in their workforce and rather it has become a matter of pride in today's world.

DIVERSITY AND INCLUSIVE PRACTICES AT COGNIZANT TECHNOLOGIES

Organisations such as Cognizant Technologies that operates in over 80 countries over the globe in the IT services sector are constantly reinventing itself with the changing times. It employs a focused set of strategies when it comes to employee-relations with the belief that a balanced mix of process, technology and personalization is a key factor for different levels of seniority within the organization. Cognizant has a "young" workforce with the average age hovering at 25-27 years and their robust HR practices ensured that they do not discriminate or differentiate across the various diverse groups working in the organisation in terms of compensation, type of role or benefits. They actively promote an inclusive workforce strategy as it not only benefits the population that it's directed to but also ensures a harmonious workplace where everyone is able to interact with each other without any discomfort. Organizations like Cognizant continue to innovate and evolve newer ways of engagement with increasingly diverse workforce and deploy, amongst other things, awareness, technology, process, policy and physical facilitation. The company actively works with its customers to create new roles or modify current ones that cater to diverse populations and boost D&I not only at Cognizant's end but also at the Customer's.

Facility modernization for the differently-abled is also very important to them. Creating roles & employment for some differently-abled through infusion of technology is a significant item on their organization charter. In terms of skill diversity, they had employees with almost all of the technological skills based on their diverse client profiles, in addition to holding domain expertise across the functions. One third of their employees were women. However they do face challenges of gender due to local demographic dynamics in some of the countries they operate like India where there's a skew in the number of women available to take on senior roles with respect to men which is slowly straightening out over the past few years.

Some employee relation initiatives/practices followed by them to promote workforce diversity and inclusiveness include

- Creation of Diversity & Inclusion and Person with Disabilities Charters and specially focused teams to drive & execute this globally across the company
- D&I events conducted across the globe and sponsored by Cognizant
- Special recruitment drives for Women and Person with Disabilities evangelizing the roles available and the facilitation provided by the organisation
- Enhancement of benefits to make it conducive for the diverse community to continue to be successful in their roles - paternity/maternity packages, transport facilities for Person with Disabilities, investment in technology for PWD, extended medical benefits including LGBTQI community benefits
- Facility modernization investments for Person with Disabilities and LGBTQI
- Veteran Hiring in the USA
- Minority Hiring

SUGGESTIONS AND RECOMMENDATIONS

Employee Relations is an important controllable tool in the hands of the management which can be harnessed to increase employee engagement and workforce diversity. Companies can arrest employee attrition and enhance employee retention by considering workforce redeployment as a practice. Organisations can prepare employees with training and coaching and prepare them for these new roles. Showing employees the path for their career growth and supporting them with internal and external training and knowledge building will influence them to stay engaged with the organization. Initiatives that encourage employees to stay and grow in the company shows the organization's commitment to retain talent. It promotes loyalty and a culture of learning and growth. Organisations that provide opportunities for Community service engagements, volunteering for the underprivileged sections of society as a part of their Corporate Social Responsibility will be preferred over others. Some other initiatives to foster great employee relations include having Reward and Recognition programs, creating opportunities for interaction with senior team members, promoting work life balance, providing wellness and well-being service and providing career guidance. Creating infrastructure and conducive work environment to include needs of the minority population such as the differentially abled, LGBTQ community etc. will be perceived to be more progressive.

CONCLUSION

Organisations can stay relevant in this rapidly changing business environment by developing a systematic vision for embracing change, encourage multiple perspectives and develop competencies among its most important resource, its employees The concept of Employee Relations has undergone a dynamic change in the last decade. Earlier the concept of employee relations was simplistic with the clear understanding that employees were paid for the job they did and fired if they didn't perform. However, this concept has gained more traction as more and more organizations realized the link between employee relations and employee engagement leading to higher productivity. The employee relations mechanism must be made use of to get as close to employees so as to gain a better understanding of the issues faced at all levels. Boosting all types of diversity can enhance creativity and bring equitable balance in the organisation. A greater understanding and appreciation of the inherent value of diversity will go a long way in changing the culture and inculcating an inclusive mind set. Employees must be given various platforms and opportunities to create and learn on the job. Retaining talent through mentoring, maintaining employee friendly practices and being an evolving future ready organisation are some of the ways to remain relevant and survive in this rapidly changing world. The way forward for companies for the future with respect to Changing Dynamics in Employee Relations and Workforce Diversity include creating Inclusive culture, defining value proposition of employees and overcoming deep rooted prejudices and stereotypes.

REFERENCES

Allison, M. T. (n.d.). Organizational Barriers to Diversity in the Workplace: Benefits, Challenges, and the Required Managerial Tools. *Journal of Insure Research, 31*(1), 78-101.

Anitha, J. (2014). Determinants of employee engagement and their impact on employee performance. *International Journal of Productivity and Performance Management, 63*(3), 308–323. doi:10.1108/IJPPM-01-2013-0008

Bartlett, C. A., & Ghoshal, S. (2002). Building Competitive Advantage Through People. *MIT Sloan Management Review, 43*(2).

Bates, S. (2004). Getting engaged. *HRMagazine, 49*(2), 44–51.

Baumruk, R. (2004). The missing link: The role of employee engagement in business success. *Workspan, 47*, 48–52.

Chrobot-Mason, D., & Aramovich, N. P. (2013). The Psychological Benefits of Creating an Affirming Climate for Workplace Diversity. *Group & Organization Management, 38*(6), 659–689. doi:10.1177/1059601113509835

CIPD. (2019). *Research Report on 'Diversity Management that Works - An Evidence-based View*. Author.

Cliff, O. (2014). Discourses of Diversity, Equality and Inclusion: Trenchant Formulations or Transient Fashions? *British Journal of Management, 25*(1), 23–39. doi:10.1111/j.1467-8551.2012.00830.x

Cox, T. Jr, & Beale, R. L. (1997). *Developing Competency to Manage Diversity-Readings, Cases and Activities*. Berrett Koehler Publishers Inc.

Daniel, T. A. (2003). *Tools for Building a Positive Employee Relations Environment*. Wiley Periodicals, Inc. www.interscience.wiley.com doi:10.1002/ert.10086

Daniels, K., & Macdonald, L. (2005). *Equality, Diversity and Discrimination - A student Text*. The Chartered Institute of Personnel and Development.

De Vos, A., & Meganck, A. (2009). What HR Managers do versus What Employees Value: Exploring Both Parties' Views on Retention Management from a Psychological Contract Perspective. *Personnel Review*, *38*(1), 45–60. doi:10.1108/00483480910920705

Effron, M., Gandossy, R., & Goldsmith, M. (2003). Human Resources in the 21st Century. John Wiley & Sons.

Ferdman, B. M., & Sagiv, L. (2012). Diversity in Organizations and Cross-Cultural Work Psychology: What If They Were More Connected? *Industrial and Organizational Psychology: Perspectives on Science and Practice*, *5*(3), 323–345. doi:10.1111/j.1754-9434.2012.01455.x

Ferdman, B., M., & Sagiv, L. (2012). Diversity in Organizations and Cross-Cultural WorkPsychology: What If They Were More Connected? *Industrial and Organizational Psychology: Perspectives on Science and Practice, 5*(3).

Futrell, C.M., & Parasuraman, A. (1984). The Relationship of Satisfaction and Performance to Salesforce Turnover. *Journal of Marketing*.

Goldsmith, M., & Thomas, R. R. (2003). *Understanding Referent Groups and Diversity: A Key Challenge for Human Resource Leaders. In Human Resources in the 21st Century*. John Wiley & Sons.

Green, K. A., López, M., Wysocki, A., & Kepner, K. (2012). *Diversity in the Workplace: Benefits, Challenges, and the Required Managerial Tools, University of Florida IFAS Extension. This document is HR022, one of a series of the Food and Resource Economics Department, Florida Cooperative Extension Service*. Institute of Foodand Agricultural Sciences, University of Florida.

Harter, J. K., Schmidt, F. L., & Hayes, T. L. (2002). Business-unit-level relationship between employee satisfaction, employee engagement, and business outcomes: A meta-analysis. *The Journal of Applied Psychology*, *87*(2), 268–279. doi:10.1037/0021-9010.87.2.268 PMID:12002955

Jackson, S. E., Joshi, A., & Erhardt, N. L. (2003). Recent Research on Team and Organizational Diversity: SWOT Analysis and Implications. *Journal of Management*, *29*(6), 801–830. doi:10.1016/S0149-2063(03)00080-1

John, G., & Graham, J. (2005). *Employee Relations* (4th ed.). Published by Chartered Institute of Personnel and Development.

Johnston, W., & Packer, A. (1987). *Workforce 2000*. Hudson Institute.

Kalev, A., Dobbin, A. F., & Kelly, E. (2006). Best Practices or Best Guesses? Assessing the Efficacy of Corporate Affirmative Action and Diversity Policies. American Sociological Review, 71, 589–617. doi:10.1177/000312240607100404

Kaye, B., & Jordan-Evans, S. (2008). *2003, Love 'Em or Lose'Em – Getting Good People to Stay*. Berett Koehler Publishers Inc.

Kelly, E., & Dobbin, F. (1998). *How Affirmative Action Became Diversity Management- Employer Response to Antidiscrimination Law, 1961 to 1996. Princeton University - American Behavioral Scientist*. Sage Publications.

Kossek, E. E., & Lobel, S. A. (1995). *Managing Diversity Human Resource Strategies for Transforming the Workplace. Introduction: Transforming Human Resource Systems to Manage Diversity - an Introduction and Orienting Framework*. Blackwell Publishers Ltd.

Kreitz, P. A. (2007). *Best Practices for Managing Organizational Diversity*. SLAC-PUB-12874.

Lewis, P., Thornhill, A., & Saunders, M. (2003). Employee Relations: Understanding the Employment Relationship Harlow. *Financial Times*.

Nishii, L. H., & Mayer, D. M. (2009). Do Inclusive Leaders Help Reduce Turnover in Diverse Groups? The Moderating Role of Leader-Member Exchange in the Diversity to Turnover Relationship. *The Journal of Applied Psychology*, *94*(6), 1412–1426. doi:10.1037/a0017190 PMID:19916652

Pless, N. M., & Maak, T. (2004). Building an Inclusive Diversity Culture: Principles, Processes and Practice. *Journal of Business Ethics*, *54*(2), 129–147. doi:10.100710551-004-9465-8

Pophal, L. G. (2018). *How to handle five generations in the workplace*. Retrieved from: https://hrdailyadvisor.blr.com/2018/02/26/handle-5-generations-workplace/

Prasad, P., Pringle, J. K., & Konrad, A. M. (2006). *Examining the Contours of Workplace Diversity - Concepts, Contexts and Challenges. In Handbook of Workplace Diversity*. Sage Publications.

Puritty, C., Strickland, R., Alia, E., Blonder, B., Klein, E., Kohl, M. T., McGee, E., Quintana, M., Ridley, R. E., Tellman, B., & Gerber, L. (2017). Diversity in Science - Without Inclusion, Diversity Initiatives May Not Be Enough - Focus on minority experiences in STEM, not just numbers. *Science*, *357*(6356), 1101–1102. doi:10.1126cience.aai9054 PMID:28912234

Reeves, T. C., McKinney, A. P., & Azam, L. (2013). Muslim women's workplace experiences: Implications for Strategic Diversity Initiatives. Equality, Diversity and Inclusion: An International Journal, 32(1), 49-67.

Tansel, A., & Gazioglu, S. (2013). *Management-Employee Relations, Firm Size and Job Satisfaction. IZA Discussion Papers, No. 7308. Institute for the Study of Labor*. IZA.

Zanoni, P., & Janssens, M. (2007). Minority Employees Engaging with (Diversity) Management: An Analysis of Control, Agency, and Micro-Emancipation. *Journal of Management Studies*, *44*(0), 8. doi:10.1111/j.1467-6486.2007.00700.x

Chapter 2
Managing Employee Relations in Multinational Firms:
Challenges and Opportunities

Sandeep Yadav
https://orcid.org/0000-0002-5030-6724
Indian Institute of Management, Kozhikode, India

Latasri Hazarika
Indian Institute of Management, Kozhikode, India

ABSTRACT

Employee relations management has become an important intangible asset for the firm in today's employee-centered business environment. The multinational firm (MNCs) operating in various countries or institutional contexts face a unique form of employee relationship management challenges. This chapter focuses on the various employee relation issue in MNCs and provides a conceptual understanding. The chapter identifies language differences in various cultural contexts, staffing mix in various foreign subsidiaries, employee turnover in the global labor market, work-life balance, power conflict between parent firm and subsidiary, and virtual teams management as major employee-relation challenges for MNCs. The chapter explores strategic management of these challenges to have competitive advantages and practical recommendations for the MNCs managers based on the existing literature. Finally, the chapter also provides various gaps in the literature to be explored by future researchers.

DOI: 10.4018/978-1-7998-3515-8.ch002

INTRODUCTION

The world has become a shopping mall availing simultaneous ideas, products, and services at every place. Globalization explains a phenomenon of the borderless world with the integration of the global value chain, product markets, financial market, and corporate structures (Ohmae, 1990). Internationalization of the firms is one aspect of globalization. Dicken (1992) makes a qualitative difference between globalization and firm internationalization. Globalization is a complex and advanced form of internationalization with the integration of dispersed and multiple economic activities by firms. A multinational enterprise (MNCs) is a firm that owns and controls the activities in different countries (Buckley & Casson, 2016). This chapter is mainly focused on employee relationship management challenges faces by MNCs. The first section of the chapter introduces the concepts of globalization and firm internationalization. The process of Internationalization comes up with several advantages and challenges. The second section of the chapter discusses various employee management challenges faced by MNCs and provide a broad framework based on theoretical literature. The third section of the chapter provides solutions for managing employee relations in MNCs and road ahead for future research. The final section of the paper concludes with findings, implications for practitioners, and theoretical contributions for academicians.

Multinational firms have several advantages by achieving economies of scale and scope, by using their slack resources across boundaries, which increase firm profitability (Franko, 1989; Kobrin, 1991) and also by acquiring a new strategic asset from foreign markets. The establishment of foreign subsidiaries causes reverse spillover of knowledge and innovation to improve firm survival and profitability (Barkema & Vermeulen, 1998; Kogut & Zander, 1992). Firms can reap profit by exploiting low-cost labor and tax benefits in the imperfect markets (S. H. Hymer, 1976; Rugman, 1979) and can spread the fixed cost of R&D and marketing over several firms units (Franko, 1989). Internationalization provides a market power based competitive advantage of serving products and services across borders (Sapienza et al., 2006). The internationalization process comes up with certain unique challenges due to the liability of foreignness (LOF). It is the cost of doing business abroad which resulted from the firm competitive disadvantage of firms in the overseas market in comparison to the local host county firms (Zaheer, 1995). LOF arises from differences in cultural, geographical, political, practices and consumer behavior, labor practices, and laws. This chapter is mainly focused on employee relationship management challenges faced by MNCs. The chapter explores the multinational firm's challenges in strategic decisions of hiring and training new employees, deciding staffing mix of local, home or third-country based employees, retention of the talent and sustaining employee, resolving language barriers, maintaining work-life management, resolving MNCs power games and employee compromises and virtual team management (e.g. managing virtual teams relations during a crisis like present Covid-19 spread).

First, As employee relation involves managing interactions between employees/ workers or their representatives and employers or their representatives (Sapienza et al., 2006), communication is one of the key tools in maintaining the much-needed interactions. However, the very essence of MNCs is in existing across multiple nations with multiple languages speaking people. Hence, MNC employees must frequently switch among various languages such as parent firm country, host country, and the common corporate languages (e.g. English) while communicating among them (Aichhorn & Puck, 2017). Lack of proficiency due to language differences can impede efficient and effective communication within MNCs employees (Brannen, 2004; Rogerson-Revell, 2007). Such shortcomings in communication can lead to various other serious issues such as mistrust, asymmetric information, power disputes, dysfunctional conflict, and a complete communication breakdown among employees (Harzing & Feely, 2008). Language disparity within MNCs further impacts the power dynamics (Tenzer & Pudelko, 2017). Second, MNCs face challenges in maintaining a proper ratio of employees of different nationalities. MNCs have the option of selecting employees from a pool of host countries, home country, and third countries (Michailova et al., 2016). Usually, the expatriate employees are from top management divisions of MNCs who are assigned to spread the already established home country advantages, to construct corporate identity, to integrate management policies, to create organizational learning capacity and knowledge transfer, and to exercise control on behalf of the home country headquarter (Bonache et al., 2001). However, such deployment of the home country employee in a foreign subsidiary has to face the changing legal regulations and restrictions of both home and host country institutions such as national and regional governments, schools, trade unions, employment agents, and so on (Zheng & Smith, 2019). Furthermore, MNCs must deal with multiple allegiances of subsidiary employees split across the focal subsidiary, the headquarters, and the subsidiary host country (Michailova et al., 2016). Simultaneous allegiances towards multiple entities lead to a conflict of interests, most of the time resulting in potential damage for all the entities involved (Michailova et al., 2016). Another type of tension between local knowledge (by employing host country nationals) and global linkage (by employing expatriates) of the MNCs must be maintained while formulating the staffing mix (Thompson & Keating, 2004).

Third, Increasing competition and market globalization have opened alternative employment options for skilled and talented resources (Paillé et al., 2013; Schiemann & Guenther, 2013; Yamamoto, 2011) and resulting employee turnover across organizations. The MNCs face the additional challenge of having to compete for dynamic human talents both at national and international levels (Tlaiss et al., 2017). The human capital competitive advantage suggested by RBV thus moves from one company to another through employee turnover. Additionally, the cost of hiring and training employees can cost up to five times an employee' s yearly salary (Bryant & Allen, 2013), turning employee turnover as a significant issue faced by MNCs. On top of the cost issue, employee turnover disturbs the organizational routines by loss of tacit knowledge and organizational memory within individuals, loss of individual-specific business networks and collaborations, reducing firm productivity and service efficiency, loss of the mentors and leaders, loss in diversity of employees and the fact that other valuable employees follow the leavers cause the organization work disruption (Ballinger et al., 2011; Bryant & Allen, 2013). Yet another challenge of employee retention in MNCs is the different categories of employees with a different need. The younger lot of employees do not seek long term employment or traditional organizational career rather focusses on work-life balance (Festing & Schäfer, 2014). The more experienced employees however seek job security and stability and comfort in their organization (Tlaiss et al., 2017). Forth, MNCs face issues in the management of work-life balance policies for employees with different nationalities. Incorporating work-life management for the employees has become an important aspect of employee relation in MNCs (McCarthy et al., 2010; Ryan & Kossek, 2008). Work-life management includes activities such as flexibility in working time and conditions, various leave option (e.g. parental, adult care, bereavement, etc.), and child and dependent care (e.g. childcare centers, afterschool care support, etc.) facilitating the balance of employees work and personal or social life demand (McCarthy et al., 2010). Implementation of such policies is complex as it requires sensitive handling of local culture, tradition, and legislation (Bardoel, 2016). While the organizational context demands MNCs to respond to the global competition by putting more pressure on employees, the institutional context is characterized by changing intuitional environment (e.g. entry of women and particularly mothers into the workforce) demanding policies supporting work-life balance of employees (Hein, 2005; Moen & Roehling, 2005).

Fifth, MNCs subsidiaries must also juggle between flexibility and security of employee relation management (Pulignano et al., 2018). Flexibility demands employment practices to be efficient and profit-driven in the face of cut-throat global competition, while security demands quality jobs and fair wages for the employees in the social interest (Crouch, 2012). The compromises arise from the trade-off depend on the intention of the two power axes of MNCs— subsidiary-subsidiary and subsidiary-Headquarters relations (Pulignano et al., 2018). Balancing flexibility and security can yield a positive-sum flexibility-security compromise, where all parties gain a shared goal or a negative sum compromise where one party gains at the expense of others. Both positive-sum and negative-sum compromises are influenced by the power axes mentioned above. The power capabilities of the actors (i.e. management and labor) enable them to negotiate with each other on trading off flexibility and security. The MNC power exercising structure depends a great deal on the home country culture. The headquarter may exercise direct control by setting policy or opt for indirect control by monitoring outcomes (Pulignano et al., 2018). Hence, maintaining a healthy balance between power games and compromises in the flexibility vs security trade-off is a persisting issue of MNCs. Sixth, Geographically distributed teams are a key characteristic of MNCs. Rapid globalization and technological innovation have increased multiculturism at the workplace through geographically dispersed team membership (Algesheimer et al., 2011). Virtual Teams (VT) can solve difficult problems serving as a network of experts irrespective of the physical location of their members. However, to have an efficient VT process, MNCs should manage the impact of multinational cultural diversity on the performance of the virtual teams (Han & Beyerlein, 2016). Having multiculturally diverse teams works as a double-edged sword for MNCs. On one hand, diversity of various nations cultures in the team improve creating, innovation, member satisfaction (Stahl et al., 2010), and improve team performance by reduced groupthink and diverse ideas (Shachaf, 2008). On the other hand, it creates potential for misinterpretations as team members perceive the information wearing their cultural lenses (Dreo et al., 2003). The employees perceived differences in national cultures may lead to unhealthy stereotypes in MNCs (Au & Marks, 2012). Additionally, the heterogeneity in attitude, belief, and values among team members can reduce the performance (Mannix & Neale, 2005). Cultural and national heterogeneity in the VTs can increase the complexity of employee relation management, collaboration dynamics, and team performance of MNCs (Pauleen, 2004). Hence it becomes a crucial issue for MNCs to identify and manage critical factors impacting their VTs (Han & Beyerlein, 2016).

The above-mentioned challenges require MNCs to balance the costs and benefits of employee management. MNCs mix of staff based on the home host and host country should be based on the cost and control. The higher ratio of the home country employee provides control over foreign operations and the higher ratio host (and third) country provides cost-based advantages by accessing the low cost and knowledgeable resources. The retention of employees requires balancing the work-life, paying the competitive salary and benefits, providing the opportunity to grow, and resolving power conflicts between the parent firm and their subsidiaries. This has a greater implication for the practitioners and strategic decisions making of the firm. Future studies need to contextualize the research based on employee relationship management in MNCs. The difference in institutional context bases on culture, practices, and norms requires a contextual examination of employee relationship management research.

This chapter has the following objectives:

- Explain the concept of globalization and firm internationalization with opportunities and challenges
- Potential challenges of employee relationship management in MNCs
- Strategic solutions to manage employee relations in MNCs
- Implications for managers and future research directions

BACKGROUND

Globalization and Multinational Firms

Globalization includes both the process of internationalization and its outcomes. The term globalization is defined in various contexts. The world has become a shopping mall availing simultaneous ideas, products, and services at every place. Globalization explains a phenomenon of the borderless world with the integration of the global value chain, product markets, financial market, and corporate structures (Ohmae, 1990). Globalization represents the exchange of products and services in multiple forms across the boundaries. The economies have become more interdependent as a consequence of globalization. Wyatt-Walter (1995) defined globalization as a social process of receding cultural and social settings from geographical distance constraints. Globalization causing a political process of conversing cultural, political, and economic aspects in the world. Internationalization of the firms is one aspect of globalization. Dicken (1992) makes a qualitative difference between globalization and internationalization. Globalization is a complex and advanced form of internationalization with the integration of dispersed and multiple economic activities.

A multinational enterprise (MNC) is a firm that owns and controls the activities in different countries (Buckley & Casson, 1976). Firms can use both equity and non-equity based modes of foreign entry (Pan & David, 2000, p. 200). The equity-based entry modes include wholly-owned subsidiary and international joint ventures. The non-equity based entry modes include contractual agreements (e.g., license, franchisee) and export. The equity-based modes have a higher commitment, risk, and control in comparison to non-equity based entry modes. Internationalization is a strategic process of orderly and sequential outward orientation of firm international activities (Bilkey & Tesar, 1977; Johanson & Vahlne, 1977). Traditionally, developed market multinationals are assumed to start internationalization from lower commitment modes such as import or export and after gaining a certain level of experiential knowledge they increase their international commitment. The recent theoretical framework on internationalization of emerging market multinationals (EMNCs) such as springboard internationalization (Luo & Tung, 2007), and LLL (Linkage, Learn and Leverage) perspective (Mathews, 2006) identify a unique pattern of internationalization. Luo & Tung (2007) explained the aggressive asset seeking internationalization pattern of EMNCs with higher risk and commitment mode such as acquisition and joint ventures. EMNCs found to show the radical approach of internationalization by making their first international investment in distant developed markets. This shows a higher risky process of internationalization by leapfrogging the incremental step of the internationalization process model. EMNCs form linkages with technology advanced developed market multinationals to overcome the absence of firm-specific advantages for foreign expansion (Mathews, 2006). These linkages help to learn and leverage MNCs global competitiveness if the host and home market (Mathews, 2017). The emergence of international entrepreneurship literature through new challenges to the traditional understanding of large MNCs (Oviatt & McDougall, 1994). The small entrepreneurial firms show early internationalization with covering a broad scope of markets and international commitment since inception gives birth to concept born globals and international new ventures.

Firm degree of internationalization can be measured using the following (Sullivan, 1994):

- Foreign sales as a percentage of total sales
- Export sales as a percentage of total sales
- Foreign profit as a percentage of total profit
- Number of foreign subsidiaries
- Foreign employees as a percentage of total employees
- Foreign asset as a percentage of total asset

Internationalization is a multidimensional construct with three main dimensions of scale, scope, and speed of internationalization (Hilmersson, 2014). The scale of internationalization can be measured as foreign sales as a percentage of total sales, export sales as a percentage of total sales or foreign assets as a percentage of total assets. The scope of internationalization is the number of the foreign market served by the firm. The speed of internationalization includes both the time to first international activity since firm inception and post-entry speed of international expansion (Oviatt & McDougall, 2005). The process of Internationalization comes up with several advantages and challenges. Advantages of firm internationalization are as follows:

1. The firm can achieve economies of scale and scope by using their slack resources across boundaries, which increase firm profitability (Franko, 1989), and also acquire a new strategic asset from foreign markets
2. Establishment of foreign subsidiaries cause reverse spillover of knowledge and innovation to improve firm survival and profitability (Barkema & Vermeulen, 1998; Bartlett & Ghoshal, 1989; Kogut & Zander, 1992)
3. The firm can reap profit by exploiting low-cost labor and tax benefits in the imperfect markets (S. Hymer, 1970; Rugman, 1979)
4. Firm internationalization spread the fixed cost of R&D and marketing over several firms units (Franko, 1989)
5. Internationalization provides a market power based competitive advantage of serving product and services across borders (Sapienza et al., 2006)

Internationalization process comes up with certain unique challenges as follows:

1. Liability of foreignness (LOF): It is the cost of doing business abroad which resulted from the firm competitive disadvantage of firms in the overseas market in comparison to the local host county firms (Zaheer, 1995). Zaheer (1995) argued various reasons for LOF as:
    a. Cost of geographical distance associated with foreign travel, transportation of product, services and human resources, communication from distance over diverse time zones
    b. The firm-specific cost of understanding culture, practices and customers behavior in the foreign market
    c. The cost associated with the unfamiliarity of the foreign business, political and economic environment and low legitimacy of the outside firms in a foreign market
    d. The cost associated with home country barriers such as constraints of transfer of technology and resources
2. New firms lack the required resources for survival in a highly competitive foreign market and face liability of newness (Stinchcombe, 2000), and liability of smallness (Aldrich & Auster, 1986)
3. The firm faces additional challenges of adopting host nation culture, practices, systems, operating processes and the organizational structures (Bartlett & Ghoshal, 1989)
4. Emerging market firms (e.g. India) face the liability of origin due to weak institutional, legal, and governance protection in home countries.
5. Multinational firms face challenges of employee relations such as hiring and training new employees, retention of the talent, and sustaining employee welfare in the international context. Hyman (1999) mentioned the various

threat to employees, employees representatives, and the institutional employee regulations due to globalization:

a. The internationalization of financial market have reduced dependence of MNCs on a particular market
b. The shift of low skilled based manufacturing industries from developed to emerging markets due to trade liberalization has reduced MNCs dependence on the specific market
c. MNCs freedom to exit the host country put pressure on the government and threaten the employees for obtaining the personal benefit of favorable tax incentives, regulations, and investment opportunities

CHALLENGES AND ISSUES IN MNCs EMPLOYEE RELATION

Globalization and the consequent increase in the multinational environment of running a business have shaped various issues and challenges in the maintenance of employee relations in multinational companies/firms (MNC). Some of the key issues are discussed below:

Language Barriers

As employee relation involves managing interactions between employees/workers or their representatives and employers or their representatives (Trif & Paolucci, 2019), communication is one of the key tools in maintaining the much-needed interactions. However, the very essence of MNCs is in existing across multiple nations with multiple languages speaking people. MNCs can be viewed as a "multilingual community" with native speakers of different mother tongues(Luo & Shenkar, 2006). Hence, MNC employees must frequently switch among various languages such as home country language, the various host country languages, and the common corporate language (e.g. English) while communicating among them (Aichhorn & Puck, 2017). Good communication depends a great deal on the proficiency of the communicators over the language of communication. Lack of proficiency due to language differences can impede efficient and effective communication within MNCs employees (Rogerson-Revell, 2007). Such shortcomings in communication can lead to various other serious issues such as information asymmetries, increased mistrust, power contests, dysfunctional conflict, and a complete communication breakdown (Harzing & Feely, 2008). Language disparity within MNCs further impacts the power dynamics (Tenzer & Pudelko, 2017). Lack of language proficiency comes in the way of exercising positional or expert-based power sources as no one can establish their position by talking over others and no one can engage in impression building through the use of good communication skills. In sum, there is a strong consensus that linguistic differences among employees cause significant challenges for an organization (Tenzer et al., 2014; Tenzer & Pudelko, 2017).

Subsidiary Staffing Mix

MNCs face challenges in maintaining a proper ratio of employees of different nationalities. MNCs have the option of selecting employees from a pool of host countries, home country, and third countries (Michailova et al., 2016). MNCs deploy expatriates to a foreign subsidiary for various reasons. One of the earlier views regarded expatriate employees as "expensive resources in crucial positions" (Brewster et al., 2014). In many cases, technical and operational expertise of home country employees drives the deployment of expatriates (sometimes outnumbering local employees) in foreign subsidiaries especially in developing nations (Rui et al., 2017; Wang et al., 2017). Other drivers of choosing home country employees over the host country are the low labor cost in the home country, shortage of skilled employees in the home country, the early stage of internationalization of the MNCs (Zheng & Smith, 2019). Usually, the expatriate employees are from top management divisions of MNCs who are assigned to spread the already established home country advantages, to construct corporate identity, to integrate management policies, to create organizational learning capacity and knowledge transfer, and to exercise control on behalf of the home country headquarter (Bonache et al., 2001). However, such deployment of the home country employee in a foreign subsidiary has to face the changing legal regulations and restrictions of both home and host country institutions such as national and regional governments, schools, trade unions, employment agents, and so on (Zheng & Smith, 2019). Furthermore, MNCs must deal with multiple allegiances of subsidiary employees split across the focal subsidiary, the headquarters, and the subsidiary host country (Michailova et al., 2016). Organizational psychology literature posits that employees allegiances drive employees' attachment to particular organizational entities through organizational commitment, organizational identification, and intention to remain in the organization (retention) (Banai & Reisel, 1993; Guzzo et al., 1994). The allegiance tensions of expatriate managers in MNCs often hinder the germination and build-up of organizational attachment (Richardson & McKenna, 2006; Van Oudenhoven et al., 2001). Simultaneous allegiances towards multiple entities lead to a conflict of interests, most of the time resulting in potential damage for all the entities involved (Michailova et al., 2016). Another type of tension between local knowledge (by employing host country nationals) and global linkage (by employing expatriates) of the MNCs must be maintained while formulating the staffing mix (Thompson &

Keating, 2004). Hence MNC staffing strategies face the challenge of achieving an optimum mix of advantages and disadvantages of expatriate staffing.

Employee Turnover

Skilled employees are one of the most essential assets for any organization. The resource-based view suggests human assets as an important source of achieving competitive advantage (Wright et al., 2001). Increasing competition and market globalization have opened alternative employment options for skilled and talented resources resulting in employee turnover across organizations. The MNCs face the additional challenge of having to compete for dynamic human talents both at national and international levels. The human capital competitive advantage suggested by RBV thus moves from one company to another through employee turnover. Additionally, the cost of hiring and training employees ranges from 25 to 500 percent of an employee' s yearly salary (Bryant & Allen, 2013), turning employee turnover as a significant issue faced by MNCs. On top of the cost issue, employee turnover causes work disruptions, loss of organizational memory, loss of tacit knowledge, disrupted informal networks, elimination of critical collaborations, loss in productivity and customer service, loss of mentors, diminished diversity, and the fact that other valuable employees follow the leavers. Hence it is very crucial to maintain an efficient employee retention system in MNCs to avoid drainage of talented human capital (Earnest et al., 2011; Gavino et al., 2012). Although MNCs agree unequivocally about the necessity of retaining talent, they struggle in formulating effective employee retention strategies (Tlaiss et al., 2017). Mostly this struggle can be attributed to the ambiguity surrounding the concept of talent. On one hand, talent is considered as natural or inborn, stable, and innate (Govaerts et al., 2011), and on the other hand, it is considered as something which can be nurtured through training and development (Meyers & Van Woerkom, 2014). The other tension exists between inclusivity and exclusivity of talent. While some argue that talent development should be directed to the entire workforce, others opine that it should be directed towards an exclusive elite group (Mellahi & Collings, 2010). Yet another challenge of employee retention in MNCs is the different categories of employees with a different need. The younger lot of employees do not seek long term employment or traditional organizational career rather focusses on work-life balance (Festing & Schäfer, 2014). The more experienced employees however seek job security and stability and comfort in their organization (Tlaiss et al., 2017). This diversity of needs by organizational employees makes it difficult to plan a uniform talent retention strategy.

Work-Life Balance

MNCs face issues in the management of work-life balance policies for employees with different nationalities. Incorporating work-life management for the employees has become an important aspect of employee relation in MNCs (McCarthy et al., 2010). Work-life management includes activities such as flexible working conditions, leave options (e.g. parental, adult care, bereavement, etc.), and child and dependent care (e.g. childcare centers, afterschool care support, etc.) facilitating the balance of employees work and non-work demands. Implementation of such policies is complex as it requires sensitive handling of local culture, tradition, and legislation (Bardoel, 2016). While dealing with work-life management in MNCs, tension arises from three sources— Strategic vs Operational consideration, centralization vs decentralization and institutional vs organizational demand (Bardoel, 2016). The first source of tension arises when a strategic policy change (e.g. Flexible working hours, lower-cost producer or providing superior customer service) with long term goal is put in place to improve work-life management of employees compromising some of the effects already operational short-term approaches (e.g. inflexible and long work hours) (Lobel & Faught, 1996). The second source of tension is one of the most well-documented issues of MNCs i.e. a balance between centralization and decentralization of decision-making related to employees spread across multiple geographies locations (Brewster et al., 2005). The headquarter Human Relation department is the one which comes up with new initiatives to the work-life management policies and passed them over to the regional Human relations departments, which generate routine employment contracts and policies. However, different layers of human relations have their focus set in different allegiances and results in tension in implementing effective work-life management policies. The final source of tension for MNCs in implementing work-life management policies is the trade-off between organizational and institutional. While the organizational context demands MNCs to respond to the global competition by putting more pressure on employees, the institutional context is characterized by changing institutional environment (e.g. entry of women and particularly mothers into the workforce) demanding policies supporting work-life balance of employees (Moen & Roehling, 2005).

Power Games and Compromises

MNCs subsidiaries must also juggle between flexibility and security of employee relation management (Pulignano et al., 2018). Flexibility demands employment practices to be efficient and profit-driven in the face of cut-throat global competition, while security demands quality jobs and fair wages for the employees in the social interest (Crouch, 2012). The compromises arise from the trade-off depend on the intention of the two power axes of MNCs— subsidiary-subsidiary and subsidiary-Headquarter relations (Pulignano et al., 2018). Balancing flexibility and security can yield a positive-sum flexibility-security compromise, where all parties gain a shared goal or a negative sum compromise where one party gains at the expense of others. Both positive-sum and negative-sum compromises are influenced by the power axes mentioned above. The power capabilities of the actors (i.e. management and labor) enable them to negotiate with each other on trading off flexibility and security. The MNCs power exercising structure depends a great deal on the home country culture. The headquarter may exercise direct control by setting policy or opt for indirect control by monitoring the outcome. Hence, maintaining a healthy balance between power games and compromises in the flexibility vs security trade-off is a persisting issue of MNCs.

Virtual Team Effects

Geographically distributed teams are a key characteristic of MNCs. Rapid globalization and technological innovation have increased multiculturism at the workplace through geographically dispersed team membership (Algesheimer, Dholakia, & Gurău, 2011). Virtual Teams (VTs) can solve difficult problems serving as a network of experts irrespective of the physical location of their members. However, to have an efficient process, MNCs should manage the impact of multinational cultural diversity on virtual team performance (Han & Beyerlein, 2016). Having multiculturally diverse teams works as a double-edged sword for MNCs. On one hand, national cultural diversity enhances creativity and satisfaction (Stahl et al., 2010) and increases team effectiveness because of multiple ideas and reduced groupthink (Shachaf, 2008). On the other hand, it creates potential for misinterpretations as team members perceive the information wearing their cultural lenses (Dreo et al., 2003). Perceived differences in national cultures may lead to unhealthy stereotypes in MNCs (Au & Marks, 2012). Additionally, culturally diverse teams demonstrate lower team performance due to a mismatch in values, beliefs, and attitudes among team members (Mannix & Neale, 2005). Complexity arises in employee relations, collaboration dynamics, and team performance of MNCs due to the national and cultural heterogeneity in VTs. Hence it becomes a crucial issue for MNCs to identify and manage critical factors impacting their VTs employee relations.

THE ROAD AHEAD: SUGGESTIONS AND MANAGERIAL IMPLICATIONS

The above section of the chapter highlights the major challenges of employee relationship faces by MNCs. These challenges also come up with certain opportunities to the focal firms. MNCs can use these challenges as a source of competitive advantage by managing strategically. This section provides a deeper view of opportunities and implications for the theory and practice.

Language Diversity Advantages

Language barriers also provide a certain opportunity for MNCs. The positive aspect of language diversity is having a different perspective on problem-solving and decision making (Aichhorn & Puck, 2017). Individuals with different languages challenge the status quo and provide an effective solution to an organization's problem. This reduces the groupthink and biasness due to similarity of the thinking horizon with homogeneous language. The cognitive and emotional challenges from language diversity can be resolved through the use of common corporate language and simplification of the language. The firm managers can have a common corporate language between the parent firm and foreign subsidiary to reduce the communication barriers and improve the shared understanding. MNCs can also simplify the language by having an agreement on common words and speeches. This reduces the language barriers and has greater implications for practice.

Strategic use of Staffing Mix

Staffing mix is a strategic issue in international business management research. Gong (2003) argues that the staff mix of foreign subsidiaries has both intermediate and final performance outcomes. The intermediate outcomes of the subsidiary staffing mix are strategic and learning outcomes. The strategic outcomes include the control and coordination of MNCs with subsidiaries. The firms with higher foreign ownership have higher control over the resources and the higher proportion of the home country employee ensures better coordination. The cognitive outcome of the subsidiary staffing mix includes learning and innovation outcomes. The author further argues that the final performance implication of the subsidiary staffing mix depends on the motives of internationalization. The MNCs can have both exploration and exploitation motives of internationalization. The firms with strategic resources (firm-specific advantages, Dunning (2001)) internationalize in the attractive foreign market for the exploitation of unique resources. The firm lacking the strategic resource advantage(e.g. emerging market firms) explores the international markets in search of knowledge and technological resources. The exploitation of the resources requires control over the foreign subsidiary by a higher proportion of the expatriates. The firms with explorative motives having a heterogeneous mix of subsidiary staff with a higher proportion of host country based employees. The host country bases employee provides access to the various business network in the host market and improves the performance of MNCs. These arguments have an important implication for MNCs managers in deciding the firm staffing mix as per the strategic motives of internationalization.

Employee Turnover and Work-Life Balance

A good organizational climate and morale help in balancing work-life stress and reduce employee turnover. The importance of creating a better working culture and normative powers is well documented in the existing literature (Tlaiss et al., 2017). The role of the top management team becomes important in identifying these issues related to employee management in MNCs. They need to understand the generation, firm, and institutional context-specific employee turnover related issues in the MNCs (Tlaiss et al., 2017). The notion of talent retention strategies requires a close temporal fit between firm strategic architecture and difference in employee generations, work-related value, and country cultural factors in the MNCs. The young talent has a higher expectation of rapid career development. The disappointment to young generation employees leads to turnover if the firms are not able to pay close attention to understand the pre-employment belief and expectations of the young employee (Festing & Schäfer, 2014). The firm managers in the human resource department need to match the expectation of young employees by integrating the expected path of career development in the training orientation and firm strategy (Tlaiss et al., 2017). Firm strategy meeting the expectation of employees will reduce the stress of managing work-life balance. MNCs are further challenged by the contextual difference in employee expectations from different countries. MNCs need to consider employee direct and indirect voice to resolve conflicts (Belizón, 2019). The direct voice channels include forming a problem-solving team, employee surveys, appraisal systems, and face to face interaction of employees with management over various issues. The indirect form of employee voices can be directed by having collecting representations of employees like labor unions. This help in resolving conflicts by direct involvement of employee in MNCs strategies. Multinationals firms employees trust in the leadership also provides psychological safety and stability at job (Rao-Nicholson et al., 2016).

Virtual Teams and Times of Crisis

Virtual teams enable work by geographically distributed people with the help of digital communication technologies. The recent development in the technology and the adaptation of internet-based communication technologies is further facilitating the importance of the virtual teams. The MNCs operating in multiple countries adopt the mode of communications like electronic mails, telephones, video conferencing, and others for instant communication and decision making. MNCs can work with their foreign subsidiaries by employing virtual teams over various projects. Virtual teams exist both at the upstream and downstream of the value chain such as sourcing teams, research & development teams, marketing teams, and customer service teams. The diversity of the virtual teams not only increases the team effectiveness by a variety of ideas and minimize the groupthink problems but also improve team satisfaction and creativity (Han & Beyerlein, 2016).

The crises make the role of virtual teams more realistic. The present Coronavirus disease 2019 (COVID-19) pandemic is an unprecedented health crisis that has shaken the management practices of firms. The MNCs operating in the various affected countries are the poorest victim of the crisis. The social distancing and the unavailability of the workers in the offices and on-field workspace have challenged the sustainability of the firm operations. Gunnigle et al. (2019) find a major role of the human resource practice in settling the management issue by Irish firm during the financial crisis in 2008. The firm follows a bottom-up approach by prioritizing the employee needs above the financial outcomes. These short term initiatives are followed by the long term growth of the firm. A similar practice is getting followed by the MNCs during the present COVID-19 crisis. The firms are supporting employees for work from home and managing virtually with internal as well as external stakeholders. The crisis has shown that MNCs don't need global offices and work in different ways like virtual teams. This has not only reduced the fixed cost of managing big corporate offices but made a major readjustment in the employee culture.

THEORETICAL IMPLICATIONS AND FUTURE RESEARCH DIRECTIONS

The chapter highlights various opportunities for unfolding employee management issues in the context of MNCs. First, future researchers can explore the complexity of virtual teams. Virtual teams come up with various challenges of the difference in language, culture, time zones, and physical distance. Future research needs to explore, how MNCs overcome these barriers in the virtual team setup. Second, research on the strategic mix of the subsidiary employee mainly focuses on the balance of the employee from parents in a single host country. In practice, the subsidiaries of MNCs have employees from various third countries also. At the same time, the geographically dispersed MNCs have subsidiaries in various countries. There are common practices of transferring employees from one subsidiary to another subsidiary located in the same or different country. This further complicates the problem of staffing mix and needs exploration in future research. Third, research on employee turnover and work-life balance management is mainly focused financial aspect of employee needs. The globalization and growth of the world economies have opened various opportunities for the employee seeker and their focus has shifted toward emotional, motivational, and mental aspects in addition to financial gains. Future researchers can study the changing needs of the world labor market and employee relationship management in MNCs. Forth, the growth of small entrepreneurial firms called born global (BG) and international new ventures(INVs) having small management teams and dependent mainly on the founder's vision. These firms are innovation-focused and have very small teams of employees. It is an opportunity for future researchers to explore the employee management issue in INVs and BG. Finally, employee management practices differ significantly in the emerging and developed economies. Emerging economies are characterized by higher environmental uncertainty, market inefficiencies, active intervention by the government (Xu & Meyer, 2013), less developed technological and managerial knowledge (Chang, 2007), less developed institutional environment, and governance structure (Khanna & Rivkin, 2001). This makes the emerging market an interesting and unique context to examine employee relations in MNCs. Rao-Nicholson et al., (2016) show that in case of emerging market multinationals the trust and visibility of leadership play important role in employees psychological safety management. Future research need to accommodate the importance of employees-leadership interaction of strategic success(e.g. performance of cross-border acquisition) of multinationals firms. Research also need to focus on, how various human resource management model evolve in emerging market multinational and how they are different from developed market multinationals (Horwitz, 2017; Horwitz & Budhwar, 2015).

CONCLUSION

The changing business scenarios in today's environment are emphasizing the employee as an important resource of competence for the firm. Firms with the positive climate of employee relations management can encourage employee involvement by creating an employee-centered and social atmosphere at the workplace (Ali et al., 2018). This chapter highlights the employee management issues in the MNCs operating in multiple institutional contexts. The chapter has identified language differences due to culture, staffing mix in the foreign subsidiaries, employee turnover, work-life balance, power conflict between the subsidiary and parent firm, and virtual team management as a major issue of employee relationship management in MNCs. These issues are also seen as an opportunity by MNCs to have a competitive advantage. The firm managing employee relations can make their employee comfortable, loyal, efficient, and lead contributors to firm performance. The shared perception of organizational climate in MNCs employees reduces the conflict between parent firms and subsidiaries. The chapter also provides various managerial implications and future research directions.

REFERENCES

Aichhorn, N., & Puck, J. (2017). Bridging the language gap in multinational companies: Language strategies and the notion of company-speak. *Journal of World Business*, *52*(3), 386–403. doi:10.1016/j.jwb.2017.01.002

Aldrich, H., & Auster, E. R. (1986). Even dwarfs started small: Liabilities of age and size and their strategic implications. *Research in Organizational Behavior*.

Algesheimer, R., Dholakia, U. M., & Gurău, C. (2011). Virtual team performance in a highly competitive environment. *Group & Organization Management*, *36*(2), 161–190. doi:10.1177/1059601110391251

Ali, M., Lei, S., & Wei, X.-Y. (2018). The mediating role of the employee relations climate in the relationship between strategic HRM and organizational performance in Chinese banks. *Journal of Innovation & Knowledge*, *3*(3), 115–122. doi:10.1016/j.jik.2016.12.003

Au, Y., & Marks, A. (2012). Virtual teams are literally and metaphorically invisible": Forging identity in culturally diverse virtual teams. *Employee Relations*, *34*(3), 271–287. doi:10.1108/01425451211217707

Ballinger, G., Craig, E., Cross, R., & Gray, P. (2011). A stitch in time saves nine: Leveraging networks to reduce the costs of turnover. *California Management Review*, *53*(4), 111–133. doi:10.1525/cmr.2011.53.4.111

Banai, M., & Reisel, W. D. (1993). Expatriate managers' loyalty to the MNC: Myth or reality? An exploratory study. *Journal of International Business Studies*, *24*(2), 233–248. doi:10.1057/palgrave.jibs.8490231

Bardoel, E. A. (2016). Work–life management tensions in multinational enterprises (MNEs). *International Journal of Human Resource Management, 27*(15), 1681–1709. doi:10.1080/09585192.2015.1074089

Barkema, H. G., & Vermeulen, F. (1998). International expansion through start-up or acquisition: A learning perspective. *Academy of Management Journal, 41*(1), 7–26.

Bartlett, C. A., & Ghoshal, S. (1989). *Managing across boarders*. Harvard Business School Press.

Belizón, M. J. (2019). Employee voice in Spanish subsidiaries of multinational firms. *European Journal of Industrial Relations, 25*(1), 75–90. doi:10.1177/0959680118776076

Bilkey, W. J., & Tesar, G. (1977). The export behavior of smaller-sized Wisconsin manufacturing firms. *Journal of International Business Studies, 8*(1), 93–98. doi:10.1057/palgrave.jibs.8490783

Bonache, J., Brewster, C., & Suutari, V. (2001). Expatriation: A developing research agenda. *Thunderbird International Business Review, 43*(1), 3–20. doi:10.1002/1520-6874(200101/02)43:1<3::AID-TIE2>3.0.CO;2-4

Brannen, M. Y. (2004). When Mickey loses face: Recontextualization, semantic fit, and the semiotics of foreignness. *Academy of Management Review, 29*(4), 593–616. doi:10.5465/amr.2004.14497613

Brewster, C., Bonache, J., Cerdin, J.-L., & Suutari, V. (2014). *Exploring expatriate outcomes*. Taylor & Francis. doi:10.1080/09585192.2013.870284

Brewster, C., Sparrow, P., & Harris, H. (2005). Towards a new model of globalizing HRM. *The International Journal of Human Resource Management Group, 16*(6), 949–970. doi:10.1080/09585190500120590

Bryant, P. C., & Allen, D. G. (2013). Compensation, benefits and employee turnover: HR strategies for retaining top talent. *Compensation and Benefits Review, 45*(3), 171–175. doi:10.1177/0886368713494342

Buckley, P. J., & Casson, M. (1976). A long-run theory of the multinational enterprise. In *The future of the multinational enterprise* (pp. 32–65). Springer. doi:10.1007/978-1-349-02899-3_2

Buckley, P. J., & Casson, M. (2016). *The future of the multinational enterprise*. Springer.

Chang, J. (2007). International Expansion Path, Speed, Product Diversification and Performance Among Emerging-Market MNEs: Evidence from Asia-Pacific Multinational Companies. *Asian Business & Management*, *6*(4), 331–353. doi:10.1057/palgrave.abm.9200228

Crouch, C. (2012). Beyond the Flexibility/Security Trade-Off: Reconciling Confident Consumers with Insecure Workers. *British Journal of Industrial Relations*, *50*(1), 1–22. doi:10.1111/j.1467-8543.2010.00825.x

Dicken, P. (1992). *Global shift: The internationalization of economic activity*. Paul Chapman.

Dreo, H., Kunkel, P., & Mitchell, T. (2003). *Virtual teams guidebook for managers*. Quality Press.

Dunning, J. H. (2001). The Eclectic (OLI) Paradigm of International Production: Past, Present and Future. *International Journal of the Economics of Business*, *8*(2), 173–190. doi:10.1080/13571510110051441

Earnest, D. R., Allen, D. G., & Landis, R. S. (2011). Mechanisms linking realistic job previews with turnover: A meta-analytic path analysis. *Personnel Psychology*, *64*(4), 865–897. doi:10.1111/j.1744-6570.2011.01230.x

Festing, M., & Schäfer, L. (2014). Generational challenges to talent management: A framework for talent retention based on the psychological-contract perspective. *Journal of World Business*, *49*(2), 262–271. doi:10.1016/j.jwb.2013.11.010

Franko, L. G. (1989). Global corporate competition: Who's winning, who's losing, and the R&D factor as one reason why. *Strategic Management Journal*, *10*(5), 449–474. doi:10.1002mj.4250100505

Gavino, M. C., Wayne, S. J., & Erdogan, B. (2012). Discretionary and transactional human resource practices and employee outcomes: The role of perceived organizational support. *Human Resource Management*, *51*(5), 665–686. doi:10.1002/hrm.21493

Gong, Y. (2003). Toward a dynamic process model of staffing composition and subsidiary outcomes in multinational enterprises. *Journal of Management*, *29*(2), 259–280. doi:10.1177/014920630302900207

Govaerts, N., Kyndt, E., Dochy, F., & Baert, H. (2011). Influence of learning and working climate on the retention of talented employees. *Journal of Workplace Learning*, *23*(1), 35–55. doi:10.1108/13665621111097245

Gunnigle, P., Lavelle, J., & Monaghan, S. (2019). Multinational companies and human resource management in Ireland during recession: A retrospective from a highly globalized economy. *Thunderbird International Business Review*, *61*(3), 481–489. doi:10.1002/tie.21978

Guzzo, R. A., Noonan, K. A., & Elron, E. (1994). Expatriate managers and the psychological contract. *The Journal of Applied Psychology*, *79*(4), 617–626. doi:10.1037/0021-9010.79.4.617

Han, S. J., & Beyerlein, M. (2016). Framing the Effects of Multinational Cultural Diversity on Virtual Team Processes. *Small Group Research*, *47*(4), 351–383. doi:10.1177/1046496416653480

Harzing, A.-W., & Feely, A. J. (2008). The language barrier and its implications for HQ-subsidiary relationships. *Cross Cultural Management*, *15*(1), 49–61. doi:10.1108/13527600810848827

Hein, C. (2005). *Reconciling work and family responsibilities: Practical ideas from global experience*. International Labour Organization.

Hilmersson, M. (2014). Small and medium-sized enterprise internationalisation strategy and performance in times of market turbulence. *International Small Business Journal: Researching Entrepreneurship*, *32*(4), 386–400. doi:10.1177/0266242613497744

Horwitz, F. (2017). International HRM in South African multinational companies. *Journal of International Management*, *23*(2), 208–222. doi:10.1016/j.intman.2017.01.005

Horwitz, F., & Budhwar, P. (2015). *Handbook of Human Resource Management in Emerging Markets*. Edward Elgar Publishing. doi:10.4337/9781781955017

Hyman, R. (1999). National industrial relations systems and transnational challenges: An essay in review. *European Journal of Industrial Relations*, *5*(1), 89–110. doi:10.1177/095968019951006

Hymer, S. (1970). The efficiency (contradictions) of multinational corporations. *The American Economic Review*, *60*(2), 441–448.

Hymer, S. H. (1976). *The international operations of national firms: A study of foreign direct investment*. Mit Press.

Johanson, J., & Vahlne, J.-E. (1977). The internationalization process of the firm—A model of knowledge development and increasing foreign market commitments. *Journal of International Business Studies, 8*(1), 23–32. doi:10.1057/palgrave.jibs.8490676

Khanna, T., & Rivkin, J. W. (2001). Estimating the performance effects of business groups in emerging markets. *Strategic Management Journal, 22*(1), 45–74. doi:10.1002/1097-0266(200101)22:1<45::AID-SMJ147>3.0.CO;2-F

Kobrin, S. J. (1991). An empirical analysis of the determinants of global integration. *Strategic Management Journal, 12*(S1), 17–31. doi:10.1002mj.4250120904

Kogut, B., & Zander, U. (1992). Knowledge of the Firm, Combinative Capabilities, and the Replication of Technology. *Organization Science, 3*(3), 383–397. doi:10.1287/orsc.3.3.383

Lobel, S. A., & Faught, L. (1996). Four Methods for Proving the Value of Work/Life interventions: Here is advice on choosing the most appropriate business methods for demonstrating that work/life interventions add value to the organization. *Compensation and Benefits Review, 28*(6), 50–57. doi:10.1177/088636879602800609

Luo, Y., & Shenkar, O. (2006). The multinational corporation as a multilingual community: Language and organization in a global context. *Journal of International Business Studies, 37*(3), 321–339. doi:10.1057/palgrave.jibs.8400197

Luo, Y., & Tung, R. L. (2007). International expansion of emerging market enterprises: A springboard perspective. *Journal of International Business Studies, 38*(4), 481–498. doi:10.1057/palgrave.jibs.8400275

Mannix, E., & Neale, M. A. (2005). What differences make a difference? The promise and reality of diverse teams in organizations. *Psychological Science in the Public Interest, 6*(2), 31–55. doi:10.1111/j.1529-1006.2005.00022.x PMID:26158478

Mathews, J. A. (2006). Dragon multinationals: New players in 21 st century globalization. *Asia Pacific Journal of Management, 23*(1), 5–27. doi:10.100710490-006-6113-0

Mathews, J. A. (2017). Dragon multinationals powered by linkage, leverage and learning: A review and development. *Asia Pacific Journal of Management, 34*(4), 769–775. doi:10.100710490-017-9543-y

McCarthy, A., Darcy, C., & Grady, G. (2010). Work-life balance policy and practice: Understanding line manager attitudes and behaviors. *Human Resource Management Review, 20*(2), 158–167. doi:10.1016/j.hrmr.2009.12.001

Mellahi, K., & Collings, D. G. (2010). The barriers to effective global talent management: The example of corporate elites in MNEs. *Journal of World Business*, *45*(2), 143–149. doi:10.1016/j.jwb.2009.09.018

Meyers, M. C., & Van Woerkom, M. (2014). The influence of underlying philosophies on talent management: Theory, implications for practice, and research agenda. *Journal of World Business*, *49*(2), 192–203. doi:10.1016/j.jwb.2013.11.003

Michailova, S., Mustaffa, Z., & Barner-Rasmussen, W. (2016). Subsidiaries of Multinational Corporations: A Framework for Analyzing Employee Allegiances. *Journal of Leadership & Organizational Studies*, *23*(2), 116–127. doi:10.1177/1548051816633071

Moen, P., & Roehling, P. (2005). *The career mystique: Cracks in the American dream*. Rowman & Littlefield.

Ohmae, K. (1990). The borderless world. *The McKinsey Quarterly*, *3*, 3–19.

Oviatt, B. M., & McDougall, P. P. (1994). Toward a theory of international new ventures. *Journal of International Business Studies*, *25*(1), 45–64. doi:10.1057/palgrave.jibs.8490193

Oviatt, B. M., & McDougall, P. P. (2005). Defining International Entrepreneurship and Modeling the Speed of Internationalization. *Entrepreneurship Theory and Practice*, *29*(5), 537–554. doi:10.1111/j.1540-6520.2005.00097.x

Paillé, P., Boiral, O., & Chen, Y. (2013). Linking environmental management practices and organizational citizenship behaviour for the environment: A social exchange perspective. *International Journal of Human Resource Management*, *24*(18), 3552–3575. doi:10.1080/09585192.2013.777934

Pan, Y., & David, K. T. (2000). The hierarchical model of market entry modes. *Journal of International Business Studies*, *31*(4), 535–554. doi:10.1057/palgrave.jibs.8490921

Pauleen, D. (2004). *Virtual teams: Projects, protocols and processes*. IGI Global. doi:10.4018/978-1-59140-166-7

Pulignano, V., Tregaskis, O., Doerflinger, N., & Bélanger, J. (2018). The distinctiveness of employment relations within multinationals: Political games and social compromises within multinationals' subsidiaries in Germany and Belgium. *The Journal of Industrial Relations*, *60*(4), 465–491. doi:10.1177/0022185618769963

Rao-Nicholson, R., Khan, Z., & Stokes, P. (2016). Making great minds think alike: Emerging market multinational firms' leadership effects on targets' employee psychological safety after cross-border mergers and acquisitions. *International Business Review, 25*(1), 103–113. doi:10.1016/j.ibusrev.2015.09.007

Richardson, J., & McKenna, S. (2006). Exploring Relationships with home and host countries. *Cross Cultural Management, 13*(1), 6–22. doi:10.1108/13527600610643448

Rogerson-Revell, P. (2007). Using English for international business: A European case study. *English for Specific Purposes, 26*(1), 103–120. doi:10.1016/j.esp.2005.12.004

Rugman, A. M. (1979). *International diversification and the multinational enterprise*. Academic Press.

Rui, H., Zhang, M., & Shipman, A. (2017). Chinese expatriate management in emerging markets: A competitive advantage perspective. *Journal of International Management, 23*(2), 124–138. doi:10.1016/j.intman.2017.01.002

Ryan, A. M., & Kossek, E. E. (2008). Work-life policy implementation: Breaking down or creating barriers to inclusiveness? *Human Resource Management, 47*(2), 295–310.

Sapienza, H. J., Autio, E., George, G., & Zahra, S. A. (2006). A capabilities perspective on the effects of early internationalization on firm survival and growth. *Academy of Management Review, 31*(4), 914–933. doi:10.5465/amr.2006.22527465

Schiemann, F., & Guenther, T. (2013). Earnings predictability, value relevance, and employee expenses. *The International Journal of Accounting, 48*(2), 149–172. doi:10.1016/j.intacc.2013.04.001

Shachaf, P. (2008). Cultural diversity and information and communication technology impacts on global virtual teams: An exploratory study. *Information & Management, 45*(2), 131–142. doi:10.1016/j.im.2007.12.003

Stahl, G. K., Maznevski, M. L., Voigt, A., & Jonsen, K. (2010). Unraveling the effects of cultural diversity in teams: A meta-analysis of research on multicultural work groups. *Journal of International Business Studies, 41*(4), 690–709. doi:10.1057/jibs.2009.85

Stinchcombe, A. L. (2000). *Social structure and organizations*. Emerald Group Publishing Limited. doi:10.1016/S0742-3322(00)17019-6

Sullivan, D. (1994). Measuring the degree of internationalization of a firm. *Journal of International Business Studies, 25*(2), 325–342. doi:10.1057/palgrave.jibs.8490203

Tenzer, H., & Pudelko, M. (2017). The influence of language differences on power dynamics in multinational teams. *Journal of World Business*, *52*(1), 45–61. doi:10.1016/j.jwb.2016.11.002

Tenzer, H., Pudelko, M., & Harzing, A.-W. (2014). The impact of language barriers on trust formation in multinational teams. *Journal of International Business Studies*, *45*(5), 508–535. doi:10.1057/jibs.2013.64

Thompson, K., & Keating, M. (2004). An empirical study of executive nationality staffing practices in foreign-owned MNC subsidiaries in Ireland. *Thunderbird International Business Review*, *46*(6), 771–797. doi:10.1002/tie.20035

Tlaiss, H. A., Martin, P., & Hofaidhllaoui, M. (2017). Talent retention: Evidence from a multinational firm in France. *Employee Relations*, *39*(4), 426–445. doi:10.1108/ER-07-2016-0130

Trif, A., & Paolucci, V. (2019). Employee Relations in Context: Globalization, Uncertainties, and Dynamics of Change. In K. Koch & P. Manzella (Eds.), International Comparative Employee Relations (pp. 14–38). Edward Elgar Publishing. doi:10.4337/9781788973229.00011

Van Oudenhoven, J. P., van der Zee, K. I., & Van Kooten, M. (2001). Successful adaptation strategies according expatriates. *International Journal of Intercultural Relations*, *25*(5), 467–482. doi:10.1016/S0147-1767(01)00018-9

Wang, D., Fan, D., Freeman, S., & Zhu, C. J. (2017). Exploring cross-cultural skills for expatriate managers from Chinese multinationals: Congruence and contextualization. *Asia Pacific Journal of Management*, *34*(1), 123–146. doi:10.100710490-016-9474-z

Wright, P. M., Dunford, B. B., & Snell, S. A. (2001). Human resources and the resource based view of the firm. *Journal of Management*, *27*(6), 701–721. doi:10.1177/014920630102700607

Wyatt-Walter, A. (1995). Globalization, corporate identity and European technology policy1. *Journal of European Public Policy*, *2*(3), 427–446. doi:10.1080/13501769508406996

Xu, D., & Meyer, K. E. (2013). Linking theory and context: 'Strategy research in emerging economies' after Wright et al. (2005). *Journal of Management Studies*, *50*(7), 1322–1346.

Yamamoto, H. (2011). The relationship between employee benefit management and employee retention. *International Journal of Human Resource Management*, *22*(17), 3550–3564. doi:10.1080/09585192.2011.560871

Zaheer, S. (1995). Overcoming the liability of foreignness. *Academy of Management Journal, 38*(2), 341–363.

Zheng, Y., & Smith, C. (2019). Tiered expatriation: A social relations approach to staffing multinationals. *Human Resource Management, 58*(5), 489–502. doi:10.1002/hrm.21937

ADDITIONAL READING

Bücker, J. J. L. E., Furrer, O., Poutsma, E., & Buyens, D. (2014). The impact of cultural intelligence on communication effectiveness, job satisfaction and anxiety for Chinese host country managers working for foreign multinationals. *International Journal of Human Resource Management, 25*(14), 2068–2087. doi:10.1080/09585192.2013.870293

Dewhurst, M., Pettigrew, M., Srinivasan, R., & Choudhary, V. (2012). How multinationals can attract the talent they need. *The McKinsey Quarterly, 3*(8), 92–99.

Ferner, A., Almond, P., & Colling, T. (2005). Institutional theory and the cross-national transfer of employment policy: The case of 'workforce diversity' in US multinationals. *Journal of International Business Studies, 36*(3), 304–321. doi:10.1057/palgrave.jibs.8400134

Ferner, A., Quintanilla, J., & Varul, M. Z. (2001). Country-of-origin effects, host-country effects, and the management of HR in multinationals: German companies in Britain and Spain. *Journal of World Business, 36*(2), 107–127. doi:10.1016/S1090-9516(01)00050-5

Lawler, J. J., Chen, S., Wu, P.-C., Bae, J., & Bai, B. (2011). High-performance work systems in foreign subsidiaries of American multinationals: An institutional model. *Journal of International Business Studies, 42*(2), 202–220. doi:10.1057/jibs.2010.42

Leung, K., Zhu, Y., & Ge, C. (2009). Compensation disparity between locals and expatriates: Moderating the effects of perceived injustice in foreign multinationals in China. *Journal of World Business, 44*(1), 85–93. doi:10.1016/j.jwb.2008.03.010

Meardi, G. (2006). Multinationals' heaven? Uncovering and understanding worker responses to multinational companies in post-communist Central Europe. *International Journal of Human Resource Management, 17*(8), 1366–1378. doi:10.1080/09585190600804754

Tung, R. L. (1984). Human Resource Planning in Japanese Multinationals: A Model for U.S. Firms? *Journal of International Business Studies, 15*(2), 139–149. doi:10.1057/palgrave.jibs.8490487

Tüselmann, H.-J., McDonald, F., & Thorpe, R. (2006). The emerging approach to employee relations in German overseas affiliates: A role model for international operation? *Journal of World Business, 41*(1), 66–80. doi:10.1016/j.jwb.2005.10.004

KEY TERMS AND DEFINITIONS

Employee-Turnover: The rate at which existing employees leave the firm.
Expatriates: The people leaving outside their native or home country.
Internalization: A process of making transaction within firm boundaries.
Internationalization: A process by which firms operate in multiple countries.
Multilingual: A person who know multiple languages.
Multinationals: A firm operating in multiple countries.
Staffing: A process of recruiting new employees based on the organization need.
Subsidiary: A firm controlled by a parent or holding company.

Chapter 3
Employee Relations as a Tool of Strategic Competitive Environment

Saloni Pahuja
https://orcid.org/0000-0002-0500-0777
Amity School of Business, Amity University, Noida, India

Kadiyala Mounica Chowdary
Amity School of Business, Amity University, Noida, India

Sakshi Mittal
Amity School of Business, Amity University, Noida, India

ABSTRACT

Challenging and ever-changing market scenarios made it difficult for organisations to be different and sustain in the market. While having innovative products, USP (unique selling proposition) and the like are on one side of the competition, attracting and retaining employees have emerged to become key concerns of the organizations. This chapter explains how employee relations help organisations in retaining employees and gain competitive edge. One of the major threats of competition with relation to employees is the changes it brings along with it in terms of the company's policies, strategies, and the pressure it brings to the employees. It is important to maintain employee relations so that these changes do not impact employee performance negatively. The authors further show how these changes will impact the work and how management can overcome the aftereffects by maintaining good employee relations.

DOI: 10.4018/978-1-7998-3515-8.ch003

INTRODUCTION

Due to the heavy competition in the market, it is becoming important to realise the value of resource of sustained competitive advantage. According to (Barney, 1991), for a resource to qualify as a source of competitive advantage or to hold the potential of sustained competitive advantage, the resource should possess the following traits- a) it must be valuable, in the sense that it either should exploit opportunities or neutralize threats or do both in the firms environment; b) it must be rare among the firm's current and potential competitors; c) it must be imperfectly imitable, and d) there shouldn't be any equivalent substitutes.

Human Resource meets all criteria of being source of sustained competitive advantage that a firm needs. Thus it is important to focus on talent management, healthy relations and welfare aspect. Traditionally HR was not given much importance but after realizing their worth as true contributor in Organisational success firms started investing in them. Many firms talk about the importance of HR but fail to implement the HR strategies effectively. Almost all successful firms invest in managing employees and having good employee relations. Employee relations start right from procurement. It includes transparent communication, fair policies for improving cooperation, having effective grievance redressal mechanism, involving then and encouraging employee participation and thus creating High performance and high involvement work system.

In this chapter, we will further see how these employee relations are helping/ will help the firms use their human resources as sources of competitive advantage.

EMPLOYEE RELATIONS

Employee relation is a word that recently evolved from the word industrial relations. Even though many authors use the two words interchangeably, there is a slight difference between the two words. Industrial relations deal with workplace relations between industrial workers and employers and bargaining between them regarding wages and other terms of employment. The term is now replaced by the word employee relations which covers all kinds of workplaces. Employee relations is defined as "a study of relationships between employees, as well as the relationship between employer and employee so as to find ways of resolving conflict and to help in improving productivity of the organization by increasing motivation and morale of the workers" (Nikoloski, Dimitrova, Koleva, Kacarski, 2004). In simple words, employee relations can be defined as the relation that the employee has with their subordinates, reporting managers, superiors and organization as a whole. Employee relations concern the welfare of employees through solving their grievances and helping them grown and develop.

In an organization, the goals of the employee and employer are different. Employer's interest is regarding minimizing the labor cost whereas; the employee's interest is in maximizing the labor cost. Objectives of employees at work are not synonymous with that of the employer (Blyton, Turnbull, 2004). Employees want high income, security, satisfaction, work-life balance, career growth and development of self, sense of belongingness etc. whereas, employer wants a good pool of talent with the least possible cost which makes the highest possible return. The organizations can achieve these goals by maintaining good employee relations. While framing policies there must be alignment between business strategy and HR strategy. The organizations should frame Human Resource Management Policies and practices such that they are all aligned with the growth, survival and success of the organization. With the help of these HRM policies and employee relation practices, the organization will be able create a positive environment in the organization which pushes employees to work with their full potential to give maximum results and thus motivates them to bring value to the organization, its products and services. Effective HR practices and healthy work culture having sound employee relations attracts the talent. If the employer and employee relations are not taken care of, right from the beginning, the basic goals of the organization will be compromised.

In this challenging environment where the environment keeps on changing due to various political, social, technological, cultural, economic and legal factors, organization must revise its strategies timely which will help the firm to cope up with changes and survive in market leading to optimum utilization of resources. When there is organizational change, it will cause employees the feeling of anxiety, stress, and insecurity and will result in impacting employee's productivity, satisfaction and commitment to the organization (Ashfort, Lee, Bobko, 1989). The employees generally resist to the changes thus organizations should try to gain the trust and acceptance of the employees through effective leadership, transparent communication, and proper awareness. To implement any of these changes firm should maintain good relations with the employee's right from the start. As good relations helps in creating a culture of mutual trust which will further leads to less resistance to change.

Handling such situations through employee relations help the organizations maintain their competitive edge and managing such problems in a better way that the competitors help the organization stay ahead in the race.

COMPETITIVE ENVIRONMENT

Every business survives in a dynamic business environment (George 2012). Business environment refers to the surroundings and circumstances which influences business operations. This environment keeps on changing due to various factors and it is important to understand these changes to survive the competition. (Scherer, 1980) defines competition as a conscious striving of business firms against one another for patronage. Few authors refer this competition as rivalry between sellers, where everyone tries to gain profits and market share by offering goods and services. Every business competes and functions in such a dynamic external environment called as competitive environment. The profits, growth and survival of any firm depend on the way they react to the changes in this environment. If any organization is unable to adapt to the changes of the environment, they tend to get losses. (Lanisiluto, 2004) Firms can avoid or minimize the impacts of negative happenings by understanding the development of competitive environment.

Firms create different strategies to survive in the competitive environment. They are made with respect to the environment and, as the environment changes; the strategies must also be modified. The firm must make critical decisions regarding their functions, strategies, products etc. to always maintain/improve their performance in the market to stay ahead in the race. So, the HR policies must be made considering these strategies and managers should identify the importance of these policies and they should act accordingly. HR should make sure that everyone in the organization, right from the top management to the smallest employee, is committed to the strategy and the HR must understand the relationship between HR practices and performance with strategies. According to (Hemmasi, 1983) the essence of formulating competitive strategy is relating a firm to its environment and a key aspect of the firm's environment is the industry in which it competes. This means that the goal of making any competitive strategy is to link the organization with its environment. It also highlights that the main component of the firm's environment is the type of industry in which it functions. When we understand the type of industry in which we are competing, we can understand the characteristics of the industry that affect the type of external issues (Hemmasi, 1983). Also it helps us understand the importance attributed to strategic factors which differ from industry to industry (Steiner's, 1969). For example, automobile industry competes on manufacturing, technology, product features and development. Whereas, clothing industry competes on quality, price, marketing etc.

Thus, it is important for the firms to constantly analyze the changes taking place in their competitive environment. (Eisenhardt, 1989 and Judge, Miller, 1991) agree that high performing companies scan their environments more frequently compared to low performing companies. With the high environmental pressure, organizations are required to make changes to their strategies constantly which impact the employer employee relations as well as the functioning of the business. The firms must constantly use SWOT analysis, PEST analysis or other analytical tools to check their current strategies and relationships in their organizations and should make changes accordingly to maximize organizational performance (Subramanian, 2017). The change in such strategies can sometimes change the structure of the competitive environment; usually by big firms. These changes can be carried out peacefully only if there is cooperation from the employees.

(Pfeffer, Leblebici, 1973) competitive environment requires tighter coordination and more orderly use of firm's resources. This means that the firms should have more levels of organizational hierarchy, frequent reporting, oral communication and advanced decision making procedure and all of these are positively related with competition (Pfeffer, Leblebici, 1973). Many researchers also feel that firms should decentralize their decision making. Firms must decentralize authority and decision making, give autonomy to be more efficient during high competition (Bosemans, Simonetti, 1975). By decentralizing, the management can focus on controlling the important and critical decisions. They will have more time to design strategies to survive and excel in the competition. Also decentralizing decision-making process of the organizations helps the organization to secure the loyalty, commitment, and dedication of the employees (Nwokocha, Izidor, Iheriohanma, 2012). (Hemmasi, 1983) believes decentralization of specific types of decisions are strongly related to objective structural dimensions of the competitive environment.

In the competitive environment, it is difficult to attract the right staff for organizations but at the same time it is highly important to have the right employee for the right job. To achieve this the firms should try to find the best match according to the job description as the employee doing a particular job can do it in the most efficient manner only if they have proper knowledge and good experience in the same area as they are working. This is the reason every organization should conduct job analysis and should make job description and job specification which helps the organizations narrow down their applications and choose the right person for the right job. This will ensure efficiency and effectiveness in performance, job satisfaction (as they are doing the job that they know), loyalty, motivation etc. These will emerge to become sources of competitive advantage.

EMPLOYEE RETENTION

Success of any organization depends on the human capital. Therefore the organizations should be conscious about their job satisfaction and retention of employee's to sustain valuable and efficient human resources (Jehnzeb, Bashir, 2013). Employee retention is a process which encourages the employees to remain within the organization for a maximum duration of time or until the completion of the project (Balamurgan, Abinaya, 2016). When there is high employee turnover, it decreases the efficiency of the work and increases the cost for the organization. This is the reason the organization had to maintain effective retention strategies. Effective retention strategies will help the organizations ensure the customers are satisfied, there is increase in sales, staff is satisfied and there is deeply embedded organizational knowledge and learning (Mathimaran, Kumar, 2017). It also reduces the cost of recruitment and selection of new employees. It is not possible to measure the exact cost associated with employee turnover for an organization but when an employee leaves an organization, they take with them their relation with the clients, knowledge regarding company and their projects (Balamurgan, Abinaya, 2016).

(Das, Baruah, 2013) mentioned in their study that organizations use various techniques like rewards and recognition, participation in decision making, work-life balance and employee retention to make employees satisfied and decrease employee turnover. One of the main disadvantages of employee turnover is customer/ client service interruption (Ghansah, 2011). Retaining employees will create more committed and satisfied workforce which will give the company competitive advantage (Pahuja, Dalal, 2016). (Sharma, 2016) employees usually prefer career development opportunities followed by compensation, type of work, company culture, overseas assignment, family circumstances and so on. Employees must be provided with proper training and development programs from time to time based on the requirement of the organization. They should try to develop the employees and increase their skills. Skill development will increase the satisfaction of employees as they are developing themselves and this will stop them from leaving the organization. Skill development will directly impact on better personnel and performance as the new skills will increase their capabilities. To maintain competitive advantage the companies must focus on enhancing the performance of employees through continual learning. Also having effective leadership at all levels can motivate individuals, teams and human networks to achieve peak performance (Jassim, 1998). This is because employees lookup to their superiors for support and feel that they are responsible for communicating information (Cole, 2006). Since there are many ways to retain the employees, the organization should focus on brining a positive change in all the factors rather than one or two factors (Sanevirathna, Yapa, 2017). This will help create positive relationships and environment in the organization.

According to (Singh, 2019) the new generations of employees are finding social initiatives by the companies more attractive. This is the reason many companies are using corporate social initiative as a tool for employee retention. Also the company should continuously do performance reviews and appraisal from time to time as it decreases the confusion and resentment in the employees. Rewards must be given based on the performance so that the employees will create a perception that better performance will lead to better rewards. This will ultimately drive the employees to work more efficiently. These rewards should not only be monetary, there should also be non-monetary rewards because different employees have different requirements and expectations: like hike, promotion, recognition, on-site etc. So the employee's motivation to perform better can be by providing various rewards like awards, promotion, on-site opportunities etc. Such activities help management reach the expectation of the employees and maintain good employee relations in such a way that employee needs are satisfied and they don't leave the organization. Also, few particular cultural activities help create obstacles in retaining most productive employees of the organization (Sheridon, 1992). So the organizations carry out such vide range of activities to maintain positive employee relations and to create a sense of belongingness to the employees so that they don't leave the organization (Sheridon, 1992).

BENEFITS TO THE ORGANIZATION

One of the main parts of employee relations is communication. It involves communicating the concerned information to the employees in a right way so that trust is built among the employees. Proper communication ensures that the objectives of the organization are clear and fastens decision making process. (Rahman, Taniya, 2017) explained employee relations as the management of communication between enterprise and staff. They expressed that this kind of communication adopts flexibility, improves employee satisfaction and inspires organization to realize its goal. When the employees are properly communicated about everything, they start trusting the organization, their decisions and will show more loyalty towards the organization. Many authors believe that employee relations is all about effective communication which helps build confidence, trust and loyalty among employees enabling the management to realize the potential skills and knowledge that is available in the organization.

There are many advantages of maintaining good employee relations. (Bajaj, 2013) observed that employee relations promote commitment, facilitates employees to achieve organizational objectives, increases trust and reduces conflicts. When employee relations are good it helps organizations maintain harmony by reducing conflicts. The employees will tend to be more understanding and this peaceful environment will help employees concentrate and increase their productivity. When there is no peace in the workplace, the employees will get disturbed and their efficiency will decrease. Even if the organization has competent, qualified and motivated employees, their performance will be in danger as long as there is no peace and harmony (Samwel, 2018). When there is harmony in the organization it is easier for the management to promote team spirit among the employees. (Sanyal, Hisam, 2018) team spirit / team work has the ability to increase the level of emotional stability; self-confidence and the like among the members and it creates a healthy environment and increases the creativity and efficiency. The organization benefits a lot through this as team structures have proven to have higher labor productivity, flatter management structures and reduced employee turnover. It also increases the quality of products and services, reduces the level of absenteeism, increases learning and development with increased industrial harmony which will all lead towards improved workplace performance (Glassop, 2002). It also creates a sense of belongingness among the employees. All these advantages not only help in attracting and retaining the employees but they also increase the attractiveness of the organization as an employer (Urbancova, Saydrova, 2017). It means that the organization will now have a bigger pool of talented employees to choose from. This also improves the image of the organization.

Employee relations focus on performance, growth and development of employees. This will ensure that the employees are satisfied. (Samwel, 2018) through his study proved that there is a positive significant relationship between employee relations and employee performance as well as between employee relations and organizational performance. As when the employee performance increases, it automatically improves the organization's performance. The stronger the relations, the stronger will be the satisfaction of the employees. As long as the employees are not satisfied they cannot produce the results that satisfy the customer/clients. (Sequeira, Dhriti, 2015) concluded from their study that the employees with high level of job satisfaction were more productive, were able to complete their tasks on time and were motivated to give their opinions which contributes towards organization's development and improvement of performance. So it is understood that the profit of the organization and their image depends upon the satisfaction of their employees and it can be achieved through maintaining good employee relations. They drive the organization towards achieving their goals and objectives and help them function at their full potential which helps them survive and stay ahead in the competition.

GLOBALIZATION

Economic globalization is one of the most powerful forces to have shaped the post-war world (Frankel, 2000). Globalization refers to the growing integration of economies and societies around the world. Globalization led to advances in communication, transportation and technology combined with free- marketed ideology and has given rise of free mobility of goods, services and capital (Irani, Nouru, Nouzi, 2011).

Globalization led to an increase in employment opportunities and the increase in competition benefitted the consumers by providing large variety of products and brands and also made sure procedures maintained their quality. Although the increase in competition had increased the competitive pressure, it also made sure there is large market base for good quality products. (Jha, Varkker, 2017) competition followed by globalization has given rise to the introduction of the 'Human' aspect to employee relations practices. Globalization made sure that there is increased level of connectivity and integration. It made it possible and easier for employees to look for job in other countries and made it easier for organizations to find pool of talented workforces. High skilled labors who invest in education and research started entering and taking jobs in high technology sectors of different parts of the world.

It is believed that globalization is resulting in the whole world becoming a global village. It is believed by few researchers that globalization would lead to the merging of employee relation practices globally (Jha, Varkker, 2011). It is also believed that the post-globalization world is/will witness new trade union structures, new patterns of behavior and increased HRM orientation of managing employees. Globalization sets conditions for managerial decision making which constraints the choices they make. It also leads to the firms changing their structures, strategies, practices etc. which leads to organizational change and the management should deal with it through proper employee relation practices like effective leadership, communication etc. Globalization also forces the companies to constantly change their products, services, increase quality, reduce cost etc. The nature of the jobs would constantly change due to the introduction of new technologies, change in products and services, innovation etc. So the management should prepare its employees for such situations by providing them with training and development programs as it would make it easier for the management to cope up with the changes and will let them be prepared to face the competitive environment and maintain competitive advantage.

There is increase in the level of competition due to globalization, liberalization and privatization and market had now become a competitive one which means that the sellers no longer have the power over the market and prices (Swaminathan, Rajkumar, 2013). They have to now compete with other similar products. This increased the complexity of each job due to which the employees feel certain level of stress in their job. (Du, Zhang, Tekhleah, 2018) Globalization intensifies competition in the market and employees of organization face increasing levels of job stress and the organizations constantly try searching for an alternative which can reduce the negative consequences of stress. It is proved that stress can drain out the physical and mental ability of an employee to perform their job. (Du, Zhang, Tekhleah, 2018) Moreover stress also weakens the motivation and drains the energy of the employees and does not allow them to perform at their full potential. In such times having job control will help employees reduce the negative consequences posed by job stress. Job control is a person's ability to influence what happens at his/her work environment especially the matters of personal interest. (Shutherland, 2017) defines job control as autonomy and effective total control over the job. To reduce such negative consequences, the organization should concentrate on providing work-life balance to the employees. (Tiwari, Tyagi, 2014) feel that in the era of globalization, the word 'work-life balance' became an important and inseparable part of any organization. They also mentioned that there are 3 main factors of work-life balance for any organization; they are- global, competition, personal lives/family values. The organizations should try to balance these three for the employees.

The importance of the relationship between globalization and employees especially in developing countries is increasing. (Dogan, 2016) feels there are many ways in which globalization effects labor. It is affected through increased sales, Foreign Direct Investment (FDI) and technological transfer. Increased sales will slowly raise the number of jobs and the employment will increase. FDI also creates new jobs. Employment creation is regarded as an important potential contribution from FDI to the economy (Tenkins, 2006). The technology transfer will ensure new technology is available in all parts of the world. It will create requirement for people with new skills. It will impose stress on employees to constantly learn new skills but the organization can reduce this stress and at the same time create loyalty by providing training and development programs from time to time. The changes caused due to globalization lead to increase in number of tasks of each job which result in job redesigning. (Kelly, 1992) Job redesigning is perceived by the employees as the improvement of their old job content. They look into it as job enrichment and empowerment because of which they tend to get satisfied and motivated. Management also sees flexibility as a way to become a global player (Porter, 1986). They maximize the use of flexible labor practices at all levels as it helps reduce the pressure and is an active response to a pattern of constrained behavior.

Globalization is leading to an increase in competition and is adding pressure on to the organizations to survive and grow in this ever changing environment which has high levels of uncertainty. If there are no proper employee relations in the organizations it would be difficult for the organizations to cope up with this change and survive in the competitive environment as the success of the organization depends on the employees (Jenzeb, Bashir, 2013).

EMPLOYEE PERCEPTION

Perception is a process by which an employee interprets their impressions and organizes them to give a proper explanation to their workplace behaviors (Langton, Robbins, 2006). Employees, just like anyone, have their perception towards everything that happens around them. Different groups of employees (departments, teams, divisions etc) have different types of perceptions which might be influenced by the discussion of the group. When they feel they are not receiving the monetary and non-monetary benefits that they deserve, it would lead to de motivation (Ullah, Khan, Siddique, 2017). They want to get compensated for their work in a fair manner. They also expect the organization to constantly support them and such support could lead to increase in motivation level and will develop a sense of belongingness. (Zhong, Wayne, Liden, 2016) also agreed that if the organizations provide support their employees on a regular basis, it will increase their motivation level which would lead to the improvement of individual and organizational performance in terms of profitability and growth. (Ullah, Khan, Siddique, 2017) also proved through their study that high perception of workplace support leads to high levels of employee motivation. Top management, HR managers and immediate supervisors should realize and understand the importance of workplace support and motivation. When management provides such kind of support to the employees they try to put their best efforts to the job and when these efforts are noticed and rewarded they will try to maintain the efficiency and will try to improve. (Tiwari, Lenka, 2016) Constant motivational support from the management would encourage the employees to put in their best efforts and when management provides clear value proposition to recognize and reward such employees, it motivates them to work enthusiastically.

(Rahman, Taniya, 2017) through their study revealed that if employee relation components like leadership, training, communication, rewards etc. are properly implemented in organizations and if managers give it high priority, it will help employees achieve tasks and targets that are set for their job positions and will help them in developing effective communication. Developing proper communication channels and systems help the employees fulfill their information needs. Employees look up to supervisors to be responsible for providing information and support (Tiwari, Lenka, 2016). They blame their supervisors if the information is not being communicated to them (Cole, 2006). Over a period of time they would develop negative relations with their superiors for not communicating properly. Employees also want to be heard, they want the management to listen to their concerns and problems. When management listens to their issues, especially when they provide support for personal issues, it creates greater sense of loyalty from the employees and that will increase their interest in work. Also when the problems of employees are solved, their stress level will reduce which will improve their concentration at work. In the same way when employees are involved in decision making, it helps creating a sense of belongingness among the employees, which helps in creating good congenial working environment and contributes towards building good employer-employee relationship (Das, Baruah, 2013).

The continual change in the competitive environment is making it important for organization to adapt to the changing environment. The organizations constantly have to change their structures, technology, manpower, managers etc. as per the requirements. When such changes are taking place, employees usually tend to worry and panic about their roles, career, new tasks and they experience fear and anxiety. But, if the employees have good perception of the organization and there are good relations between them, they trust the organization and their decisions and will try not to panic or worry in such situations. When employee has good impression, the same is reciprocated to the external environment. Such organizations not only perform well and attract prospective employees but they also retain their potential workforce which helps them achieve sustainable competitive advantage.

A study by (Blyton, 2008) revealed that employees do not give their best performance when they are not satisfied or when they are un-happy with their management, superiors, government or even their colleagues. Sometimes when employees are not satisfied with the policies or/and when there is bad relationship between employees and management, it can lead to strikes, lockout or such drastic actions. Employees sometimes take such drastic actions to express their grievances or when they feel management is doing nothing to solve their grievances even after having knowledge about it. Such problems can be avoided by management by maintaining relations and incorporating loyalty and trust on the organizations and their decisions. (Murali, Poddar, Seema, 2017) through their research proved that there is positive relationship between loyalty and performance. Loyalty also ensures that the employees stick to the organization for long. Whereas, when they are satisfied with their job, it is reflected in their performance. It not only increases the productivity but also satisfies the customers and clients. It does not only make the organization attractive for prospective employees but also increases the customer base. According to Fortune magazine, 40% of companies listed under top 100 "America's Best Companies to Work For" also appeared on Fortune top 500 companies. All these factors clearly show the importance of maintaining employee relations and these benefits help the organizations maintain their competitive advantage even during tough situations.

EMPLOYEE RELATIONS AND COMPETITIVE ADVANTAGE

Companies make strategies and policies to survive in the competition and they try to be innovative so that no other firm can copy their strategies. Making such strategies will give competitive advantage to the firm. (Barney, 1991) A firm is said to have competitive advantage when it is implementing a value creating strategy not simultaneously being implemented by any current or potential competitor. Earlier these strategies were limited to technology and financial resources. Companies used to focus on technological and financial resources as a source for competitive advantage but, the source of competitive advantage has shifted from financial resources to technological resources to human capital. This means that the emphasis is now on human capital and the firm's actual success and prosperity lie on the employee's skills, efficiencies, motivation, loyalty, satisfaction etc. (Jassim, 1998) Even though this is widely accepted, many firms still do not give utmost importance to human resources. They might talk about the importance of HR but they do not show it through their actions. But big companies like Google, Wipro and the like have realized the worth of Human Resource and thus started treating them as strategic partner and source of sustained competitive Advantage. As performance, productivity, quality and services all depend on the human resources. A firm is said to have sustained competitive advantage when it is implementing a value creating strategy not simultaneously being implemented by any current or potential competitors and when these other firms are unable to duplicate the benefits of the strategy (Barney, 1991). Sustained competitive advantage exists only when other organizations are unable to duplicate the benefits of the firm's competitive advantage (Jassim, 1998). A company might imitate the HR policies used by a successful firm, but during cases of difficulty they wouldn't know what to actually do. This is because the problem faced by every organization is different in many ways, the internal and external environment changes from organization to organization and the way the environment reacts to the actions taken by the organization also changes. (Hemmasi, 1983) different competitive environments and various strategies beget different organizational responses.

Many authors feel that the resources responsible for having competitive advantage, changes from organization to organization and it is not really easy to find the main resource responsible for gaining the sustained competitive advantage. Each manager in the firm believes in different possibilities. Everyone might have different theories but it is almost not possible to prove them. According to (Barney, 1991) as long as the link between resources controlled by a firm and competitive advantage remains ambiguous, it is not possible for other firms to imitate the successful firm's strategy.

Employee relations help in creating a culture of mutual respect and trust which is very difficult to imitate. No other firm can be able perfectly imitate the culture and create same level of understanding and trust. Employee relations help gain trust, establishing confidence and loyalty of employees towards the organization. (Bajaj, 2013) observed that employee relations promote commitment, facilitates employees to achieve organizational objectives, increases trust and reduces conflicts. All of these will lead to smooth functioning of the firm and will help in creating an environment which will result in better performance and satisfied workforce. When the employees are satisfied, their efficiency increases which further increases the organization's performance. Positive and healthy environment will enhance the organization's reputation leading to the success. Thus, maintaining positive employee relations is very crucial to have competitive advantage and be successful.

CONCLUSION

From this chapter we can understand the importance of employee relations in an organization. It is crucial for an organization to consider both employer and employee's goals. The survival, growth and prosperity of the organization depend on maintaining harmonious employee relations (Samwel, 2018). It is high time the organizations realize that their success depends on its employees and importance of maintaining good employee relations as it can lead to better performance, loyal employees, satisfied workforce and clients. Many successful organizations are constantly trying to understand the needs of the employees for the very same reason.

Satisfied, competent and committed employees give extraordinary performance. Organizations can use many techniques like fair rewards and recognition; encourage employee participation in decision making, taking care of work-life balance and employee relations to ensure higher retention and decrease in employee turnover (Das, Baruah, 2013). It is important for the organizations to focus on bringing a positive change in the organization instead of focusing on one or two factors since the needs of each employee varies.

In the era of globalization it would be difficult for organizations to survive the competition and the changes it brings along with it if there aren't good employee relations. Globalization is leading to the merging of employee relations practices globally (Jha, Varkker, 2011). It is paving way towards new problems like increased complexity of jobs, increase in stress level; constant change in strategies and technology etc. and such problems requires new solutions and better relationship management. This is the reason many companies are creating new role of employee relations/ retention specialist (Singh, 2019). It is understandable that every organization should realize the benefits of employee relations and should invest in it to maintain their competitive edge since it helps organizations to convert employees into sources of competitive advantage in such a way that no other firm can perfectly imitate the resources of the organization. It is important for every to focus on maintaining proper employee relation practices to leverage best out of its employees and thus gain competitive edge.

REFERENCES

Ashford, S. J., Lee, C., & Bobko, P. (1989). Content, cause, and consequences of job insecurity: A theory- based measure and substantive test. *Academy of Management Journal, 32*(4), 803–828. doi:10.2307/256569

Bacong, C.I.M., & Encio, H.A. (2017). Effect of employee relation to job performance in engineering, construction and manufacturing company. *Asia Pacific Journal of Educational, Arts and Sciences, 42*(2), 103-110.

Bajaj, R. (2013). Suggestions to implement human relations and its determinants in public sector. *American Journal of Engineering Research, 2*(12), 91–97.

Balamurugan, G., & Abinaya, R. (2016). A study on employee retention strategies in leading IT companies at Trichy. *Intercontinental Journal of Human Resource Research Reviews, 4*(3), 42-47.

Barney, J. (1991). Firms resources and sustained competitive advantage. *Journal of Management, 17*(1), 99–117. doi:10.1177/014920639101700108

Barrett, M., & McCallum, C. (1996). Globalization and the employment relationship: towards an explanatory framework. Research papers in international business, 4-95.

Blyton, P., & Turnbull, P. (2004). *The dynamics of employee relations (3rd ed.)*. Palgrave Macmillan.

Cole, M. S., Bruch, H., & Vogel, B. (2006). Emotion as mediators of the relations between perceived supervisor support and psychological hardiness on employee criticism. *Journal of Organizational Behavior, 27*(4), 463–484. doi:10.1002/job.381

Das, B. L., & Baruah, M. (2013). Employee retention: A review of literature. *IOSR Journal of Business and Management, 14*(2), 8–14. doi:10.9790/487X-1420816

Dogan, B. (2016). The effects of globalization on employment: Bounds test approach in Turkey sample. *Asian Economic and Financial Review, 6*. doi:18488/journal.aefr/2016.6.10/102.10.620.633

Du, Y., Zhang, L., & Tekleab, A.G. (2018). Job strains, job control, and POS on employee performance: an interactionist perspective. *Journal of Business Research*, 213-216. doi:10.1016/j.jbusres.2017.09.040

Eisenhardt, K. M. (1989). Making fast strategic decisions in high- velocity environments. *Academy of Management Journal, 32*(3), 543–576.

Frankel, J. A. (2000). *Globalization of the economy*. National Bureau of Economic Research. https://www.nber.org/papers/w7858

George, A. (2012). Business environment factors- a conceptual frame work. Academic Press.

Ghansah, E. (2011). *The role of employee retention on job performance* (Unpublished dissertation). Kwame Nikrumah University of Science and Technology.

Glassop, L. I. (2002). The organizational benefits of teams. *Human Relations, 55*(2), 225–247. doi:10.1177/0018726702055002184

Hemmasi, M. (1983). Competitive environment, business strategy, and organizational structure, an analysis of firm performance. LSU Historical Dissertations and Theses, 5-30.

Irani, F. N. H. A., & Noruzi, M. R. (2011). Globalization and challenges; what are the globalization's contemporary issues? *International Journal of Humanities and Social Science, 1*(6), 216–217.

Jassim, R. K. (1998). *Competitive advantage through the employee* (Unpublished doctoral dissertation). Reg. Eng. College of Technology at Jeddah.

Jehanzeb, K., & Bashir, N. A. (2013). Training and development program and its benefits to employee and organization: A conceptual study. *European Journal of Business and Management, 5*(2), 243–250.

Jenkins, R. (2006). Globalization, foreign investment and employment in Vietnam. *Transactional Corporations, 15*(1), 115-142.

Jha, J. K., & Varkkey, B. (2017). Convergence or divergence: The impacts of globalization on employee relations in India and China. *IJES, 25*(2), 44–57.

Judge, W. Q., & Miller, A. (1991). Antecedents and outcomes of decision speed in different environmental contexts. *Academy of Management Journal, 34*(2), 449–463. PMID:10111313

Kelly, J. (1992). Does job re-design theory explain job re-design outcomes? *Human Relations, 45*(8), 753–774. doi:10.1177/001872679204500801

Langton, N., & Robbins, S. (2006). *Organizational behaviour.* Toronto: Pearson Prentice Canada.

Lansiluoto, A. (2004). *Economic and competitive environment analysis in the formation of strategy.* Publications of the Turku School of Economics and Business Administration.

Mathimaran, K.B., & Kumar, A.A. (2017). Employee retention strategies-An empirical research. *Global Journal of Management and Business Research: E Marketing, 17*(1), 17-21.

Murali, S., Poddar, A., & Seema, A. (2017). Employee loyalty, organizational performance and performance evaluation- a critical survey. *IOSR Journal of Business and Management, 19*(8), 62–73. doi:10.9790/487X-1908036274

Nikoloski, K., Dimitrova, J., Koleva, B., & Kacarski, E.M. (2014). From industrial relations to employment relations with focus on employee relations. *International Journal of Sciences: Basic and Applied Research, 18*(2), 117-122.

Nwokocha, I., & Iheriohanma, E. B. J. (2012). Emerging Trends in Employee Retention Strategies in a Globalizing Economy: Nigeria in Focus. *Asian Social Science, 8*(10), 198–202. doi:10.5539/ass.v8n10p198

Pahuja, S., & Dalal, R.C. (2016). *Study of human resource system, competitive advantage status and their relation in Indian public sector banks*. doi:10.5958/0976-173X.2013.00027.0

Pfeffer, J., & Leblelici, H. (1973). The effects of competition on some dimensions of organization structure. Social forces, 52, 268-279.

Porter, M. (1986). *Competition in global industries*. Harvard University Press.

Rahman, M.S., & Taniya, R.K. (2017). Effect of employee relationship management (ERM) on employee performance: a study on private commercial banks in Bangladesh. *Human Resource Management Research, 7*(2), 90-95. doi:10.5923/j.hrmr.20170702.03

Samwell, J.O. (2018). Effects of employee relations on employee performance and organizational performance- study of small organizations in Tanzania. *Global Journal of Management and Research: Administration and Management, 18*(8).

Sanyal, S., & Hisam, M. W. (2018). The impact of teamwork on work performance of employees: A study of faculty members in Dhofar University. *IOSR Journal of Business and Management, 20*(3), 15–21. doi:10.9790/487X-2003011522

Scherer, F. M. (1980). *Industrial market structure and economic performance*. Rand McNally.

Senevirathna, G.A.B.E. (2017). *Factors affecting employee retention*. Academic Press.

Sequeira, A.H., & Dhriti, A. (2015). *Employee relations and its impacts on employee performance: a case study*. doi:10.13140/RG.2.1.3942.5446

Sharma, V. (2016). Exploring employee retention in IT industry in India: Study based on multi response analysis. *IJCEM*, *2*(12), 86–97.

Sheridan, J. E. (1992). Organizational culture and employee retention. *Academy of Management Journal*, *35*(5), 1036–1049.

Simonetti, J. L., & Boseman, F. G. (1975). The impact of market competition on organization structure and effectiveness: A cross- cultural study. *Academy of Management Journal*, *18*(3), 631–638.

Singh, D. (2019). A Literature Review on Employee Retention with Focus on Recent Trends. *International Journal of Scientific Research in Science, Engineering and Technology*, 425–431. doi:10.32628/IJSRST195463

Steiner, G. (1969). *Strategic factors in business success*. New York: Financial Executive Research Foundation.

Subramaniam, K.R. (2017). Employer employee relationship and impact on organization structure and strategy. *International Journal of Innovative Trends in Engineering*, *27*(43), 39-44.

Sutherland, J. (2017). Job control, job demands and job satisfaction in Britain: trends and inter- relationships. In *Scottish centre for employment research* (pp. 1–18). SCER.

Swaminathan, P.S., & Rajkumar, S. (2013). Stress levels in organizations and their impact on employees' behaviour. *BVIMR Management Edge*, *6*(1), 79-87.

Tiwari, B., & Lenka, U. (2015). Building and branding talent hub: An outlook. *Industrial and Commercial Training*, *47*(4), 208–211. doi:10.1108/ICT-11-2014-0077

Tiwari, D.N., & Tyagi, S. (2014). Impact of globalization on work life balance in IFFCO, AONLA, BAREILLEY. *International Journal of Research in Commerce and Management*, *5*(8), 55-57.

Ullah, Z., Khan, M. Z., & Siddique, M. (2017). Analysis of employees' perception of workplace support and level of motivation in public sector healthcare organization. *Business and Economic Review*, *9*(3), 240–256. doi:10.22547/BER/9.3.10

Urbancova, H., & Snydrova, M. (2017). Remuneration and employee benefits in organizations in the benefits in organizations in the Czech Republic. *Acta Universitatis agriculturae et Silviculturae mendelianae Brunsis*, *65*, 357-363. . doi:10.11118/actaun201765010357

Zhong, L., Wayne, S. J., & Liden, R. C. (2016). Job engagement, perceived organizational support, high- performance human resource practices, and cultural value orientations: Across- level investigation. *Journal of Organizational Behavior*, *37*(6), 823–844. doi:10.1002/job.2076

Chapter 4
The Relationship Between Ethical Climate, Workplace Deviance, and Mindfulness:
A Theoretical Framework

Meltem Akca
https://orcid.org/0000-0001-5544-5929
Alanya Alaaddin Keykubat University, Turkey

Meltem Yavuz
Mind Crafting Academy, Turkey

İhsan Akca
Sakarya University, Turkey

ABSTRACT

Development of postmodern organizational approaches in the knowledge-based business environment plays a major role on the gaining importance of knowledge-based talents and skills. Moreover, corporate governance-related progress impacts structures and implications of organizations. Enterprises must follow the rules required by the age and regard the innovations in order to maintain their assets and provide competitive advantage. For that reason, human-related innovations and practices are popular in the management area. In this perspective, ethics is one of the most significant issues in both business and social life. Enhancement of negative work outcomes triggers the efforts for the establishment of ethical climates. Increase of the workplace deviance of employees also influences the need of moderating variables in the relationship between ethical climates and deviance. This chapter mentions ethical climate, workplace deviance, and mindfulness. Moreover, relations between variables are discussed in reference to the literature.

DOI: 10.4018/978-1-7998-3515-8.ch004

INTRODUCTION

Due to the rapid development of the knowledge-based economy with the new capitalism, the knowledge-based skills that businesses have; started to constitute the basis for creating organizational success and sustainable competitive advantage (Spanos & Lioukas, 2001). As it is known, efficiency and effectiveness criteria generally determine the performance of the enterprise. While these criteria may consist of financial values, they may also consist of non-financial values (Kor & Mesko, 2013). As the current literature points out, it is emphasized that the main sources that increase the performance of the organizations are human resources and human-based skills (Luthans et al., 2004; Ambrosini & Bowman, 2009; Acquaah, 2012). If one of the most important sources determining performance is human talent or attitudes, this may be both an advantage and it may also appear as a disadvantage. Therefore, humanitarian attitudes or values can be constructive for an organization as well as they may lead to devastating consequences. In this chapter, we aim to make an assessment on variables that can lead to both negative and positive outputs, and to develop a theoretical framework to empirically test the proposed model. In this context, we have determined variables that are ethical climate, workplace deviant and mindfulness. As the theoretical background supports, it is proposed that there is a significant relationship between ethical climate dimensions and workplace deviant behavior and mindfulness positively moderates these relationships.

THEORETICAL BACKGROUND

Ethical Climate

The concept of ethical climate was first proposed by Victor and Cullen (1988). The ethical climate is the employee's perception of whether the norms, rules, principles, values, and beliefs that exist in the organization are ethical (Jaramillo, Mulki & Solomon, 2006: 272). In addition, it is the ethical climate that guides employees in their decision-making processes regarding acceptable and unacceptable behaviors (Ulrich et al., 2007; Huang, You & Tsai, 2012; Karagözlü, Özden & Yıldırım, 2014: 35).

Arnaud (2010) stated that most of the ethical climate related studies refers to the Victor and Cullen's (1987-1988) typology. While forming ethical climate dimensions, Victor and Cullen (1987-1988) used Kohlberg (1984) Theory of Cognitive Moral. Kohlberg (1984) defined ethical standards as; self-interest, caring and principle. Victor and Cullen (1987-1988) focused on these standards while explaining ethical climate theories. Victor and Cullen (1988) also stated that ethical climate relates to the employees 'perceptions about whether the organizations' policies, rules, practices, and principles are ethical or not. In this context, employees' perceptions and thoughts about the principles and procedures that exist in their organizations create an ethical climate (Elçi & Alpkan, 2006; Şahin & Dündar, 2011). Accordingly, the ethical climate is a business climate that the organization has and consists of ethical values (Mulki, Jaramillo & Locander, 2009). In addition, ethical climate is considered as a part of organizational climate that may shape the behavior and implementations in the workplace (Wimbush & Shepard,1994; Appelbaum et al., 2005). In this perspective, organizational climate is perceived as which employee expectation from the organization is met (Isaac, 1993). If employees' expectations are met by the organization, perception of organizational climate exists as good. On the other side, if expectations of employees about work or life are not met, organizational climate perception transforms to negative (Vardi, 2001). Due to the moral issues are especially important for individuals' behaviors, employees' perceptions about ethical values, policies, practices, and norms have a major role on their reactions towards organizational climates (Cullen et al., 2003). Furthermore, the strong ethical climate is accepted as an informal control mechanism within the institution. Perception of ethical climate examines that how employees deal with ethical choices that confront them (Appelbaum et al., 2005). The clearness and transparency of the rules, principles, and values for knowing ethical and unethical behaviors within the organization are effective in the positive attitude of employees (Mccabe, Trevino & Butterfield, 2001). Therefore, it is possible to say that the ethical climate also performs a psychological function by guiding the employees (Demir, 2019).

Schneider and Rentsch (1998) and Vardi (2001) and Victor and Cullen (1988) defined that multiple types of climates may exists in organizations. According to Victor and Cullen (1998), organizations and subgroups have different rules, systems, and standards. In this case, the ethical climate differs from organization to organization. The different identity of each organization is effective in the differentiation of the ethical climate structure. Besides, differences in ethical climate perception may occur between internal units and departments (Yeşil, Mavi & Ceyhan, 2017; Yurdakul, 2013; Rothwell & Baldwin, 2006; Tuna & Yeşiltaş, 2014; Elçi &Alpkan, 2009).

In their study, Victor and Cullen (1988) created a model consisting of two dimensions, three types and nine principles regarding ethical climate. The first dimension is the classification of the structure of ethical criteria used in organizational decision making. Kohlberg (1967) Cognitive Moral Development Theory was effective in the creation of this classification (Parboteeah et al., 2010; Tuna & Yeşiltaş, 2014). The egoist, benevolent and principle climate types are covered under this typology. On the other side, the locus of analysis used in ethical decision making is considered as the second dimension. Goldner's (1957) Social Role Theory was used to base the locus of analysis (Thompson & Greene,1994; Schminke, Ambrose & Neubaum,

2005). Individual, local, and cosmopolitan levels are assigned as the base of the locus of analysis. While the ethical climate is referred for decision making in the organization, the local of analysis is used to determine the level of decision making (Victor & Cullen, 1988). According to this model, ethical climate dimensions are comprised of instrumental, caring, independence, rules, laws, and codes (Akdoğan & Demirtaş, 2014; Ismail & Yuhanis, 2018).

Table 1. Principles of ethical climate

			Locus of Analysis	
		Individual	Local	Cosmopolitan
	Egoism	Self-Interest	Company Profit	Efficiency
Ethical Criterion	Benevolence	Friendship	Team Interest	Social Responsibility
	Principle	Personal and Morality	Company Rules and Procedures	Law and Professional Codes

Egoism is the organizational behavior in search of drying out and rewarding for individuals and organizations. Elçin and Alpkan (2009) compared egoism to hedonism and evaluated it in a hedonic approach such as searching for things that would provide personal benefit and avoiding painful things. In the egoist climate type, it is seen that employees exhibit behaviors in their own favor and interests to avoid reward or punishment. These behaviors lead to a climate where competitive, cost-effective targets are set for increasing individual and organizational efficiency (Akkoç, 2012). Contrary to the egoist climate type, it is explained with benevolence that individuals, colleagues, and colleagues want to be good and care about them. In this ethical climate type, organizational behaviors are adopted, which least disturb the members of the organization and will benefit them. Utilitarianism for many people in the benevolent climate type comes to the fore (Elçin & Alpkan, 2009). Benevolent climate type is a climate type that encourages friendship, benevolence, strengthening interpersonal relationships and loyalty (Akkoç, 2012). Considering the best for everyone in the organization reflects the benevolent climate (Deshpande, 1996). It is emphasized that the organizational climate is mentoring, educational, benevolent in participatory, group-based cultures. Relationships between individuals and departments are strong in this type of organizational climates and labor turnover is low (Mohr, Young, & Burgess, 2012).

The type of ethical criteria that employees depend on the rules created by the organization is principle. Principle is a deontological approach and it is based on the adoption and compliance with certain principles as reference (Elçi & Alpkan, 2009). Despite teleological approaches in egoistic and benevolent climate types, principle focuses on abstract behavior associated with the organization, as opposed to personal and team satisfaction and interests. It is envisaged how the employees working in the ethical climate of principle should decide in line with organizational value, principles, rules, and norms (Akkoç, 2012). In the climate of principle, it is nourished from the approach that a morally inaccurate behavior will bring positive results for others will not justify the person. In the climate type, it is emphasized that the individual's own moral values in the individual field, organizational principles in the local field, and the legal system will be the reference in the universal field (Yılmaz & Yıldırım, 2019).

Table 2. Dimensions of ethical climate

			Locus of Analysis	
		Individual	**Local**	**Cosmopolitan**
	Egoism	Instrumental		
Ethical Theory	Benevolence	Caring		
	Principle	Independence	Rules	Law and Code

Self-interest is related with egoism and individual needs. Self-interest is comprised of strength, well-being, happiness, digestion, and individual interests. Organizational interest (corporate profit) also feeds from egoistic ethical criterion that requires ethical decision-making by groups of employees who accept organizational interests more than everything. Efficiency criterion also takes place in egoist structure and ethical decisions are evaluated accordance with economic and social interests. Moreover, friendship refers to benevolent criteria and emphasizes the importance of caring of all organizational members in the focus of individual analysis. Team spirit is also supported by benevolent criteria that cares about others' well-being in the organization. Similarly, social responsibility also related with cosmopolitan focus of analysis that aims provide welfare of others (Maloof, 2018). Furthermore, personal and morality, law, and professional codes feeds from principle theory whereas they have different bases for locus of analysis in the decision-making process.

In an instrumental climate, ethical decisions are made based on individual or organizational self-interest, even if those decisions work to the detriment of others (e.g., In this company, people are mostly out for themselves) (Martin & Cullen, 2006; Simha & Cullen, 2012). Despite any potential benefits, this type of climate tends to be least preferred among employees (Tsai & Huang, 2008). In a caring climate, ethical decisions are made based on what is best for others (e.g., The most important concern is the good of all the people in the company). Employees typically prefer this type of climate (Deshpande & Joseph, 2009). In an independent climate, ethical decisions are made based on personal principles and judgment, regardless of the organization's stance (e.g., In this company, people are expected to follow their own personal and moral beliefs) (Martin & Cullen, 2006; Simha & Cullen, 2012). In a rules climate, ethical decisions are made based on the internal laws of the organization or rules of the company (e.g., It is very important to follow strictly the company's rules and procedures here) (Martin & Cullen, 2006; Simha & Cullen, 2012). Lastly, in a law and code climate, ethical decisions are made based on external laws (e.g., People are expected to comply with the law and professional standards over and above other considerations.) (Martin & Cullen, 2006; Simha & Cullen, 2012). Although these five climates are presented as distinct, an organization can have multiple climates present (Victor & Cullen, 1987).

Workplace Deviance

Negative behaviors in the literature have been described in different studies as; non-compliant behavior (Puffer, 1987), delinquency (Hogan & Hogan, 1989), negative citizenship behavior (Fisher, Locke & Henne,1992), workplace deviance (Robinson & Bennett, 1995; Robinson & Greenberg, 1998), organizational delinquency (Hogan & Hogan, 1989), tyranny (Ashforth,1997), antisocial behavior (Giacalone & Greenberg, 1997; Robinson and O'Learly-Kelly,1998), workplace aggression (Baron & Neuman, 1996), organizational misbehavior (Vardi & Wiener, 1996), dysfunctional behavior (Griffin, O'Leary-Kelly & Collins, 1998) organizational vice (Moberg, 1997), workplace counterproductivity (Sackett & DeVore, 2002), counterproductive behavior (Fox, Spector & Miles, 2001; Marcus, Schuler, Quell, & Hümpfner, 2002).

Kılıçarslan-Gökoğlu and Öztürk (2020) defined that employee behaviors that comprised of violate and damage intentions are called as deviant behaviors. Mehda (2020) also reported that deviant behavior means a behavior which is not productive for organizational sustainability that has harmful intentions in it. Peterson (2002) emphasized that workplace deviance behaviors are voluntary employee behaviors. In addition to that, workplace deviance is considered as "any organizational member action that violates widely accepted (societal) moral norms (Kish-Gephart, Harrison & Treviño, 2010:2). Moreover, workplace deviance is an undesirable concept for organizations which consists of harassment, fraud, sabotage, theft, drug-alcohol use, vandalism, absenteeism, slow working, long breaks and counterproductive work behaviors (Yavuz, Ozbilgin & Kamasak, 2020; Kwok, Au & Ho, 2005; Bennett & Robinson, 2000).

In the deviance typology, Robinson and Bennett (1995) classified workplace deviance in to two categories as organizational deviance (aims to harm organization and its processes) and interpersonal deviance (targets to damage personal relations). Moreover, Mehra (2020) reported that deviance can be formal (robbery) or informal (leg pulling). Robinson and Greenberg (1988) also noticed five important features for announcing a behavior as deviant. These are, perpetrator, intentionality, target of the behavior, nature and execution of the behavior and consequence of behavior. Scholars informed that analyzing these features, it is easier to call a behavior as a deviance or something else (Yüksel, 2012).

Reference to the Robinson and Bennett (1995), the implementations or actions related with individual behaviors of employees were announce as interpersonal deviance. In this context, interpersonal deviance targets to harm others, co-workers, subordinates and supervisor relations in the workplace. On the other side, organizational deviance is associated with intentions that aims to damage organization itself or its processes. (Robinson & Bennett, 1995). In this perspective, it should be emphasized that while organizational deviance aims to harm organization with theft, sabotage and unsuitable working hours related actions, interpersonal deviance focuses on other employees, colleagues and supervisors or leaders that includes gossiping, fun, physical aggression behaviors (Akca, 2020; Bennett and Robinson, 2000). Furthermore, scholars mentioned about four types of deviant behaviors by determining two main deviant dimensions. While production deviance and property deviance are related with organizational deviance, political deviance and personal aggression are classified under interpersonal deviance. Production deviance behaviors are comprised of actions like slow working, wasting resources, leaving workplace early and long breaks which have minor impacts in organization. Despite that, property deviance plays a major role in the occurrence of problems as sabotaging, stealing, bribery, lying behaviors that negatively correlated with job outcomes. In addition to these, political deviance can explain by actions and behaviors connected with blaming, gossiping, and unfair competing with colleagues. It is also significant to note that political deviance related conflicts have minor impressions on interpersonal relations and organization. On the other hand, personal aggression includes serious harmful intentions towards organizational members. Endangering, sexual harassment, verbal abuse and stealing other's equipment or and organizational things are some of instances of personal aggression.

Roots of workplace deviance goes back to Industrial Revolution (Klotz & Buckley, 2013). Mehra (2020) stated that supervisors' harassment on employees triggered the progress of deviant behaviors in organizations. Alias and Rasdi (2015) classified deviance antecedents in to three factors as: individual, organizational, and work-related. In this classification, ethical climate is evaluated under organizational factors that leads to the deviance (Mehra, 2020, Singh, 2020; Appelbaum et al,

2007). Moreover, Agwa (2018) noticed the antecedents of workplace deviance as unfair treatment, job stressors. Ambrose and colleagues (2002) also reported that injustice in organizations influence the existence of deviant behaviors. In addition to that, negative attitudes and workload in the work environment also play role on deviant behaviors (Litzky et al, 2006). Mehra (2020) also emphasized that negative perception of organizational climate, injustice in practices, and abusive supervision are some of determinants of deviant behaviors.

Kılıçarslan-Gökoğlu and Öztürk (2020) stated that deviant behaviors have been considered as a problem in the workplace in the past two decades. Deviant behaviors like stealing, violence, sabotage, aggressive behaviors are generally observed in today's most of organizations (Harper, 1990). Yavuz, Ozbilgin and Kamasak (2020) and Sharma and Singh (2020) expressed that deviant behaviors can directly or indirectly influence organizational outcomes at the workplace. Simons and Roberson (2003) determined that deviant behaviors need to be solved to minimize negative impacts on job outcomes related with unethical practices. Robinson and Greenberg (1998) documented that negative workplace behaviors both causes financial losses and deterioration at social and psychosocial relations in the organizations. Appelbaum and colleagues (2005) also reported that deviant workplace behaviors result with revenue losses and damage organizational environment. In addition to financial costs of deviance behaviors it is also important to note that deviance connected social costs have increased in organizations (Kidwell & Martin, 2005). Litzky and colleagues (2006) determined that higher production costs, inconsistent pricing and service quality, poor reputation are also some of consequences of workplace deviance in organizations.

Mindfulness

Mindfulness is a state of awareness of moment experiences, which includes consciousness and non-judgmental attentiveness (Bishop et al., 2004; Kabat-Zinn, 1994). The concept does not only involve recognizing what is in the present, but also the way we meet what we recognize (Segal, Williams, and Teasdale, 2002). Therefore, mindfulness can be called as the combination of perception and acceptance of judgment since perception itself can merely be considered as an ongoing process including unconsciousness. Although mindfulness relies on the Buddhist philosophy and has a history that traces back to nearly 3000-years, it is not connected with any religious or philosophical movement in its current form. However, the most potent aspect of mindfulness relies on scientific evidence, which supports its effectiveness across different contexts such as psychology, psychiatry, medicine, sports, nutrition etc. (Creswell, 2017). Latterly, mindfulness-based intervention techniques to improve emotional intelligence and enhance active collaboration and leadership skills have started to be used widely in the workplace settings (Hülsheger et al., 2012). There is strong evidence that show mindfulness-based interventions have a positive impact on different employee outcomes. For example, according to the results obtained from 62 literature review studies mindfulness interventions have positive effects on several outcomes that are cognitive, attitudinal, behavioral, psychological health, physical health (Yavuz, 2019).

Yavuz (2019) found 431.000 results that include the word "mindfulness" at Google Scholar on 14 January 2019. Besides, the search yields up to 3328 studies that include the word "mindfulness-based interventions", "mindfulness meditation", and "mindfulness training" in organizational settings at the databases such as PsycINFO, Business Source Premier, CINAHL Plus with Full Text and ERIC. One of the reasons why the mindfulness movement has gained such momentum in the past decade is that we have been performing more multitasking than ever before and feel the negative effects of constant shifting (Panno et al., 2018). While our brains are technically able to focus on one thing at a time, our transition from thought to thought is surprisingly high for a lot of people, especially white-collar workers. Increasing screen usage and faster-paced life are two important contributions of this epidemic. In general, the brains of the white-collar employees are at extreme speed, as they focus on many things at the same time. This can quickly consume limited mental energy and greatly affect overall well-being (Vu and Gill, 2018). By adopting mindfulness and using what we want to be careful about, we can slow down our thoughts, regulate our minds, and lead quieter, more productive lives (Williams and Seaman, 2016). Focusing on the present allows individual to calmly accept the feelings, thoughts and bodily sensations. Mindfulness allows people to be gentle even in the difficult situations they encounter during the day, to stand for a while instead of reacting quickly to a destructive reaction, and even to grow compassion even those who are challenging us (Christensen-Salem et al., 2020).

For many people, the workplace can be incredibly stressful and not a pleasant place to spend their days. The time spent there is considered a requirement to make money. However, today workplaces are trying to become places to have fun, not feared places to go. One reason is that many introduce and apply mindfulness and change the way people work together and the environments in which they work. Mindfulness is an excellent tool to help enterprises run smoothly and effectively. By increasing awareness in the workplace, it becomes a more effective environment where greater success can be achieved at many levels. If employees can communicate with their colleagues or executives carefully and thoughtfully at the workplace, it encourages them to be more focused and productive, which is exactly what mindfulness does (Barrett et al., 2016). It teaches individuals how to find it in an instant with full awareness and how best to bring it to themselves. When people try to do this, they may reduce stress, increase productivity and efficiency, and establish a better connection with their colleagues in the workplace settings (Valentine, Godkin, and Varca, 2010). By increasing mindfulness in the workplace, it becomes a more effective environment where greater success can be achieved at many levels.

A PROPOSED MODEL FOR RELATIONSHIP BETWEEN ETHICAL CLIMATE, WORKPLACE DEVIANCE AND MINDFULNESS

Ethical Climate and Workplace Deviance Behavior

In the literature, there are studies that reveal out the ethical climate is an antecedent of workplace deviance in organizations (Andreoli & Lefkowitz, 2008; Appelbaum et al., 2005; Appelbaum, Iaconi & Matousek, 2007; Peterson, 2002; Vardi, 2001). Wimbush and Shepard (1994) and Peterson (2002) also stated that ethical climate may be used to predict the deviant and counterproductive workplace behaviors. Besides, Harder (2019) defined that deviance behaviors can be caused by two main antecedents as organizational factors and situational factors. In this opinion, ethical climate is considered as an organizational factor while personality is evaluated as situational factor. Scholars also obtained in their empirical studies that ethical climate is negatively correlated with deviance behaviors (Deshpande & Joseph, 2009; Mayer et al., 2010; Smith, Thompson & Iacovou, 2009).

Social Exchange Theory is generally referred by the researchers who analyses the relationship between organizational related factors and workplace deviance (Obalade & Aragundade, 2019; Mitchell & Ambrose, 2007). Accordance with the theory, employees react as how they perceive the organizational conditions towards to them. Bandura's (1973) Social Learning Theory emphasized that individuals' behaviors are influenced by the behaviors of others where he/she belongs to. For that reason, if organization has an ethical climate, behaviors of employees tend to form as ethic. Moreover, Social Information Processing Theory (SIPT) can explain the relationship between ethical climate and workplace deviance. Reference to the theory, it is stated that individuals analyze their environment to learn how to behave in that environment (Salancik & Pfeffer, 1978). Besides, environment guides employees which behaviors are more valued and appropriate in the organization (Maloof, 2018). Besides, Trevino (1986) emphasized that organizational and situational factors impact employees' attitudes and behaviors at the workplace. In this context, Turnipseed (1988) also underlined the role of organizational climate on the employees' behavior.

Organizational climate is considered as the shared perceptions of practices, policies, implementations, and procedures (Reichers & Schneider,1990). Ethical climate is one of the organizational climate types that refers to shared perceptions about what is ethic and correct in organization that leads employees to behave better and ethic (Victor and Cullen, 1987-1988, Peterson, 2002). However, it is expected to have ethical behaviors with the design of ethical climate, if the climate is not perceived as ethical, employees' behaviors tend to occur as negative and deviant (Wimbush & Shepard, 1994). For that reason, ethical climate is both the antecedent of ethical behaviors and existence of deviance in the workplace (Peterson, 2002).

Determining how and which climate type minimize deviant behavior is an important issue for the managers (Harder, 2019). Climates that promote selfish structures easily tends to deviant behavior (Harder, 2019). Appelbaum and colleagues (2005) defined that instrumental climate is related with employees' own interest with production. Ismail and Yuhanis (2018) emphasized that in generally while egoist and instrumental climate types have a negative impact on ethical work behaviors; caring, independence, rules and company codes and law climates tend to have positive relations. Reference to Peterson (2002) independent and caring climates, were found negatively correlated with production deviance. On the other side, Pagliaro, Presti, Barattucci and Barreto (2018) explained that development of prosocial behavior in work environment in caring climate decrease deviance more than instrumental climate. Kaur (2017) obtained that independence, law and code, rules climates positively impact organizational commitment that discourage deviance behaviors. Riggle (2007) also obtained positive relationship between ethical climate and ethical behavior. Furthermore, Yüksel (2012) revealed out that caring climate has a negative impact on organizational deviance.

Vardi (2001) also obtained that there is a negative relationship between ethical climate and organizational misbehavior. Mayer and colleagues (2010) obtained that there is a negative relationship between ethical climate and employee misconduct. Aryati and colleagues (2018) found that ethical leadership impact the formation of ethical climate that negatively affect deviant behaviors in organizations. Yasir and Rasli (2018) analyzed the relationship between ethical climate and deviance behaviors of healthcare officers. With the participation of 289 healthcare officials it was found that organizational ethical climate has a negative impact on deviance behavior. Kılıç (2013) revealed out that increase of perception of ethical climate has a negative effect on production deviance. Moreover, he noticed that selfish and egoist climates has a positive correlation with deviance. Alias and Rasdi (2015) analyzed the relationship between ethical climate and deviance in an empirical study with the participation of Malaysian government employees and obtained that there is a negative correlation with ethical climate and interpersonal and organizational deviance. Moreover, it was stated that unethical practices both influence employee behavior and organizational reputation negatively (Alias & Rasdi,2015).

Kohlberg's (1984) Theory of Moral Development, emphasized that caring leads the employees job outcomes positively because of ethical standards that includes inside it. Benevolent climate is also related with moral philosophy (Martin & Cullen, 2006). Reference to Ethical Climate Theory, benevolent climate leads employees to behave for the welfare of all ones in the organization (Goldman & Tabak, 2010). Hollingworth and Valentine (2014) reported that employees tend to work harder to have a benevolent climate that leads welfare of all ones in the organization.

Kuenzi and Schminke (2009) determined that benevolent climate may be considered as a moderator due to its positive effects on employees' job outcomes. Sims and Keon (1997) also expressed that if employees perceived ethical climate as benevolent, they focus on their duties more and more. Reference to Liu and Chiu (2018) benevolent climate enforce employees to work harder to provide all individuals welfare and organizational success. Cullen and colleagues (2003) found that caring climate perceived as a positive by employees that supports employees for working better and preventing threats in the organization.

Lopez, Babin and Chung (2009) expressed that ethical climate questionnaire of Victor and Cullen (1988) is easily used for in different nations. Caring climate has positive impact on ethical behaviors in organization (Huang et al., 2012; Yener, Yaldıran & Ergun, 2012). Thus, it is proposed that:

P_1: Ethical climate dimensions significantly associated with workplace deviance behavior.

Moderating Effect of Mindfulness

The ethical climate in an organization includes common perceptions of what is ethically correct, including a 'team' psychology. Recent empirical studies showed that ethical climate promoted ethical leadership and performance outcomes, including labor turnover, organizational citizenship behavior, job satisfaction, and job performance, and compassion (Williams and Seaman, 2016). Undeniably, these are admirable benefits for practitioners; in fact, it would not be unreasonable to predict that such performance results will also support the improvement of administrative performance. The findings of another study showed that an ethical climate can also provide positive conditions to facilitate compassion that contribute corporate success (Zoghbi-Manrique-de-Lara & Guerra-Baez, 2016). It may be assumed that if employees feel more compassion, they may also avoid deviant behaviors.

Mindfulness enhances employees' understanding of workplace situations, monitoring and reacting to them, and further enhancing their senses throughout the organization. Awareness can also affect individuals' perceptions of their work because a stronger sense of corporate purpose has been created to link business activities within the firm.

It is collective awareness that unites employees under the assumptions of collaboration (Weick and Sutcliffe, 2006). Mindfulness includes a person's ability to evaluate conditions in a realistic and accurate way, making it easier to build important ideas (Brown, Ryan & Creswell, 2007).

Self-controlled regulation, which is the process of directing individuals' own feelings, thoughts and behaviors to achieve a specific and particularly demanding goal, is very common in modern Western cultures. It is even emphasized that self-regulation is an indispensable tool to focus on success in both professional and personal life. Unlike self-regulation, however, mindfulness is not a tool for individuals to move themselves in a predetermined direction. Rather, it is the capacity of the person to be aware of current thoughts and feelings, including self-control attempts. Mindfulness is a positive feature that allows individuals to respond more effectively to environmental demands (Valentine, Godkin & Varca, 2010).

Based on the literature, organizational characteristics affect ethical climate perception and workplace deviant behavior since these factors regulate the dynamics of the working situation that employees experience. It probably includes the level of organizational ethics based on ethical values and codes that raise awareness and reduce bullying (Ferrell and Ferrell, 2008). The negative relationship between perceived ethical climate will decrease when employees have higher levels of mindfulness. As a result, mindfulness resulting from perceived ethical climate may decrease deviant behaviors. Therefore, it can be proposed that:

P_2: Mindfulness positively moderates the relationship between ethical climate dimensions and workplace deviance behavior, such that ethical climate dimensions are associated with fewer workplace deviance behavior in employees with a high level of mindfulness.

CONCLUSION

Martin and Cullen (2006) stated that ethical work climates influence employees' work outcomes. Barnett and Vaicys (2000) also expressed that ethical climate affects employees' behavior and job outcomes. However, ethical climate is an important factor shaping intra-organizational relationships and employee behavior, and the interactions of ethical climate with organizational outputs and interactions need to be analyzed well (Elçi & Alpkan, 2009: 297). Although, effects of ethical work climates on negative behaviors were analyzed in a number of studies (Appelbaum

Figure 1. A model proposal

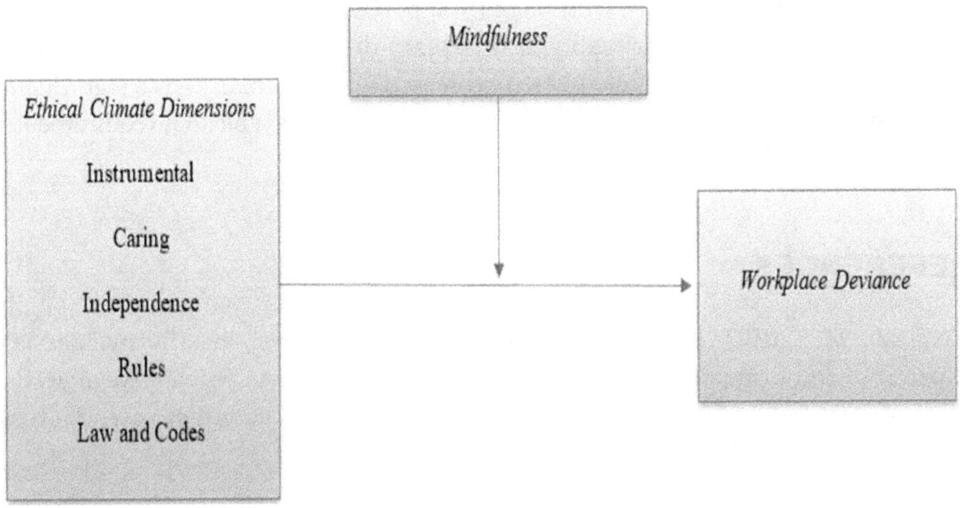

et al., 2007; Martin & Cullen, 2006; Appelbaum et al., 2005; Peterson, 2002; Vardi, 2001; Robinson & O'Leary-Kelly, 1998;Wimbush & Shephard, 1994), it has not been figured this interaction with the relationship of mindfulness.

Peterson (2002:50) expressed that ethics emphasized the behavior which is right or wrong in the reference of law, justice, or policies while deviance significantly violates organizational norms. Appelbaum and colleagues (2005) advised that having an ethical climate in organizations, may solve and manage the deviant behaviors in the workplace. Moreover, Robinson and Bennett (2000) and Henle and colleagues (2005) defined that lack of ethical climate in organizations causes unethical and deviant behaviors. Andreoli and Lefkowitz (2008) also reported in their empirical study that lower perception of ethical climate results with workplace deviance.

It is required to create an ethical climate both to control and reduce deviance behaviors in the workplace (Singh, 2020). Vardi (2001) emphasized that overall positive organizational climate results with less misconduct behavior. Peterson (2002) expressed that when an organization focuses on employees' well-being and welfare, deviance related behaviors tend to decrease.

Principle climates focus on ethical standards that lead these rules are beneficial for all organizational members (Kaur, 2017). Deshpande and Joseph (2009) expressed that preventing egoist climate may transform employee behaviors more ethic in the workplace.

Truthful about employees expectations, integration of ethical decision making or performance processes, ethical training programs, creating an ethical climate, building trust based relations, being fair at reward and punishment systems, training of supervisors, effective leadership implementations are some of advises that can reduce deviant behaviors in the workplace (Singh, 2020; Howald et al., 2018; Baucus & Near, 1991). Besides, spirituality at workplace discourage deviant behaviors in organizations. Ahmad and Omar (2016) expressed that spirituality has a significant impact on employees' behaviors. Satisfaction of employees' spiritual requirements can decrease tendency of workplace deviance (Sign, 2020).

REFERENCES

Acquaah, M. (2012). Social networking relationships, firm-specific managerial experience and firm performance in a transition economy: A comparative analysis of family owned and nonfamily firms. *Strategic Management Journal*, *33*(10), 1215–1228. doi:10.1002mj.1973

Agwa. (2018). *Workplace Deviance Behaviors, Leadership, Suleyman Davut Göker*. IntechOpen. Available from: https://www.intechopen.com/books/leadership/workplace-deviance-behaviors doi:10.5772/intechopen.75941

Ahmad, A., & Omar, Z. (2016). Workplace spirituality among Malaysian community service employees in the public sector. *Asian Social Science*, *12*(9), 193–201. doi:10.5539/ass.v12n9p193

Akca, M. (2020). An Investigation of the Relationship Between Favoritism and Workplace Deviance: Meditation Role of Negative Emotions. In*Analyzing Workplace Deviance in Modern Organizations* (pp. 114–138). IGI Global. doi:10.4018/978-1-5225-9996-8.ch007

Akdoğan, A., & Demirtaş, Ö. (2014). Etik Liderlik Davranişlarinin Etik İklim Üzerindeki Etkisi: Örgütsel Politik Algilamalarin Araci Rolü. *Afyon Kocatepe Üniversitesi İktisadi ve İdari Bilimler Fakültesi Dergisi*, *16*(1), 107–124.

Akkoç, İ. (2012). Gelişim Kültürü ve Etik İklimin Yenilikçiliğe Etkisinde Dağıtım Adaletinin Rolü. *Journal of Alanya Faculty of Business*, *4*(3), 45–60.

Alias, M., & Rasdi, R. M. (2015). Organizational predictors of workplace deviance among support staff. *Procedia: Social and Behavioral Sciences*, *172*, 126–133. doi:10.1016/j.sbspro.2015.01.345

Ambrose, M. L., Seabright, M. A., & Schminke, M. (2002). Sabotage in the workplace: The role of organizational injustice. *Organizational Behavior and Human Decision Processes*, *89*(1), 947–965. doi:10.1016/S0749-5978(02)00037-7

Ambrosini, V., & Bowman, C. (2009). What are dynamic capabilities and are they a useful construct in strategic management? *International Journal of Management Reviews*, *11*(1), 29–49. doi:10.1111/j.1468-2370.2008.00251.x

Andreoli, N., & Lefkowitz, J. (2009). Individual and organizational antecedents of misconduct in organizations. *Journal of Business Ethics*, *85*(3), 309–332. doi:10.100710551-008-9772-6

Appelbaum, S. H., Deguire, K. J., & Lay, M. (2005). The relationship of ethical climate to deviant workplace behaviour. *Corporate Governance: The International Journal of Business in Society,5*(4), 43-55.

Appelbaum, S. H., Deguire, K. J., & Lay, M. (2005). The relationship of ethical climate to deviant workplace behaviour. *Corporate Governance*, *5*(4), 43–55. doi:10.1108/14720700510616587

Appelbaum, S. H., Iaconi, G. D., & Matousek, A. (2007). Positive and negative deviant workplace behaviors: causes, impacts, and solutions. *Corporate Governance: The International Journal of Business in Society, 7*(5), 586-598.

Arnaud, A. (2010). Conceptualizing and measuring ethical work climate: Development and validation of the ethical climate index. *Business & Society*, *49*(2), 345–358. doi:10.1177/0007650310362865

Aryati, A. S., Sudiro, A., Hadiwidjaja, D., & Noermijati, N. (2018). The influence of ethical leadership to deviant workplace behavior mediated by ethical climate and organizational commitment. *International Journal of Law and Management*, *60*(2), 233–249. doi:10.1108/IJLMA-03-2017-0053

Ashforth, B. E. (1997). Petty tyranny in organizations: A preliminary examination of antecedents and consequences. *Canadian Journal of Administrative Sciences*, *14*(2), 126–140. doi:10.1111/j.1936-4490.1997.tb00124.x

Bandura, A. (1973). *Aggression: A social learning analysis*. Prentice-hall.

Barnett, T., & Vaicys, C. (2000). The moderating effect of individuals' perceptions of ethical work climate on ethical judgments and behavioral intentions. *Journal of Business Ethics*, *27*(4), 351–362. doi:10.1023/A:1006382407821

Baron, R. A., & Neuman, J. H. (1996). Workplace violence and workplace aggression: Evidence on their relative frequency and potential causes. *Aggressive Behavior: Official Journal of the International Society for Research on Aggression*, *22*(3), 161–173. doi:10.1002/(SICI)1098-2337(1996)22:3<161::AID-AB1>3.0.CO;2-Q

Barrett, B., Grabow, M., Middlecamp, C., Mooney, M., Checovich, M. M., Converse, A. K., Gillespie, B., & Yates, J. (2016). Mindful climate action: Health and environmental co-benefits from mindfulness-based behavioral training. *Sustainability, 8*(10), 1040. doi:10.3390u8101040 PMID:28008371

Baucus, M. S., & Near, J. P. (1991). Can illegal corporate behavior be predicted? An event history analysis. *Academy of Management Journal, 34*(1), 9–36.

Bennett, R. J., & Robinson, S. L. (2000). Development of a measure of workplace deviance. *The Journal of Applied Psychology, 85*(3), 349–360. doi:10.1037/0021-9010.85.3.349 PMID:10900810

Bishop, S. R., Lau, M., Shapiro, S., Carlson, L., Anderson, N. D., Carmody, J., Segal, Z. V., Abbey, S., Speca, M., Velting, D., & Devins, G. (2004). Mindfulness: A proposed operational definition. *Clinical Psychology: Science and Practice, 11*(3), 230–241. doi:10.1093/clipsy.bph077

Brown, K. W., Ryan, R. M., & Creswell, J. D. (2007). Mindfulness: Theoretical foundations and evidence for its salutary effects. *Psychological Inquiry, 18*(4), 211–237. doi:10.1080/10478400701598298

Christensen-Salem, A., Walumbwa, F. O., Babalola, M. T., Guo, L., & Misati, E. (2020). A Multilevel Analysis of the Relationship Between Ethical Leadership and Ostracism: The Roles of Relational Climate, Employee Mindfulness, and Work Unit Structure. *Journal of Business Ethics*, 1–20. doi:10.100710551-020-04424-5

Creswell, J. D. (2017). Mindfulness interventions. *Annual Review of Psychology, 68*(1), 491–516. doi:10.1146/annurev-psych-042716-051139 PMID:27687118

Cullen, J. B., Parboteeah, K. P., & Victor, B. (2003). The effects of ethical climates on organizational commitment: A two-study analysis. *Journal of Business Ethics, 46*(2), 127–141. doi:10.1023/A:1025089819456

Demir, S. (2018). Etik iklim ve okuldan ayrılma niyeti arasındaki ilişki: Örgütsel bağlılığın aracılık rolü. *Hacettepe Üniversitesi Eğitim Fakültesi Dergisi, 34*(3), 824–838.

Deshpande, S. P. (1996). Ethical Climate and the Link between Success and Ethical Behavior: An Empirical Investigation of a Non-Profit Organization. *Journal of Business Ethics, 15*(3), 315–320. doi:10.1007/BF00382957

Deshpande, S. P., & Joseph, J. (2009). Impact of emotional intelligence, ethical climate, and behavior of peers on ethical behavior of nurses. *Journal of Business Ethics, 85*(3), 403–410. doi:10.100710551-008-9779-z

Elçi, M., & Alpkan, L. (2006). The influences of ethical climate on organizational citizenship behaviors. *Hacettepe University Journal of Economics and Administrative Sciences*, *24*(1), 141–170.

Elçi, M., & Alpkan, L. (2009). The impact of perceived organizational ethical climate on work satisfaction. *Journal of Business Ethics*, *84*(3), 297–311. doi:10.100710551-008-9709-0

Ferrell, O. C., & Ferrell, L. (2008). A macromarketing ethics framework: Stakeholder orientation and distributive justice. *Journal of Macromarketing*, *28*(1), 24–32. doi:10.1177/0276146707311290

Fisher, C. D., Locke, E. A., & Henne, D. L. (1992). The new look in job satisfaction theory and research. In *Job satisfaction: Advances in research and applications* (pp. 165–194). The Free Press.

Fox, S., Spector, P. E., & Miles, D. (2001). Counterproductive work behavior (CWB) in response to job stressors and organizational justice: Some mediator and moderator tests for autonomy and emotions. *Journal of Vocational Behavior*, *59*(3), 291–309. doi:10.1006/jvbe.2001.1803

Giacalone, R. A., & Greenberg, J. (1997). Antisocial behavior in organizations. *Sage (Atlanta, Ga.)*.

Gökoğlu, S. K., & Öztürk, E. B. (2020). A Cross-Cultural Review of Workplace Deviance Research. In *Analyzing Workplace Deviance in Modern Organizations* (pp. 23–46). IGI Global. doi:10.4018/978-1-5225-9996-8.ch002

Goldman, A., & Tabak, N. (2010). Perception of ethical climate and its relationship to nurses' demographic characteristics and job satisfaction. *Nursing Ethics*, *17*(2), 233–246. doi:10.1177/0969733009352048 PMID:20185447

Griffin, R. W., O'Leary-Kelly, A., & Collins, J. (1998). Dysfunctional work behaviors in organizations. *Journal of Organizational Behavior*, *5*, 65–82.

Harder, T. (2019). *Antecedents of Workplace Deviance*. Celebration of Student Scholarship.

Harper, D. (1990). Spotlight abuse-Save profits. *Industrial Distribution*, *79*, 47–51.

Henle, C. A., Giacalone, R. A., & Jurkiewicz, C. L. (2005). The role of ethical ideology in workplace deviance. *Journal of Business Ethics*, *56*(3), 219–230. doi:10.100710551-004-2779-8

Hogan, J., & Hogan, R. (1989). How to measure employee reliability. *The Journal of Applied Psychology*, *74*(2), 273–279. doi:10.1037/0021-9010.74.2.273

Hollingworth, D., & Valentine, S. (2014). Corporate social responsibility, continuous process improvement orientation, organizational commitment and turnover intentions. *International Journal of Quality & Reliability Management*, *31*(6), 629–651. doi:10.1108/IJQRM-09-2012-0131

Howald, N., Lortie, B., Gallagher, C., & Albert, M. A. (2018). *Preventing and Deterring Organizational Deviance. Society for Industrial and Organizational Psychology.* White Paper Series.

Huang, C. C., You, C. S., & Tsai, M. T. (2012). A multidimensional analysis of ethical climate, job satisfaction, organizational commitment, and organizational citizenship behaviors. *Nursing Ethics*, *19*(4), 513–529. doi:10.1177/0969733011433923 PMID:22753457

Hülsheger, U. R., Alberts, H. J., Feinholdt, A., & Lang, J. W. (2012). Benefits of mindfulness at work: The role of mindfulness in emotion regulation, emotional exhaustion, and job satisfaction. *The Journal of Applied Psychology*, *98*(2), 310–325. doi:10.1037/a0031313 PMID:23276118

Isaac, R. G. (1993). Organizational culture: Some new perspectives. Handbook of organizational behavior, 99.

Ismail, S., & Yuhanis, N. (2018). Determinants of ethical work behaviour of Malaysian public sector auditors. *Asia-Pacific Journal of Business Administration*, *10*(1), 21–34. doi:10.1108/APJBA-07-2017-0068

Jaramillo, F., Mulki, J. P., & Solomon, P. (2006). The role of ethical climate on salesperson's role stress, job attitudes, turnover intention, and job performance. *Journal of Personal Selling & Sales Management*, *26*(3), 271–282. doi:10.2753/PSS0885-3134260302

Kabat-Zinn, J. (1994). *Wherever you go, there you are*. Hyperion.

Karagözoğlu, Ş., Özden, D., & Yildirim, G. (2014). Yoğun bakım hemşirelerinin hastane etik iklim algısı. *Turkish Journal of Research & Development in Nursing*, *16*(1), 34–45.

Kaur, J. (2017). Exploring relationships among ethical climate types and organizational commitment: A case of Indian banking sector. *Journal of Indian Business Research*, *9*(1), 20–40. doi:10.1108/JIBR-02-2015-0022

Kidwell, R. E., & Martin, C. L. (2005). The prevalence (and ambiguity) of deviant behavior at work. *Managing Organizational Deviance*, 1-21.

Kılıç, S. (2013). *Algılanan örgütsel etik iklim ile üretkenlik karşıtı iş davranışları arasındaki ilişkiler*. Niğde Üniversitesi Sosyal Bilimler Enstitüsü Yayınlanmamış Doktora Tezi.

Kish-Gephart, J. J., Harrison, D. A., & Treviño, L. K. (2010). Bad apples, bad cases, and bad barrels: Meta-analytic evidence about sources of unethical decisions at work. *The Journal of Applied Psychology*, *95*(1), 1–31. doi:10.1037/a0017103 PMID:20085404

Klotz, A. C., & Buckley, M. R. (2013). A historical perspective of counterproductive work behavior targeting the organization. *Journal of Management History*, *19*(1), 114–132. doi:10.1108/17511341311286222

Kohlberg, L. (1967). Moral and religious education and the public schools: A developmental view. *Religion and Public Education,* 164-183.

Kohlberg, L. (1984). *The psychology of moral development*. Essays on moral development. Harper & Row.

Kor, Y., & Mesko, A. (2013). Dynamic managerial capabilities: Configuration and orchestration of top executives' capabilities and the firm's dominant logic. *Strategic Management Journal*, *34*(2), 233–244. doi:10.1002mj.2000

Kuenzi, M., & Schminke, M. (2009). Assembling fragments into a lens: A review, critique, and proposed research agenda for the organizational work climate literature. *Journal of Management*, *35*(3), 634–717. doi:10.1177/0149206308330559

Kwok, C. K., Au, W. T., & Ho, J. M. (2005). Normative controls and self-reported counterproductive behaviors in the workplace in China. *Applied Psychology*, *54*(4), 456–475. doi:10.1111/j.1464-0597.2005.00220.x

Litzky, B. E., Eddleston, K. A., & Kidder, D. L. (2006). The good, the bad, and the misguided: How managers inadvertently encourage deviant behaviors. *The Academy of Management Perspectives*, *20*(1), 91–103. doi:10.5465/amp.2006.19873411

Liu, C. M., & Chiu, C. K. (2020). Modeling turnover intention and job performance: The moderation of perceived benevolent climate. *Review of Managerial Science*, *14*(3), 611–631. doi:10.100711846-018-0302-3

Lopez, T. B., Babin, B. J., & Chung, C. (2009). Perceptions of ethical work climate and person–organization fit among retail employees in Japan and the US: A cross-cultural scale validation. *Journal of Business Research, 62*(6), 594–600. doi:10.1016/j.jbusres.2008.05.018

Luthans, F., Luthans, K. W., & Luthans, B. C. (2004). Positive psychological capital: Beyond human and social capital. *Business Horizons, 47*(1), 45–50. doi:10.1016/j.bushor.2003.11.007

Maloof, A. D. (2018). *The Moderating Effects of Ethical Leadership and Ethical Climate on the Relationship Between Employee Integrity and Workplace Deviance* (Doctoral dissertation). Alliant International University.

Marcus, B., Schuler, H., Quell, P., & Hümpfner, G. (2002). Measuring counterproductivity: Development and initial validation of a German self-report questionnaire. *International Journal of Selection and Assessment, 10*(1-2), 18–35. doi:10.1111/1468-2389.00191

Martin, K. D., & Cullen, J. B. (2006). Continuities and extensions of ethical climate theory: A meta-analytic review. *Journal of Business Ethics, 69*(2), 175–194. doi:10.100710551-006-9084-7

Mayer, D. M., Aquino, K., Greenbaum, R. L., & Kuenzi, M. (2012). Who displays ethical leadership? An examination of antecedents and consequences of ethical leadership. *Academy of Management Journal, 55*(1), 151–171. doi:10.5465/amj.2008.0276

Mayer, D. M., Kuenzi, M., & Greenbaum, R. L. (2010). Examining the link between ethical leadership and employee misconduct: The mediating role of ethical climate. *Journal of Business Ethics, 95*(1), 7–16. doi:10.100710551-011-0794-0

McCabe, D. L., Treviño, L. K., & Butterfield, K. D. (2001). Cheating in academic institutions: A decade of research. *Ethics & Behavior, 11*(3), 219–232. doi:10.1207/S15327019EB1103_2

Mehra, S. (2020). Organizational Culture, Climate, and Workplace Deviance. In *Analyzing Workplace Deviance in Modern Organizations* (pp. 66–78). IGI Global. doi:10.4018/978-1-5225-9996-8.ch004

Mitchell, M. S., & Ambrose, M. L. (2007). Abusive supervision and workplace deviance and the moderating effects of negative reciprocity beliefs. *The Journal of Applied Psychology, 92*(4), 1159–1168. doi:10.1037/0021-9010.92.4.1159 PMID:17638473

Moberg, D. J. (1997). On employee vice. *Business Ethics Quarterly*, *7*(4), 41–60. doi:10.2307/3857208

Mohr, D. C., Young, G. J., & Burgess, J. F. Jr. (2012). Employee turnover and operational performance: The moderating effect of group-oriented organisational culture. *Human Resource Management Journal*, *22*(2), 216–233. doi:10.1111/j.1748-8583.2010.00159.x

Mulki, J. P., Jaramillo, J. F., & Locander, W. B. (2009). Critical role of leadership on ethical climate and salesperson behaviors. *Journal of Business Ethics*, *86*(2), 125–141. doi:10.100710551-008-9839-4

Obalade, G. O., & Arogundade, K. K. (2019). Ethical climate and deviant behavior among employees of selected public and private universities: The case of the emerging country. *Corporate Governance and Organizational Behavior Review*, *3*(2), 30–39. doi:10.22495/cgobr_v3_i2_p3

Pagliaro, S., Lo Presti, A., Barattucci, M., Giannella, V. A., & Barreto, M. (2018). On the effects of ethical climate (s) on employees' behavior: A social identity approach. *Frontiers in Psychology*, *9*, 1–10. doi:10.3389/fpsyg.2018.00960 PMID:29951022

Panno, A., Giacomantonio, M., Carrus, G., Maricchiolo, F., Pirchio, S., & Mannetti, L. (2018). Mindfulness, pro-environmental behavior, and belief in climate change: The mediating role of social dominance. *Environment and Behavior*, *50*(8), 864–888. doi:10.1177/0013916517718887

Parboteeah, K. P., Chen, H. C., Lin, Y. T., Chen, I. H., Lee, A. Y., & Chung, A. (2010). Establishing organizational ethical climates: How do managerial practices work? *Journal of Business Ethics*, *97*(4), 599–611. doi:10.100710551-010-0527-9

Peterson, D. K. (2002). Deviant workplace behavior and the organization's ethical climate. *Journal of Business and Psychology*, *17*(1), 47–61. doi:10.1023/A:1016296116093

Puffer, S. M. (1987). Prosocial behavior, noncompliant behavior, and work performance among commission salespeople. *The Journal of Applied Psychology*, *72*(4), 615–621. doi:10.1037/0021-9010.72.4.615

Reichers, A. E., & Schneider, B. (1990). Climate and culture: An evolution of constructs. *Organizational Climate and Culture, 1*, 5-39.

Riggle, R. J. (2007). *The impact of organizational climate variables of perceived organizational support, workplace isolation, and ethical climate on salesperson psychological and behavioral work outcomes*. University of South Florida, Graduation Thesis.

Robinson, S., & Bennett, R. (1995). A typology of deviant workplace behaviors: A multi-dimensional scaling study. *Academy of Management Journal, 38*, 555–572.

Robinson, S., & Bennett, R. (1997). Workplace deviance: Its definition, its manifestations, and its causes. *Research on Negotiations in Organizations, 6*, 3–27.

Robinson, S., & Greenberg, J. (1999). Employees behaving badly: Dimensions, determinants and dilemmas in the study of workplace deviance. In D. M. Rousseau & C. Cooper (Eds.), *Trends in organizational behavior* (Vol. 5, pp. 1–23). Wiley.

Robinson, S. L., & O'Leary-Kelly, A. M. (1998). Monkey see, monkey do: The influence of work groups on the antisocial behavior of employees. *Academy of Management Journal, 41*(6), 658–672.

Rothwell, G. R., & Baldwin, J. N. (2006). Ethical climates and contextual predictors of whistle-blowing. *Review of Public Personnel Administration, 26*(3), 216–244. doi:10.1177/0734371X05278114

Sackett, P. R., & DeVore, C. J. (2002). Counterproductive behaviors at work. In N. Anderson, D. S. Ones, H. K. Sinangil, & C. Viswesvaran (Eds.), Handbook of industrial, work and organizational psychology, Vol. 1. Personnel psychology (p. 145–164). Sage Publications Ltd.

Şahin, B., & Dündar, T. (2011). Sağlık sektöründe etik iklim ve yildirma (mobbing) davranişlari arasindaki ilişkinin incelenmesi. *Ankara Üniversitesi SBF Dergisi, 66*(01), 129–159. doi:10.1501/SBFder_0000002198

Salancik, G. R., & Pfeffer, J. (1978). A social information processing approach to job attitudes and task design. *Administrative Science Quarterly, 23*(2), 224–253. doi:10.2307/2392563 PMID:10307892

Schminke, M., Ambrose, M. L., & Neubaum, D. O. (2005). The effect of leader moral development on ethical climate and employee attitudes. *Organizational Behavior and Human Decision Processes, 97*(2), 135–151. doi:10.1016/j.obhdp.2005.03.006

Schneider, B., & Rentsch, J. (1988). Managing Climates and Cultures: A Futures Perspective. In J. Hage (Ed.), *Futures of Organizations*. San Francisco: New Lexington Press.

Segal, Z., Williams, M. R., & Teasdale, J. (2002). *Mindfulness-based cognitive therapy for depression: A new approach to preventing relapse*. Guilford Press.

Sharma, N., & Singh, V. K. (2018). Psychological empowerment and employee engagement: Testing the mediating effects of constructive deviance in Indian IT Sector. *International Journal of Human Capital and Information Technology Professionals*, *9*(4), 44–55. doi:10.4018/IJHCITP.2018100103

Simha, A., & Cullen, J. B. (2012). Ethical climates and their effects on organizational outcomes: Implications from the past and prophecies for the future. *The Academy of Management Perspectives*, *26*(4), 20–34. doi:10.5465/amp.2011.0156

Simons, T., & Roberson, Q. (2003). Why managers should care about fairness: The effects of aggregate justice perceptions on organizational outcomes. *The Journal of Applied Psychology*, *88*(3), 432–443. doi:10.1037/0021-9010.88.3.432 PMID:12814293

Sims, R. L., & Keon, T. L. (1997). Ethical work climate as a factor in the development of person-organization fit. *Journal of Business Ethics*, *16*(11), 1095–1105. doi:10.1023/A:1017914502117

Singh, Y. (2020). Workplace Deviance: A Conceptual Framework. In *Analyzing Workplace Deviance in Modern Organizations* (pp. 1–22). IGI Global. doi:10.4018/978-1-5225-9996-8.ch001

Smith, H. J., Thompson, R., & Iacovou, C. (2009). The impact of ethical climate on project status misreporting. *Journal of Business Ethics*, *90*(4), 577–591. doi:10.100710551-009-0062-8

Song, X. (2017). *The Impact of Regulatory Focus and Perceived Organizational Benevolent Climate on Innovative Behaviors of Knowledge Workers*. Academic Press.

Spanos, Y. E., & Lioukas, S. (2001). An examination into the causal logic of rent generation: Contrasting Porter's competitive strategy framework and the resource-based perspective. *Strategic Management Journal*, *22*(10), 907–934. doi:10.1002mj.174

Tannenbaum, S. I., & Yukl, G. (1992). Training and development in work organizations. *Annual Review of Psychology*, *43*, 399–441.

Thompson, K. H., & Greene, R. R. (1994). Role theory and social work practice. *Human behavior theory: A diversity framework*, 93-114.

Trevino, L. K. (1986). Ethical decision making in organizations: A person-situation interactionist model. *Academy of Management Review*, *11*(3), 601–617. doi:10.5465/amr.1986.4306235

Tsai, M. T., & Huang, C. C. (2008). The relationship among ethical climate types, facets of job satisfaction, and the three components of organizational commitment: A study of nurses in Taiwan. *Journal of Business Ethics, 80*(3), 565–581. doi:10.100710551-007-9455-8

Tuna, M., & Yeşiltaş, M. (2014). Etik iklim, işe yabancılaşma ve örgütsel özdeşleşmenin işten ayrılma niyeti üzerindeki etkisi: Otel işletmelerinde bir araştırma. *Anatolia: Turizm Araştırmaları Dergisi, 25*(1), 105–117.

Turnipseed, D. L. (1988). An integrated, interactive model of organisational climate, culture and effectiveness. *Leadership and Organization Development Journal, 9*(5), 17–21. doi:10.1108/eb053644

Ulrich, C., O'Donnell, P., Taylor, C., Farrar, A., Danis, M., & Grady, C. (2007). Ethical climate, ethics stress, and the job satisfaction of nurses and social workers in the United States. *Social Science & Medicine, 65*(8), 1708–1719. doi:10.1016/j.socscimed.2007.05.050 PMID:17619068

Valentine, S., Godkin, L., & Varca, P. E. (2010). Role conflict, mindfulness, and organizational ethics in an education-based healthcare institution. *Journal of Business Ethics, 94*(3), 455–469. doi:10.100710551-009-0276-9

Vardi, Y. (2001). The effects of organizational and ethical climates on misconduct at work. *Journal of Business Ethics, 29*(4), 325–337. doi:10.1023/A:1010710022834

Vardi, Y., & Wiener, Y. (1996). Misbehavior in organizations: A motivational framework. *Organization Science, 7*(2), 151–165. doi:10.1287/orsc.7.2.151

Victor, B., & Cullen, J. B. (1987). A theory and measure of ethical climate in organizations. In W. C. Frederick (Ed.), *Research in corporate social performance and policy* (pp. 51–71). JAI Press.

Victor, B., & Cullen, J. B. (1988). The organizational bases of ethical work climates. *Administrative Science Quarterly, 33*(1), 101–125. doi:10.2307/2392857

Vu, M. C., & Gill, R. (2018). Is there corporate mindfulness? An exploratory study of Buddhist-enacted spiritual leaders' perspectives and practices. *Journal of Management, Spirituality & Religion, 15*(2), 155–177. doi:10.1080/14766086.2017.1410491

Weick, K. E., & Sutcliffe, K. M. (2006). Mindfulness and the quality of organizational attention. *Organization Science, 17*(4), 514–524. doi:10.1287/orsc.1060.0196

Williams, J. J., & Seaman, A. E. (2016). The influence of ethical leadership on managerial performance: Mediating effects of mindfulness and corporate social responsibility. *Journal of Applied Business Research, 32*(3), 815–828. doi:10.19030/jabr.v32i3.9659

Wimbush, J. C., & Shepard, J. M. (1994). Toward an understanding of ethical climate: Its relationship to ethical behavior and supervisory influence. *Journal of Business Ethics, 13*(8), 637–647. doi:10.1007/BF00871811

Yasir, M., & Rasli, A. (2018). Direct and indirect effects of ethical leadership on workplace deviance in public healthcare sector of Pakistan. *Journal of Advances in Management Research, 15*(4), 558–574. doi:10.1108/JAMR-11-2017-0109

Yavuz, M. (2019). *Mindfulness-based interventions for the organisational outcomes: a systematic literature review* (Unpublished master thesis). University of Leicester.

Yavuz, M., Ozbilgin, M. F., & Kamasak, R. (2020). Exploring the Interplay Between Deviance and Loneliness at Work. In *Analyzing Workplace Deviance in Modern Organizations* (pp. 48–65). IGI Global. doi:10.4018/978-1-5225-9996-8.ch003

Yener, M., Yaldıran, M., & Ergun, S. (2012). The effect of ethical climate on work engagement. *Procedia: Social and Behavioral Sciences, 58*, 724–733. doi:10.1016/j.sbspro.2012.09.1050

Yeşil, S., Mavi, Y., & Ceylan, S. (2017). Etik İklim Algisi ve Bireysel Sonuçlar Üzerine Etkileri. *Dumlupınar Üniversitesi Sosyal Bilimler Dergisi*, (51), 19–38.

Yilmaz, A. T., & Yildirim, A. (2019). Bir Üniversite Hastanesinde Çalişan Hemşirelerin Etik İklim Algisi. *Elektronik Sosyal Bilimler Dergisi, 18*(69), 162–176.

Yüksel, S. (2012). *The impact of perceptions of ethical work climates and organizational justice on workplace deviance* (Unpublished Doctoral Dissertation). Ankara: Middle East Technical University.

Yurdakul, M. (2013). *İş ahlakında etik iklim: Bireysel ve kurumsal özellikler açısından etik iklimin bankacılık sektöründe araştırılması*. İstanbul Üniversitesi Sosyal Bilimler Enstitüsü Uluslararası İşletmecilik Anabilim Dalı Yayınlanmamış Yüksek Lisans Tezi.

Zoghbi-Manrique-de-Lara, P., & Guerra-Baez, R. (2016). Exploring the influence of ethical climate on employee compassion in the hospitality industry. *Journal of Business Ethics, 133*(3), 605–617. doi:10.100710551-014-2415-1

Chapter 5
Ignoring Commitment of Labor's Welfare:
Evidence in State-Owned Enterprise Cement Holding of PT Semen Indonesia (Persero) Tbk

Effnu Subiyanto
https://orcid.org/0000-0001-7879-2499
Widya Mandala Surabaya Catholic University, Indonesia

ABSTRACT

Despite many challenges ahead, the state-owned enterprises' roadmap to establish several new forms of holdings are still progressing in Indonesia. Indonesia's government believes that holdings are the best answer to manage all of 143 remaining state-owned enterprises for ease of control, efficiency, effectiveness in operations, and as a driver to boost bigger profit as well. Based on evidence in the state-owned enterprise PT Semen Indonesia's holding, the holding is tending to ignore labor's welfare. Welfare attention has diverted, and unfortunately, only a few are discussing about labor and its rights, especially in justifying distributing annually bonuses. This chapter investigates that holdings' implementation in Indonesia is significantly contrary in terms of labor's views compared with the original theory to build strong corporations for developing better welfare for all parties.

DOI: 10.4018/978-1-7998-3515-8.ch005

INTRODUCTION

Several rush new forms of State-owned Enterprise (SOE) holdings are again sparking concerns and attracting high public attention throughout Indonesia. Amidst uncertainty within laws and politics - worsen by many leaders' vested personal interest - establishment many holdings based on the PT Semen Indonesia (PTSI) holding is unavoidably triggering fierce disputes. Many mandatory tasks require adjustments and the consequences are wasting time and expensive; even more, organization is severely suffer, especially leadership issues.

Within period 2014-2019, the Indonesia SOEs' Ministry plans to establish at least six holdings, which only two of them have been indicating on stream as planned. The new two holdings recently established are Mining's holding led by the Indonesia Aluminum (PT Inalum), and Oil and Gas Holding led by PT Pertamina. The other four holdings respectively holding for banks, constructions, highways, and housings; all were failed to be established in due time. However, the Ministry again has stated to establish new other kinds of holding of pharmacy and holding of aviation.

The most issues then occurred within intern organization especially coming from labor. Due confidential information and strictly access, they collect information by their own and some of them gather information by learn and share through its union, union federation, and union confederation as well. The effective way to assembly information and knowledge according their considerations is visiting or making comparation study, benchmarking each other, seminar, or establish certain focus group discussion (FGD) to the other Union's colleagues who earlier had made their corporations as holding company.

LITERATURE REVIEW

Understanding Holding

In term of definition, a holding company is a company that does not have any operations, activities, or other active business itself. Instead, the holding company owns assets (Kennon, 2018). These assets can be shared as capital, inventories, or stock in other corporations, limited liability companies, limited partnerships, private equity funds, hedge funds, publicly traded stocks, bonds, real estate, song rights, brand names, patents, trademarks, copyrights, or virtually anything else that has value.

Holdings are shall controlling several groups of its businesses without directly operate of them day-to-day. The different things, holdings elect a board of directors to protect and assure their interests. That board, among its other responsibilities such as determining the dividend, managing effective operational, centralizing corporate strategy, deploying finance policies, information technologies, ERP, control rights, hiring the CEO of holding's member, and many other things. The CEO, in turn, when required can hire his direct subordinates. These executives have the power to determine the CEOs and key other executives at the holding's group.

Due to decide to invest, executives then create a new subsidiary. Holdings elect a board of directors. The next day, the subsidiary company do several things in operational. Subsidiary company can incorporate a new business with majority share ownership. It can also contribute amount capital to run or open its subsidiary company indeed. Various core businesses can be accessed with measurable projection. By end of year it businesses' branches then consolidated into balance sheet to measure each of business performance. It then compensates each others, if one of business channel went loss, it will be compensated with other channel business that contributing profit.

This holding's model is implementing in Procter & Gamble, the Burlington Northern Santa Fe (BNSF) railroad (Kennon, 2018). It is also had been implemented by Warren Buffett in his holding company, Berkshire Hathaway. BNSF has billions of dollars in debt, which help fund its massive capital expenditure budget for railroad track, railroad cars, and other infrastructure. The holding's advantage is none of these debts are guaranteed by Berkshire Hathaway.

Unlikely with Kenon (2018), holdings' model generally nowadays in world is distributing power with elaborating of top-down command. Agustiawan (2015) best describing in Temasek's holding structure as mentioned at Figure 1. The Temasek devided its member holdings into 5 categories respectively financial services, telecom, media & technology, transportation & industrial, life sciences, consumer & real estate, and energy & resources. The BOD at the headquarter office while operational company's BOD at every branches offices. Command had been hold at the central, while operational becomes holding's member rights.

According to Subiyanto (2019), to avoid overlapping tasks between holding and operational companies, holding then decided to distribute tasks into two strategic functions. A part of them to be responsibility at the holding, while rest of it be concerned by operational companies. A 12 numbers of functions that belonging at the holding is;

1. Marketing
2. Procurement
3. Capital expenditure
4. Production
5. Finance and accounting
6. Information and technology
7. Human capital

8. Secretary of company
9. Legal and risks
10. Controlling
11. Research and development
12. Corporate and social responsibility

Figure 1. Structure of Temasek's Holding
Source: Agustiawan, 2015

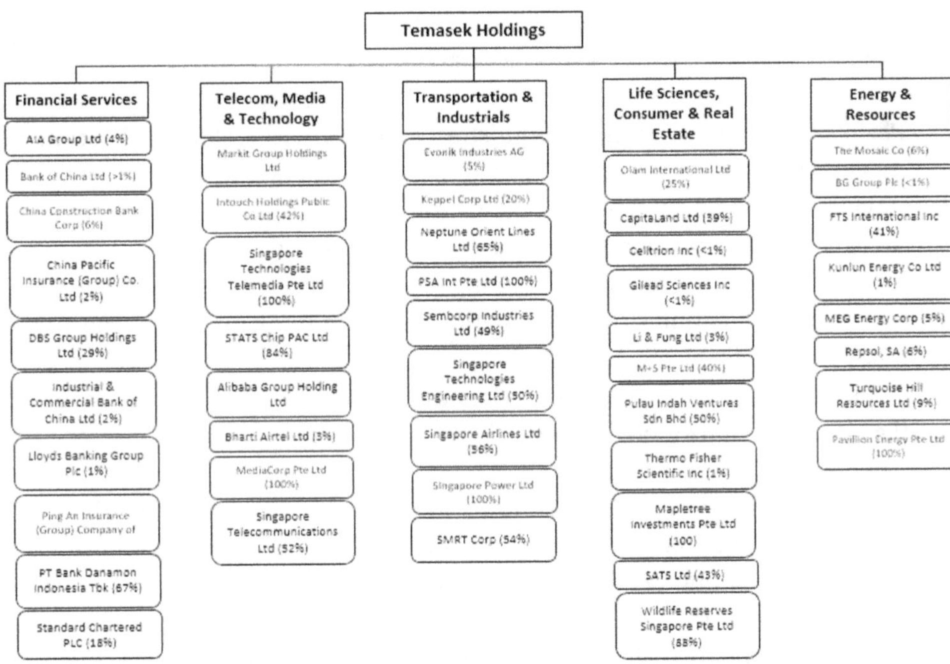

HOLDING AS STRATEGIC'S TOOLS

New forming SOEs' Holdings in Indonesia are widespread campaigned as a new strategic tool recently. Despite the theme is still being fierce debate among leaders within the businesses, a part of them are insisting to only implementing urgently in organization; as they thought it had been strategically decided by the board management. Generally, as the leaders understanding, beside they are representing formal organization; they must also be able to translate its strategy within vision and mission into concrete steps for easily implemented by subordinates. This is uneasy, as the strategy formulation generally entails heavy doses of visions, difficult analysis, and entrepreneurial judgments.

A successful strategy implementation into concrete steps depend on the skills over others in which not limitation respectively organizing, motivating, culture building, and creating stronger fits between strategy and daily operational. The further challenge is how the organization operates ingrained leadership's behavior remains without change just because a new strategy has announced (Biazin, Solano-Charris, & Quintero, 2017).

These are things respectively requiring adjustments as following the organization's overall conditions, to the nature of the strategy, the amount of strategic changes involved, and to the manager's own skills, styles, and methods. Four broad areas must carefully elaborate within every leaders;

1. Performing the recurring administrative tasks associated with strategy implementation.
2. Revisiting between strategy and the various internal interests in order to align the whole organization behind strategy accomplishment.
3. Figuring out an agenda and determining set of action priorities that synchronize with the organization's overall situation in which implementation must take place.
4. Deciding what managerial approach and leadership style to adopt in inducing the needed organizational changes.

For implementing leadership's strategy in an existing organization, the most challenging is to bring and conduct internal operations into good alignment and to unite within. Building enthusiasm and commitment are important to perform and carry out chosen strategy. Following further must be addressed respectively is organizational skills and capabilities, functional area activities, organization structure, reward systems and incentives, policies and procedures, information systems and control mechanisms, budgets and programs, and shared values and cultural norms.

It must be comprehended that forming holdings in SOEs will affect inside and outside companies, directly and indirectly as well into societies. Holdings are conglomerate-corporation-formed for the purpose of controlling interests in several companies. The holding company enables a corporation to diversify its investments, manage other firms, and contribute to the growth of companies in different business sectors. Although there are many advantages to the holding company form, there are also lot of disadvantages for management, its subsidiaries, investors, and labor.

According Figure 2 developed by Aguilera & Jackson (2003) and David (2011), even holdings must without exception meet governance aspect strictly. There are three intersection interests between management, capital, and labor. The labor's participant is correlating with its welfare's rights through transformation SOEs into new holdings must assure they rights; they even hopefully expect that the new form of businesses will increase their welfare significantly future. They are easily thought as an economic scope and economic scale are growing, it shall affect to the increase of revenue, leveraging profit for the holdings, bringing effective and efficient, and finally will increase welfare for labor. According scheme drawn by Aguilera & Jackson (2003), these economic scale and economic scope best describe as capital.

Figure 2. Corporate governance concept
Source: Aguilera & Jackson, 2003

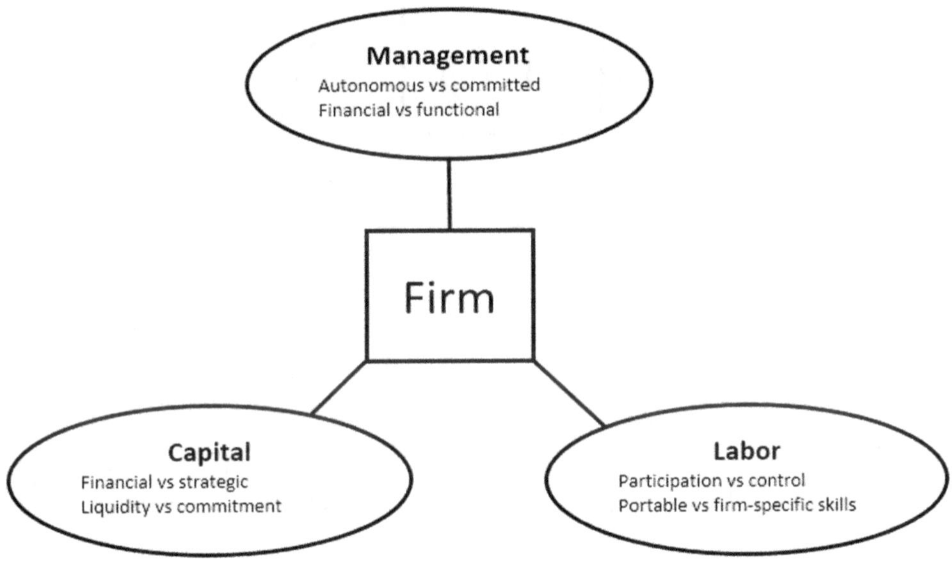

Detail institusional's relation had been further developed (Aguilera & Jackson, 2003) as seen at Figure 3. Especially; labor is concerning with three important things respectively representation rights (welfare), skill formation, and union organization as formal representing labor in the holdings. The three aspects can be incorporated by solid teamwork to meet targets. The ultimate goal of every holdings is imposible achieved without compromising with them. Management has responsibility to maintain all of them in harmonize tone, capital as source of operational and labor is operators and or workers who day-to-day standby at nearby production center to run machineries. Labor's responsibility is not only dealing with daily operational, but not limitation involving in various duties that reflect firm's interests.

Figure 3. Institusional relation within governance
Source: Aguilera & Jackson, 2003

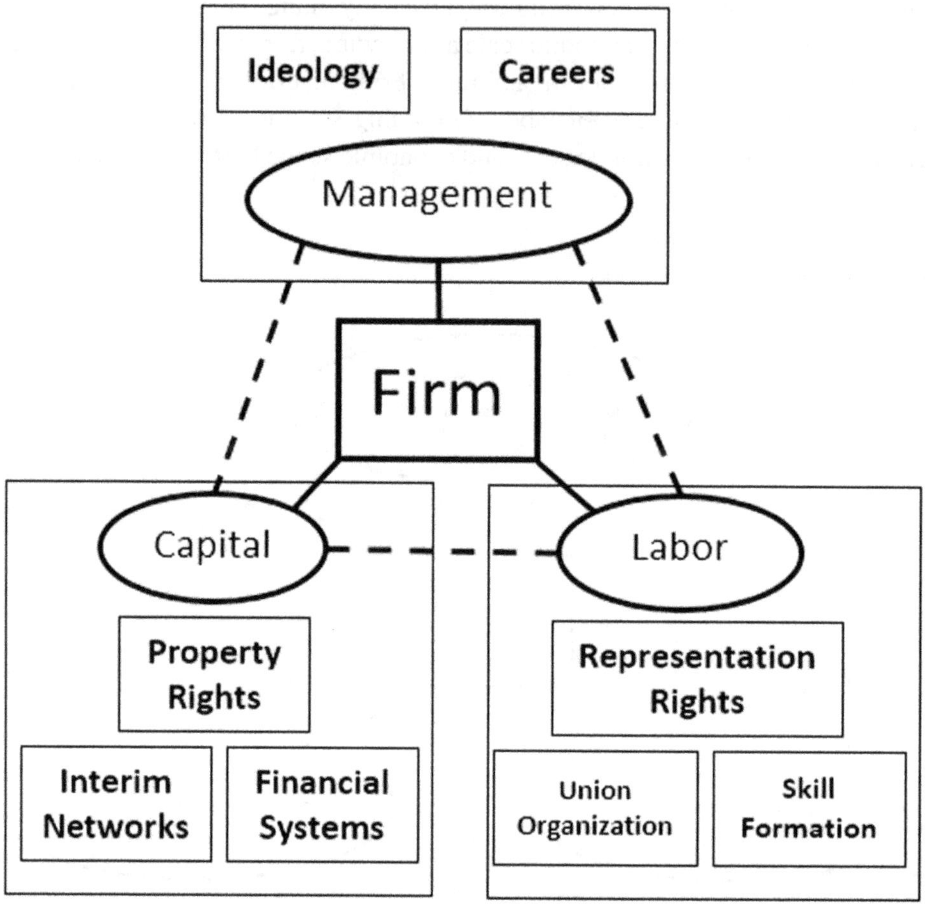

According to Kennon (2018), Hudson (2019), and Exner (2012) labor is expected its involvement to making working climate meaningful (Harikrishnan, 2014).

HOLDINGS IN INDONESIA'S SOE

According Exner (2012) the benefits of using a holding company in conjunction with an operating company can be numerous and span everything from tax savings, to added creditor protection, until to making a business more saleable. On the other side, the disadvantages of having a holding company are for the most part limited to the added legal and accounting costs and complexity associated with incorporating, operational and maintenance management. In deciding on whether or not to incorporate a holding company into an existing corporate structure, it basically comes down to whether or not the various benefits they offer outweigh the added costs and complexity of having them. A thorough understanding of the potential benefits is key to making this decision, as there will be many instances where a holding company may be quite beneficial and many instances where they may offer minimal benefit.

Following disadvantages in forming holdings are comprising: (1) Disadvantages for management, (2) Disadvantages for subsidiaries, (3) Disadvantages for shareholders, and (4) Other disadvantages.

Disadvantages for Management

At this disadvantage, the BOD face several challenges with a holding company form relating with organization. Since the holding company likely has a controlling interest in several corporations, the BOD may have limited knowledge in the industry climate, operations and investment decisions of the variety members of holdings. Such limitations may result in ineffective decision-making. New BOD may often less equipped knowledge to tackle the challenges of the company's day-to-day operations and slow respond to quick address competition and market conditions.

Due the BOD generally at the cockpit, management aspects have been done through remote with top-down approach only. Two ways communication have limited, operators at the operational channels only concentration to perform production with less engagement personally. This kind situation will emerge a principle-agent relationship and prone to drive conflicts.

Disadvantages for Subsidiaries

The newly owned subsidiary of a holding company also faces challenges with a change of control. With a new reporting structure in place, subsidiaries businesses in practically have limitation room for improvement and innovation. Between subsidiaries often unavoidable to severely compete each other and destroy market share finally. Therefore, competing interests between management may result in contention and poor decision-making, which can negatively affect to the subsidiaries.

Disadvantages for Shareholders

Minority shareholders may also face challenges with a holding company form of organization. While the holding company pays taxes on profits from its subsidiary companies, shareholders pay taxes on dividends received from the holding company.

Shareholders may also disagree with the new management's approach and decision-making. Also, with a new controlling shareholder, minority shareholders must pay more to maintain their previous shareholding and replace the directors. This change of control may cause contention between the shareholders and the management of holding company.

Other Disadvantages

The holding company form of organization also faces liquidity issues. Since the conglomerate owns a controlling interest in many corporations, in a highly volatile market or market crisis, the holding company may find it difficult to remain profitable, solvent, or convert its assets in a timely manner to avoid substantial unnecessary losses. Additionally, many of the strategic holding company may have unprofitable assets or business lines. If the holding company engages in similar industry sectors, management may face systemic risks, or conversely if the company is engaged in different industry sectors, the holding company may fall susceptible to several volatile market changes that make it difficult to mitigate risk. This can result in residual losses that the holding company may not have envisioned before purchasing the corporations.

The other disadvantages is labor issues. This theme often ignored due to labor issues can be discussed later while on going progress. This kind is becoming further trap for labor, in many cases as in Indonesia situates today, conflicts between the BOD and labor are frequently occurred. Source of conflicts are various starting due to miscommunication, unclear career planning for labor, un-answer issues relating with future strategic that have impact to the labor's welfare, wages, and annually bonuses.

RESEARCH METHODOLOGY

This study has been thoroughly analyzed by mining information and organizing data from real happened within at a State-owned Holding of PT Semen Indonesia since 2010 to 2018. It has been combining with semi-structured interviews and explanatory design of various level labor, unions and executives. Their opinions and views have been gathered, selected, and analyzed carefully to get closely visualization to the phenomenon generally. This study also utilizing mixed study both in quantitative and in qualitative analyses to build comprehensive conclusion for advice and recommendation.

Combining qualitative tools are gathered which are consisting phenomenon, cases studies, histories, and grounded theory. Phenomenon has been considered as willingness' issues that spread over the nations due to recent development (James H Watt, 1995). Author considers to lift-it-up State-owned holding's cases as Author well knowledge of the issues and interacting day-to-day with all of them. Based on previous qualitative tools, explanatory and argument theory are presented which are influenced direct indirect with induction, deduction, and verification observations.

ANALYSIS

Existence of over than 143 Indonesia's SOEs have recently are tending to be important in the daily national discussion. The SOEs is evidently stronger in many aspects such as building infrastructure, banking, maritime, logistics, and many more. In terms of its assets, Figure 4 shows ascending trend of total amount Rp 8,902 trillion (US$635.86 billion) by end of 2018, while amount dividend reached Rp 44.7 trillion (US$3.19 billion). SOEs' dividends are a part of income source of Indonesia annually budget. Growing assets of the cases imply that SOEs demanded to be handling more efficient and effectively.

The first ten SOEs have recorded as the biggest amount assets per end of 2018 are following;

1. Electrical State Company (PLN) with its asset Rp 1,311 trillion (US$93.64 billion).
2. Bank of People Indonesia (BRI) Rp 1,296 trillion (US$92.57 billion).
3. Bank of Mandiri (Bank Mandiri) Rp 1,202 trillion (US$85.86 billion).
4. Oil & Gas Company (Pertamina) Rp 923 trillion (US$65.93 billion).
5. Bank of State Indonesia (BNI) Rp 808 trillion (US$57.71 billion).
6. Bank of State Saving (BTN) Rp 285 trillion (US$20.36 billion).
7. Indonesia Telecommunication (Telkom) Rp 204 trillion (US$14.57 billion).
8. Sriwijaya Fertilizer (Pusri) Rp 128 trillion (US$9.14 billion).
9. State Gas (PGN) Rp 120 trillion (US$8.57 billion).
10. Semen Indonesia (PTSI) Rp 52 trillion (US$3.71 billion).

Figuring out the positive trending of the SOEs' assets that recently have drawn attention of Indonesian's public can be seen at Figure 4. Managing is keyword, the big questions then how to utilize huge potential, giant opportunity for public interests as big as possibly. Experts believe that organizing and transforming into new platform of SOEs' holdings will be next step to be taken. The ultimate future goals is easy control, help distress national budget, market intervention due to as biggest as possibly to people welfare stipulated by Constitutional 1945.

Figure 4. Indonesia state-owned assets and amount dividend (in Rp trillion)
Source: Subiyanto, 2018

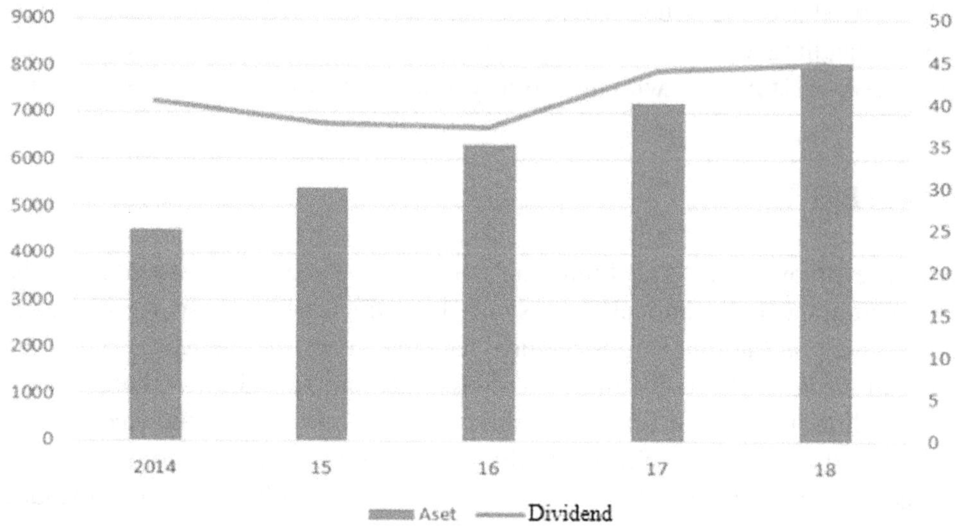

Learning from previously early holding of Indonesia's Fertilizer (2012), Semen Indonesia Holding (2013) and National Farming (2014) (Subiyanto, 2019), following by two additional new holdings of mining, and oil and gas (2018); the SOE's ministry has declared to form of few SOEs' holdings as mentioned at Table 1.

Holding of Infrastructure is viewed an urgent as Indonesia is entering strategic phase to develop and manage huge infrastructure projects. The leader of the projected holding will be the SOE Hutama Karya which expertise as contractor and project builder in the country. Following planned holding is housing to assure cheap prize of housing for people. The SOE Perumnas will lead the holding. Further planned holdings are banking and food to assure financing and food for people. Indonesia is experiencing with lack of finance that triggering enourmous debts (Subiyanto, 2019) and frequently facing shortage of food with consequently to reopen import. Managing of them well is a goal to be expected to help improve things that decades ignored. The most problems is government had lack in developing sustain strategy for future but only focus in short terms as extinguisher. Formation numbers of holdings to cope uncertain future development and at the same time to organizing hundreds of SOEs.

Table 1 shows of four kind of holdings in Indonesia that recently published into public but so far still under fierce discussion with many parties. According to Indonesia's laws, first party which is Ministry of SOE will become first source the transformation. After being planned, drawn, learning various schemes or options

Table 1. Planning of Few Next Indonesia's state-owned holdings

Type of Holding	Holding of Infrastructure (Toll Road and Construction)	Holding of Housing and Regional Development	Holding of Banking, Finance and Insurance	Holding of Food
Lead holding	**PT Hutama Karya (Persero)**	**Perum Perumnas**	**PT Danareksa Persero**	**Perum Bulog**
Member	1. PT Jasa Marga (Persero) Tbk	1. PT Adhi Karya (Persero) Tbk	1. PT Bank Mandiri (Persero) Tbk	1. PT Sang Hyang Seri (Persero)
	2. PT Waskita Karya (Persero) Tbk	2. PT PP (Persero) Tbk	2. PT Bank Negara Indonesia (Persero) Tbk	2. PT Pertani (Persero)
	3. PT Indra Karya (Persero)	3. PT Virama Karya (Persero)	3. PT Bank Rakyat Indonesia (Persero) Tbk	3. PT Bhanda Ghara Reksa (Persero)
	4. PT Wijaya Karya (Persero) Tbk	4. PT Nindya Karya (Persero).	4. BTN	4. PT Perusahaan Perdagangan Indonesia (Persero)
	5. PT Yodya Karya (Persero).		5. PT Pegadaian (Persero)	5. PT Perikanan Nusantara (Persero)
			6. PT Pembiayaan Nasional Madani (Persero)	6. PT Perikanan Indonesia (Persero)
			7. PT Jalin Pembayaran Nasional	7. PT Berdikari (Persero)

Source: compiling by Author (2018)

with number of experts, academicians, then its propose to be presented at the House of Representative to get permission.

By the above planning according Table 1. several schemes of State's ownerships have been examined with consideration to avoid against the laws. The SOEs is strongly indeed becoming part of the Constitution 1945 and already derivative to several number of laws. Once it enactment, SOEs have been controlled by public and demanded members of House of Representative involvement to make change and amendment. The most challenge in terms of establishing holdings is adaptation of share distribution in justified majority. Figure 5 is showing schemes offered the SOEs ministry as proposal to be discussed with the House.

Beside share's right, based on operational there were matrixed of four possibility proposed holdings and four considerations accordance Figure 6. SOEs' Indonesia so far have only experienced in strategic's holding and projected in near future years to come will be financial holdings' type.

Figure 5. Draft Structure of Indonesia state-owned holdings
Source: SOE ministry, 2018

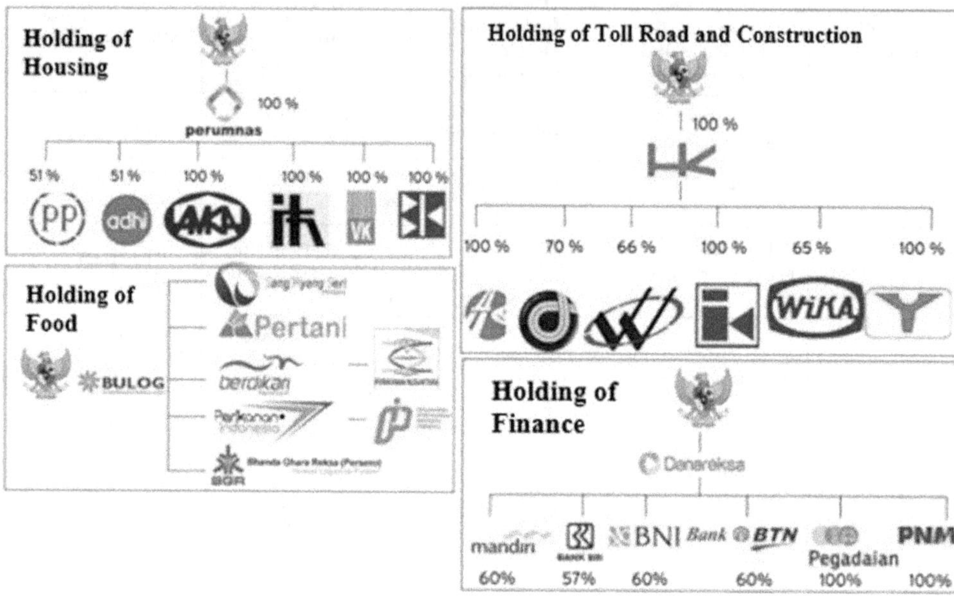

Due to lack consideration involving labor's participation according Figure 6, Semen Indonesia's holding then elaborated strategic's holding type with propose to enhancing in operational approach only. Operational and justify aspects were

Figure 6. Proposed Matrixed of Indonesia's state-owned holdings
Source: Subiyanto, 2018

	1. Financial Holding	2. Strategic Management Holding	3. Active Management Holding	4. Operating Holding
	We just want to know your results	***We want to know what you do***	***We want to know how you do it***	***We will work with you to do it***
Who we are	▸ We are an investment company	▸ We are the strategic leadership of a collection of management entities	▸ We are both consultants to and the strategic leadership of management entities	▸ We are the key managers of all business units
Underlying Philosophy	▸ Create/enforce a disciplined management model ▸ Value is created by individual companies closest to customers	▸ Add value in the linkages between BUs ▸ Value is created by individual companies closest to customers	▸ Provide guidance to BUs via expertise ▸ Value is created by individual companies using corporate expertise	▸ Make key decisions for BUs ▸ Value is created by corporate expertise and control
Key Characteristics	▸ Core sets high financial goals. BUs are completely accountable for achieving results ▸ BUs commit to multi year strategy plans which if met no annual review is necessary	▸ Core sets key financial and operational metrics. BUs are accountable for results ▸ BUs commit to multi year plans - core ensures strategy coherence across units and performs annual review	▸ Core and BUs share responsibility for broad set of financial and operating metrics ▸ Core proactively reviews business unit strategic plans and annual budgets	▸ Core is responsible for financial and operating performance ▸ Core dictates business unit strategic plans and budgets
Examples	▸ Ineos	▸ BP, ICI, Total Fina Elf	▸ Shell Chemicals	▸ LG (Before restructuring)

diverting as top attention with operational approach while ignoring labor aspects that substantially deterioting level of welfare.

Figure 7 shows that originally Semen Gresik has majority share of 99.99% both in Semen Padang and Semen Tonasa since 1998. To capture nation's spirit, Semen Gresik then transformed to Semen Indonesia but with consequence dissapearing "Gresik" (see Figure 8) by end of 2012.

By first designed, Authors found that labors interests were ignoring in all documents. The issues were forgotten by design as at the time it had not sparked yet became urgent and attention. The Indonesia's government is only focus how to strengthen businesses to compete at market. Beside, the other consideration, labors issues are traditionally difficult to be ignored as SOEs and or holdings' executive will be originally come from career staffs. At the time planning, the BOD will guarantee from internal staffs who traditionally well understanding emotional and psycological of labors. Development then quickly changed as SOEs and Holdings' executives have been mixed with number of fit and proper tests. The BOD with totally different background and experience is often to led different type of SOEs. Executive with finance background for example led cement holding, while executive with cement experience chair as BOD of aviation industries.

Figure 7. PT Semen Gresik (Persero) Tbk's first structure
Source: Subiyanto, 2018

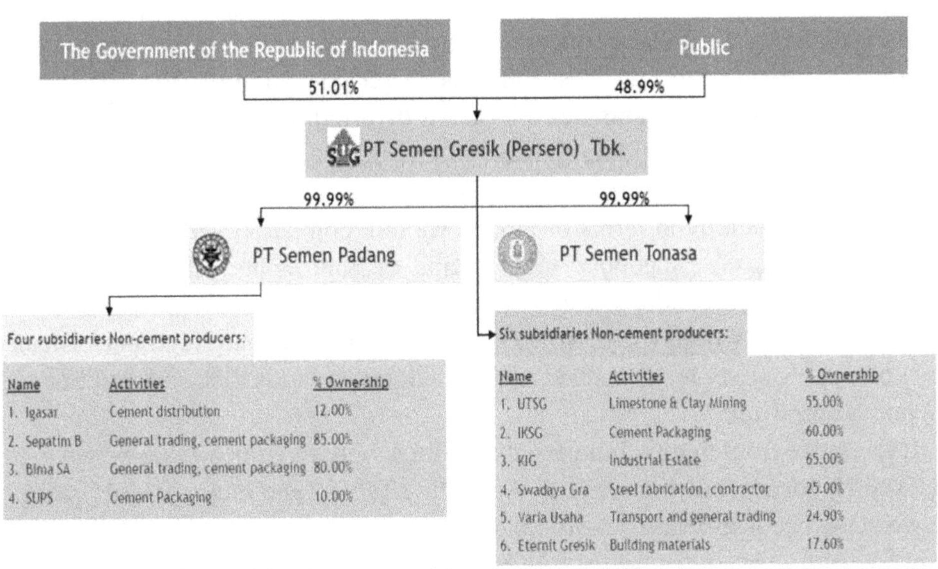

For reason to win-win-solution and leaving sectoral and municipal mark, Semen Gresik then transform to Semen Indonesia as we acknowledge today. The new structure of Semen Indonesia's holding best describing at Figure 8.

Figure 8. Process of Transforming PT Semen Gresik to PT Semen Indonesia
Source: Subiyanto, 2018

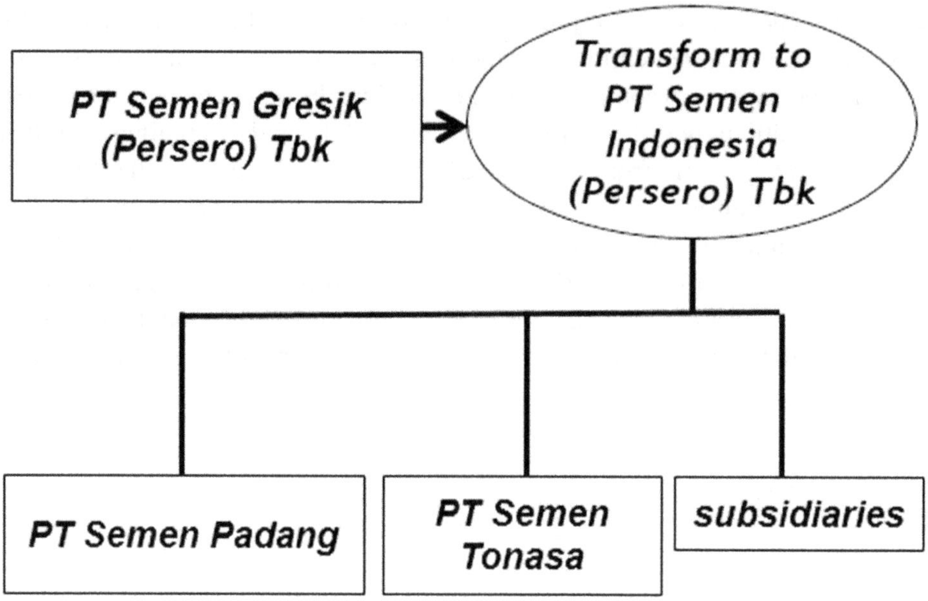

Unfortunately, due to lack concepts of holdings since beginning, only focusing in daily operational, concentrate as much as bigger portion in legally aspects, then issues relating with labor rights were obviously diverted. The symptom has occurred at the Semen Indonesia's holding and tainted as dark side success' history of holdings formation as general. The distinctive phenomenon that unusual things happened in the holdings especially in terms of labor's welfare compared with the benchmark Holding of Temasek Singapore and Holding of Khazanah Malaysia. There are many things to be immediately addressed in connection with compromising level of welfare. Labor's obligations in norm terms such as keeping high performance and company's target have reached as planned, but rewards, benefits and bonuses are not awarded yet.

Experience from Semen Indonesia's holding, welfare comparation between the BOD and labor are showing unequal. According Table 2 and Figure 9, welfare's gap between the two is growing year-to-year and getting wider even after establishing a holding. This evidence is ironic due to forming of holdings in advance to keep and maintain prosperous for all stake holders, but the case had shown that commitment against labors' rights are easily ignored. The table clearly showing the gap between the BOD and labors.

Table 2. Welfare distribution employees and board of directors

Year	Net profit (Rp billion)	Employees' Scope						BOD's Scope
		Quarterly bonus for employees (times of monthly salary)				Annually bonus for employees (times of monthly salary)	Total bonus for employees (times of monthly salary)	Total tantiem for Board of Directors (times of monthly salary)
		Q1	Q2	Q3	Q4			
2010							5.56	28.71
2011	3,955.27	1	1	1	1.26	5.96	10.22	25.48
2012	4,926.64	1.5	1	1.5	1.75	6.95	12.70	20.26
2013	5,354.30	1.25	1.2	1	2.25	7.25	12.95	29.45
2014	5,573.58	1	1.09	0.75	0.75	7	10.59	42.17
2015	4,525.44	0.75	1	0.5	0.75	6.9	9.90	49.67
2016	4,535.04	0.95	0.75	0.75	0.5	6.97	9.92	47.25
2017	2,043.03	0.5	0	0.25	0.2	2.97	3.92	47.25
2018	3,082.49	0.24	0.25	0.13	0.19	3.97	4,59	57.44

Source: compiling by Author, 2019

By Table 2, Authors can read that total amount bonuses are trending to decrease year-to-year. Due Semen Indonesia's holding was formally formed in early 2013, statistically found that total amount bonuses for labors respectively 5.56 time of gross monthly salary (2010), 10.22 (2011), 12.7 (2012) and 12.95 (2013). However after Semen Indonesia's holding officially formed 2013, total bonuses for labor then fall gradually to 10.59 (2014), 9.9 (2015), 9.9 (2016), 3.95 (2017) and finally only to 0.92 (2018).

In opposite, Authors see other things different to the total bonuses for the BOD that showing to increase year-to-year. While total bonuses in 2013 is 29.45 time of monthly gross salary, it then significantly increases to 57.44 time of monthly gross salary in 2018. This is dramatically things happen as bonuses for labor decrease while bonuses for the BOD in contrast increase. The best to depict the welfare gap situation can be seen at Figure 9.

Author proposes that the anomaly phenomenon of the Semen Indonesia's holding due to caused respectively: (1) Employees' absenteeism since first developing, (2) Neglecting employees' participatory due to the BOD's vested interest, (3) Utilizing

Figure 9. Welfare's gap between The BOD and employees after holding
Source: compiling by Author, 2019

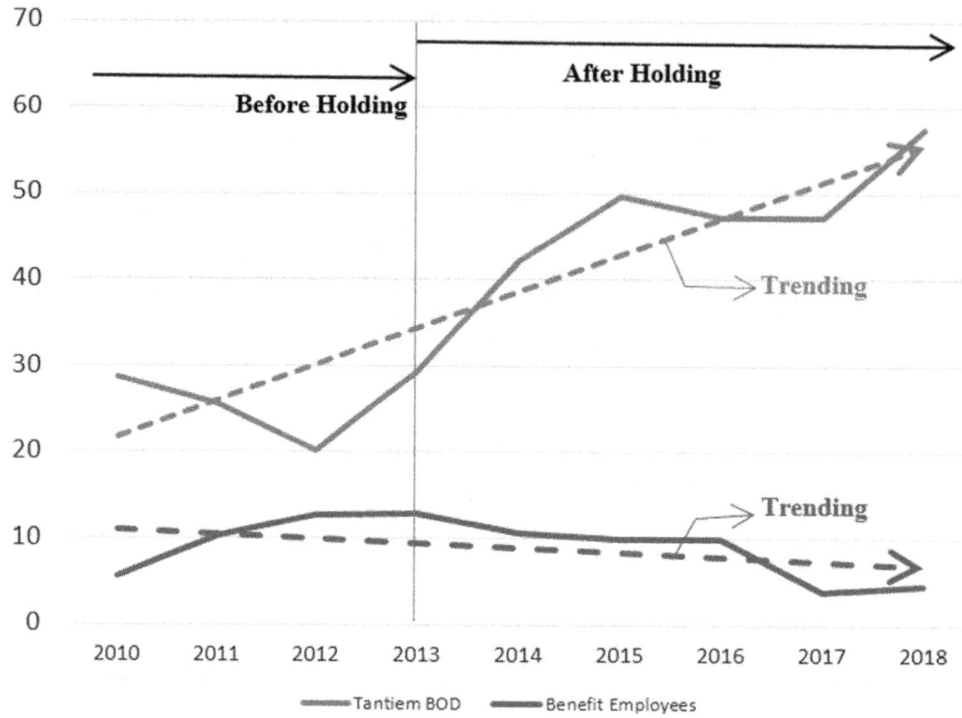

power approach in terms of principle-agent relationship, (4) Opportunistic interested of both Management and labor, and (5) Different view of disparity span-level welfare of Management and labor.

CONCLUSION

Despite of sound success establishing SOEs' holdings in Indonesia, there are found that welfare's commitment for labors have been showing ignored. Basic concepts operational in industries should maintain equal rights between stake holders is inapplicable in the case within Semen Indonesia's holding. For the case, government's commitment, preliminary campaign by SOEs' ministry to build SOEs' better is untrue.

There is needed revisiting, repositioning of establishing SOEs' holding future to acknowledge labors engagement as equal partner not as principal-agent relationship. When the BODs and BOCs are enjoying lure benefit annually, same treatment should apply for labors. Employees are not expecting to get same amount benefits as much as the BODs and BOCs, but at least coherently equal proportion or in equal percentage with management. This is to avoid wider welfare's gap between two, to strengthen teamwork, to increase belonging and finally to bolster SOEs holdings itself today and future.

ACKNOWLEDGMENT

This research received no specific grant from any funding agency in the public, commercial, or not-for-profit sectors.

REFERENCES

Aguilera, R. V., & Jackson, G. (2003). The Cross-national Diversity of Corporate Governance Dimensions and Determinants. *Academy of Management Review*, *28*(3), 447–465. doi:10.5465/amr.2003.10196772

Agustiawan, K. (2015). *Transforming the BUMN into an Indonesian State Holding Company*. Ash Center Harvard Kennedy School.

Biazin, C., Solano-Charris, E. L., & Quintero, J. A. (2017). Supply Chain and Operations Strategies for Problem-Solving in Latin American Countries: An Introduction. *Journal of Operations and Supply Chain Management*, 1-5.

Burma, A. Z. (2014). Human Resource Management and Its Important for Today's Organizations. *International Journal of Education and Social Science*, 85–94.

David, F. R. (2011). *Strategic Management: Concepts and Cases* (13th ed.). Prentice Hall.

ExnerR. (2012, December 12). *MNP*. Retrieved from MNP: https://www.mnp.ca/en/posts/do-i-need-a-holding-company

Geissler, C., & Krys, C. (2013). The Challenges of Strategic Management in the Twenty-first Century. *@Springer Fachmedien Wiesbaden*.

Harikrishnan, G. (2014). Study on Labour Welfare Measures - With Special Reference to Rubber Board of India. *Global Journal of Commerce & Management Perspective*, 82-85.

Hudson, S. (2019). *Hearst*. Retrieved from Chron: https://smallbusiness.chron.com/disadvantages-holding-company-form-organization-22665.html

James, H., & Watt, S. A. (1995). *Research Methods for Communication Science*. Allyn and Bacon.

Jiang, X. (2009). Strategic Management for Main Functional Areas in an Organization. *International Journal of Business and Management*, *4*(2). Advance online publication. doi:10.5539/ijbm.v4n2p153

Kennon, J. (2018, October 29). *The Balance*. Retrieved from The Balance: https://www.thebalance.com/understanding-a-holding-company-357341

Kingsford, R. T., & Biggs, H. C. (2012). Strategic Adaptive Management. Academic Press.

Kreitz, P. A. (2007). Best Practices for Managing Organizational Diversity. *SLAC-PUB-12499*.

Nickols, F. (2016). *Strategy, Strategic Management, Strategic Planning and Strategic Thinking*. Distance Consulting.

Papadakis, V. M., Lioukas, S., & Chambers, D. (1998). Strategic Decision-Making Processes: The Role of Management and Context. *Strategic Management Journal*, *19*(2), 115–147. doi:10.1002/(SICI)1097-0266(199802)19:2<115::AID-SMJ941>3.0.CO;2-5

PricewaterhouseCoopers. (2005). *PricewaterHuman Resources Management Strategies to Support Organizational Changes*. Luxembourg: PwC.

Sluijs, E., & Kluytmans, F. (2017). *Business Strategy and Human Resource Management: Setting the Scene*. Academic Press.

Subiyanto, E. (2020). A Failure Innovation Strategy of Acquisition during Excess Capaci-ty: Financial Approach based-on Case Study at the State-owned Cement Holding PT Semen Indonesia (Persero) Tbk. *Journal of Innovation and Entrepreneurship*, *9*(1), 20. Advance online publication. doi:10.118613731-020-00134-4

Subiyanto, E. (2019). OBOR: A New Hope for Future Indonesian or a New Trap? Case Study in Indonesia. In *Foreign Business in China and Opportunities for Technological Innovation and Sustainable Economics* (pp. 143–156). IGI Global. doi:10.4018/978-1-5225-8980-8.ch007

Thomas, K. W. (2015). *Making Conflict Management a Strategic Advantage*. CPP Inc.

Wals, K. (2010). *Key Issues in Strategic Human Resources*. Cornell University.

Chapter 6
Workforce Diversity to Foster an Innovation

Rahul Baburao Waghmare
https://orcid.org/0000-0001-7245-0869
Vishwakarma University, Pune, India

ABSTRACT

In global scenario it is necessity for all the organizations to employ diversified workforces. Workforce diversity helps the organization in improving productivity and innovative performance. The workforce diversity and inclusion strategies are directly linked to innovative business; they encourage employees to have different perspectives and ideas which drive innovation. To deal with global challenges through innovative performance, organizations have robust programs and policies to recruit and retain diversified workforces. Through this chapter, the author addresses how workforce diversity is fostering innovation in contemporary organizations.

INTRODUCTION

Workforce diversity is a more disputable topic in today's global business environment. Managing workforce diversity is significant task for organizations as it affects organizations performance, productivity and innovativeness. As the term workforce diversity is became a trend after liberalization of markets many researchers have studied this topic from various perspective and disciplines. This chapter deals with conceptual review of workforce diversity and innovation and puts emphasis on how diversity will foster an innovation performance of an organization.

Research indicates that innovation gives the seeds for monetary growth. Innovation in a company context is about remodeling a thinking into a new process, product or

DOI: 10.4018/978-1-7998-3515-8.ch006

service to generate a competitive advantage. For that innovation to show up depends as much on collective difference as on combination ability. If people assume alike then no matter how clever they are, they most possibly will get stuck at the identical regionally most advantageous solutions. Finding new and better solutions, innovating, requires thinking differently. If you convey many extraordinary views to a problem, you end up with greater innovative solutions. Workplace diversity can make certain there is a giant pool of knowledge, skills, existence experience, perspectives, and expertise. That's why diversity powers innovation.

THE CONCEPT OF WORKFORCE DIVERSITY

From the time of its evolution there is little argument in defining diversity among researchers and practitioners. In the words of Cox and Beale (1997) diversity is "a mix of people in one social system who have distinctly different socially group affiliations" (p.1).

In defining the term diversity much of the inertia was towards the differences of an individuals, whereas Thomas (1999), incorporate similarities as well as differences while defining diversity: "individuals who are different in some ways and similar in others" (p.5). With the increase in the interest of researchers, teachers in studying diversity in the context of an organization the term Workforce diversity is emerged which emphasized the requirement of new ways of interactions and communication among individuals and groups in an organization.

According to Robbins and Coulter (2018): "Workforce diversity can be defined as the ways in which people in organization are different form and similar to one another "(p.158). The workforce diversity often involved characteristics like race, ethnicity, gender, religion, age, ability and sexual orientation. The workforce diversity has challenges which needs to be managed by an organization; managing diversity effectively provides various benefits to an organization in global environment which assist them in gaining competitive advantage.

Robbins and Coulter (2018) enlists the benefits of diversity that organizations are experiencing from three perspectives. (See Table 1)

Workforce Diversity and Organizational Performance

Since the inception of the term workforce diversity, its relation with organizational performance is a most debated topic among researchers. Workforce diversity and organizational culture has been frequently said to be responsible for all manner of positive and negative ills. (Shani and Lau, 2005).The relationship between job

Table 1. Benefits of workforce diversity

Benefits of Workforce Diversity		
People Management	**Organization performance**	**Strategic**
I. Better use of employee talent **II.** Increased quality of team problem-solving efforts **III.** Ability to attract and retain employees of diverse backgrounds	**I.** Reduced costs associated with high turnover, absenteeism, and lawsuits **II.** Enhanced problem-solving ability **III.** Improved system flexibility	**I.** Increased understanding of the marketplace, which improves ability to better market to diverse consumers **II.** Potential to improve sales growth and increase market share **III.** Potential source of competitive advantage because of improved innovation efforts

Source: *Adopted from* Robbins, S. P., Coulter, M., & Fernandez, A. (2018). *Management* (14th Ed.). Chennai, ID: Pearson India Education Services Pvt. Ltd. (p. 160).

satisfaction and employee performance has been studied and focused. (Agrawal, P., & Gautam, O. 2019)

Organizations have considered the issue of managing diverse workforce as an important chore in human resource management. Arokiasamy (2013) considers workforce diversity as "double-edged sword": Companies need to focus on diversity and look for ways to become totally inclusive organizations because diversity has the potential of yielding greater productivity and competitive advantages. Managing and valuing diversity is a key component of effective people management, which can improve workplace productivity. Unmanaged diversity in the workplace might become an obstacle for achieving organizational goals. (p.59)

The previous studies on workforce diversity and organizational performance tends towards showing positive effect on managing diversity on improving performance of an organization. Organizational performance can be enhanced through workforce diversity because of improved problem-solving abilities and system flexibility. Workforce diversity improves problem solving abilities and in increases system flexibility as diverse workforce requires processes and procedures to be more inclusive (Robbins & Coulter, 2018, p.162)

Saxena (2014) emphasizes the same perspective as Arokiasamy (2013) on managing workforce diversity: An organization's major objective is to earn profit and to enhance its productivity, no doubt that almost all the authors are saying that employing diversified workforce is the very essence in today's scenario but to manage such a diversified workforce is a big challenge in front of the management (p. 84).

Workforce diversity in office leads to politics (Sharma, S., & Gautam, O. 2014) which ultimately ruin the cultural and synergy among individuals. Gupta (2014) proposed the conceptual model that indicates factors which links diversity and organization performance. (See Figure 1).

Figure 1. A conceptual model that shows the factors mediating work force strategy & performance link
(Source: Gupta, R. (2013). Workforce diversity and Organizational performance. International Journal of Business and Management Invention, 2(6), 36–41. p.4)

Significance of the Study

The current study will be useful for corporate managers in terms of managing their workforce by focusing the guidelines for keeping the creativity high among a diverse group of thinkers while maintaining a positive climate. Furthermore, it will be grey area for academicians, researchers and practitioners to manage their diverse workforce. Lastly innovation leads holistic development of organization and of diverse workforce.

RESEARCH METHODOLOGY

Current study used extensive literature review (Kitchenham, et.al. 2009) on workforce diversity and innovation. 73 articles were extracted with keywords workforce, workforce diversity and innovation from Google scholar, J-gate and other reliable sources for literature. After analyzing all articles only 27 were found suitable to write a theoretical review for workforce diversity and innovation.

Theoretical Review on Workforce Diversity and Innovation

Innovation is a requisite for better organizational performance in today's global and competitive environment. As world is becoming smaller, innovation is even more challenging for an organization. Organizations are always looking for new ways for creating innovative products, services and business practices to gain competitive advantage in the market. In the view that organizations are having more diverse in workforce in in current business environment; one question is emerged as important topic for researchers and academicians to be focus on: whether workforce diversity will improve innovativeness and creativity of an organization?

In the search of answer to above question previous studies indicated that there is positive link between workforce diversity and innovation performance of an organizations. In the endeavoring the same, researcher have considered the diversity & inclusions effect on creativity, product innovation, productivity and competitive advantage. Few of the studies have emphasized on how various dimensions of diversity led to generate creative and innovative ideas and business practices.

For new Product or Services

Workforce diversity enables organization to be more innovative and helps businesses generating new products and services (Hewlett, Marshall & Sherbin, 2014). Hewlett, Marshall and Sherbin (2014) in their HBR article, *How diversity can drive innovation* proposed the concept of 2-D diversity and elaborated how it will drives innovation. The two type's diversity are inherent diversity and Acquired diversity. 2-D diversity enables the organization to create innovative environment where "outside box ideas heard". According to Hewlett, Marshall and Sherbin (2014), Companies with 2-D diversity out-innovate and out-perform others. Employees at these companies are 45% likelier to report that their firm's market share grew over the previous year and 70% likelier to report that the firm captures a new market (p.2).

Fostering Innovation

The report of Forbes Insights (2011) *Global Diversity and Inclusion: Fostering Innovation through a Diverse Workforce emphasis on:* A diverse and inclusive workforce is necessary to drive innovation, foster creativity, and guide business strategies. Multiple voices lead to new ideas, new services, and new products, and encourage out-of-the-box thinking. Today, companies no longer view diversity and inclusion efforts as separate from their other business practices, and recognize that a diverse workforce can differentiate them from their competitors by attracting top talent and capturing new clients (p. 19)

Studies had proved that better diversity management will be a valuable asset for increasing innovation in the organization. According to Lorenzo and Voigt (2017) diversity has the greatest impact on innovation at companies that reinforce diversity through five conditions in the work environment:

1. Participative leadership behavior
2. Openness to cognitive diversity
3. Strategic priority
4. Frequents interpersonal communication
5. Equal Employment practices

The review of literature indicates that innovation and workforce diversity go hand in hand, and they create the environment and outcomes that top management wants. Buitron(2019) suggest four ways to drive innovation in an organization leveraging on diverse workforce.(See table 3)

Table 2. Ways to use diversity to drive innovation

1	Promote Inclusion	Individuals need to feel that they are heard and their opinion matters.
2	Encourage Decision-making	Organizations naturally have benefits of multiple perspective when they have workforce with diverse backgrounds. Using innovative techniques organizations can enhance the better brainstorming sessions and decision making,
3	Promoting safe environment	Prompting Safe environment where individuals are encouraged to make decisions and make mistakes.
4	Boosting organization Culture	Instead of focusing on resolving the differences among individuals; organizations need to be focus on boosting organization culture where people with different dimensions are encouraged to create vibrant environment which leads to promote higher productivity and innovativeness.

(Source: Buitron, V. (2019, January 23). The Role of Diversity in Innovation. Retrieved from https://tangocode.com/2019/01/the-role-of-diversity-in-innovation/.)

While investigating the nexus between labor diversity and firm's innovation, Parrotta, Pozzoli and Pytlikova(2014) finds an evidence that ethnic diversity can facilitates the patenting activity of firms by increasing the patent applications and by enlarging the breadth of patenting technology fields.

Diversity and Creativity

This Forbes insight report includes quotes from top professional who are leveraging the benefits of workforce diversity. Few of the quotes are as follows: "Diversity fosters creativity. We need to generate the best ideas from our people in all levels of the company and incorporate them into our business practices." –Frédéric Rozé, chief executive officer, L'Oréal USA.

"We couldn't have gone through all of the mergers and acquisitions and continue to be successful without having a diverse workforce. It's important to our business strategy and it makes us more innovative and competitive." –Debbie Storey, senior vice president of talent development and chief diversity officer, AT&T. Diverse workforce brings in different skills and abilities together in an organization which helps in increasing problem-solving ability, decision making and creativity. "Creativity thrives on diversity" (Morgan, 1989).

Govendo (2005) suggests that diversity in the team led to generating different perspective which helps in generating creative solutions and opportunities for the problems of an organization. He provides five guidelines to increase creative output through idea generation. (See table 2)

Table 3. Five guidelines for keeping the creativity high among a diverse group of thinkers while maintaining a positive climate

1	Make it safe to share creative ideas
2	Clearly articulate the objectives and how they fit into the larger, strategic picture
3	Turn points of disagreement into new ideas
4	Take the time to explore unusual, intriguing ideas for their real world applicability
5	Conclude your session with a set of action items and Accountability

(Source: Govendo, A.J. (2005). Workforce, diversity and corporate creativity. Handbook of Business Strategy, 6(1), 213-218. p.5&6)

Ruthy Miller (2018) presents the five ways diversity drives innovation and out-of-the-box thinking in small businesses.

Diversity Fuels Creativity

Organizations having diverse workforce brings multiple backgrounds and different perspectives which fosters an environment where ideas with out of box thinking are accepted.

Diversity Helps to Take Better Decisions

Diversity in teams brings multiple perspectives, creative debate and constructive conflicts which help organization in taking better decisions.

Diversity Helps Recruitment and Hiring

In competitive business environment, it is perilous task of an organization to have diverse workforce and inclusion. Organizations must look for hiring workforce with diverse backgrounds and skillsets.

Diversity Leads to Better Products and Services

Multicultural perspective and different worldviews, experiences of individuals in diverse workforce create products and services which will better serve the problems of communities.

Diversity Boosts Profitability

In today's competitive business environment, diverse workforce for organizations no longer nice-to-have, it is a must-have for organizations who are looking for growth and competitive advantage.

The finding from the study on workforce composition and innovation (Mohammadi et.al, 2017) indicates that ethnic and educational diversity increases the success in radical innovation. And study suggests that organizations should pursue hiring policies inspired by greater diversity as a tool for fostering innovativeness of the organization.

Workforce Diversity and Inclusion

Sollner (2010) in his working paper finds that there is a positive relationship between occupational diversity and the propensity to innovate for both manufacturing and services firms. (p.21). Mohammadi, Brostorm and Franzoni (2017) argues that ethnic and higher education diversity within the workforce is associated with superior performance in radical innovation. (p. 32). An inclusive workplace that understands the needs of their employees, making them feel valued and respected has a significant and positive impact on employee retention. Perhaps most importantly, research suggests companies that openly articulate values of inclusion and have a diverse workforce tend to appeal to a wider customer and supplier base.

To turn diversity into organizations advantage Salomon and Schork (2016) suggests effective diversity program by providing training at all levels of organization which should have more focus on inclusion. According to Catherine Phillips (2019), "The fact is that if organizations want to build teams or organizations capable of innovating, they need diversity. Diversity enhances creativity. It encourages the search for novel information and perspectives, leading to better decision making and problem solving.

Diversity can improve the bottom line of companies and lead to unfettered discoveries and breakthrough innovations". Organizations must invest their time in cultivating diversity and inclusion strategy as these will not built in one day. According to PwC's 18th Annual Global CEO Survey, 85% of CEOs whose organizations have a diversity and inclusion strategy say it has enhanced performance. Highly inclusive organizations rate themselves 170% better at innovation, according to Bersin by Deloitte. (Mitschein, 2018). Firstly, it seems that too many organizations make the elemental error of failing to align their diversity practices with their organizational goals. And in such situations, regardless of what proportion good will there's towards the concept of diversity, the tough realities of running the business on a day-to-day basis, of keeping customers satisfied, of selling and delivering the merchandise or service will keep undermining it. And secondly, there's often a mismatch between how organizations design diversity policies and the way they implement them. Or to place it differently, what looks good on paper too often falls apart in practice.

Steele and Derven,(2015) in their paper expands the discussion around the relationship between Diversity & Inclusion and innovation by exploring not only how diversity & inclusion can be leveraged for better outcomes in innovation, but also how innovation can be leveraged for better outcomes in Diversity & Inclusion. Diversity means various things to different people, and organizations must apply those definitions to their companies accordingly. Diversity and inclusion can't be a one-time campaign or a one-off initiative. Promoting them within the workplace may be a constant work-in-progress and will be maintained and nurtured to ensure effectiveness. Empathetic leadership is vital to the present transformation. For real change to happen, every individual leader must invest the worth of belonging – both intellectually and emotionally.

Previous studies indicate that employees of the organizations who are using inclusion strategy effectively are more likely to takes risk, challenges a status quo and embrace diverse arrays of creative ideas. Baumgartner (2010) in his blog states that diversity is important ingredients for creative thinking. And it its proven that diversity in teams helps in producing creative results.

Scope for Future Research

The study emphasis on how workforce diversity will be a driving force for innovation and creativity. In recent duration researcher and practitioner have not focused on creating knowledge on the way's workforce diversity will foster innovation and growth of organizations, hence there is necessity of conceptual as well as empirical studies for identifying the diversity among and

CONCLUSION

In this chapter, author has provided a conceptual review on workforce diversity and its relations with organizational as well as innovation performance. From the papers reviewed author indicates that its necessity for an organization to manage diversity effectively and leverage on the differences and homogeneity of an individuals to enhances the decision making and problem-solving ability. The major outcome from this review is organization is should look for identifying diversity at different levels of organization and to concentrate on the executing inclusion programmes effectively. The key determinant of success is the effective administration of diversity. Not only, then, does the application of equality and diversity insurance policies in such contexts limit the poor outcomes of cultural dominance, however they additionally assist to release the latent innovation conceivable of numerous staff. In other words, the innovation achievable of diversity are fine harnessed when efforts to maximize such manageable is coordinated with greater frequent methods to equality and diversity management. The application of strategies that are designed to foster exact equality practices, have confidence and inclusiveness through fantastic leadership, when mixed with creativity and innovation techniques that capitalize on range to deliver innovation, provide a groundwork for increased enterprise and monetary productiveness and competitive advantage In the concluding the chapter author suggests that diversity management and inclusion fosters the innovation in the organization.

REFERENCES

Agrawal, P., & Gautam, O. (2019). The Effects of Leaders' Behavior on Job Satisfaction, Organizational Citizenship Behavior, Deviant Behavior, and Job Performance of Employees. In Analyzing Workplace Deviance in Modern Organizations (pp. 100-113). IGI Global.

Arokiasamy, A. R. A. (2013). Literature review on workforce diversity, employee performance and organizational goals: A concept paper. Journal of Arts. *Science & Commerce*, *4*(4), 58–63.

Buitron, V. (2019, January 23). *The Role of Diversity in Innovation*. Retrieved from https://tangocode.com/2019/01/the-role-of-diversity-in-innovation/

Cox, T., & Beale, R. L. (1997). *Developing competency to manage diversity: readings, cases & activities*. Berrett-Koehler.

Global Diversity and Inclusion: Fostering Innovation Through a Diverse Workforce. (2011). *Forbes Insights*. Retrieved from https://www.forbes.com/forbesinsights/innovation_diversity/

Govendo, A. J. (2005). Workforce, diversity and corporate creativity. Handbook of Business Strategy, 6(1), 213-218. doi:10.1108/08944310510557495

Gupta, R. (2013). *Workforce diversity and Organizational performance*. Academic Press.

Hewlett, S. A., Marshall, M., & Sherbin, L. (2013). How diversity can drive innovation. *Harvard Business Review- Innovation*. Retrieved from https://hbr.org/2013/12/how-diversity-can-drive-innovation

Kitchenham, B., Brereton, O. P., Bugden, D., Turner, M., Bailey, J., & Linkman, S. (2009). Systematic literature reviews in software engineering–a systematic literature review. *Information and Software Technology*, *51*(1), 7–15. doi:10.1016/j.infsof.2008.09.009

Lorenzo, R., & Voigt, N. (2017, April 26). *The Mix That Matters: Innovation Through Diversity*. Retrieved from https://www.bcg.com/en-au/publications/2017/people-organization-leadership-talent-innovation-through-diversity-mix-that-matters.aspx

MillerR. (2018, May 2). Retrieved from https://www.salesforce.com/blog/2018/05/diversity-drives-innovation-for-small-businesses.html

Mitschein, M. (2018). *Why Diversity and Inclusion Matters – From an Innovation Perspective*. Retrieved from https://www.digitalistmag.com/future-of-work/2018/08/22/why-diversity-inclusion-matters-from-innovation-perspective-06183094

Mohammadi, A., Broström, A., & Franzoni, C. (2017). Workforce Composition and Innovation: How Diversity in Employees' Ethnic and Educational Backgrounds Facilitates Firm-Level Innovativeness. *Journal of Product Innovation Management*, *34*(4), 406–426. doi:10.1111/jpim.12388

Parrotta, P., Pozzoli, D., & Pytlikova, M. (2013). The nexus between labor diversity and firm's innovation. *Journal of Population Economics*, *27*(2), 303–364. doi:10.100700148-013-0491-7

Phillips, K. W. (2014, October 1). *How Diversity Makes Us Smarter*. Retrieved from https://www.scientificamerican.com/article/how-diversity-makes-us-smarter/

Robbins, S. P., Coulter, M., & Fernandez, A. (2018). *Management* (14th ed.). Pearson India Education Services Pvt. Ltd.

Salomon, M. F., & Schork, J. M. (2003). Turn Diversity to Your Advantage. *Research Technology Management*, *46*(4), 37–44. doi:10.1080/08956308.2003.11671575

Saxena, A. (2014). Workforce Diversity: A Key to Improve Productivity. *Procedia Economics and Finance*, *11*, 76–85. doi:10.1016/S2212-5671(14)00178-6

Shani, A., & Lau, J. (2005). *Behavior in organizations: an experiential approach.* McGraw-Hill.

Sharma, S., & Gautam, O. (2014). An empirical analysis on office politics in Indian organizations. *Human Resource Reflection*, *1*(3), 86–92.

Sollner, R. (2010). *Human Capital Diversity and Product Innovation: A Micro-Level Analysis.* JENA Economic Research Papers.

Steele, R., & Derven, M. (2015). Diversity & Inclusion and innovation: A virtuous cycle. *Industrial and Commercial Training*, *47*(1), 1–7. doi:10.1108/ICT-09-2014-0063

Thomas, R. R., & Woodruff, M. I. (1999). *Building a house for diversity: how a fable about a giraffe & an elephant offers new strategies for today's workforce.* American Management Association.

Why Diversity is the Mother of Creativity. (2019, November 13). Retrieved from https://innovationmanagement.se/imtool-articles/why-diversity-is-the-mother-of-creativity/

Chapter 7
Bringing Social Media Into Work:
The Positive and Negative Effects on Policy Implementation - An Introduction to Theory and Research

Francesca Di Virgilio
University of Molise, Italy

ABSTRACT

This study develops an integrative model in order to identify the underlying factors that drive employees to engage in social media at work for businesses. More specifically, the model explains the interplay between employment statuses, motivation, job satisfaction, and social activities for the purpose of analyzing the positive effects of social media use and the negative effects of social media overload on social media policy implementation. Nevertheless, the model proposes a research roadmap can be examined by utilizing a framework for the assessment of the use of social media at work, as a tool to improve business organizations. Finally, it concludes with the discussion of several open issues and cutting-edge challenges.

Social media is tool at work was developed during the last few years. A ground-breaking phenomenon has become intertwined with many organization's daily lives and is therefore also essential for private and public organizations that strive towards gaining a competitive advantage in the business environment (Bizzi, 2018; Di Virgilio, et al. 2019). The new idea of social media at work is distinct from the traditional marketing approach to social media. This "revolution in the measurement

DOI: 10.4018/978-1-7998-3515-8.ch007

of collective human behaviour" (Kleinberg, 2008, p.66) gives managerial decision makers unprecedented opportunities such as collecting information about purchasing behaviors, reaching out to new customers, promoting brands, acquiring and building a reputation of trustworthiness, with overall positive effects on financial performance (Berthon, et al., 2012; Paniagua & Sapena, 2014).

Organizations can advertise their services and products through sponsored posts on social media and brand awareness through their corporate pages, can stimulate active dialogue with their customers, and potential customers, and can observe their social media behaviors to analyse the common characteristics of customer-centered and identify their main social media initiatives success drivers, then combine the current knowledge on social media success drivers with social media projects at minimal cost (Hanna, et al., 2011; Kohli, et al., 2015).

Recently, organizations have started encouraging employees to use social media not only for customers but also for their workers, to interact with coworkers in order to empower collaboration and knowledge sharing.

Current studies suggest that social media can be beneficial to facilitate the work of employees, O'Connor, Schmidt, and Drouin (2016) found that 86% of employees have coworker friends on social media, that 77% of them use social media while working, and that in 44% of cases they talk about their jobs; Tiago and Veríssimo (2014) found in their study that 82% of employees believe that a digital presence in social media promotes internal and external relationships, and 60% believe social media usage supports their decision-making processes.

Social media offers the opportunity to interact with coworkers in the organization, the possibility to build friendships, to gain access to resources, to share information necessary, to get support or advice and to execute task activities (Liu, et al., 2015).

The studies reviewed indicate the increasing need to investigate social media within the workplace, in particular there is an urgency for studies with a strong theoretical foundation that might offer a last in guidance within a phenomenon that evolves significantly on day to day basis. The available literature has been criticized for lacking a bonding theory to organize the findings and guide future research (Miao et al., 2007; Hansen & Levin, 2016; Di Virgilio, et al., 2019).

Yet, there is a hidden problem that has been neglected by managers, the use of social media to facilitate work and benefit organizations could paradoxically risk fostering withdrawal intentions and turnover, which damage organizations. More precisely, two missing links emerge: first of all, relatively little attention has been paid to as well as employee use of social media for workplace and corresponding behaviors. The second missing link concerns on how companies adopt and use social media.

In this scenario, the purpose of this chapter is an attempt to take on this challenging task. This research aims to study the factors associated with the technological and organizational, context that relates to social media usage in organizations as the extent to which social media benefits organizations is still not clear. By extending the findings of social connectedness from interpersonal use of social media in the workplace.

This study develops an integrative model in order to identify the underlying factors that drive employees to engage in social media at work for businesses. More specifically, the model explains the interplay between employment status, motivation, job satisfaction and social activities, for the purpose of analyzing the positive effects of social media use and the negative effects of social media overload on social media policy implementation.

However, to better understand the relationship between these factors and to be able to give actionable recommendations to both organizations and employees, is necessary an integrative model within a comprehensive social media strategy for business opportunity based on employee motivation and job satisfaction.

In this scenario, we organized the chapter in different parts. In the first part we make a contribution to the body of literature by examining components the functionalities of social media practice and user behavior at work. Then we analyze a review of the variables which have been discussed in employee motivation and job satisfaction literatures will be presented with the goal of identifying key constructs that influence employee to use social media at work. Given the vast literature examining employee motivation and job satisfaction, this review will be selective with only the most relevant concepts being included. In the second part, we analyze the hidden problems related to risk of employees' abuse of social media at work. Utilizing these key variables and concepts, an integration of both literatures with the goal of generating an integrative model will be attempted. Finally, we identify five propositions which are the results of the literature review. We close the paper by discussing future research directions for this work.

Thanks to this chapter, we have a good amount of information about the role of social media policy implementation for businesses, and as a useful guide to future research on social media strategy as a whole.

SOCIAL MEDIA PRACTICE AND USER BEHAVIOR AT WORK

A burgeoning body of research conducted over the last few decades has shown that companies have paradigmatically changed the way they are organized and managed, as well as how they compete (Ngai et al., 2015; Di Virgilio, 2018a; Enders et al., 2008; Kietzman, et al., 2011). The effectiveness of social media for business embeds a number of new tools and approaches that have the potential to support or enhance these strategic, organizational and managerial modifications, to innovate their business models and managerial practices (He et al., 2013; Luo et al., 2013, Ghezzi et al., 2016).

New, bold theoretical perspectives are needed to enhance our understanding of these phenomena.

In October 2016, Facebook launched one of its major innovations: Facebook at Work (Bizzi, 2018). Facebook at work offers a new platform to facilitate communication and collaboration among employees in the organization. Instead of using long and inefficient chains of emails, employees can efficiently communicate through the website, exchange messages and files, and engage in video conferences and meetings. The interface is similar to that of the traditional website, leveraging the familiarity of employees with Facebook. The service offers a vast array of functionalities that outcompete traditional intranet services, and hundreds of companies have already been successfully using its test version. In short, the technology is not crucial to performing their jobs. This can lead to multiple outcomes.

In this regard, Treem and Leonardi (2012) support the use of social media for internal task-efficiency within organizations. They advance the argument to support the available social media options for the purposes of visibility of tasks, work behavior, and the workflow of work-related activities. In fact, they note that social media, like Facebook, lists the interests and hobbies of other workers. This provides an easy way for an individual to see who knows what in an organization.

In recent years, there has been an increasing interest to examine the role of benefits, costs, and experience with social media in relation to individual factors to share knowledge among employees using social media. Positive results can be achieved only through proper training and control of those users and employees who are in charge to use companies' social media platforms or to gather customer related information (Kaplan & Haenlein, 2010; Martini, et al., 2013; Di Virgilio, 2018b, Di Virgilio & Antonelli, 2018). In particular employees communicate in social media and contribute to the company's image and reputation.

The external public perceives the employees as true ambassadors of the company and thus feedback takes on a major role in building its reputation (Badea, 2014).

If people use social media for work, their contacts are likely to be coworkers. The contents shared will pertain to work activities, job advice, and career opportunities. Employees can leverage their coworkers' social networks to build professional ties outside of the organization and gain exposure to job opportunities. Social media can help an employee connect with his or her coworkers' social networks, expanding professional ties and opportunities. In addition, employees who use social media for work may be exposed to career opportunities from their contacts or from their contacts' networks. Personal friendship networks tend to cluster in closed groups with limited reach, while professional networks tend to be more open, sparser, and allow for greater awareness of and access to job opportunities (Granovetter, 1995).

Social media is inherently about engagement and collaboration, the benefits cannot be unidirectional or one-sided. Leftheriotis and Giannakos (2014) note that social media may offer benefits to organizations by stimulating work performance. Sun and Shang (2014) maintain that companies should encourage employees to use social media for work-related tasks. In particularly, intention to use social media appears to be amplified in the case of employees in marketing/sales versus diminished in the case of individuals in other departments, consistent with the idea that the customer facing nature of some jobs impacts intention to use social media technologies for businesses (Agnihotri et al. 2012; Behringer & Sassenberg, 2015; Bharadwaj, 2000; Di Virgilio, 2018a,b).

Before a firm can enter in the social media policy, it must determine the appropriate goals associated with the social media implementation. It needs to identify and understand the value proposition for the employee and for the firm.

EMPLOYEE MOTIVATION TO USE SOCIAL MEDIA

Current arguments suggest that social media can be beneficial to facilitate the work of employees.

However, not all employees will be equally inclined and motivated to use social media at work. Some individuals see social media as a private tool to be used for leisure and do not want it to interfere with their jobs, while other individuals use social media as a tool to enable job activities and facilitate work interactions (McDonald & Thompson, 2016). The different behaviors of these two types of individuals could explain the potential to deploy a social media policy implementation by organization.

Nevertheless, some employees use social media technology on behalf of the organization less than other employees could be their job role/focus, specifically regarding the difference in the "customer-facing" nature of their jobs (Robertson & Kee, 2017; Hansen & Levin, 2016). Engaging in discussion with consumers in social media on behalf of a business is inherently a marketing/sales activity. And while some may agree with the concept espoused by Peter Drucker that firms do two things innovation and marketing, the reality exists that goals and mentalities can differ across the organization's departments or within a company's strategic business units (e.g., Kahn & Mentzer, 1994). As stated by Dougherty (1992, p. 179), different departments can be viewed as "different thought worlds." Indeed, we note that a common sample focus of the motivation model in business research is that of sales or marketing employees (Miao et al., 2007).

Thus, while a business may hope that all of its employees would equally engage in social media discussions about the organization, we posit that individuals in marketing and sales-related positions are more likely to act on intentions to engage in social media technology usage. Indeed, the marketing and sales employees might frequently use social media technology because they perceive an expectation and motivation to do so. That is, the technology would appear to be crucial to performing their jobs, perhaps even mandatory at times (Levin et al., 2012). Conversely, other employees might infrequently use social media technology because they perceive a lack of expectation and motivation to use it.

The most important issue to understand when determining whether employees will be motivated to engage at work through social media is the work-life boundary associated with the use of social media. (Sánchez Abril, Levin, & Del Riego, 2012). Research on social media has shown that its use can lead to positive feelings and emotions. People who actively participate on Facebook (e.g., write Facebook posts, comment on other's status updates, click the 'Like' button to show support of updates) are more likely to experience feelings of connectedness and higher levels of happiness (Valkenburg, Peter, & Schouten, 2006). In fact, Kim and Lee (2011) state that individuals report greater levels of happiness from the number of Facebook friends they have. This may be due to the frequent visualization of Facebook friends, as a visualization can remind users of their social connections, and of subsequent affirmation or enhancement of self-worth and self-esteem.

Positive results can be achieved only through proper social media policy implementation. The challenge for organizations is whether they will make their structures flexible and harmonized so as to successfully integrate social media into the communication policy.

JOB SATISFACTION AT WORK AND THE LINK WITH EMPLOYMENT STATUS

Locke (1976, p. 1297) defines job satisfaction as "a pleasurable or positive emotional state resulting from the appraisal of one's job or job experiences". Employees who are more satisfied with their daily work are more likely to help organizations reach their goals efficiently (Scott & Stephens, 2009). Job satisfaction is a frequently studied dependent variable in communication research in the workplace (Staw, 1984).

In other words, job satisfaction can reap positive benefits within workplace tasks, roles, and relationships. Organizational research has generally viewed job satisfaction as a variable that is created internally through workplace interactions, practices, routines, and policies.

Social media has infiltrated the traditional workplace: social uses of Facebook at work, task-based uses of social media at work, context collapse concerns, and strategies for managing context collapse. It is not uncommon for coworkers to be friend each other on Facebook, although some people are still cautious about this practice. These themes suggest that social media is blurring the boundary between the social and the professional.

Within the workplace, these benefits could include one's satisfaction of their job. Perhaps by allowing employees time to utilize social media for businesses, both during the workday as a break, and outside of work, job satisfaction may flourish.

Recently studies shift focus to economic aspects such as the gender gap, and relative income, showed that there are numerous psychological factors determinants of job satisfaction such as the place of residence (Asadullah, Xiao, & Yeoh, 2015).

For instance, employees are by definition not employed in their hometowns. Long distances from their families cause emotional exhaustion. Therefore, employees are less satisfied with their jobs if they are far away from their families (Qin, Hom, Xu, & Ju, 2013). However, their working stress is reduced when they have more friends and acquaintances in the same working cities (Jin, Wen, Fan, & Wang, 2012).

In this case, social media tend to contact more friends and improve their job satisfaction (contacting that people from the same hometown are the most likely to become friends), social media became an emotional support and is significantly associated with the subjective well-beings.

By extending the findings of social connectedness and psychological happiness from interpersonal use of Facebook to the workplace, many studies higlight if Facebook use among co-workers (who spend varying amount of Facebook time and who are of different employment statuses) is associated with employees' job satisfaction (Robertson & Kee, 2017). Job satisfaction can be influenced by several factors where employment status can be one of them.

Communication researchers have addressed contractual obligation (or short-term employment) to an organization (Gossett, 2001), explaining that temporary or contract employees may identify with organizations differently, as compared to those with differing employment statuses. Dailey (2016) explores the role of internship socialization into full time employment.

Taken together, these new inclinations about how workers are employed justifies the need to study employment status as a factor related to social media use and job satisfaction.

USER BEHAVIOUR AND NEGATIVE SOCIAL MEDIA USAGE: SOCIAL OVERLOAD

When discussing the outcomes and impacts of the above-mentioned applications of social media, there is a hidden problem that organizations may have overlooked and could require adjusting our recommendations for businesses.

While social media use can be beneficial to an organization, it can pose increased risks due to its interactivity, spontaneity, and likelihood of unedited content (Scott & Jacka, 2011).

Given that social media is complex and touches have an impact on many areas of an organization. Specifically, social media risks can stem from the organization's use of it, from employees' use, from external sources to the organization, or from a combination of these sources.

The negative effects of social media usage, like the so called "social overload" determined by an excessive use of and reliance on technological tools, thus leading to social exhaustion or the intention to discontinue social media use (Maier et al., 2015).

The possible drawbacks may be associated to the use of these tools and instruments, such as: the decrease of real-life interactions and the subsequent impoverishment of actual experience as social media replace other face-to-face, less-mediated communication channels (Hanna et al., 2011).

The risk that a wrong usage of social media could bring tensions among the employees within a company, where a bad reputational impact may lead to distrust on colleagues and bosses (Kumar & Devi, 2014).

An excessive reliance on social media-related information may create perception biases, as a person could base his thoughts only on the basis of social media reputation, avoiding the real knowledge of colleagues' strengths and weaknesses (Nagendra, 2014).

Employees who use social media for work or leisure have different public or private preferences for social media access. Individuals can regulate the privacy settings and web search indexing of their online published content. The more people use social media for leisure, the more they prefer keeping high privacy (McDonald & Thompson, 2016). Individuals who use social media for work may be less motivated to keep their contents private since they are already visible to coworkers and supervisors.

Additionally, social media use may threaten employee productivity. Social media presents employees with the challenge of navigating the boundaries between their personal and professional identities (Ollier-Malaterre et al., 2013). An overuse of social media for personal purposes during working hours may result in productivity losses and misuse of resources (Field & Chelliah, 2012; Khansa et al., 2017). Finally, damage to an organization's reputation may occur when employees post negative comments about its products or policies (Brivot et al., 2017; O'Leary, 2011a). In addition to reputational risk concerns that can arise from negative, embarrassing, or incriminating employee comments, hackers may infiltrate an organization's social media accounts and post false or misleading information (Castillo et al., 2011). Brivot et al. (2017) further note that controlling reputational risk is difficult as there are multiple, conflicting viewpoints on how social media risk should be controlled and if at all.

Despite the understandable concerns discussed above, another hidden problem about who use social media in the organization to facilitate their work are more likely to become exposed to the opportunities that social media offers to create new work connections and to search for jobs (Bozzi, 2018).

The use of social media to facilitate work may not only enrich the relationships an employee develops inside the organization but also the relationships that an employee develops outside of the organization, eventually increasing the risk that employees will engage in job search behaviors and develop new work connections to find an alternative occupation (Bizzi, 2018). There is a fundamental trade-off that creates a dilemma for organizations.

Strong social media interactions to facilitate work also mean creating more opportunities to find alternative jobs and to either leave the organization.

Social media could activate job search intentions or behaviors in employees and make them the target of recruitment campaigns. Although job search behaviors are primarily determined by one's dissatisfaction with one's job (Bretz, Boudreau, & Judge, 1994), employees are also incentivized by the cost to search for jobs, access to job opportunities, and by the perception of available employment in other organizations (Direnzo & Greenhaus, 2011).

Social media lowers these costs and increases the opportunities to search for new jobs and to augment employability. Employees can be easily attracted by other companies that use social media for recruitment; quickly develop ties with employees in other companies through interest groups, blogs, or communities of interest; have easier access to HR professionals working for other companies; and, therefore, increase their employability in other organizations, which could spur job search behaviors and intentions.

Making social media content public is an easier way to be reached by new work contacts or HR professionals who acquire in-formation from social profiles to contact and recruit new hires. Furthermore, people who use social media for work in their organization may develop more professionally oriented social media profiles with information about employment history making them appealing to HR recruiters.

People who use social media only to relate to close friends and to share personal content may not accept requests from unknown individuals. People who already use social media to work may be more inclined to respond positively to requests from unknown professionals or recruiters, even if there is no pre-existing personal tie. If the use of social media to facilitate work in the organization is related to the use of social media to develop ties outside of the organization and search for new jobs, there could be a problem.

The social media research still lacks sufficient quantitative and qualitative analysis of negative social media usage.

Even so, a gap exists within many organizations between concerns about negative social media usage and the existence of formal social media policy implementation that are applied throughout the organization.

SOCIAL MEDIA USE AND EFFECTS ON SOCIAL MEDIA POLICY IMPLEMENTATION

Social media policy implementation refers to the existence of policies designed to manage social media, to identify how they implement and use social media across all areas, where the purpose is to identify a research road map how organizations and their employees use social media externally and internally to improve business. Policy implementation reflects the degree to which an organization has implemented specific policies regarding social media use.

Social media use addresses how organizations employ social media both externally and internally (Demek et al., 2018). Measures of social media external use address the use of social media to communicate with customers, increase sales, develop and maintain the organization's brand, and recruit and communicate with new employees. Internally, organizations use social media as an interactive internal communication, collaboration and knowledge-sharing tool between co-workers, to brainstorm about new product development, and obtain employee feedback about the organization (Eschenbrenner et al., 2015; Schaupp & Bélanger, 2014). The analysis treats social media use as a formative construct, since changes in the various indicators are assumed to determine changes in the value of this construct (Hair et al., 2011) and these indicators are not necessarily correlated.

In addition, organizations use social media as a recruiting tool to attract new employees and prescreen potential future employees. Further, organizations use social media to build brand reputation, increase sales, and obtain consumer feedback in order to improve products and customer service (Eschenbrenneret al., 2015). Managers perceive that these external and internal uses of social media add value to the organization by increasing sales contacts, reducing marketing costs, improving customer service, increasing productivity and improving the company external perception (Schaupp & Bélanger, 2014). Devereux et al. (2017) also underlined how social media can reveal corporate identity of organizations who choose to adopt them, summarizing the relationship between corporate identity and social media according to five stages of social media including social media adoption, choice of platform/s, choice of content, stakeholder engagement and organization interaction.

Organizations use social media to increase efficiencies within the supply chain, monitor the market and competition, and communicate with investors and analysts (O'Leary, 2011b; Trinkle et al., 2015).

It is a second-order reflective construct, with two underlying first-order constructs that address policies on: (i) employees' personal use of social media, (ii) employees' work-related use of social media.

For example, an employee may actively engage with social media to show an image of engagement and high work, while maintaining energy levels that might otherwise be expended on work or reducing stress-related energy depletion (Andreassen, et al., 2014). On the other hand, some employees may view their social media use as a "guilty pleasure," an outlet for personal interests, non-work interests, or something that needs to be hidden or concealed at work.

Although various forms of social media were ostensibly developed as tools to augment relationship building, many argue that using social media at work actually degrades relationship and connectivity, and also decreases productivity. For example, if social media use is something that employees feel they must hide, or if they use social media in ways that are not always fully truthful, such use may impede trust at work. Studies have shown that social media users may exaggerate their success, happiness, or productivity (Zywica & Daniwski, 2008), which may also prove detrimental to honest, productive relationships at work. Research on the impacts of social media use indicates that the difference between meaningful relationships in the real world and the casual relationships common to social media may become unclear to users. Additionally, the time and energy spent on social media may come at the expense of time spent on task as well as time that would otherwise be used in maintaining real time relationships, thereby damaging the authenticity of relationships over time (Turkle, 2012). Thus, while it is possible to use social media for building one's resource of a professional network, it also may be a mechanism whereby employees' distance themselves from workplace relationships in favor of less present on-line relationships.

Thus, as intensity of social media use increases, we argue that users may expand their knowledge of the medium and progressively learn to use it in ways that may be dysfunctional for organizational life (Carlson et al. 2016).

Social media policy implementation depends on organization's social media use. While the correlation between social media use and policy implementation is given for granted, prior academic and practice research suggests that a social media policy implementation depend on whether an organization takes a proactive or reactive approach to use social media at work.

THEORIZED MODEL

Considering the research literature, we have constructed a theoretical integrative model: to explore the relationship between individual level (motivation, job satisfaction and employment status) to use social media on behalf of businesses. There are also the negative effects of social media usage (social overload), that to highlight potential negative outcomes of social media policy implementation.

In this section we outline the descriptions of our proposed logic, resulting in the theorized model illustrated in Figure. 1.

Figure 1. The theoretical integrative model

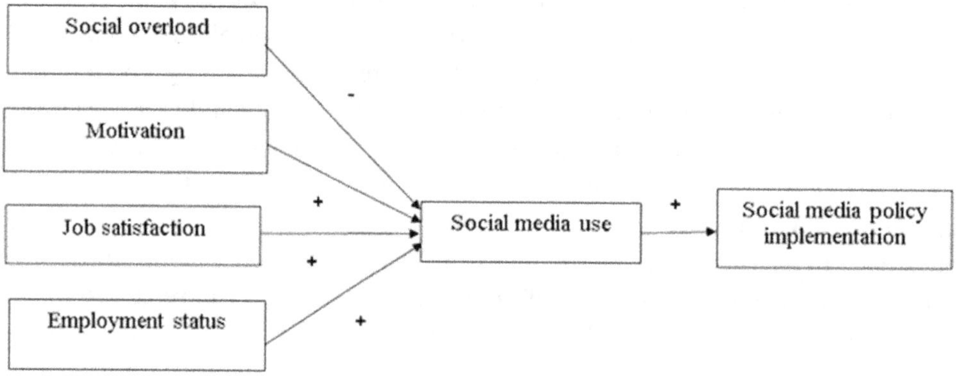

The following propositions come from the following statements which are:

- Motivation has a significant positive effect on an employee's intention to use social media at work.
- Full time employees experience the highest degree of job satisfaction and they spend more time on social media compared to their non-full time counterparts.
- Job satisfaction has a significant positive effect on an employee's intention to use social media at work.
- Social media use has a direct positive impact on social media policy implementation.
- Social overload has a direct negative effect on the decision to implement a social media policy.

In summary, we posit that employees more satisfied and motivated performing are more likely to intend to use the social media technology for the businesses.

Thus, while the extent of social media use will directly influence social media policy implementation, and social overload will influence negatively social media policy implementation. Specifically, as the organization's social media use increases, the influence of social media use on policy implementation will increase, and influence positively firm value creation.

CONCLUSION

The use of social media has become one of the most dominant companies' tools for organizations and networking. However, reviewing and synthesizing the literature we found that there is a gap in the area of social media firms' use behavior in terms of policy.

This chapter suggested that more research was needed in the field of social media management in order to achieve a better understanding the main social media initiatives success drivers to business, as bad management of social media at work would lead to an incomplete understanding of phenomena occurring as employee levels.

The theoretical model we are proposing will accomplish one important goal with respect to social media: the variables of our model (Fig. 1) indicates that in order to manage social media use, organizations first need to identify how they implement and use social media across all areas. Normatively, organizations should assess and balance opportunities and costs when deciding on a social media policy implementation (Haimes, 2012; Carlson et al. 2016). The right approach is to invest in specific ways to encourage social media for work purposes in such a way that benefits both the organization and employees. If employees use social media to facilitate work on their own, without support from the organization, the likelihood of focusing on outside relationships and job searches is higher. However, if the organization takes an active and supportive stance to help employees use social media for work, the likelihood of job searches decreases (Bizzi, 2018).

A supportive environment that provides resources leads to lower withdrawal behaviors than a controlling and punishing environment that prevents or represses withdrawal intentions (Heavey, Holwerda, & Hausknecht, 2013). Enabling effective work collaboration produces affective responses in employees, who develop positive attitudes toward and become more embedded in the organization (Totterdell, Wall, Holman, Diamond, & Epitropaki, 2004). If companies leverage social media appropriately, they can increase attachment to the organization, decrease withdrawal intentions, and neutralize the attractiveness of external employment options.

Following these premises, the recommendation would be to encourage the use of social media to facilitate work. Furthermore, there is the necessity to avoid the abuse of social media at work, which may distract employees, or employees are not sensitized toward the nondisclosure of private information and the risk of reputational damage (O'Connor et al., 2016; Rosen & Samuel, 2015).

If employees receive support, they increase their satisfaction with the organization and their attachment to it (Shore & Wayne, 1993). Our study shows that there are some important potential applications of the model in the study of social media policy, with an outline of the major theoretical approaches to these applications. Practitioners can use this theoretical model to evaluate behaviour of firms and employees and better target future social media interventions towards those groups most likely to benefit. This study opens a new path of research on how social media policy implementation can affect firm benefits. This chapter started by identifying an organizational trend, more and more, companies are suggesting that employees use social media to interact with each other. The chapter illustrates a research road map for organizations, proposing recommendations to minimize the problem and to turn the problem into an opportunity. The chapter offers theoretical contributions and practical recommendations, shedding light on the unexplored effects of social media and helping companies respond to unexplored challenges.

The ideal recommendation would be to develop a research road map on social media policy implementation that minimize the risks of reputational damage or the leaking of sensitive information and inhibit the abuse of social media, but which overall encourage employees' social media use under the perception that it can benefit their work.

FUTURE RESEARCH DIRECTIONS

From a research perspective, this chapter sets a broad agenda for future research. Use of social media has become one of the most dominant tools for marketing and networking for firms operating in the business system. However, reviewing and synthesizing the literature indicate that there is a gap in the area of social media use behavior of firms in dealing with online networks to increase their performance. Social media technologies permit many opportunities for businesses to compete or fail in the market. It is important for employees to engage with customers in social media about the business. However, wanting employees to use social media does not equate to usage. Even behavioral intention does not always translate into behavioral usage of social media technologies on behalf of businesses by employees. Rather, it appears that the connection between intention and usage is amplified or diminished depending on the employee's status, motivation, job satisfaction consistent with the idea that goals and mentalities differ across business departments and units (Hansen & Levin, 2016; Dougherty, 1992; Kahn & Mentzer, 1994). Thus, the practice of simply expecting employees across all departments to equally act on intentions given the same set of organizational policies (to encourage motivations) would appear to be ineffective. Also, job satisfaction plays an important role in the formation of intention to use the social media on behalf of business.

Given the increasing prominence of social media phenomenon, there are many interesting opportunities for new researches. A future research direction is to test our model with real data and to test our set of hypotheses to understand how social media can be successfully applied in order to interpret the role of the variables.

Future studies should compare firms that social media control policies to those that do not and determine the impact on firm performance. The issue of how to effectively design and deploy social media management model in this approach is an additional future research direction to follow.

A future research direction can assess the model empirically by targeting a panel of employees in order to observe them on social media behavioral usage.

Future studies may also examine our model in different cultural contexts and generations, in which employees will have different job roles and employment statuses. Also, a more complex construct of time is organizational temporality, which can be measured to understand how employees experience time at work (e.g., urgency, pace, scarcity, nonlinearity). Last, scholars can take a qualitative approach to understand how co-workers use Facebook, beyond simply in terms of the amount of clock time. This will help us further grasp what social media interactions look like inside and outside the workplace. The model assumes unidirectional relationships among constructs, yet bidirectional linkages exist and need further investigation.

REFERENCES

Agnihotri, R., Kothandaraman, P., Kashyap, R., & Singh, R. (2012). Bringing "social" into sales: The impact of salespeople's social media use on service behaviors and value creation. *Journal of Personal Selling & Sales Management*, *22*(3), 333–348. doi:10.2753/PSS0885-3134320304

Andreassen, C. S., Torsheim, T., & Pallesen, S. (2014). Predictors of Use of Social Network Sites at Work - A Specific Type of Cyberloafing. *Journal of Computer-Mediated Communication*, *19*(4), 906–921. doi:10.1111/jcc4.12085

Asadullah, M. N., Xiao, S., & Yeoh, E. (2015). Subjective well-being in China, 2005–2010: The role of relative income, gender, and location. *China Economic Review*.

Badea, M. (2014). Social Media and Organizational Communication. *Social and Behavioral Sciences*, *149*, 70–75.

Behringer, N., & Sassenberg, K. (2015). Introducing social media for knowledge management: Determinants of employees' intentions to adopt new tools. *Computers in Human Behavior*, *48*, 290–296. doi:10.1016/j.chb.2015.01.069

Berthon, P. R., Pitt, L. F., Plangger, K., & Shapiro, D. (2012). Marketing meets Web 2.0, social media, and creative consumers: Implications for international marketing strategy. *Business Horizons*, *55*(3), 261–271. doi:10.1016/j.bushor.2012.01.007

Bharadwaj, A. S. (2000). A resource-based perspective on information technology capability and firm performance: An empirical investigation. *Management Information Systems Quarterly*, *24*(1), 169–196. doi:10.2307/3250983

Bizzi, L. (2018). The hidden problem of Facebook and social media at work: What if employees start searching for other jobs? *Business Horizons*, *61*(1), 23–33. doi:10.1016/j.bushor.2017.09.002

Bretz, R. D., Boudreau, J. W., & Judge, T. A. (1994). Job search behavior of employed managers. *Personnel Psychology*, *47*(2), 275–301. doi:10.1111/j.1744-6570.1994.tb01725.x

Brivot, M., Gendron, Y., & Guenin, H. (2017). Reinventing organizational control: Meaning contest surrounding reputational risk controllability in the social media area. *Accounting, Auditing & Accountability Journal*, *30*(4), 795–820. doi:10.1108/AAAJ-06-2015-2111

Carlson, J. B., Zivnuska, S., Harris, R. B., Harris, K. J., & Carlson, D. S. (2016). Social Media Use in the Workplace: A Study of Dual Effects. *Journal of Organizational and End User Computing*, *28*(1), 15–31. doi:10.4018/JOEUC.2016010102

Castillo, C., Mendoza, M., & Poblete, B. (2011). Information credibility on twitter. In *Proceedings of the 20th International Conference on the World Wide Web*. Association for Computing Machinery.

Dailey, S. L. (2016). What happens before full-time employment? Internships as a mechanism of anticipatory socialization. *Western Journal of Communication*, *80*(4), 453–480. doi:10.1080/10570314.2016.1159727

Demek, K. C., Raschke, R. L., Janvrin, D. J., & Dilla, W. N. (2018). Do organizations use a formalized risk management process to address social media risk? *International Journal of Accounting Information Systems*, *28*, 31–34. doi:10.1016/j.accinf.2017.12.004

Devereux, L., Melewar, T., & Foroudi, P. (2017). Corporate Identity and Social Media: Existence and Extension of the Organization. *International Studies of Management & Organization*, *47*(2), 110–134. doi:10.1080/00208825.2017.1256161

Di Lauro, S., Tursunbayeva, A., Antonelli, G. & Martinez, M. (2018). Measuring organizational identity via LinkedIn: The role played by employees' tenure, type of employment contract and age. *Studi Organizzativi,* (2), 114–129.

Di Virgilio, F. (Ed.). (2018a). *Social Media for Knowledge Management Applications in Modern Organizations*. IGI Global. doi:10.4018/978-1-5225-2897-5

Di Virgilio, F. (2018b). Exploring determinants of knowledge sharing: the role of social media in business organizations. Overview and new direction. In F. Di Virgilio (Ed.), *Social Media for Knowledge Management Applications in Modern Organizations* (pp. 1–30). IGI Global. doi:10.4018/978-1-5225-2897-5.ch001

Di Virgilio, F., & Antonelli, G. (2018). Consumer behavior, trust and electronic word-of-mouth communication: toward a model of understanding of consumer's purchase intentions online. In F. Di Virgilio (Ed.), *Social Media for Knowledge Management Applications in Modern Organizations* (pp. 58–80). IGI Global. doi:10.4018/978-1-5225-2897-5.ch003

Di Virgilio, F., Valderrama Santomé, M., & López Bolás, A. (2018). Social media strategy within organizational communication: major open issues and challenges. In F. Cantoni & G. Mangia (Eds.), *Human Resource management and digitalization* (pp. 205–225). Giappichelli Routledge.

Di Virgilio, F., Valderrama Santomé, M., & Toural, C. (2019). The roles of job satisfaction and motivation on employees' intentions to use social media for businesses: towards a multilevel and integrative organizational model. In Advances In Global Business And Economics, ANAHEI Publishing, LLC.

Direnzo, M. S., & Greenhaus, J. H. (2011). Job search and voluntary turnover in a boundaryless world: A control theory perspective. *Academy of Management Review*, *36*(3), 567–589.

Dougherty, D. (1992). Interpretive barriers to successful product innovation in large firms. *Organization Science*, *3*(2), 179–202. doi:10.1287/orsc.3.2.179

Enders, A., Hungenberg, H., Denker, H. P., & Mauch, S. (2008). The long tail of socialnetworking: Revenue models of social networking sites. *European Management Journal*, *26*(3), 199–211. doi:10.1016/j.emj.2008.02.002

Eschenbrenner, B., Nah, F. F. H., & Telaprolu, V. R. (2015). Efficacy of social media utilization by public accounting firms: Findings and directions for future research. *Journal of Information Systems*, *29*(2), 5–21. doi:10.2308/isys-50894

Field, J., & Chelliah, J. (2012). Social-media misuse a ticking time-bomb for employers: Robust policies and procedures needed to reduce the risks. *Human Resource Management International Digest*, *20*(7), 36–38. doi:10.1108/09670731211270301

Ghezzi, A., Gastaldi, L., Lettieri, E., Martini, A., & Corso, M. (2016). A role for startups in unleashing the disruptive power of social media. *International Journal of Information Management*, *36*(6), 1152–1159. doi:10.1016/j.ijinfomgt.2016.04.007

Gossett, L. M. (2001). The long-term impact of short-term workers. *Management Communication Quarterly*, *15*(1), 115–120. doi:10.1177/0893318901151007

Granovetter, M. S. (1995). *Getting a job: A study of contacts and careers*. University of Chicago Press. doi:10.7208/chicago/9780226518404.001.0001

Haimes, Y. Y. (2012). Systems-based guiding principles for risk modeling, planning, assessment, management, and communication. *Risk Analysis*, *32*(9), 1451–1467. doi:10.1111/j.1539-6924.2012.01809.x PMID:22548671

Hair, J. F., Ringle, C. M., & Sarstedt, M. (2011). PLS_SEM: Indeed a silver bullet. *Journal of Marketing Theory and Practice*, *19*(2), 139–150. doi:10.2753/MTP1069-6679190202

Hanna, R., Rohm, A., & Crittenden, V. L. (2011). We're all connected: The power of the social media ecosystem. *Business Horizons*, *54*(3), 265–273. doi:10.1016/j.bushor.2011.01.007

Hansen, J. M., & Levin, M. L. (2016). The effect of apathetic motivation on employees' intentions to use social media for businesses. *Journal of Business Research*, *69*(12), 6058–6066. doi:10.1016/j.jbusres.2016.06.009

He, W., Zha, S., & Ling, L. (2013). Social media competitive analysis and text mining: A case study in the pizza industry. *International Journal of Information Management*, *33*(3), 464–472. doi:10.1016/j.ijinfomgt.2013.01.001

Heavey, A. L., Holwerda, J. A., & Hausknecht, J. P. (2013). Causes and consequences of collective turnover: A meta-analytic review. *The Journal of Applied Psychology*, *98*(3), 412–453. doi:10.1037/a0032380 PMID:23668597

Jin, L., Wen, M., Fan, J. X., & Wang, G. (2012). Tans-local ties, local ties and psychological well-being among rural-to-urban migrants in Shanghai. *Social Science & Medicine*, *75*(2), 288–296. doi:10.1016/j.socscimed.2012.03.014 PMID:22546316

Kahn, K., & Mentzer, J. (1994). The impact of team-based forecasting. *Journal of Business Forecasting*, *13*(2), 18–21.

Kaplan, A. M., & Haenlein, M. (2010). Users of the world, unite! The challenges and opportunities of social media. *Business Horizons*, *53*(1), 59–68. doi:10.1016/j.bushor.2009.09.003

Khansa, L., Kuem, J., Siponen, M., & Kim, S. S. (2017). To cyberloaf or not to cyberloaf: The impact of the announcement of formal organizational controls. *Journal of Management Information Systems*, *34*(1), 141–176. doi:10.1080/07421222.2017.1297173

Kietzman, J. H., Hermkens, K., McCarthy, I. P., & Silvestre, B. S. (2011). Social media? Get serious! Understanding the functional building blocks of social media. *Business Horizons*, *54*(3), 241–251. doi:10.1016/j.bushor.2011.01.005

Kim, J., & Lee, J. E. R. (2011). The Facebook paths to happiness: Effects of the number of Facebook friends and self-presentation on subjective well-being. *Cyberpsychology, Behavior, and Social Networking*, *14*(6), 359–364. doi:10.1089/cyber.2010.0374 PMID:21117983

Kleinberg, J. (2008). The Convergence of Social and Technological Networks. *Communications of the ACM*, *51*(11), 66–72. doi:10.1145/1400214.1400232

Kohli, C., Suri, R., & Kapoor, A. (2015). Will social media kill branding? *Business Horizons*, *58*(1), 35–44. doi:10.1016/j.bushor.2014.08.004

Kumar, K. V., & Devi, V. R. (2014). Social media in financial services a theoretical perspective. *Procedia Economics and Finance*, *11*, 306–313. doi:10.1016/S2212-5671(14)00198-1

Leftheriotis, I., & Giannakos, M. N. (2014). Using social media for work: Losing your time or improving your work? *Computers in Human Behavior*, *31*, 134–142. doi:10.1016/j.chb.2013.10.016

Levin, M. A., Hansen, J. M., & Laverie, D. (2012). Toward understanding new sales employees' participation in marketing-related technology: Motivation, voluntariness, and past performance. *Journal of Personal Selling & Sales Management*, *32*(3), 379–393. doi:10.2753/PSS0885-3134320307

Liu, D., Brass, D., Lu, Y., & Chen, D. (2015). Friendships in online peer-to-peer lending: Pipes, prisms, and relational herding. *Management Information Systems Quarterly*, *39*(3), 729–742. doi:10.25300/MISQ/2015/39.3.11

Locke, E. A. (1976). The nature and causes of job satisfaction. In M. D. Dunnette (Ed.), *Handbook of industrial and organizational psychology*. Rand McNally College.

Maier, C., Laumer, S., Eckhardt, A., & Weitzel, T. (2015). Giving too much social support: Social overload on social networking sites. *European Journal of Information Systems*, *24*(5), 447–464. doi:10.1057/ejis.2014.3

Martini, A., Massa, S., & Testa, S. (2013). The Firm, the platform and the customer: A'double mangle' interpretation of social media for innovation. *Information and Organization*, *23*(3), 198–213. doi:10.1016/j.infoandorg.2013.07.001

McDonald, P., & Thompson, P. (2016). Social media(tion) and the reshaping of public/private boundaries in employment relations. *International Journal of Management Reviews*, *18*(1), 69–84. doi:10.1111/ijmr.12061

Miao, C. F., Evans, K. R., & Zou, S. (2007). The role of salesperson motivation in sales control systems Intrinsic and extrinsic motivation revisited. *Journal of Business Research*, *60*(5), 417–425. doi:10.1016/j.jbusres.2006.12.005

Nagendra, A. (2014). Paradigm shift in hr practices on employee life cycle due to influence of social media. *Procedia Economics and Finance*, *11*, 197–207. doi:10.1016/S2212-5671(14)00188-9

Ngai, E. W., Tao, S. S., & Moon, K. K. (2015). Social media research: Theories, constructs, and conceptual frameworks. *International Journal of Information Management*, *35*(1), 33–44. doi:10.1016/j.ijinfomgt.2014.09.004

O'Connor, K. W., Schmidt, G. B., & Drouin, M. (2016). Helping workers understand and follow social media policies. *Business Horizons*, *59*(2), 205–211. doi:10.1016/j.bushor.2015.11.005

O'Leary, D. E. (2011a). Blog mining-review and extensions: From each according to his opinion. *Decision Support Systems*, *51*(4), 821–830. doi:10.1016/j.dss.2011.01.016

O'Leary, D. E. (2011b). The use of social media in the supply chain: Survey and extensions. *Intelligent Systems in Accounting, Finance & Management*, *18*(2-3), 121–144. doi:10.1002/isaf.327

Ollier-Malaterre, A., Rothbard, N. P., & Berg, J. (2013). When worlds collide in cyberspace: How boundary work in online social networks impacts professional relationships. *Academy of Management Review*, *38*(4), 645–669. doi:10.5465/amr.2011.0235

Paniagua, J., & Sapena, J. (2014). Business performance and social media: Love or hate? *Business Horizons*, *57*(6), 719–728. doi:10.1016/j.bushor.2014.07.005

Qin, X., Hom, P., Xu, M., & Ju, D. (2013). Applying the job demands resourcesmodel to migrant workers: Exploring how and when geographical distance increase quit propensity. *Journal of Occupational and Organizational Psychology*, *87*(2), 303–328. doi:10.1111/joop.12047

Robertson, B. W., & Kee, K. F. (2017). Social media at work: The roles of job satisfaction, employment status, and Facebook use with co-workers. *Computers in Human Behavior*, *70*, 191–196. doi:10.1016/j.chb.2016.12.080

Rosen, L., & Samuel, A. (2015). Conquering digital distraction. *Harvard Business Review*, *93*(6), 110–113.

Sánchez Abril, P., Levin, A., & Del Riego, A. (2012). Blurred boundaries: Social media privacy and the twenty-first-century employee. *American Business Law Journal*, *49*(1), 63–124. doi:10.1111/j.1744-1714.2011.01127.x

Schaupp, L. C., & Bélanger, F. (2014). The value of social media for small businesses. *Information Systems*, *28*(1), 187–2. doi:10.2308/isys-50674

Scott, C. R., & Stephens, K. K. (2009). It depends on who you're talking to: Predictors and outcomes of situated measures of organizational identification. *Western Journal of Communication*, *73*(4), 370–394. doi:10.1080/10570310903279075

Scott, P. R., & Jacka, J. M. (2011). *Auditing Social Media: A Governance and Risk Guide*. John Wiley & Sons.

Shore, L. M., & Wayne, S. J. (1993). Commitment and employee behavior: Comparison of affective commitment and continuance commitment with perceived organizational support. *The Journal of Applied Psychology*, *78*(5), 774–780. doi:10.1037/0021-9010.78.5.774 PMID:8253631

Staw, B. M. (1984). Organizational behavior: A review and reformulation of the field's outcome variables. *Annual Review of Psychology*, *35*(1), 627–666. doi:10.1146/annurev.ps.35.020184.003211 PMID:19400627

Strauss, A., & Corbin, J. M. (1990). *Basics of qualitative research: Grounded theory procedures and techniques*. Sage.

Sun, Y., & Shang, R. A. (2014). The interplay between users' intraorganizational social media use and social capital. *Computers in Human Behavior*, *37*, 334–341. doi:10.1016/j.chb.2014.03.048

Tiago, M. T. P. M. B., & Veríssimo, J. M. C. (2014). Digital marketing and social media: Why bother? *Business Horizons*, *57*(6), 703–708. doi:10.1016/j.bushor.2014.07.002

Totterdell, P., Wall, T., Holman, D., Diamond, H., & Epitropaki, O. (2004). Affect networks: A structural analysis of the relationship between work ties and job-related affect. *The Journal of Applied Psychology*, *89*(5), 854–867. doi:10.1037/0021-9010.89.5.854 PMID:15506865

Treem, J. W., & Leonardi, P. M. (2012). Social media use in organizations: Exploring the affordances of visibility, editability, persistence, and association. *Communication Yearbook*, *36*, 143–189.

Trinkle, B., Crossler, R., & Bélanger, F. (2015). Voluntary disclosures via social media and the role of comments. *Journal of Information Systems*, *29*(2), 101–122. doi:10.2308/isys-51133

Turkle, S. (2008). Always-on/Always-on-you: The Tethered Self. In J. E. Katz (Ed.), *Handbook of Mobile Communication Studies*. MIT Press. doi:10.7551/mitpress/9780262113120.003.0010

Valkenburg, P. M., Peter, J., & Schouten, A. P. (2006). Friend networking sites and their relationship to adolescents' well-being and social self-esteem. *Cyberpsychology & Behavior*, *9*(5), 584–590. doi:10.1089/cpb.2006.9.584 PMID:17034326

Zywica, J., & Danowski, J. (2008). The faces of Facebookers: Investigating social enhancement and social compensation hypotheses; Predicting Facebook and offline popularity from sociability and self-esteem, and mapping the meanings of popularity with semantic networks. *Journal of Computer-Mediated Communication*, *14*(1), 1–34. doi:10.1111/j.1083-6101.2008.01429.x

Chapter 8
I Am Here to Stay:
Customer and Employee Engagement in an M-Commerce World

Kirti Sharma
Gurukula Kangri Vishwavidyalaya, India

Deeksha Ahuja
Gurukula Kangri Vishwavidyalaya, India

Ashish Arya
Gurukula Kangri Vishwavidyalaya, India

Aditya Dhiman
Gurukula Kangri Vishwavidyalaya, India

ABSTRACT

The advent of m-commerce has contributed significantly to the evolution of the digital media environment. Today, almost everything (i.e., the exchange of goods, services, payments, and access of information) is growing fast via electronic media. The purpose of this chapter is to find the relationship between the customers and employees engaged in the m-commerce world. For doing this, researchers did a systematic review of the literature and found that if the digital companies provide a good quality of services to their employees and customers, they both engaged in the m-commerce world. As the digital world has a two-way communication mode, companies should work upon different types of strategies (i.e., to provide a better platform to their current offerings and should incorporate the valuable customers and employee feedback for improving the image of their offerings). There are several techniques that help the companies to engage their customers like gamification and artificial intelligence.

DOI: 10.4018/978-1-7998-3515-8.ch008

INTRODUCTION

As we know, technology is changing more rapidly in this digital era and being the king customers' expectations from the companies are shaping this incremental technical transformation. In today's digital era e-commerce companies are trying their best to tap on these expectations earlier as well as better than their competitors to gain competitive advantage and utilize the same for their success. Here, customer engagement indicates the deliberate efforts of the firms to inspire, motivate, empower, and measure the customers' contribution to marketing functions and marks a shift in marketing research and business practices (Harmeling, Moffett, Arnold & Carlson, 2017). Whereas, employee engagement is an uplifting frame of mind held by the representative (employee) towards the association. A company representative knows about business setting, and works with colleagues to improve execution inside the activity to support the association. The association must work to create and support commitment, which requires a two-path connection among business and worker (Robinson et al., 2004).

With the advent of new technologies and faster data rates on the internet, ecommerce platformers are making considerable efforts in augmenting the 4ps (product, place, price and promotion) to engage customers and give them an overall good experience. If a company is not paying attention to its website, or not responding to its customers' questions, that company will not survive in this digital era. Today if customers have had a bad experience from any of the e-commerce website, they immediately stop using the same. Some may instantly post a negative review (this can greatly influence the buying decision of a potential customer) and will never ever recommend to his/ger circle, which will hamper the image of brand in the market. Cut-throat competition in this industry is at such a level where margin for errors are very less. Today, customers' reviews are considered as a guide/suggestion by the potential customers to decide whether to finally buy a product or not.

The wireless world has been experiencing tremendous growth. We have seen the various advancements in network generations, network service qualities, growing availability of wireless applications and the emergence of wireless hand-held devices such as PDAs, Smart Phones, etc. These devices are becoming part of our daily lives today (Liu & Chlamtac, 2004). Today, smartphones are the most prominent medium for reaching to the customers and it needs to be woven throughout the entire digital shopping journey to deliver that flawless experience to customers. Companies leading the retail pack such as Amazon, Wal-Mart, Snapdeal, Myntra and Alibaba etc., are taking advantage of new technology. All these new innovations in e-industry attract the customers to engage in M-commerce world. To cater and provide the best user experience to the mobile customers, companies must have to understand the context in which their customers are using smartphones, so that they can enhance the services they already offer (Watson et al., 2013).

According to Statista, there is 3.5 billion smartphone users in the world today, which means that in the world of wireless, 45.12% of the world's population have a smartphone today ("How Many People Have", n.d.). A report by techjury depicts that Mobile accounts for over 40% of e-commerce in terms of number of transactions in the world. And the number of users, using mobile devices for M-commerce purposes, are increasing day by day. According to s today almost everyone is using mobile devices for M-commerce purposes. So, customers are expecting more or more from the businesses. On the other hand, businesses have come to realize that customer experience does not limited to sales result, website clicks and social media presence: instead knowing what prompts customers to behave the way they do – what are the different types of customer behaviour exist, how different issues impact these behaviour and how this can help e-businesses to improve overall online customer experience.

EMPLOYEE ENGAGEMENT IN M-COMMERCE

In today's era, companies are very much concerned with gaining the trust of their employees and keep them motivated and committed towards the work as well as the organization, so that they can contribute their best effort for the achievement of the organizational goals (Sarangi, 2016).

Employee engagement postulates the level of commitment, passion and participation an employee is willing to put in (also termed as employee productivity), that make an organization successful and provides competitive advantage over competitors.

As propounded by Sarangi (2016) engaged employees:

- Are emotionally attached to their work & the organization.
- Tend to stay for a long period of time and their chances of moving out of the organization are very less.
- Perform 20% better than their colleagues and enhance the profitability of the firm.
- Always vouch for their organization.
- Always stay happy in their life, both in social as well as in professional life.
- Helps organization in adapting changes anytime they want efficiently and effectively. Which is a competitive advantage for an organization over the competitors.

Engagement level of employees varies with respect to their personality, seniority, type of work and duration of service in an organization; and not by sector. Young blood (Younger employees) shows great enthusiasm during initial days when they join the organization, but soon they lose the grip and become disengaged. So, retaining the young blood is a challenging task for employers and they strive to keep them motivated and engaged. Whereas, senior employees have the greater chance of getting engaged and they are the ones who stay for long in the organization. Adaptable individuals also get easily engaged.

Top and middle level managers considered as most engaged professionals. On the other side, support staff and employees at lower level carries the tag of least engaged individuals.

Common drivers of employee engagement are (Sarangi, 2016; Ambler, 2007):

- Type of work/Job
- Clear job description
- Career development opportunities
- Acknowledgement and rewards
- Respectful relationships inside and outside the organisation
- Two way communication
- Inspiring leadership/employee participation.

Engaged employees are the 'backbone' of an organization and people are industrious, accountable and ethical. It is crucial to profitable business performance.

Types of Employees

In the context of engagement, there are three types of employees in any organisation (Govindappa, 2017). They are:

- **Engaged Employees** are passionate about their work and feel a sense of attachment to their company. They drive innovation, enhance profitability reputation, have a positive attitude towards the organization and keep the firm move forward.
- **Not-Engaged Employees** are the sleepwalkers. They come to the office (put time) but not the energy or passion in their work. They are neither engaged nor disengaged. Such employees perform the desired tasks but are not concerned with the productivity (quality & quantity of work).
- **Actively Disengaged Employees** are the most unhappy individuals in an organisation; neither they perform their work nor let others perform their work and instead undermine what engaged coworkers accomplish. Company

should try to reinforce the attitude of employees towards the organization, otherwise they will dilute the hard work of engaged employees.

Human resource leaders play a significant role in employee engagement. HR manager sets the principles, system of beliefs and creed of their company and spread that positive morale to the employees in the organisation.

10 C's of Employee Engagement

George Ambler (2007) defines Employee engagement is the combination of - passion of employees, effective leadership skills, and support from the top management to the employees. 10 C's for employee engagement are given by George Ambler in 2007. He pulled the facts and highlights from the full story in the Ivey Business Journal and also summarized the explanation of the 10 C's as follows:

- **Connect:** There is an immense need of establishing positive relation/ connection between employees and their boss. If an employee has a negative attitude towards his boss or vice versa, then employee engagement cannot be exercised within the organisation. On the other side, leader should also always value his employees and convey a feeling of belongingness
- **Career:** Management and leaders should provide challenging as well as meaningful work to their employees. It is believed that most employees enjoy performing new or challenging tasks, as they get bored performing same tasks again and again. Leaders should also provide opportunities for career advancement to employees because an organisation can grow only when its employees are growing.
- **Clarity:** Communication is the key for successful implementation and execution of a plan. Hence, top level managers should clearly communicate the vision and mission of the firm to the employees, so that the effort of all the employees can be directed towards the organizational objective (unity of direction can be achieved). Managers should be very clear about- what they want from the employees and how their jobs affect the organization.
- **Convey:** Managers should timely provide the feedback of the functioning of the employees. This point emphasizes the two-way communication approach – employer to employee and vice versa.
- **Congratulate:** Outperformed employees will always be rewarded and acknowledged. These types of activities motivate the employees to perform better and better.

- **Contribute:** Taking insights and suggestions of employees in the decision making, makes them feel like they are an important part as well as the key contributors of the organization and they will be much more engaged.
- **Control:** It is obvious that an employee performs better when he takes the complete ownership of his task. So, giving an employee control over his work create a sense of trust and a level of engagement is created.
- **Collaborate:** Bringing the efforts of all the employees together. A good leader always creates a team in which there is healthy competition, trust and cooperation. He stresses upon the synergized effort of all the team members and encourages team members to maximize the potential to the fullest.
- **Credibility:** A credible organization has good reputation and high ethical standards. And leaders always try to maintain a good reputation. If an employee is disengaged, it means he is not credible and coworkers and clients will not trust him; and this will severely impact the image of the company.
- **Confidence:** A confident individual always performs better. If employees see their leader as a confident and ethical person, they will try to be like him.

Employee Engagement in Digital Companies

In this digitized world, where day today technological advancements and innovations are making a customer's life even more convenient, hassle free and easy. These digital companies are actually shaping our future. Along with their focus on customer, they should also embrace the advance technologies to create a friendly working culture for their employees within the organization. They should find new ways of keeping their employees happy and passionate about their work.

Digital companies, like Google, facebook, etc. are well known for their ability to take care of employees and strongly believe that employee engagement is an essential ingredient for businesses to boost the performance and productivity.

So, why (and how) are digital companies getting employee engagement right? Here are some points to be considered:

Some points advocating -How digital companies are exercising employee engagement:

- **Employee Growth and Recognition:** Engaged employees know that they will grow within an organization, both professionally and personally.

These companies frequently organise training and development programs to keep their employees well updated with the latest developments in the industry. This gives a powerful message to the employees that the company values them as an asset. Additionally, the importance of recognition, acknowledgement and praise for good work can't be overlooked.

The more we feel appreciated for our work, the more motivated we become and the better we perform.

Dreamworks, an animated studio, often hosts parties and events for its employees, to discuss their personal projects. The idea is to find all possible ways to appreciate and boost the motivation of the employee. It boosts morale and innovative thinking at workplace.

- **Flexible and Informal Environment:** Most digital organisations (also referred as forward-thinking companies), recognize their employees as people and not as machine/asset. Employees can - come in casual outfit, no formal dress code, work from home, come at 11am after dropping the kids at school. Ultimate, objective of the employer is to help you be a happy and productive member of the organization.

Companies like Facebook and Google take necessary steps to create flexible and informal working environment, where a motivated employee will contribute his best. There are a large number of remote employees on Facebook and are connected through video conferencing tools.

Google initiated a program where it offers its employees 'one day' a week free time to work on their side projects that keep them curious and engaged.

- **Perks and Benefits:** Ultimately employees serve in consideration of remuneration, which is monetary in terms. And additional monetary value in terms of perks and benefits make an employee even happier and satisfied with his job, as we know, happy employee is far more productive.

Perks and benefits are non-wage compensation and includes – Vacation time, Medical insurance, Dental insurance, Stock options, Gym membership, In-office snacks, Standing desks, Employee retreats, Staff dinners, Hotel suites, Company car, etc.

Many digital companies understand the impact that physical and mental wellness has on company culture.

Shopify, a canadian ecommerce company, in perks and benefits it offers the latest Apple products, full health coverage, dental coverage, share options, leave, and free tickets.

- **Feedback:** The best ways to ensure employee engagement is regular & transparent communication and providing continuous feedback on employees' work that will keep them moving towards their individual as well as organizational goal.

Instead of relying on structured annual performance review, companies are adopting practice of frequent check-ins/review (monthly or quarterly) to keep employees motivated, on-track and happy. This way the problem is identified and corrected at initial stage itself using feedback.

Buffer, a social media software company has a 'default to transparency' rule. According to them - transparency can strengthen the company and help in making important decisions. It is part of their culture that employees should 'state their thoughts immediately and with honesty' – they even publish all internal emails that can be universally accessible.

- **Practical use of technology:** These days, not only millennials are familiar with advanced innovation – but nearly everybody. Digital companies are great at finding viable (practical) uses for technology that offer convenience and effectiveness.

Unlike traditional companies, where employers find it difficult to bring technological shift in the organization (using traditional training and development program) because most employees resist learning the technological changes, Digital companies are applying game based rules for daily tasks & activities to help employees learn new things.

In this digital era, whatever is happening in the field of employee engagement is just a beginning and there is a lot to be explored in this field. In the future, organisations will embrace the digital technologies and provide employees the tools, support and freedom they need to become fully engaged and motivated.

Customer Engagement in M-Commerce

MaryLau Costa (2010) states that upto ⅔ of a brand's profit may rely on effective consumer engagement.

"Customer engagement is the ongoing interactions between company and customer, offered by the company, chosen by the customer" (Greenberg, 2014).

Paul Greenberg focused on the 'choice'. In order to find the type of interaction that consumer values, companies usually let their customers choose freely, how they would like to engage with the company. By making it easier for customers to engage in way they feel like/valuable, companies strengthen customer's emotional investment in their company's brand.

"Customer engagement is an estimate of the degree and depth of visitor interaction against a clearly defined set of goals" (Peterson, 2006).

Eric Peterson here implies that there are different levels of customer engagement. Some customers have a deep level, and some have shallow level of engagement. For example, a customer, who first time comes across our brand on social media and places the order- have different level of engagement than someone who's placed 10 orders in the last year.

Ultimately, Peterson clarifies that the more valuable and frequent the engagement is, the more invested your customer will be with your brand in the long term.

"Customer engagement is the degree and depth of brand-focused interactions a customer chooses to perform." ("What is Customer Engagement", 2019)

Practitioners believe that this definition accurately articulates quality and quantity of engagements that customers have with company's brand are equally important.

In order to drive more valuable engagement, companies should find new ways to add value to customer experience. The ideal situation for the companies is, when customers feel like they have just as much to gain from engaging with company's brand, company can manage to keep customers emotionally connected to company's brand.

It has been identified that today, consumers are in the seat of the driver, and they are moving forward at a wonderful or great speed. The companies which test and learn how to be with the customers will be amply rewarded and those who are sitting to take a wait-and-see approach will have a hard time to survive in this catching up world (Martin, 2011).

STEPS FOR EFFECTIVE CUSTOMER ENGAGEMENT

1. Companies need to define their customers' journey map. It means that companies must need to know who their customers are and where they came from.
2. After knowing customers, companies need to know how their customers interact with, which will help in identifying the customer engagement platforms.
3. Companies should need to observe the behaviour of their customers in real time. These analytics will help better for understanding and fulfilling the customers' requirement.
4. Companies should need to offer and give personalised services, which will enhance their sales. This is not the time of giving generic services, as each and every customer has different preferences; so, by giving the personalised services the company's sales turnover will be enhanced.

5. After that company should need to observe that how many prospects accept the offer and take action for it. By giving the customized offerings to the customers.
6. Now after observing this, companies need to determine the engaged customers bounced rates. Bounce rate tells about which type of services we are giving to our customers and experience your customer's engagement platforms offer.
7. After completing the above steps last is to take the feedback from the customers for future dealings, so that you are able to know what are the future demands of the customers and what are the challenges they have faced while doing online transactions. And if there is any challenge faced by the customer then company should have to take necessary actions so that the problem will be solved and the customers will retained.

Empirical Investigation of Relationships Between Customer Engagement and Employee Engagement

In regard to this, various practitioners, academicians and experts have contributed immense with their studies.

Menguc et al. (2013) finds that employee engagement is positively associated with customer satisfaction and customer loyalty which leads to active customer engagement. According to the study engagement or disengagement of employees affect how they behave and interact with customers.

Iqra Shaheen and Nadia Naseem (2015) conclude in their study that customer satisfaction is possible only when employees are satisfied and finally this will lead to increase in company's performance.

Bakker and Demerouti (2007) concluded in their study that levels of employee engagement is positively correlated to customer loyalty. An engaged employee performs his duties/tasks more dedicatedly than a disengaged one. Hence the performance of an employee is a good predictor of customer engagement (Salanova et al., 2005).

Chi and Gursoy (2009) suggest that customers tend to have a better experience with organisations that have higher levels of employee engagement. An employee is said to be an engaged one (characteristics of an engaged employee) when he is enthusiastic, energetic, motivated and passionate about his/her work (Menguc et al., 2013).

The level of a firm's employee engagement is suggested as an influencer of the success factors of decreased employee turnover, increased profitability and an increased customer service level (Gallup, 2013).

Although the importance of employee engagement is emphasised in the literature, it is posited that only thirteen percent of employees around the globe are engaged

(Gallup, 2013). This suggests that a customer experience, although holistic in nature, may be strongly influenced by an employee in providing a customer a product or service.

Fleming et al. (2005) highlighted a study on call centre agencies that shows that customer experience depends entirely on the engagement level of the employees (customer service representative) of an organization.

Factors Affecting M-commerce adoption in Customer Engagement and Employee Engagement

Customer and Employee engagement matters for both, as the dedication of employees towards their workplace can help them to gain a lot of lively and satisfied customers which further by word of mouth can help them gain more customers, which can be their future lively and satisfied customers. Remarkably it's a win-win situation. Where committed employees lead to satisfied customers, the opposite is also true. Satisfied customers also play a role in employee commitment. If the customers have the positive experiences, it can reinforce how employees feel about the assessment and purpose of their work.

Whereas, the M-Commerce concept was given by Kevin Duffey in 1997 at the beginning of the Global mobile Commerce forum. It was developed for providing all the capabilities in the hands of the customers anywhere, anytime by using wireless technology. The factors listed below are based on the literature concerning technology acceptance models. Next section investigated the factors affecting the adoption of M-commerce by consumers (users), which can further affect the customer and employee engagement.

Perceived usefulness: According to Davis (1989) perceived usefulness of a system is defined as "the degree to which individuals believe that the use of new technology to improve their performance on the task". There are many studies in the field of information systems and mobile commerce that demonstrated a significant effect of perceived usefulness on intention to use or adopt (Kim & Garrison, 2009; Khalifa & Shen, 2008). They identified that the perceived usefulness has the positive influence on the m-commerce adoption.

Perceived Ease of Use: Dholakia & Dholakia (2004) defined Perceived ease of use as the "degree to which a person believes that using a particular system would be free of effort". While, Teo (2001) defined it as "the degree to which the user expects the use of the system to be user friendly". The perceived ease of use has been integrated as a significant factor in adopting Mobile commerce (Bhatti, 2007; Davis, 1989; Wei, Marthandan, Chong, Ooi, & Arumugam, 2009). There are many previous empirical studies which showed that perceived ease of use had a positive influence for m-commerce adoption (Khalifa & Shen, 2008; Kim & Garrison, 2009;

Wei, Marthandan, Chong, Ooi, & Arumugam, 2009). Thus, perceived ease of use reflects the efforts resulting from the use of mobile commerce (Khalifa & Shen, 2008).

Perceived Trust: Cho, Koon, & Lee (2007) defined trust as "buyer-seller relationships as the perception by a prospective buyer of credibility and benevolence in the target of trust". Perceived trust is a significant concept affects consumer behavior and decides the achievement of m-commerce (Wei, Marthandan, Chong, Ooi, & Arumugam, 2009). It is a significant analytical factor in explaining the adoption of m-commerce in many existing technology adoption studies (Cho, Koon & Lee, 2007; Wei, Marthandan, Chong, Ooi & Arumugam, 2009). In addition, it helps build suitable favorable expectations of acting and other preferred benefits (Cho, Koon & Lee, 2007). The researcher proposed that perceived trust of use will have a positive influence on the adoption of m-commerce. Therefore, it is essential to engage perceived trust into the model.

Perceived Cost: Perceived cost is the key points in the creation and delivery of M-commerce (Sadi & Noordin, 2011). The serious concern for the user is a perceived cost to determine whether to use m-commerce or not (Hong, Thong, Moon & Tam, 2008). Wei, Marthandan, Chong, Ooi & Arumugam (2009) pointed out that one of the causes that might slow expansion of the M-commerce is perceived cost factor. Li, Fu & Li (2007) found that cost is supposed to be a significant predictor of the use of M-commerce. Anil, Ting, Moe & Jonathan (2003) found that the cost is a factor influencing the use of mobile commerce.

Muthaiyat (2004) reported that in turn to obtain an effective penetration level of mobile technology; it was required for a certain minimum level of income. The researcher proposed that the perceived cost of use will have a positive influence on the adoption of m-commerce.

Perceived Privacy: According to Chaffey (2003) privacy is defined as "the right of an individual to control the information held about them by third parties". Khalifa & Shen (2008) stated that the privacy concerns with the next strong influence after the cost on the result of the use of m-commerce. Furthermore, Sheng, Nah & Siau (2008) found a strong association between privacy and intentions to adopt of m-commerce. Korzaan & Boswell (2016) found that privacy strongly influenced the behavioral intentions. The researcher proposed that perceived privacy of use will have a positive influence on the adoption of m-commerce. Hence, it is necessary to involve perceived privacy into the model (Nassuora, 2013).

CONCLUSION

After doing the systematic literature review researchers found that for engaging the customers company should strive to engage and win the loyalty of their employees and employees and that can be done by embracing innovative technologies and abandoning the traditional outdated technologies. Companies should also adopt the 10 c's of employee engagement (Ambler, 2007) for better employee engagement followed by the customer engagement.

From the past studies, it has been found that there are six dimensions which affect the M-commerce and these are: perceived usefulness, perceived ease of use, perceived privacy, perceived trust, and perceived cost (Bowden, 2009; Sashi, 2012; Sawhney, Verona & Prandelli, 2005; Demangeot & Broderick, 2016). Sashi (2012) found that there are various types of customers in virtual world and these are: delighted customers, fans, transactional customers and loyal customers and these all have different expectations. If a customer likes a particular website and has been using it for long, it means he is an engaged customer and then the 'customer engagement' converts that particular customer into a fan. But the customers who become fans they have to progress through the customer engagement life cycle. In addition to this, for current fans, online sellers need a mix of transactional, delighted, and loyal customers who can be turned into fans in the future. So, a mix of digital and non-digital technologies can be used to smoothen the progress of customers' transition through the stages in the customer engagement cycle.

The researchers have also found that there is one big challenge for e-commerce companies i.e. to tap on and win the faith of those potential customers who only visit e-commerce (online) for browsing the product related information and purchase the product offline. This can be done by identifying the interest of visitors and understanding the possible reasons -why customers are dropping off or not making final purchase from a particular website.

They also identified that the customer and employee satisfaction play an important role in customer and employee engagement respectively. It is a way to capitalise on, in order to ensure high customer and employee engagement on companies' e-commerce website. Primarily, this means that companies' website should not only look appealing but should also focus on various key points, like: clear website navigation, enhanced search, flexible payment options, tracking facility, and better return policy. In addition to this, shipping cost is one of the important determinants of consumer satisfaction in M-commerce world and it should be clearly mentioned in the companies' website, along with how speedily the delivery of goods and services can be made, all this synergies efforts will help in customer engagement. And for employee engagement Career development opportunities, Flexible working hours, Fair pay structure, Learning culture, Cultural diversity, Transparency and honesty, Autonomy, Inspiration, Communication, and Employee recognition play a significant role.

Digital wallets are also playing an important role in customer satisfaction which influences customer engagement (Castrechini, Helgeson & Malko, 2014; Epstein,

2018). Today, Consumers are progressively more using their mobile devices to carry out transactions with various e-commerce platforms. But, customer loyalty in the e-commerce industry is very less because of some factors like insufficiency or lack of flexibility in payment options and slow checkout process among others, etc. So, digital wallets aim at enhancing the shopping experience of customers by offering them new modes to expedite and secure transactions in the e-commerce industry. Apart from this, digital wallets or M-wallets and mobile payment solutions improve business performance and facilitate strategic decision-making in the e-commerce industry. The electronic commerce companies can fulfill their customers' experience by offering them easy-to-use and quick payment solutions through different channels such as apps, digital wallet, virtual payment solutions, and other contactless technologies. With every single passing day, mobile technology is improving with its regular improvements; today mobile payment method has gone to a completely new level. In this way, mobile wallets offer an efficient way to enhance the customer engagement, which in turn allows them to have a competitive edge over other entities.

Significance of the Study:

The study has numerous managerial implications for companies to look upon, such as -how to improve customer experience as well as employee engagement, what are the prevailing innovative technologies companies are using to engage their customers and also the employees, how employee's engagement or disengagement influences his/her performance and customer experience, seeking ways to establish good interaction between employees and customers, assessing gaps in the current customer experience levels and overcoming the same by capitalizing the strengths of employee engagement.

All these questions are critical to the success of an organisation and by answering the questions companies can gain competitive advantage over their competitors.

Along with its implications in the current scenario this study also has its significance in the future as well. Day by day customers are getting more and more knowledgeable and informed; and because of this they are deriving the trend in the industry by expecting even more from the companies. So, to win the faith of these customers, companies are devising their strategies around employee engagement to establish a long-term relationship with the customers.

The study contributes in the field of customer and employee engagement. The study also has its implications on academic fraternity by way of sharing its contribution and recommending further research that can be conducted in this field. Recommendations for the study includes: A concise measure for customer experience, firm specific or industry specific studies relating to influence & impact of consumer and employee engagement on each other.

REFERENCES

Bakker, A., & Demerouti, E. (2007). The Job Demands-Resources model: State of the art. *Journal of Managerial Psychology*, *22*(3), 309–328. doi:10.1108/02683940710733115

Bowden, J. L. H. (2009). The process of customer engagement: A conceptual framework. *Journal of Marketing Theory and Practice*, *17*(1), 63–74. doi:10.2753/MTP1069-6679170105

Castrechini, M., Helgeson, H., & Malko, M. (2014). *U.S. Patent Application No. 14/363,765*. US Patent Office.

Chaffey, D. (2003). E-Business and E-Commerce Management. Academic Press.

Chi, C., & Gursoy, D. (2009). Employee satisfaction, customer satisfaction, and financial performance: An empirical examination. *International Journal of Hospitality Management*, *28*(2), 245–253. doi:10.1016/j.ijhm.2008.08.003

Cho, D. Y., Koon, H. J., & Lee, H. Y. (2007). Analysis of trust in internet and mobile commerce adoption. In *Proceedings of the 40th Hawaii International Conference on System Science* (p. 50). IEEE. 10.1109/HICSS.2007.76

Costa. (n.d.). *Customer engagement improves brand profits*. Retrieved from https://www.marketingweek.com/customer-engagement-improves-brand-profits/

Davis, F. D. (1989). Perceived usefulness, perceived ease of use and user acceptance of information technology. *Management Information Systems Quarterly*, *13*(3), 319–340. doi:10.2307/249008

Demangeot, C., & Broderick, A. J. (2016). Engaging customers during a website visit: A model of website customer engagement. *International Journal of Retail & Distribution Management*, *44*(8), 814–839. doi:10.1108/IJRDM-08-2015-0124

Epstein, M. J. (2018). Adapting For Digital Survival. *Strategic Finance*, *99*(8), 26–33.

Fleming, J. H., Coffman, C., & Harter, J. K. (2005). Manage your Human Sigma. *Harvard Business Review*, *83*(7), 106–114. https://hbr.org/2005/07/manage-your-human-sigma PMID:16028821

Gallup. (2013). *State of the Global Workplace: Employee Engagement Insights for Business Leaders*. Gallup Inc.

Govindappa. (2017). Impact of employee engagement on organizational success: A study in TATA Advanced Materials. *International Journal of Academic Research and Development*, 1202-1207.

Harmeling, C. M., Moffett, J. W., Arnold, M. J., & Carlson, B. D. (2017). Toward a theory of customer engagement marketing. *Journal of the Academy of Marketing Science*, *45*(3), 312–335. doi:10.100711747-016-0509-2

Hong, S. J., Thong, J. Y., Moon, J. Y., & Tam, K. Y. (2008). Understanding the behaviour of mobile data services consumers. *Information Systems Frontiers*, *10*(4), 431–445. doi:10.100710796-008-9096-1

How Many Phones Are in the World. (n.d.). Retrieved from https://www.bankmycell.com/blog/how-many-phones-are-in-the-world

Khalifa, M., & Shen, K. N. (2008). Drivers for transactional B2C m-commerce adoption: Extended theory of planned behavior. *Journal of Computer Information Systems*, *48*(3), 111–117.

Liu, J. J., & Chlamtac, I. (2004). Mobile Ad-Hoc Networking with a View of 4G Wireless: Imperatives and Challenges. In S. Basagni, M. Conti, S. Giordano, & I. Stojmenovic (Eds.), Mobile Ad Hoc Networking (pp. 1-46). John Wiley & Sons, Inc.

Martin, C. (2011). *The third screen: Marketing to your customers in a world gone mobile*. Academic Press.

Menguc, B., Auh, S., Fisher, M., & Haddad, A. (2013). To be engaged or not to be engaged: The antecedents and consequences of service employee engagement. *Journal of Business Research*, *66*(11), 2163–2170. doi:10.1016/j.jbusres.2012.01.007

Nassuora, A. B. (2013). Understanding Factors Affecting the Adoption of M-commerce by Consumers. *Journal of Applied Sciences*, *13*(6), 913–918. doi:10.3923/jas.2013.913.918

Naware, M., A. (2016). M-Commerce in India. *International Journal of Advanced Research in Computer and Communication Engineering*, 913–915.

Petrov, C. (2019). *50 M-Commerce Statistics For 2020*. Retrieved from https://techjury.net/stats-about/mcommerce/#gref

Robinson, D., Perryman, S., & Hayday, S. (2004). *The Drivers of Employee Engagement. Report 408*. Institute for Employment Studies.

Sadi, S. A., & Noordin, M. F. (2011). Factors influencing the adoption of M-commerce: An exploratory Analysis. *Proceeding of the 2011 International Conference on Industrial Engineering and Operations Management.*

Salanova, M., Agut, S., & Peiró, J. M. (2005). Linking Organizational Resources and Work Engagement to Employee Performance and Customer Loyalty: The Mediation of Service Climate. *The Journal of Applied Psychology*, *90*(6), 1217–1227.

Sarangi, D. (2016). *Employee Engagement and Its Impact on Organizational Success – A Study in Manufacturing Company* (pp. 52–57). India: IOSR Journal of Business and Management.

Sashi, C. M. (2012). Customer engagement, buyer-seller relationships, and social media. *Management Decision*, *50*(2), 253–272.

Sawhney, M., Verona, G., & Prandelli, E. (2005). Collaborating to create: The Internet as a platform for customer engagement in product innovation. *Journal of Interactive Marketing*, *19*(4), 4–17.

Shaheen & Naseem. (2015). A Review of Customer Satisfaction, Employee Satisfaction and their impact on Firm Performance. *International Journal of Management & Organizational Studies, 4*(1).

Teo, T. S. (2001). Demographic and motivation variables associated with internet usage activities. *Internet Research*, *11*(2), 125–137.

Wei, T. T., Marthandan, G., Chong, A. Y.-L., Ooi, K. B., & Arumugam, S. (2009). What drives Malayasian m-commerce adoption? An empirical analysis. *Industrial Management & Data Systems*, *109*, 370–388.

WhatI. C. E. WhyI. I. I. (2019). Retrieved from https://blog.smile.io/what-is-customer-engagement-and-why-is-it-important

Chapter 9
Employees' Attitudes and Perceptions Towards Electronic Monitoring Surveillance Affecting Employee Behavior:
An Exploratory Evidence From the Airline Industry

Omvir Gautam
Vishwakarma University, India

Pooja Agrawal
https://orcid.org/0000-0003-0971-5451
Vishwakarma University, India

ABSTRACT

Electronic monitoring surveillance (EMS) has emerged as a mechanism to monitor the behavior of the employees. Fast-growing organizations are adopting this strategy in an expeditious way. EMS deals with the CCTV, internet surfing control, and check on emails. The chapter is an attempt to diagnose the employees' attitudes and perceptions towards EMS and its impact. For this research purpose, a sample was drawn from the population of the selected airports Chandigarh, Pune, Goa, and New Delhi. Sample data of 237 respondents was done by using Smart-PLS.

DOI: 10.4018/978-1-7998-3515-8.ch009

The findings revealed that employees show that attitude and perception towards EMS were significant. It also influenced their work behavior positively. This chapter suggests managerial implications for organizations in understanding the appropriate implementation and use of EMS strategy as future scope of study. Moreover, this chapter also provides a platform for the researchers to study the different HR practices like commitment, loyalty, job satisfaction, and engagement.

INTRODUCTION

Electronic Monitoring, Surveillance (EMS) is contemplating a wider scope in the 21st century. This century is known as technology and automated century. Many researchers like (Aiello, 1993; Aiello and Svec, 1993; Vorvoreanu and Baton, 2000) propounded that for the last two decades the use of Electronic Monitoring Surveillance (EMS) at workplace gradually increased and its prevalence still rising in a good pace. Moreover, (Lane, 2003; Allen et al., 2007; Ball, 2010) postulated that the use of EMS in the organizations was enormous because it decline the cost involved in work activities and enhancing the organizations' complexity. It is a considerable concern as technological and automated era are either a boon or bane for the society. This technology has some pros and cons, like EMS makes employers capable for trace and monitors the undesired behavior of their employees in the working premises. EMS could be referring as the use of the computerized mechanism in collecting, retaining, analyzing, and assimilating the information on employees' behavior at the workplace.

Author (Wen et al. 2007) propounded that EMS is a controlling strategy which strengthen the organizations to monitor employees' movement and provide reports about their mobility from the workplace. Furthermore, its use also explained for harnessing of technology in capacity to take photos of an employee's screen at regular time intervals, provides the information to the employer regarding different websites employees were visiting, email content and confidential information they might probably disclose.

In this regard, American Management Association (2007) surveyed 304 organizations in the United States, which used EMS to check the behavior of their employees during their work hours. The survey results, revealed that 28 percent of the organizations terminated their employees for the inappropriate use of official email ids and other social media sites in official time, In addition to other reasons for employee's termination include wrong or offensive language, violation of confidentiality rules, and breach of any company policy. Furthermore, 30 percent of organization terminated their employees' job because of the wrong use of internet downloading or uploading of inappropriate content, use social networking sites during working hours, etc.

Ball (2010) reported that a little research had been conducted on the impact of EMS on work related dimensions such as attitude, trust among employee and employer relationship. Surprisingly in the middle of the last century, some researchers like (Strickland, 1958; Kruglanski, 1970) were proclaiming that minimum trust management demands high EMS and be elaborated by employees as managerial distrust and would led a negative impact on harmonious relationship among employees and employers . D' Urso, (2006) postulated that viability of EMS in the advanced organization demanded further studies. Similarly, Ball (2010) noticed that minimum work had been considerate on the influence of EMS on prominent work associated attitude. In this study, the main intention was to analyze the employees' attitude and perception towards EMS and its impact on their work behavior.

Research Issue

The present paper is an attempt to investigate the attitude and perception of employees towards the Electronic Monitoring Surveillance (EMS) and its impact on employees' behavior.

RQ 1: What is the employee's attitude and perception towards EMS?
RQ 2: What is the inter relationship between employee's attitude and perception towards EMS and employees' behavior?

Theoretical Framework and Hypotheses Development

EMS has been considered as one of the divergent strategy from the other strategies of Human Resource Management (HRM). Enormous researchers put their efforts to identify the validity of EMS strategy in an organization and concluded their different perspectives. For example, Oz et al., (1999) analyzed the employees' attitude towards EMS and also measured the difference between employers'-employees' attitude towards EMS. For this purpose, a cross sectional research conducted by using a structured questionnaire and collected data from 823 respondents was analyzed. The result indicated that superiors were having a positive attitude towards EMS because they thought that it would be an effective way to reduce theft in the organization. On the other way employees (subordinates/non-supervisors) holding a negative attitude towards EMS because they thought it creates controlled behavior which led stress in the workplace. It was also found that females were holding a positive attitude as compared to males towards EMS.

Alder (2001) diagnosed that employed in democratic organizations revealed a positive attitude towards EMS as compared to the employees of bureaucratic organizations. It was also concluded that employees' positive attitude established when EMS was only restricted to observe their job behavior and not disturbed their secrecy. Rousseau et al. (1998) generated a positive association between trust, work behavior and employees' attitude. It was diagnosed that the use of EMS led a feeling of distrust among employees, which established a negative attitude towards this, added diminishing behavior like organizational citizenship behavior (Dirks and Ferrin, 2002; Connell et al., 2003 and Agrawal, P., and Gautam, O., 2019).

H1: Attitude of Employees Positively Influences Electronic Monitoring Surveillance.

It is very contradictory and controversial that attitude leads perception or perception leads attitude. There are enormous researches available to point out that perception is the base of attitude, but on the other side of the coin some researchers pointed out that attitude influence the perception of people. Authors (Balzer & Sulsky, 1990; Ostroff, 1993) propounded that employees perceived the objective of performance assessment program differently which led the development of their attitude differently. The present paper considered that attitude of employees towards EMS positively influences their perception. To support this hypothesis, there is no direct literature available both on attitude and perception. Researchers like Sherif & Cantril, (1945) postulated that a person perceived selectively when he/she considering extrinsic stimuli by interpreting his/her opinion depends on beliefs, experience and attitudes. Furthermore, researchers like (Tuncel - Sümer, 2000; Oz - Sumer, 2004 and Agrawal, P., and Gautam, O., 2018) identified job attitude acted as a predictor of perceived performance and job satisfaction.

H2: Attitude of Employees Positively Influences Their Perception Towards Electronic Monitoring Surveillance.

Apart from different researches which highlighted an attitudinal perspective towards EMS, it was also perceived by enormous researchers that employees led the different perception towards EMS. Some of were like; Jenson and Raver (2012) proved that EMS helped in the development of smooth relationship between employees and employers, employees' job engagement and empowerment. As similarly, (Samaranayake and Gamage, 2011) collected research data from 380 respondents of an IT company in order to evaluate their job satisfaction as well as their perception towards work satisfaction, invasion of secrecy, rationale of employer and judgmental effectiveness. The results revealed that job satisfaction was positively associated with those employees who perceived a positive perspective towards EMS. Author like (Alder and Ambrose, 2005) posited that if employees' perceived EMS as a fair technique to control their behavior, then it was highly connected with the employees' higher productivity which led their higher job satisfaction.

On the other side, some researches reflected that job satisfaction negatively associated with those employees who perceived a negative perspective towards EMS and thought that it disrupted their privacy and made their work more complex and cumbersome. Ericson and Haggerty (1997) propounded that EMS led a feeling of distrust in the mind of the employees and resulted in disharmonious relationship between employees and employers. Zureik (2003) postulated that when EMS practiced became a part of organizational policy then it developed employees' perception that we are not trusted by the organization. Additionally, Meyers(2003) justified that if employees' perceived differently like considered that it is an unacceptable technique to monitor their behavior than its impact on employees' performance may be inverse which led lower job satisfaction of employees.

H3: Perception of Employees Positively Influences Electronic Monitoring Surveillance.

To accomplish the second research objective, the past literature was analyzed to understand the impact of employees' attitude and perception of their work behavior. A few research studies were available on this like; (Lee and Kleiner, 2003) suggested that employers had the privilege to monitor employees' behavior during working timings in the organization because they were accountable for all the considerable tasks like organization's confidential information and safety of the employees during the scheduled work time. Likewise, Samaranayake and Gamage, 2001; Alder and Ambrose, 2005 and Jenson and Rever, 2012 posited that EMS was an appropriate technique to observed the behavior.

On the other side, a segment of past studies like; Flanagan (1994) propounded that employers' perceived that EMS was a complex technique to expect employees' higher performance because it led a phenomenon of distrust among the employees. Authors Flangan (1994) and Vorvoreanu and Baton (2000) postulated that EMS led employees' negative behavior because they thought that EMS system decreased workplace privacy and increased stress and resulted in deterioration in interest towards their work, increase truancy rate, distrust and work pressure. Furthermore, analysis suggested that this type of behavior can have a significant impact on employee's work life and resulted in employees' lower rate of performance. Moreover, Rousseau et.al (1998) was propounded a positive relationship between employees' behavior, trust and attitude. Similarly, Alder (2001) extended the research in tune with Aiello and Kolb (1995) that employees' holding a positive attitude towards EMS and the sign9ficanat contribution of EMS in creation of employee's stress.

H4: Electronic Monitoring Surveillance Positively Influences Employees' Work Behavior.

Figure 1. Conceptual model

Objectives of the Study

1. To measure the attitude and perception of employees towards Electronic Monitoring Surveillance.
2. To analyze employees' perception and attitude towards EMS and its impact on their work behavior.

Methodology

The population for present study catered employees working in the airline industry. The sample consists of employees working at airports (Chandigarh, Pune, Goa and New Delhi). A purposive sampling method was used to identify the respondents for fulfillment of present research. The research was done since July 2019 to August, 2019. A total of 360 questionnaires were distributed to potential employees from these four airports. The rationale used for only these mentioned airports was high pedestrian density and tourism connecting centers (TCC) in order to link with various nearby tourist destinations. The questionnaires were gathered from all airports. Only 237 questionnaires were returned, constituting a response rate of 65.83 percent. Out of these 237 usable questionnaires, 93 (39.24 percent) were from ground staff (baggage handlers, baggage clerks, or fleet service agents), 31 (13.08 percent) from security officers, and 113 (47.67 percent) from front desk executives (air ticket issuer and housekeeping staff). A total of 169 (71.31 percent) responses were from males while 68 (28.69) were from females.

Furthermore, under the education level 17 respondents were higher secondary, 109 were graduate, 77 were post graduate and 34 respondents were holding education in different domains. Out of 237 questionnaires, 29 employees were associated from less than 1 year, 17 employees were holding their work tenure from 1-3 years, 45 employees had experience from 3-5 years, 78 employees were associated with the organization from 5-7 years and 68 employees were connected with the organization from more than 7 years. 61.16 percent respondents were holding work experience from 5-7 or more than 7 years which revealed that employees were associated with the organization from a longer span of time.

Table 1, illustrates a bifurcation of respondents by nature of duty perform, gender, education qualification and work tenure.

Table 1. Demographical attributes

	Demographical Attributes	Frequency	Percent
Nature of duty perform	Ground Staff	93	39.24
	Security Staff	31	13.08
	Front Desk Staff	113	47.67
Gender	Male	169	71.31
	Female	68	28.69
Educational Qualification	Higher secondary	17	7.17
	Graduate	109	45.99
	Post graduate	77	32.49
	Others(diploma, certification)	34	14.35
Work tenure (Experience)	Less than 1 year	29	12.23
	1-3 year	17	7.17
	3-5 year	45	18.98
	5-7 year	78	32.91
	More than 7 year	68	28.69

The data collection instruments used is derived from Attitude Measurement Scale (Spector, 1992), Perception, EMS and Employees' behavior and blended with the demographic profile of respondents. The questionnaire used in this study employed on dimensions Attitude, Perception, EMS and Employees' behavior. Each item in the seven point Likert's scale was measured in a range of 1 (strongly disagree) to 7 (strongly agree). There were 3 scales to measure overall employees' behavior. The nature of duty performs; gender, education qualification and work tenure were considered as demographic questions to respondents. To assure confidentiality and camouflaged, the tool were coded and only complete questionnaires were considered for analysis.

The validity of the data collection tool that is questionnaire was done by expert panel. The panel was given a questionnaire and requested to review the content of the items (Employees Behavior) and other three were adopted (Mention citation). The discriminant validity with respect to convergent validity had been established in the current study. The pilot testing was done to established reliability analysis for small sample (n=29) of randomly selected respondents. The internal consistency (Cronbach's alpha was found as 0.89, depicting the reliability of the used research instruments. For analysis purpose the Structural Equation Modeling (SEM) was adopted with incorporation of Partial Least Square (PLS) Method for validating our study. The measurement model and structural model were tested and results has been explained in next subsequent headings.

Data Analysis, Results and Findings

For analyzing the data, Structural Equation Modeling (SEM) technique was utilized. Smart PLS software, which uses the Partial Least Square (PLS) Method, was used in the study. There are two types of model which can be evaluated by this method. The two models are Measurement Model and Structural Model. The association of latent construct and their related variables can be represented by measurement model. The structural model represents the relationship between different constructs.

Measurement Model

The values of the measurement model have been represented in table 2. The results are used to evaluate the convergent validity and internal consistency. Table 2, represents the result of measurement model based on PLS algorithm. The output obtained from the analysis was used to assess the convergent validity, and internal consistency. To assess the convergent validity, Average Variance Extracted (AVE) was used while the internal consistency was evaluated by using Composite Reliability (CR). A value of AVE less than 0.5 is not acceptable because it could not explain more than half of the variance by its items or variables (Henseler, Ringle, & Sinkovics, 2009). Therefore some items from the constructs were deleted to gain the AVE value of 0.5. Initially the construct Attitude is represented by 16 items but 10 items have been deleted to make the AVE value of construct greater than 0.5. One item from Perception constructs and two items from Employees Behavior construct have been also deleted but no item from EMS construct has been deleted. After modification in constructs, a value of AVE greater than 0.5 has been obtained for each construct.

For attaining the internal consistency, Fornell & Larcker (1981) suggested the measurement of CR value. The author suggested that a construct with CR value more than 0.7 is considered internally consistent.

Table 2. Measurement model

Construct	Item	Loading	AVE	CR
Attitude	A2	0.7532	0.5638	0.8857
	A5	0.7529		
	A12	0.7670		
	A13	0.7553		
	A14	0.7650		
	A15	0.7103		
Perception	P1	0.7512	0.5551	0.8617
	P2	0.7673		
	P3	0.6994		
	P4	0.7284		
	P6	0.7765		
Electronic Monitoring Surveillance (EMS)	EMS1	0.5862	0.5234	0.8434
	EMS2	0.8106		
	EMS3	0.8240		
	EMS4	0.6111		
	EMS5	0.7511		
Employees Behavior	EB2	0.7818	0.5256	0.8154
	EB3	0.7280		
	EB4	0.7149		
	EB5	0.6710		

The results from table 2, clearly demonstrate an acceptable level of convergent validity and internal consistency as the values of AVE and CR are more than 0.5 and 0.8 respectively.

Table 3. Discriminant validity

	Attitude	Perception	EMS	Employees' Behaviour
Attitude	**0.7508**			
Perception	0.7180	**0.7450**		
EMS	0.6476	0.6800	**0.7234**	
Employees Behavior	0.7037	0.6976	0.6022	**0.7249**

Note: The diagonals represent the square root of the AVE, while the off-diagonals represent the correlations.

To check the discriminant validity, the values of square root of AVE of different constructs and correlations between the constructs have been compared. Fornell & Larcker(1981) suggested that the square root of AVE should be greater than the correlations between construct to achieve discriminant validity. It is shown in table 3.

The results from table 3, represent a considerable amount of discriminant validity as the values of square root of AVE is more than the inter-construct correlations.

Structural Model

Figure 2 below represents the structural model. Bootstrapping procedure has been used in Smart PLS software to generate the path coefficients along with their associated T-values. The path coefficients along with T-values are provided in table 3. These T-values are used to test the developed hypotheses.

Figure 2.The structural model

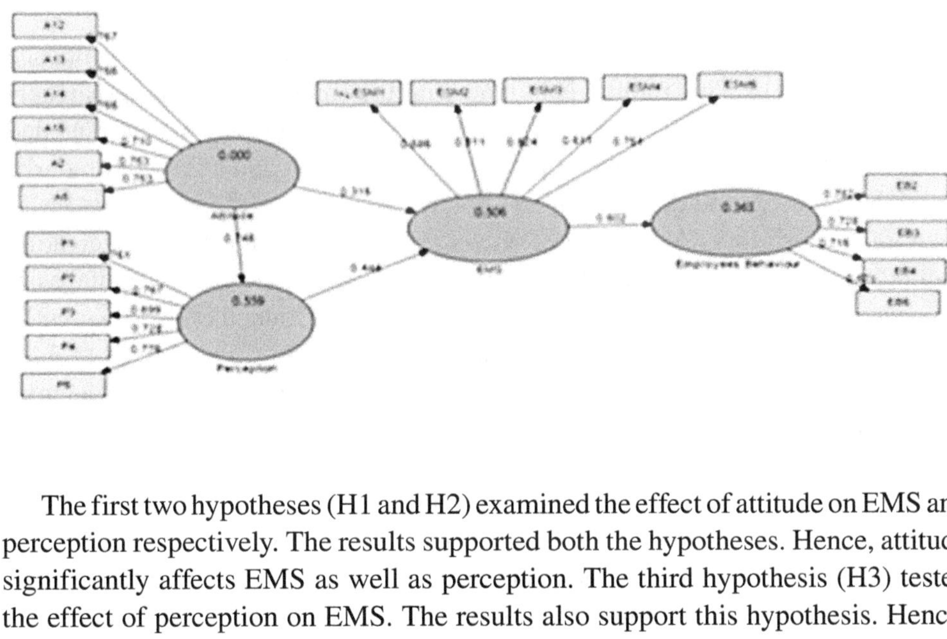

The first two hypotheses (H1 and H2) examined the effect of attitude on EMS and perception respectively. The results supported both the hypotheses. Hence, attitude significantly affects EMS as well as perception. The third hypothesis (H3) tested the effect of perception on EMS. The results also support this hypothesis. Hence, perception also has an effect on EMS. The fourth hypothesis (H4) examined the effect of EMS on Employees' Behaviour and the hypothesis is also supported as clear from the results. Hence, EMS has significant effect on Employees' Behaviour.

Discussion

The motive to conduct this research was to empirically evaluate the employees' attitude and perception towards Electronic Monitoring Surveillance (EMS) and its impact on their work behavior. After applying Smart-PLS results from table 4 depicted that the all hypotheses were significant.

Table 4. Results of hypothesis testing using structural model analysis

Hypotheses		Standard Error	Path Coefficient	T-value	Decision
H1	Attitude EMS	0.1226	0.3154	4.0325	Supported
H2	Attitude Perception	0.0576	0.7480	15.7961	Supported
H3	Perception EMS	0.1423	0.4441	5.0541	Supported
H4	EMS Employee Behavior	0.0994	0.6022	8.6731	Supported

Results from table 4 showed that employees' attitude positively influence towards EMS (H1). This finding is in tune with the findings of some researchers like Rousseau et.al, 1998 and Alder, 2001. Rousseau et.al (1998) was propounded a positive relationship between employees' behavior, trust and attitude. Similarly, Alder (2001) diagnosed that employees' holding a positive attitude towards EMS, when it perceived that EMS observed only work related behavior and not creating any bottlenecks in their personal life. On the other side, some research findings are inconsistent with the present finding like Oz et.al, 1999; Connell et al., 2003; Dirks and Ferrin, 2002; posited a negative attitude towards EMS.

Moreover, analysis revealed that attitude of employees positively influences their perception towards EMS (H2). This finding is consistent with the findings of (Sherif & Cantril, 1945; Tuncel - Sümer, 2000 and Öz - Sümer, 2004). Researchers concluded that employees' positive attitude positively influence their perception. On the other side this finding is inconsistent with the findings of (Balzer & Sulsky, 1990; Ostroff, 1993). They propounded that perception influence the attitude of an individual. It could be summarize that the employees those possessing a positive attitude towards EMS also perceiving this positively and vis-à-vis.

Furthermore, analysis revealed that employees positively influence their perception towards EMS (H3). This finding is in tune with the few researches like (Alder and Ambrose, 2005; Samaranayake and Gamage 2011 ; Jenson and Raver 2012 and Rana,S., Agrawal, P., and Jha, N.(2013) indicated that employees' perceived EMS was a fair strategy and this positive perception enhanced their productivity, job satisfaction and developed harmonious relationship among employees and employers. Moreover, Lee and Kleiner (2003) postulated that EMS helped to reduce the probability of employees' unethical or illegal behavior, more security of the information or less chance to reveal confidentiality and enhanced employees' productivity.

On the other part some research findings were not in tune with the present finding and pointed out that employees' perception negatively influence towards EMS. Ericson and Haggerty, 1997; Oz et al., 1998 and Zureik, 2003, postulated that EMS developed an unnecessary feeling of distrust and anxiety which resulted in disharmonious relationship in the industry. Additionally, Meyers (2003) postulated that when employees' perceived that EMS was an inappropriate technique to control their behavior than their performance affected differently which revealed lower performance rate along with lower job satisfaction.

Moreover, the findings indicated that employees' attitude and perception towards EMS were positively influenced and it positively affected their work behavior (H4).This finding is in tune with the findings of researchers like; Lee and Kleiner, 2003; Alder and Ambrose, 2005; Samaranayake and Gamage, 2011 ; Jenson and Raver, 2012 and Sharma, S., and Gautam,O. (2014) highlighted that an EMS was an appropriate way to observed and controlled employees' behavior. It was pointed out that if EMS application was fair, appropriate and perceived in a right manner then it led employees' higher performance, increased productivity rate, enhanced job satisfaction, high involvement and harmonious relationship in the organization.

Some researchers revealed a different perspective towards EMS and inconsistent with the present findings. Researchers like (Flanagan, 1994; Vorvoreanu and Baton, 2000) contributed that EMS plays a role of bottleneck in earning qualitative and productive work. Aiello and Kolb (1995) enlarged this research area and concluded by laboratory experiments that EMS led a higher level of stress in employees. It was also concluded that this stress level was highly secured in the employees when they were observed in the group and vis-à-vis. Moreover, Meyers, (2003) added that the negative perception towards EMS deteriorated the level of employee job satisfaction. On the basis of survey data of AMA (2007), it was highlighted that EMS included the checking of computer files, monitoring of e-mail or internet surfing, phone calls, CCTV to control employees' behavior. The findings of the survey concluded that negative perception towards EMS resulted in employees' demoralization and violation of privacy rights.

LIMITATIONS AND SCOPE FOR FURTHER RESEARCH

The research is conducted at selected airports. So, the findings of this research paper cannot be generalized in other industries. The time was limited. The sample was drawn by using purposive sampling, which is a part of non-probability sampling. It could be a limitation of this research paper.

Research is not considered as complete if it is not providing the wings for future research. The present paper is talking about the attitude and perception of employees towards EMS and its impact on their work behavior. This paper can provide a platform for the researchers to study the different HR practices like commitment, loyalty, satisfaction and engagement with this aspect. Furthermore, the findings in this study are supported by empirically and could be used to analyze employee – employer supervision with respect to other industries by the academicians and researchers.

IMPORTANCE OF THE STUDY

The current study will be useful for researchers, who wants to carry their work on pertinent issues concerned with strategic human resource management (SHRM), cultural diversity of work force and Human Resource perspectives. It will also sheds light to company managers in terms of understanding the upgrading of services in Airline industy.Lastly, the human resource managers may develop a priority matrix for critically analyzing the importance of the relevant issues.

FINAL WORDS

Generally, employees considered EMS as a disciplinary or controlling tool in an organization. The available past literature pointed out that in some organizations the purpose of EMS is not effectively communicated to the employees. This unawareness leads a negative attitude and perception towards EMS which resulted in negative work behavior. In the present research paper results revealed that employees of airline industry holding a positive attitude towards the use of EMS. This positive attitude led their positive perception and resulted in their positive work behavior. It is an indication of the other organization that if they will properly communicate their purpose of using EMS in an organization then the employees will hold a right attitude and perception towards EMS and resulted in better work behavior.

REFERENCES

Agrawal, P., & Gautam, O. (2018). Truancy and Job Satisfaction towards Sponsored Child-Care Facility in India. *Prabandhan: Indian Journal of Management, 11*(7), 23–35. doi:10.17010/pijom/2018/v11i7/129937

Agrawal, P., & Gautam, O. (2019). The Effects of Leaders' Behavior on Job Satisfaction, Organizational Citizenship Behavior, Deviant Behavior, and Job Performance of Employees. In *Analyzing Workplace Deviance in Modern Organizations* (pp. 100–113). IGI Global.

Aiello, J. R., & Kolb, K. J. (1995). Electronic performance monitoring and social context: Impact on productivity and stress. *The Journal of Applied Psychology*, *80*(3), 339–353. doi:10.1037/0021-9010.80.3.339 PMID:7797458

Alder, G. S. (2001). Employee reactions to electronic performance monitoring: A consequence of organizational culture. *The Journal of High Technology Management Research*, *12*(2), 323–342. doi:10.1016/S1047-8310(01)00042-6

Alder, G. S., & Ambrose, M. L. (2005a). An examination of the effect of computerized task specific monitoring feedback on monitoring fairness, performance and satisfaction. *Organizational Behavior and Human Decision Processes*, *97*(2), 161–177. doi:10.1016/j.obhdp.2005.03.003

Alder, G. S., & Ambrose, M. L. (2005b). Towards understanding fairness judgments associated with computer task-specific monitoring: An integration of the feedback, justice, and monitoring research. *Human Resource Management Review*, *15*(1), 43–67. doi:10.1016/j.hrmr.2005.01.001

American Management Association. (2007). *The Latest on Workplace Monitoring and Surveillance*. American Management Association of USA. Available from: http://press.amanet.org/pressreleases/177/2007electronicmonitoringsurveillancesurvey/

Ball, K. (2010). Workplace surveillance: An overview. *Labor History*, *51*(1), 87106. doi:10.1080/00236561003654776

Ericson, R. V., Ericson, R. V., & Haggerty, K. D. (1997). *Policing the risk society*. Clarendon Studies in Criminolo. doi:10.3138/9781442678590

Flanagan, J. A. (1994). Restricting electronic monitoring in the private workplace. *Duke Law Journal*, *43*(6), 1256–1281. doi:10.2307/1372857

Fornell, C., & Larcker, D. F. (1981). Evaluating structural equation models with unobservable variables and measurement error. *JMR, Journal of Marketing Research*, *18*(1), 39–50. doi:10.1177/002224378101800104

Henseler, J., Ringle, C. M., & Sinkovics, R. R. (2009). The use of partial least squares path modeling in international marketing. In *New challenges to international marketing* (pp. 277–319). Emerald Group Publishing Limited. doi:10.1108/S1474-7979(2009)0000020014

Jensen, J. M., & Raver, J. L. (2012). When self-management and surveillance collide: Consequences for employees' organizational citizenship and counterproductive work behaviors. *Group & Organization Management*, *37*(3), 308–346. doi:10.1177/1059601112445804

Lee, S., & Kleiner, B. H. (2003). Electronic surveillance in the workplace. *Journal of Management Research News*, *26*(2/3/4), 72–81. doi:10.1108/01409170310784014

Meyers, N. (2003). *Employee Privacy in the Electronic Workplace: Current Issues for IT Professionals*. In *14th Australasian Conference on Information Systems*, Perth, Western Australia.

Oz, E., Glass, R., & Behling, R. (1999). Electronic Workplace Monitoring: What Employees Think. *International Journal of Management Sciences*, *27*, 167–177.

Rana, S., Agrawal, P., & Jha, N. (2013). CRM vs. HR Issues: An Extensive. Literature Review. *Global Journal of Business Management*, *7*(2), 35–44.

Samaranayake, V., & Gamage, C. (2011). Employee Perception towards Electronic Monitoring at Work Place and Its Impact on Job Satisfaction of Software Professionals in Sri Lanka. *Telematics and Informatics*, *29*(2), 233–244. doi:10.1016/j.tele.2011.08.003

Sharma, S., & Gautam, O. (2014). An Empirical Analysis on Office Politics in Indian Organisations. *Human Resource Reflection*, *1*(3), 86–92.

Vorvoreanu, M., & Baton, C. H. (2000). Examining electronic surveillance in the workplace: A review of theoretical perspectives and research findings. Conference of the International Communication Association.

Vyas, J. H., & Shrivastava, R. (2011). Employee Perception of Corporate Social Responsibility and Job Satisfaction in Large Scale Units. *Prabandhan: Indian Journal of Management*, *4*(12), 23.

Wen, H. J., Schwieger, D., & Gershuny, P. (2007). Internet usage monitoring in the workplace its legal challenges and implementation strategies. *Information Systems Management*, *24*(2), 185–196. doi:10.1080/10580530701221072

Chapter 10
The Dynamics of Employee Relationships in a Digitalized Workplace:
The Role of Media Richness on Workplace Culture

Tanusree Chakraborty
Rajalakshmi School of Business, India

Malabika Tripathi
https://orcid.org/0000-0002-5052-2953
Amity University, Kolkata, India

Somrita Saha
Amity University, Kolkata, India

ABSTRACT

Employees of this day are not confined only to the physical space that they occupy during office hours. Today's workstations are connected environments ensuring instant access to other employees and anything that employees need for work which goes beyond any communication barriers and as a result is changing employee experiences to better engaged, innovative, and efficient ones. All these changes have given way to alterations in employee interrelation dynamics within the boundaries of technological environments. The chapter leads to an understanding of how today's work culture has changed, what the digitized workplace looks like, the where and how of task-technology fits, and the model of interpersonal relationships. The chapter also talks about the related implications of media richness theory at workplace with special reference to digitized work environment and virtual reality. Further, the chapter brings in the challenges of cyberloafing and phubbing as consequences of the digitized workplace and how those affect performance and employee relations.
DOI: 10.4018/978-1-7998-3515-8.ch010

INTRODUCTION: EMPLOYEE RELATIONS AT WORKPLACE

People spend most of their day time at the workplace and it is asserted that people who possess a best friend at work are much more engaged in their work. In a study conducted by Gallup (2017) on work relationships, it was found that people, who simply had a good friend, as compared to a best friend even, were found to be more satisfied at work in general. While asserting that man is a social animal, it is focused that men are naturally social beings and that a man desires friendship and positive connections which can be compared as equal to the need for food and water. Thus emphasizing on the fact that the better the relations are at workplace, the gladder and more industrious people would be. Dating back to some old studies, it can be said that the indication that spirits of friendship impact performance in the workplace is an old one, (Mayo, 1933). Looking back at the famous Hawthorne studies, this can be related as well, that, personal relations in industrial settings are significant (Roethlisberger and Dickson, 1939).

The average full-time employee will easily spend eight hours on the job each working day, during which they sometimes work together intensively with others. That's why it's necessary for them to engage in interpersonal relationships. The decisions that need to be made can't be made by one person. The quality of the relationships within an organization says a lot about its culture, too. A positive culture is characterized by cheerful employees who get along well. A positive corporate culture usually has a positive influence on business results. A negative culture will manifest in the form of many conflicts and useless discussions. Workplace interrelationships focus the core domain of communication, and there are various ways of improving and stimulating interpersonal relationships within an organization through improved communication (Chakraborty & Ganguly, 2019). Communication is the link to humanity. Interpersonal relationship and communication are closely inter-related. Individuals in an interpersonal relationship share the accountability for shaping the nature of a relationship by creating sense from the interaction. Looking at the workplace communication, the scenario of workplace communication has altered over the recent years.

Digital transformation is not considered as a niche concern today, as digital environment has plunged beyond just the technical departments and made its way into the boardroom of leaders; and this is true for every kind of industry and across geographical boundaries. Communication takes place a lot through digital platforms and relation get in impetus on digital platforms. Thus, anytime we communicate with another person, whether a friend, parent, coworker, or employer, we are communicating interpersonally. It is very regular for communicators to bring into play digital media to get their messages across to one another or the public with the help of blogging, texting, tweeting, Instant messaging, e-mailing, or posting in a social networking site such as Facebook. Digital tools today sanction individuals to communicate. There has been a plethora of debate and dialogue among professionals in academia and industry as to how digitization controls HRM functions, but it has not engendered the equal level of penetrating discussion as to how digitization has impacted industrial relations or employee relations. The question that here arises with respect to employee relation in digitalized economy is, whether digitalization can assist in generating, upholding and sustaining a affable, amiable and friendly employee relation, or it has some challenges along with it as well?

The present chapter makes an attempt to understand the dynamics of workplace relationships in the digitalized economy touching upon the new workplace culture, how task–technology fit has affected interpersonal relations, how digital platforms act as a boon to enhanced communication efficacy in virtual reality. It also provides insights into some of the hazards of digital transformation that leads to undesirable behaviours like cyberloafing and phubbing at workplace and finally attempts to integrate boons and hazards of workplace relations in a digitalized environment. Thus in crisp, the chapter discusses the dynamics of relations at workplace by seeing through the boons and hazards of digitalized environment.

BACKGROUND: ERA OF WORKPLACE DIGITALIZATION

According to Ray Kurzweil (2004), "*Technological developments are far reaching advancements that have gone beyond just making of tools and equipments; it is a procedure of crafting ever more robust technology using the tools from the previous rounds of innovation*" (Berman & Dorrier, 2016). With the advent of technology, all areas of society have changed. A few decades ago, people could only dream of doing half the things they do now. Digital technology has made an impact on education, business, government, political administration, medicine and so on (Naidoo, 2018). One of the areas of impact of digital technology is in the work field. Deloitte (2012) defined digital workplace as that which encompasses all the technologies people use to get work done in today's workplace-both the ones in operation and the ones yet to be implemented. It ranges from HR applications and core business applications to e-mail, instant messaging and enterprise social media tools and virtual meeting tools. Technological advancements have completely restructured the way organizations work (Prasad, 2018).

Rapid digital transformation has pushed the workplace towards digitalization in order to stay relevant (Mahler & Westergren, 2019). With the advances in technology over the years, the whole world and nature of work and workplace has changed (Naidoo, 2018). For example, the work processes in the media industry has changed because of digitalization (Rintala & Suolanen, 2017). Using the digital technology, the processes of content making, content recording and overall program production has been made much easier, quicker and more convenient (Rintala & Suolanen, 2017). Rapid developments of digital technology have led to several organizational benefits such as increase in revenue, reduction in operation costs, enhancing innovation, improving customer experience and satisfaction, rise in productivity and work efficiency, better staff satisfaction, huge improvements in employee experiences and keeping things organized (Herrera et al., 2012).

Thus, workplace digitalization aims at improving organizational performance, quality of work and wellbeing of the employees (Pot, 2017). The modern workplaces now have many innovative technologies that enhance productivity, boost efficiency, keep things organized, and improve work experience and so on (Prasad, 2018). However, with pros come the cons. These rapid developments that bring such positive benefits to the organization also bring some cons to their worker which ultimately affects the organization itself. Digitalization also prompts anxiety, stress, tension and apprehension about their future and job security in the world of fast-paced digitalization (Muro et al., 2017). Most important and perceptible impact has been felt on the interpersonal relations front. With this current rate of speed of digitalization in the workplace, it is believed that it could disrupt the work and economic sectors (Brynjolfsson & McAfee, 2014). The increase in automation and rise of artificial intelligence is resulting in job destruction (Timonen & Vuori, 2018). One of the characteristics with which new workplace has to adapt is to be more flexible and this is resulting in virtual and nonhierarchical forms in organization (Joyce, 1997). Digital technologies not only change the way an individual works but also how the collective works and its work practices in significant but "unpredictable ways" (Barley & Bechky, 2017). This is leading to unpredictable communication and interpersonal relationship patterns also. With the increasing rise in the usage of cloud services and data upload, anytime and anywhere the employees and those in the organization have access to sensitive data. With cyber-crimes growing in number, security has become a major concern in digitalized workplace (McGregor, 2018). From this perspective, interpersonal communication remains under threat, about how much information to share in communication platforms. It is true that training and grooming employees with new technologies in their digitalized workplace will enhance their efficiency and boost their productivity, however it would be unreasonable to expect that all the employees would take the training happily, will learn at the same pace as others or will be able to cope up with modern demands of the work (Weedmark, 2019). This can cause job stress or 'techno-stress', information overload, IT (information technology) addiction or IT anxiety and/or affect employees' mental health and ultimately their work efficiency and productivity (Marsh, 2019).

INDUSTRY 4.0 AND INTERPERSONAL RELATIONSHIP

The 21st century will be reminisced by generations to come as the forerunner of Industry 4.0. Besides countries like US and China, India is likely to be one of the leaders of Industry 4.0, augmenting new economic prospects. With the advent of Industry 4.0, workplace skills and interpersonal relationships are undergoing changes and the need of the hour is a wide range of skill sets. For this, corporates are also encountering a flared gap between the skills desired by them and the skills available in the workforce, particularly with respect to interpersonal relationships among the workforce. Learning strategies for the employees are undergoing changes and these are getting associated to organizational strategies to match the employees and bridge the gap. With the access to digital machines like smartphones, laptops, desktops, tabs, etc and with the access to internet, the nature of employee relation has started undergoing changes. More than physical interaction, employees relate to one another on a digital platform. Desk to desk conversations also occur over the internet. Even employees hardly spend time with one another, either for formal reasons or informal reasons. Too much use of internet and bring-your-own –device at work has also led to cyberloafing, which is a highly likely form of behaviour that occurs among the employees at work. A recent study by Hu & Hsu (2019) show that 69 percent of respondents admitted of wasting time on work unrelated activities each day. Digitalized workplace does not mean how the boss thinks employees should work but rather how the employees actually work. In order to become a digitalized workplace, the organization must actively engage in the process of digitalization (Mahler &Westergren, 2019), be it training or recruiting employees who can deal with and work in a digitalized workplace. This is progressing at a rapid rate, with this transformation at workplace, there is transformation perceived in employee relations. The Fourth Industrial Revolution is in the necessity just not to accept progressive technologies, but also to improve ethical as well as inclusive leaders, this has brought about a change in interpersonal dimensions of organizations, both at interpersonal skill level and relations level. All these are results of infiltrating digital technologies like artificial intelligence, the internet of things, cloud computing, advanced analytics and robotics.

A TASK–TECHNOLOGY FIT PERSPECTIVE

Workplace digitization is an outcome of the need to amalgamate task and technology. The advent of technology and the rapid progression of it have made huge impact on organizations. The need to splurge Information technology at workplace is the core requirement of most organizations in the present day. Business Dictionary

(2019), has defined information technology (IT) *is "a set of tools, processes, and methodologies (such as coding/programming, data communications, data conversion, storage and retrieval, systems analysis and design, systems control) and associated equipment employed to collect, process, and present information. In broad terms, IT also includes office automation, multimedia and telecommunications"*. The components of Information Systems (IS) are people, IT and business processes to achieve a business goal. IS are designed to help its users to perform their tasks more efficiently, conveniently and effectively (Irick, 2008). Organizations spend millions of dollars to provide appropriate IS to improve their organizational or individual performance (Goodhue, 1995). However, to provide appropriate IS, the organizations must better understand the relationship between IS and individual performances. In the *Task-technology fit (TTF) model*, the relationship between IT and individual performances has been depicted. Goodhue & Thompson (1995) define TTF as *"the degree to which a technology assists an individual in performing his or her tasks"* (Irick, 2008). In the context of TTF and IT, technology refers to applications of scientific knowledge in practical fields. Task refers to "*the actions carried out by individuals in turning inputs into outputs*" (Goodhue, 1995). Task and technology are important determinants of IS's success and research (DeLone & McLean, 1992; Alkhalifah & D'Ambra, 2011). These two determinants or factors can be integrated or combined and this enables new technologies to either change the nature of tasks or potentially create new tasks (Junglas et al., 2008). The third component of TTF is "fit". Goodhue specified "fit" as a match among task requirements, individual abilities, functionality and the interface of technology (Goodhue, 1997). He argued that TTF is that when a technology helps by providing features and support that "fit" the individuals and the requirements of a task. Thus, it is a matter of fact that, it order to balance the need of organizational effectiveness, the ardent requisite of the day has been to connect task and technology and employees.

GENERAL MODEL OF INTERPERSONAL RELATIONSHIP

The core focus of the chapter is how interpersonal need gets affected in the technology infiltrated workplace. Before entering into the discussion of that, it is indispensable to understand the model of interpersonal relationship. Any model which describes interpersonal relationship is known as an interpersonal relationship model. An Interpersonal relationship model elucidates an individual's stance towards relationship and how one's perception alters in due course of time.

Interpersonal relationship model has two important components in creating an individual's perception about relationships:

Figure 1. The following diagram depicts task-technology fit model
Goodhue & Thompson (1995)

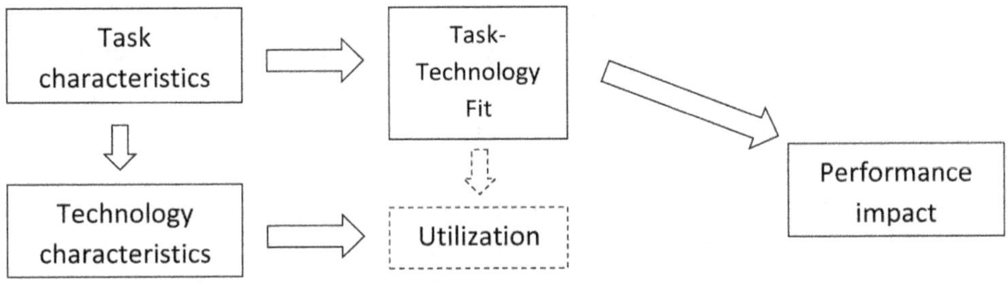

1. **Other to Self:** The component "other to self" represents an individual's awareness of another person's attitude, thoughts and beliefs towards himself.
2. **Self to Other:** The component "self to other" represents an individual's awareness of his own attitude, thoughts and beliefs towards the other person.

Like in general communication and development of interpersonal relationship, workplace interpersonal relationship model also passes through the following stages:

INTERPERSONAL RELATIONSHIPS AT WORK: THE INDISPENSABLE

Interpersonal relationships in the workplace have become an inevitable reality. It may be in the perspective of these relationships that workers find a social intention. According to Heaphy & Dutton (2008), positive interpersonal connections are linked with better individual and work-related outcomes. Positive interactions can promote positive interpersonal relationships, and it is from the growth and continuation of these relationships, that many workers find accomplishment. Employees may find

Table 1. General model of interpersonal relationship

Stage 1 Acquaintance Stage	Stage 2 The Build-up Stage	Stage 3 Maintenance Stage	Stage 4 Decline Stage	Stage 5 Termination Stage
Knowing the other individual	Coming close Being passionate Development of feelings, trust	Engaging in permanent commitments Maintenance of trust and transparency	Deterioration of relationship	End of the relationship Reasons vary

an opportunity to fulfill their "need to belong" in this positive relational context. According to Baumeister and Leary (1995), the need to belong is a fundamental human motivation, guiding both voluntary and involuntary behaviors, thoughts, and emotions. Two criteria must be met to satisfy the need to belong (Baumeister& Leary, 1995): *first*, interactions must be frequent and non-aversive and *second,* they must occur in the context of a stable and enduring relationship. The workplace encourages the development of persistent interactions and extended relationships. The positive results, for both individuals and organizations, related with positive interpersonal relationships in the workplace are well-documented. Cohen and Wills (1985) are of the view that for individual employees, at the broadest level, simply being a part of a social network (e.g., an organization) may reduce employee stress levels in terms of formal (i.e., organizationally approved) workplace relationships, leaders that are perceived as "good listeners" have been allied with employee feelings of belonging, inclusion, social significance, and togetherness (Alvesson & Sveningsson, 2003). Also, it should be noted by many that positive interpersonal relationships with mentors have been related with enhanced work-related results, such as increased remuneration, organizational promotion (Allen, Eby, Poteet, Lima, & Lentz, 2004; Dreher& Ash, 1990) career mobility (Scandura, 1992), acknowledgment, rewards, and a prospect to establish a foundation of power (Hunt & Michael, 1983), communication enhances employee engagement and to a larger extent impacts organizational effectiveness (Chakraborty & Ganguly, 2019). According to Baker & Dutton (2007), when organizations promote positive interpersonal relationships, others tend to follow the example, further creating a community of belonging.

Apart from formal workplace relationships, informal relationships are also linked with positive work-related and personal effects. Mainiero (1989) is of the opinion that attraction among co-workers augments teamwork, communication, and cooperation It has also been found that workplace friendships have been related with various positive effects, such as augmented job satisfaction, job involvement, job performance, team cohesion, organizational commitment, and decreased intention to turnover (Berman, West, & Richter, 2002; Feeley, Hwang, & Barnett, 2008; Riordan & Griffeth, 1995; Winstead, Derlega, Montgomery, & Pilkington, 1995). In addition, workplace romances have been associated with happier employees and a positive work atmosphere (Riach & Wilson, 2007).

Thus, apart from positive psychological benefits, positive social interactions have been considerably related with enhanced cardiovascular activity, immune system functioning, and hormone patterns (Heaphy & Dutton, 2008). Kramer, (1991), is of the view that employee identification with the organization has been related to increased employee compliance, motivation, job satisfaction, and group cohesion, as well as decreased turnover and in-group conflict. Also, Liden, Wayne, and Sparrowe (2000) stated that positive interpersonal relationship is a key interpreter of organizational commitment, while, Kostova and Roth (2003) report that positive interpersonal relationships should be positively related to team performance, as they promote individual behaviors that are aimed at increasing team efficacy and efficiency.

Though positive interpersonal relationship has a great impact on both the individual and the organization, nevertheless, researchers have a propensity to center on the effects and implications of negative interpersonal relationships at work on organizational and employee outcomes as well. From an employee perspective, these studies perpetually find higher levels of job dissatisfaction, intent to turnover, and negative physical and mental health effects among employees who have been facing such negative interpersonal interactions like aggression, social exclusion, and incivility (Bowling & Beehr, 2006; Cortina & Magley, 2003; K. D. Williams, 2001). But the impact of positive effects due to interpersonal relationships is far more. Thus, it can be said that the scope of these positive outcomes for both the individual and the organization emphasize the importance of fostering positive interpersonal relationships in the workplace. As the necessity of a positive workplace relationship is evidenced through so many studies, it can be asserted that, it is a strong pillar for organizational effectiveness and the retention of robust positive interpersonal relationship is inevitable.

MEDIA, TECHNOLOGY AND INTERPERSONAL RELATIONSHIP

According to the late media critic and communication theorist Marshall McLuhan (1966), the channels of communication affect both the sending and the receiving of messages. The same words convey different messages depending on whether they are sent using face-to-face interaction, print, a cell phone, a video, or a podcast. It is now almost five decades since he predicted that the introduction of new technologies would transform our world into a mobile global village. His prophecy has come true. Technology makes it increasingly possible for us to watch and listen to, introduce ourselves to, and have continuing contact with individuals across the country and around the world without ever leaving our homes. Technology is altering our sense of self, our social norms, our views of reality, our images of success and failure, our happiness, our interpersonal options, and the communication rules we adhere to. Years ago, Apple's Steve Jobs observed that computers are really personal and should be renamed "inter-personal computers." Today we use them, tablets, or smartphones to log on to Facebook, LinkedIn, or Foursquare so we can bond with others. Now, we live our lives plus sometimes a "second life," enacting a fantasy or alternative life online. However, when we form a relationship online, we are likely to view through rose-tinted glasses and create high hope for it, expectations that might not be realized if we meet face-to-face. In fact, online partners feel greater intimacy with and attraction for one another than when they actually meet one another face-to-face. In addition to broadening the network of people, we communicate with, for those who experience communication apprehension when face-to-face with another person, technology makes it possible to connect without such fear. The claims we make about internet addiction are much like the claims people used to make about television being a plug-in drug. Whether it is the television or a computer, a machine is altering our consciousness and the nature of our interpersonal interactions.

Media Richness Theory (MRT)

Daft and Lengel (1984), and later Trevino (1990) developed the *Media richness theory* and it became very popular along with the diffusion of electronic communication media (e.g., email in 1990s). The theory suggests the effective use of a communication channel by matching the richness of a medium and the equivocality of task. Daft and Lengel (1984, 1986) paid attention to the significance of uncertainty and equivocality reduction in successful information processing in organizations. More specifically, uncertainty is the lack of information, which can be reduced by the quantity or amount of information. In contrast, equivocality refers to confusion or lack of understanding, which cannot be reduced by the amount of information but can be reduced by the quality or richness of information (Daft, Lengel, & Trevino, 1987). In a mediated situation using a communication technology such as email, uncertainty reduction would not be the problem because technology can carry a large amount of information to reduce uncertainty. Equivocality reduction, on the other hand, would be problematic primarily due to the lack of nonverbal cues inherent in mediated communication.

Media richness theory, thus, determines the "richness" of a medium based on availability of:

1. Immediate feedback
2. Multiple cues
3. Language variety
4. Personal focus.

Thus, for a high level of an equivocal task, such as an explanation of a complicate technical matter, face-to-face, the richest medium, would be most effective. Whereas for a low level of an equivocal task, such as giving numerical data requested, a lean medium (e.g., an unaddressed document) would be most effective. The most important premise from the authors, which is often overlooked by the audience, is that effective managers can select the most appropriate medium by successfully matching the richness of a medium to the level of equivocality of the task (Daft et al., 1987). When media richness theory is associated with interpersonal relationship, it has a base. A relationship might be damaged because of the selection of message from an inappropriate channel (Ledbetter, 2014).But the increase of channel preferences may create pressure to users on what is believed as a morally or socially correct way to transmit a message to another individual (Madianou & Miller, 2012). Possibly for these reasons, an interpersonal relationship is one of the most extended areas of research in media richness theory. For example, in Pettegrew and Day's (2015) study, 79% of participants reported that mobile devices have changed communication in interpersonal relationships. Reflecting the alteration, numerous studies have examined the role of communication in the development of friendships with media richness theory.

On the four criteria outlined in media richness theory, diffused communication media such as webcam, texting, instant messaging, and social media would be placed as leaner channels than face-to-face communication. Investigating the association between duration of interaction and happiness as the outcome over a variety of recent channels, Vlahovic, Roberts, and Dunbar's (2012) study still reported the significance of face-to-face communication among others. The result demonstrated that an increase in duration of interaction was a positive predictor of happiness only for face-to-face communication. It was found that for learner channels, such as texting, telephone, and email, duration of interaction had no relationship with happiness. However, Kwak (2012) argued that online media could be either lean or rich depending on the communicator's use of media. For example, voice chat was considered a rich channel by allowing immediate feedback, which was used for equivocal communication. In addition, communicator motive is involved in a selection of channels. For instance, an active motive for communication led to use a richer channel (e.g., voice chat), whereas passive motive drove to a leaner channel (e.g., text-based chat).

Recent advanced technology has been enriching "lean" channels that are used in relationship development. It has been reported by Sheer's studies (2010, 2011) that adolescents in Hong Kong liked using instant messaging (e.g., MSN, ICQ) with the attached audio and video features. In addition, unlike synchronous channels (e.g., face-to-face), adolescents liked the advanced tool of "presentation control" in the asynchronous channel. Also it was found that the use of the relatively rich channel could control the quality of communication, which, in turn, contributed to friendship quality (Sheer, 2010). Sheer (2011) also reported the significance of lean media catering to different types of relationships.

Zhou, Su, Zhou, & Zhang, (2016) suggested that the interactivity in text also contributed to the development and maintenance of friendships using more recent media such as text-based social media. Liu & Yang, (2016) stated the importance of mobile-phone based texting. Liu and Yang's study also revealed that the accessibility of mobile phones facilitated immediate communication in close friendships. In contrast, internet-dependent social networking sites, including instant messaging services on the sites, were used in less intimate relationships. Although text messaging is considered a lean channel by the criteria in media richness theory, texting from a mobile phone without Internet access was used more frequently in close relationships that would expect immediate responses (Liu & Yang, 2016). These studies reveal that users have become proficient at using the text-based lean channel taking advantage of the advanced technology in the context of interpersonal communication.

Media Synchronicity Theory (MST)

Media Synchronicity Theory (MST) has been given by Dennis, et al., (2008). The theory propounds that people respond to the capability of media and engage in synchronicity. It postulates that communication will be improved when media synchronicity and communication synchronicity coincides. Conveyance and convergence are the two pillars of communication as per this theory. Conveyance refers to the passage and processing of new information in such a way that the receiver of the message alter the mental framework of the context or the situation. Media enhances the conveyance part and its synchronicity function is low. Convergence on the other hand, requires faster information transformation and has decreased need for processing of information, i.e. exactly opposite of conveyance as a process. Convergence rests on synchronicity, but convergence is free from that. Better communication results, where there is a match between communication processes and capabilities of the media. (Dennis et al.,2008). In a study by Niinimaki et al., (2012), authors found that there is a role of media synchronicity with respect to the tools chosen for communication for Global Software Development projects. In another study authors found that media synchronicity model is a preliminary point for recognizing the media requirements towards effective planning of communication (Fox, Leicht & Messner, 2010). MST training has also been found to impact technical communication projects as well as media fit communication (Lam, 2016). Another study in terms if interpersonal relationships reveal that media synchronicity moderates the given relation that exists between task characteristics and implementation of Information and Communication Technology (ICT), also between ICT and knowledge formation (Ryoo & Koo, 2010). All these leads to the understanding that multiple media channels should be considered for various aspects of communication (Dennis et al. 2008).

For successful communication, it requires to involve oneself in both transmission as well as processing activities (Dennis et al., 2008).

Media Multiplexity Theory (MMT)

Media multiplexity theory (MMT) focuses on the core of how social networks robustly impact the media we choose to use, among the various media available for communication. Also it focuses on the incidences that individuals engage in multiple media types to communicate with one another. MMT (Haythornthwaite, 2005) provides a theoretical outline for examining interpersonal relationship across social media. The theory proposes that individuals in any interpersonal relationship do not communicate with their partners via only one media, they use multiple platforms to communicate, which has been referred to as multimodality in communication (Walther & Parks, 2002).This theory also posits that, the strength, bonding and interdependence in any interpersonal relationship has positive association with the number of media used to communicate, that is the basis of media multiplexity theory (Haythornthwaite, 2000).

New Workplace Culture and Media Richness

Media richness theory was born in an organizational setting and has continued to motivate new research within the perspective of organizations and managerial practices. Nevertheless, studies in this context have also shown inconsistent results. Braun et al., (2019) examined ideal managerial communication of employees. They compared it to the actual communication practices in the workplace. Although there is a trend towards more frequent computer-mediated communication than face-to-face communication in the workplace, employees may not perceive that the use of "lean" media leads to effective leadership communication. The results indeed reported that many employees expected the use of richer channels, such as face-to-face, communication and expected less use of lean channels, such as telephone/email, by their managers. Braun et al. (2019) also found a relationship between the utilization of richer channels by leaders and positive perceptions towards the leader's effectiveness and personality which eventually supported the Media richness theory. The subjective perception towards media richness has been directly tested in different studies. Armengol, Fernandez, Simo, and Sallan (2017) compared supervisor communicative behavior, such as informing, listening, and coordinating to peer behavior via email. This was done to examine social influence on an individual's perception towards the richness of email. But, their results were contradictory with Fulk's (1993) study and demonstrated that social influence on perceived media richness was noteworthy only from a manager but not from coworkers. Successful collaboration among team members is significant to achieve organizational goals. Such collaboration often takes place online today. Aritz, Walker, and Cardon (2018) investigated how the teams collaborated using multiple, media-based communication channels, such as email, Google Docs, Facebook, texting, and phone calls, thus proving the media multiplexity theory. They also examined a team's preference for certain channels and communicative tools. On the other hand, it should also be noted that the contribution of interactivity to media richness is not always positive. In the realm of recruiting, Badger, Kaminsky & Behrend (2014) examined the effectiveness of interactivity on online recruitment systems. A comparison between a traditional website (a lean medium) and an interactive site created in a virtual platform (a rich medium) was drawn in the study. It was discovered by the researchers that as compared to the richer, interactive site, job applicants could recall more factual information from the leaner, traditional website. Apers and Derous (2017) found that the use of a richer channel to present job applicant resumes, such as video rather than the traditional paper, masked their personalities, which challenged recruiters who often judged from the resumes in the first place. However, Saat & Selamat's (2014) study on communication for corporate social responsibility still showed that richer websites with animation and videos than lean websites produced effective communication. The inconsistent support for media richness theory was also apparent in a study on communication between suppliers and buyers of a new product. Similar to past studies that did not support the theory, Thomas (2013) found that the richest face-to-face communication and lean email exchanges had no difference in the level of knowledge exchange. However, this result might be influenced by the email strategies communicators used (e.g., speedy feedback, adaptable to circumstance, and language), especially when the participants were working closely together on a project. Furthermore, this study showed different advantages from the rich and lean media. More specifically, multiple cues available in face-to-face communication allow knowledge exchange among members easily, which is, in turn, viewed as effective for new product development. On the other hand, email can overcome time and space constraints reducing costs for face-to-face meetings in the process of knowledge exchange, which, in turn, makes product development more efficient. This finding would explain the recent use of multiple media among organizational members (Stephens, Barrett, & Mahometa, 2013) and among consumers (Maity, Dass, & Kumar, 2018). Maity et al. (2018) discovered media richness involved in perceived cost in information-seeking behavior, which affected media use by consumers. Their results indicated that the richer the channel, the lower the cost of information-seeking because richer channels could automatically carry a large volume of information about the product that helped consumers' decisions.

Thus, it is evident that the Media Richness theory has grown from its original premise of effective managerial communication to more inclusive to other aspects of communication, including interpersonal relationship, and organizational practices. Media richness theory has been vastly studied across the contexts, yet these studies have also shown discrepancies in the theory, particularly with more recent media.

ENHANCED INTERPERSONAL COMMUNICATION EFFICACY IN VIRTUAL REALITY

A particular collection of technological hardware is usually described by the media as *virtual reality*. People identify virtual reality with a collection of devices. It might include a computer capable of 3D real-time animation, a head-mounted display; data gloves equipped with one or more position trackers. Nevertheless, this focus on technology is disappointing to communication researchers and software developers. According to Steuer (1992), this approach cannot provide any understanding into the procedures or effects of using these systems, it cannot provide a conceptual framework from which to make regulatory choices and even cannot provide an appealing form, from which to develop media products. Bricken (1990) is of the view that the core of virtual reality is the comprehensive relationship between the participant and the virtual environment, where direct experience of the engrossed environment comprises communication. From this point of view, virtual reality can be considered as the principal frame of a general development of present communication interfaces such as telephone, television and computer. (Kay, 1984). Biocca & Delaney (1995) states that the chief feature of this progression is the full engagement of the sensorimotor channels of humans into a bright and worldwide communication experience.

Virtual reality has been defined as a communication technology or a medium by several researchers. Virtual environments have been described as "communication media" by Ellis (1991). However, Biocca & Levy (1995) is of the view that virtual Reality "is likely to emerge as the next dominant medium - if not the ultimate medium". But it would be ambiguous, however, to think of single-user virtual reality systems in this way. Schroeder (1996) states that the concept of a communications technology normally entails that two or more people are involved and that the importance is placed on the messages that pass between them. Thus it implies that the terms 'communication' and 'medium' should only be used in the context of multi-user Virtual Reality" Nevertheless, when virtual reality is a communications medium in a multi-user configuration, it can be evaluated, as Palmer (1995) points out, "as a medium of interpersonal communication in the same way all media have been evaluated" .Multi-user Virtual Reality can be considered as a specific type of Computer-Mediated-Communication (CMC).So if interpersonal communication is a process of negotiation– the only way to understand it is by analyzing the subjects involved in it in the environment in which it operates. According to Mantovani (1996b), the early 1990s saw changes in the paradigms used in studies of person-computer and person-computer-person interaction. The main outcome of this has been the realization that interaction can only be fully understood through detailed analysis of the social context in which it occurs (Mantovani, 1996).Thus enhanced communication efficacy in virtual reality has proved to be boon of technology in today's present day scenario.

DIGITALIZATION AT WORKPLACE AND CYBERLOAFING DYNAMICS

While discussing the various dynamics of a digitalized workplace, one of the major challenges that need discussion is cyberloafing. The term 'cyberloafing' refers to the use of the internet and other services provided to the employees by their workplace for non-work related purposes during the working office hours. The evolution of the internet and other technologies in the organizations has created opportunities for deviant behaviours (Jandaghi et al., 2015). Internet, smartphones, tablets, high end desktops all boost productivity and efficiency for work. However, it also gives rise to what we call 'Cyberloafing'.

The term Cyberloafing was introduced by Tony Cummins in 1995 with the rise of cyber sciences and the World Wide Web. However, the term grew its popularity when it was used by Lim (2002) in his paper of 'Organizational Behaviour Journal' (Jandaghi et al., 2015; Selwyn, 2008). The term cyberloafing is derived from two words: 'cyber' referring to computers or the internet and 'loafing' refers to the act of slack or avoiding work (MacMillian Dictionary, 2019). Thus, from the word itself, it can be understood that cyberloafing refers to the act of avoiding work with the means of computer or using the internet. According to Lim, Teo & Loo (2002), cyberloafing is "any voluntary act of employees using their companies' internet access during office hours to surf non-work related Web sites for non-work purposes, and access (including receiving and sending non-work related email". Cyberloafing is a type of workplace deviant behaviour (Lim 2002; Lim &Teo 2005; Ugrin and Pearson 2013; Hu & Hsu, 2019). Cyberloafing is a type of counterproductive behaviour (Chen & Lim, 2009). It is so because cyberloafing is an unproductive use of time and organizational resources which detract employees from completing their actual work and meeting work demands (Chen & Lim, 2009).

Lim (2002) stated two categorizations of deviant behaviour of cyberloafing: Slacking in the web and emailing unrelated work messages. However, over the years, several other forms of such behaviour were added such as: internet incoming generation (using work internet for additional income), downloading nonbusiness information, downloading music, using chat rooms, playing games and so on (Jandaghi et al., 2015). Blanchard &Henel (2008), distinguished between minor cyberloafing behaviours (e.g., studying CNN news) and serious cyberloafing behaviours (e.g., visiting adult websites). A survey conducted by Websense.com (www.websense.com) in 2006 found that the average time an American employee spends on cyberloafing activities is about 24% of his working hours. This puts the average time spent on work unrelated activities at around 10 hours per week (Chen & Lim, 2009). From the anecdotal evidence, Fox in 2007 suggested that there are some employees who spend around 5-6 hours per day surfing the internet at work. In another research on internet use at workplace by Shrivastava, Sharma & Marimuthu (2017) found that 42% of 250 participants claimed that they have postponed their work due to internet activities. Thus, while technological innovations bring positive changes in the business, social, organizational and personal aspects, they also increase deviational activities. Such activities have detrimental effects on an organization's finances. Anecdotal records show that employees from United Kingdom who spent around 40% of their working time in engaging cyberloafing activities (Amble, 2004) cost their business organizations about £154 million a year (Hallett, 2002). Freimark in 2012 states that 'The American Management Association (2008)' found that 28% of organizations fired an employee for cyberloafing.

Cyberloafing can prove to be destructive in nature (in terms of employee productivity and organizational revenue); however it may be constructive as well if it helps the employees and the organization (Ozler et al., 2012). While cyberloafing is typically a negative form of behaviour, engaging in it for brief periods of time may have positive effects such as relief from boredom, preventing stress overload and fatigue, refreshing the mind, increase in well-being and overall happier employees (Vitak et al., 2011; Ozler&Polat, 2012; Dolan, 2018). While it is true that internet may lead to distractions in work, researches show that internet also provides much diversion at workplace which can lead to "creativity, flexibility and foster a learning environment" (Blanchard & Henle, 2008). Studies suggest that employees engage in cyberloafing when they are being 'unfairly treated' by the organizations (Mastrangelo et al., 2006). In this sense, cyberloafing is a retaliation type of behaviour of employees who rebel against 'injustice'. Studies indicate that justice perceptions are strongly related to cyberloafing (Venkatraman, 2008). Another group of studies indicate that low work demands make employees bored or high work demands make employees stressed and this makes them likely to use cyberloafing as 'an office toy' to escape from such situations (Anandarajan & Simmers, 2005). This lets employees take a break and allow them to 'zone out' then re-focus their attention back to work. In this sense, cyberloafing has a beneficial side (Lim & Chen, 2012). Furthermore, Freimark (2012) found that employees who experience a heightened role conflict in the workplace are more likely to engage in cyberloafing activities. Personal factor as a determinant of cyberloafing can also not be ignored; it has been found that personality traits are linked with cyberloafing (Jia et al., 2013). Wyatt & Philips (2005) found a positive relation between extraversion and cyberloafing. Studies indicate a positive relationship between cyberloafing and external locus of control of an employee; it is believed that employees who cyberloaf, believe that getting caught are 'outside of their control and is up to chance' (Freimark, 2012; Blanchard &Henle, 2008). When engage in cyberloafing, employees engage in chats with another, through Whatsapp, snapchat, instant messages, facebook, so on and so forth. Office colleagues exchange pleasantries through those internet platforms, rather than sitting over a cup of coffee in an office canteen or cafeteria.

DIGITALIZATION AT WORKPLACE AND PHUBBING: EFFECTS ON SOCIAL INTERACTION

Lending from the usage of the portmanteau of the words "phone" and "snubbing" by Haigh (2012), and originally coined in a campaign by the Macquarie Dictionary to characterize a mounting challenge of smartphone misuse by smartphone users in social situations (Pathak, 2013), phubbing can be described as the act of snubbing another person in a social situation by paying attention to his phone and not talking to the person directly. Because of the progression of technology, new and innovative technologies give way to virtual communication devices like tablets, mobiles laptops, and smartphones; people are working in the world of bring-your-own-device (BYOD); due to this, information and communication technologies (ICT) have become indispensible in our lives (Oberst, Wegmann, Stodt, Brand and Chamarro, 2017). This information technology, excessive use of internet through various kinds of devices at the workplace has impacted human relations at work. The impact of that, as seen through the occurrence of phubbing behaviour at workplace is considered as one of the hazards of digitalized work environment. Phubbing impacts social interaction.

In one study that extensively investigated the social concerns of "phubbing", the authors found that increased phubbing significantly and negatively impacted individual's perception about the quality of communication and satisfaction derived from the relationship (Chotpitayasunondh, & Douglas (2018). In another study it was found that men perceive phubbing as negative more than women do. It was also found that the nature of adult romantic attachment influences the extent to which partners do engage in phubbing (Kryukova & Ekimchik, 2019). In a study by Davey et al. (2018), it has been reported that phubbing prevalence was 49.3%, of 400 college youths studied. In his study Karadağ et al. (2015) saw that that using smartphones leads to phubbing behaviour among individuals. Again with the advent and advancement of digital workplace, the feelings of loneliness has increased among people;, whatever interactions they have with others occur through internet, this is identified as another contributor to phubbing, as Karadağ et al., (2015) also adds that loneliness among individuals leads to phubbing. Another phenomenon, FoMo (fear of missing out) keeps individuals more engaged to their smart devices and that they eventually engage in phubbing (Chotpitayasunondh& Douglas, 2016;

Elhai et al., 2016). Williams, (2001) asserted that not only needs get threatened and emotions get affected by phubbing, but phubbing might also impact the functioning of interpersonal relationships. Being phubbed at workplace, leads to a negative affect and in their study Levenson & Gottman, (1983) posited that negative affect does not lead to development of close relationships and having satisfaction from relationships. The Reciprocated Social Exchange (RSE) (Newman, Miao, & Hooke, 2013) outlines that posits that employees perceive their association with their managers greater than just a "standard economic contract" ((Dirks & Ferrin, 2002), to which trust is central. For a healthy relationship between the boss and sub-ordinate, there has to be trust, which in turn impacts job performance. According to Research by Nakamura (2015) if a person is found to see his mobile phone while talking to another, it undermines emotional connection. In a study, Robert, & David (2017), found that using a mobile phone in the workplace can demoralize others and impact an employee's success negatively. Employees having the feeling of being unattended to is detrimental to job engagement. The same study by Robert & David (2017) also adds that mobile phone use by managers or bosses in the company of their subordinates negatively impacts employee engagement. Thus, in the realm of changed employee relations, in a digitalized environment, the evidences of some cons are invariably observed. Though employees can connect to one another at ease and with precision, it is of course true, that behaviour like phubbing is an undesirable outcome of workplace digitalization.

FUTURE IMPLICATIONS

Being an integrative attempt to explore the dimensions of workplace interpersonal relations in the changed era of Industry 4.0, the present paper implies that technology is a boon as well as a hazard to workplace. But at this juncture we need to accentuate the strengths of technology and minimize the weaknesses. The findings of the study have managerial as well as practical implications and message for future. Interpersonal relationship in an indispensable dimension of any organization. Increased attention needs to be paid to the dynamics of healthy interpersonal relationships and workplace and also reducing undesirable effects like cyberloafing and phubbing. Too much digitalization should not leave communication patterns overly mechanical. Emphasis must be laid by organizations on interpersonal relations by having a culture of humour at workplace, inculcating a friendly ambience, being empathetic, having positive attitude and overall emphasize on teamwork. At any workplace, enthusiastically working on interpersonal relationship dimensions can lead to an immense enhancement to career development and having a satisfied workplace. At any workplace, it is the responsibility of both managers and employees to concentrate on developing hard and soft skills, besides, maintain high level of employee relations towards a positive organizational climate. Healthy employee relations would futuristically foster mutual respect and concern for colleagues. Healthy employee relations also foster happiness of coworkers and customers enhances their trust and confidence.

CONCLUSION

The present chapter has contributed to an overall understanding of how the new work culture has emerged with the advent of digitalized workplace. It has highlighted the major tenets of a digitalized work environment and has offered a body of literature on how technology, has changed workplace culture and employee relations. To be very specific, it has tried to bring into picture how internet and internet run devices impede with workplace communication. Furthermore, the chapter has discussed the relevant task–technology fit perspective at work; it has touched upon the model of interpersonal relationship at work, and shown how media richness theory leads to choice of communication medium among employees and how media multiplexity and media synchronicity theory applies to workplace setting. Striding through the nature of new workplace culture, the chapter has drawn upon how technology leads to enhanced communication efficacy in virtual reality, indicating the boon of technology. It has also posited that this new digitalized workplace has certain undesirable outcomes as well, like cyberloafing and phubbing. Both these phenomena result in negative impact on workplace social interaction. In a nutshell, the chapter has integrated the boons and hazards of workplace relations in a digitalized environment.

REFERENCES

Alkhalifah, A., & D'Ambra, J. (2011). Applying task-technology fit to the adoption of identity management systems. *Proceedings of the 22nd Australasian Conference on Information Systems*.

Allen, T. D., Eby, L. T., Poteet, M. L., Lima, L., & Lentz, E. (2004). Mentoring benefits: A meta-analysis. *The Journal of Applied Psychology*, *89*, 127–136. doi:10.1037/0021-9010.89.1.127 PMID:14769125

Alvesson, M., & Sveningsson, S. (2003). Managers doing leadership: The extra-ordinarization of the mundane. *Human Relations*, *56*(12), 1435–1459. doi:10.1177/00187267035612001

Amble, B. (2004). *Does cyberloafing undermine productivity?* Management-Issues Ltd. Retrieved from: http://www.managementissues.com /2006/8/24/research/does cyberloafing-undermining-productivity. asp

Anandarajan, M., Simmers, C. A., & D'Ovidio, R. (2011). Exploring the underlying structure of personal web usage in the workplace. *Cyberpsychology, Behavior, and Social Networking*, *14*(10), 577–583. doi:10.1089/cyber.2010.0136 PMID:21728817

Apers, C., & Derous, E. (2017). Are they accurate? Recruiters' personality judgments in paper versus video resumes. *Computers in Human Behavior*, *73*, 9–19. doi:10.1016/j.chb.2017.02.063

Armengol, X., Fernandez, V., Simo, P., & Sallan, J. M. (2017). An examination of the effects of self-regulatory focus on the perception of the media richness: The case of E-mail. *International Journal of Business Communication*, *54*(4), 394–407. doi:10.1177/2329488415572780

Badger, J. M., Kaminsky, S. E., & Behrend, T. S. (2014). Media richness and information acquisition in internet recruitment. *Journal of Managerial Psychology*, *29*(7), 866–883. doi:10.1108/JMP-05-2012-0155

Barley, S. R., & Bechky, B. A. (2017). From the editor: The changing nature of work: Careers, identities, and work lives in the 21st century. Academy of Management Discoveries, 3(2), 111-115.

Baumeister, R. M., & Leary, M. R. (1995). The need to belong: Desire for interpersonal attachments as a fundamental human motivation. *Psychological Bulletin*, *117*(3), 497–529. doi:10.1037/0033-2909.117.3.497 PMID:7777651

BBC. (2019, June 26). *Robots 'to replace up to 20 million factory jobs' by 2030*. Retrieved from: https://www.bbc.com/news/business-48760799

Berman, A., & Dorrier, J. (2016). Technology feels like it's accelerating—because it actually is. *Singularity Hub*. Retrieved from: https://singularityhub.com/2016/03/22/technology-feels-like-its-accelerating-because-it-actually-is

Berman, E. M., West, J. P., & Richter, M. N. Jr. (2002). Workplace relations: Friendship patterns and consequences (according to managers). *Public Administration Review*, *62*(2), 217–230. doi:10.1111/0033-3352.00172

Biocca, F., & Delaney, B. (1995). Immersive virtual reality technology. In F. Biocca & M. R. Levy (Eds.), *Communication in the age of virtual reality* (pp. 57–124). Lawrence Erlbaum Associates.

Biocca, F., & Levy, M. R. (1995). Virtual reality as a communication system. In F. Biocca & M. R. Levy (Eds.), *Communication in the age of virtual reality* (pp. 15–31). Lawrence Erlbaum Associates.

Blanchard, A. L., & Henle, C. A. (2008). Correlates of different forms of cyberloafing: The role of norms and external locus of control. *Computers in Human Behavior*, *24*(3), 1067–1084. doi:10.1016/j.chb.2007.03.008

Bowling, N. A., & Beehr, T. A. (2006). Workplace harassment from the victim's perspective: A theoretical model and meta-analysis. *The Journal of Applied Psychology*, *91*(5), 998–1012. doi:10.1037/0021-9010.91.5.998 PMID:16953764

Braun, S., Hernandez Bark, A., Kirchner, A., Stegmann, S., & van Dick, R. (2019). Emails from the boss—Curse or blessing? Relations between communication channels, leader evaluation, and employees' attitudes. *International Journal of Business Communication*, *56*(1), 50–81. doi:10.1177/2329488415597516

Bricken, W. (1990). *Virtual reality: Directions of growth* (HITL Technical Report R90-1). Seattle, WA: University of Washington.

Brynjolfsson, E., & McAfee, A. (2014). *The second machine age. Work, progress, and prosperity in a time of brilliant technologies.* W.W. Norton.

Chakraborty, T., & Ganguly, M. (2019). Crafting Engaged Employees Through Positive Work Environment: Perspectives of Employee Engagement. In Management Techniques for Employee Engagement in Contemporary Organizations (pp. 180-198). IGI Global.

Chotpitayasunondh, V., & Douglas, K. M. (2016). How "phubbing" becomes the norm: The antecedents and consequences of snubbing via smartphone. *Computers in Human Behavior*, *63*, 9–18. doi:10.1016/j.chb.2016.05.018

Chotpitayasunondh, V., & Douglas, K. M. (2018). The effects of "phubbing" on social interaction. *Journal of Applied Social Psychology*, *48*(6), 304–316. doi:10.1111/jasp.12506

Cohen, S., & Wills, T. A. (1985). Stress, social support, and the buffering hypothesis. *Psychological Bulletin*, *98*(2), 310–357. doi:10.1037/0033-2909.98.2.310 PMID:3901065

Cortina, L. M., & Magley, V. J. (2003). Raising voice, risking retaliation: Events following interpersonal mistreatment in the workplace. *Journal of Occupational Health Psychology*, *8*(4), 247–265. doi:10.1037/1076-8998.8.4.247 PMID:14570522

D'Ambra, J., Wilson, C. S., & Akter, S. (2013). Application of the task-technology fit model to structure and evaluate the adoption of E-books by A cademics. *Journal of the American Society for Information Science and Technology*, *64*(1), 48–64. doi:10.1002/asi.22757

Daft, R., & Lengel, R. (1984). Information richness: A new approach to managerial behavior and organization design. In B. M. Staw & L. L. Cummings (Eds.), *Research in organizational behavior* (Vol. 6, pp. 191–233). JAI Press.

Daft, R. L., & Lengel, R. H. (1986). Organizational information requirements, media richness, and structural design. *Management Science*, *32*(5), 554–571. doi:10.1287/mnsc.32.5.554

Daft, R. L., Lengel, R. H., & Trevino, L. K. (1987). Message equivocality, media selection and manager performance: Implications for information systems. *Management Information Systems Quarterly*, *11*(3), 355–366. doi:10.2307/248682

Davey, S., Davey, A., Raghav, S. K., Singh, J. V., Singh, N., Blachnio, A., & Przepiórkaa, A. (2018). Predictors and consequences of "Phubbing" among adolescents and youth in India: An impact evaluation study. *Journal of Family & Community Medicine*, *25*(1), 35. doi:10.4103/jfcm.JFCM_71_17 PMID:29386960

DeLone, W.H., & McLean, E.R. (1992). Information Systems Success: The Guest for the Dependent Variable. *Infonvation Systems Research, 3*(1), 60-95.

Dennis, A. R., Fuller, R. M., & Valacich, J. S. (2008). Media, tasks, and communication processes: A theory of media synchronicity. *Management Information Systems Quarterly*, *32*(3), 575–600. doi:10.2307/25148857

Dictionary, B. (n.d.). *Information Technology (IT).* Retrieved from: http://www.businessdictionary.com/definition/information-technology-IT.html

Dolan, E. W. (2018, May 19). *Study finds cyberloafing can help employees cope with workplace boredom.* Retrieved from: https://www.psypost.org/2018/05/study-finds-cyberloafing-can-help-employees-cope-workplace-boredom-51278

Dreher, G. F., & Ash, R. A. (1990). A comparative study of mentoring among men and women in managerial, professional, and technical positions. *The Journal of Applied Psychology*, *75*(5), 539–546. doi:10.1037/0021-9010.75.5.539

Ellis, S. R. (1991). Nature and origins of virtual environments: A bibliographical essay. *Computing Systems in Engineering*, *2*(4), 321–347. doi:10.1016/0956-0521(91)90001-L

Feeley, T. H., Hwang, J., & Barnett, G. A. (2008). Predicting employee turnover from friendship networks. *Journal of Applied Communication Research*, *36*(1), 56–73. doi:10.1080/00909880701799790

Fox, A. (2007). Caught in the Web: Internet surfing takes on addictive qualities for some employees who may be hiding their abuse at work-at a cost to both themselves and their employers. *HRMagazine*, *52*(12), 34.

Fox, S., Leicht, R. M., & Messner, J. I. (2010). Assessing the relevance of media synchronicity theory to the use of communication media in the AECO industry. *Journal of Architectural Engineering*, *16*(2), 54–62. doi:10.1061/(ASCE)AE.1943-5568.0000012

Freimark, M. (2012). *The role of organizational citizenship behavior and organizational justice on intention to cyberloaf through a general deterrence theory lens*. Southern Illinois University at Carbondale.

Fulk, J. (1993). Social construction of communication technology. *Academy of Management Journal*, *36*, 921–951.

Gallup, Inc. (2017). *State of the American Workplace*. Retrieved from https://news.gallup.com/reports/199961/7.aspx

Gebauer, J., Shaw, M. J., & Gribbins, M. L. (2010). Task-technology fit for mobile information systems. *Journal of Information Technology*, *25*(3), 259–272. doi:10.1057/jit.2010.10

Gephart, R. P. Jr. (2002). Introduction to the brave new workplace: Organizational behavior in the electronic age. *Journal of Organizational Behavior: The International Journal of Industrial. Occupational and Organizational Psychology and Behavior*, *23*(4), 327–344. doi:10.1002/job.143

Goodhue, D. L., & Thompson, R. L. (1995). Task-technology fit and individual performance. *Management Information Systems Quarterly*, *19*(2), 213–236. doi:10.2307/249689

HaighA. (n.d.). *Stop phubbing*. Retrieved from http://stopphubbing.com

Hallett, T. (2002). *Christmas cyberloafing cost UK businesses£ 154 million*. Academic Press.

Haythornthwaite, C. (2000). Online personal networks: Size, composition and media use among distance learners. *New Media & Society*, *2*(2), 195–226. doi:10.1177/14614440022225779

Heaphy, E. D., & Dutton, J. E. (2008). Positive social interactions and the human body at work: Linking organizations and physiology. *Academy of Management Review*, *33*(1), 137–162. doi:10.5465/amr.2008.27749365

Henle, C. A., & Blanchard, A. L. (2008). The interaction of work stressors and organizational sanctions on cyberloafing. *Journal of Managerial Issues*, 383–400.

Herrera, F. (n.d.). *The digital workplace: Think, share, do. Transform your employee experience*. Deloitte. Retrieved from: https://www2.deloitte.com/content/dam/Deloitte/mx/Documents/human-capital/The_digital_workplace.pdf

Hoehle, H., & Huff, S. (2012). Advancing task-technology fit theory: a formative measurement approach to determining task-channel fit for electronic banking channels. *Information Systems Foundations: Theory Building in Information Systems*, 133-170.

Hunt, D. M., & Michael, C. (1983). Mentorship: A career training and development tool. *Academy of Management Review*, *8*(3), 475–485. doi:10.5465/amr.1983.4284603

Irick, M. L. (2008). Task-technology fit and information systems effectiveness. *Journal of Knowledge Management Practice*, *9*(3), 1–5.

Jandaghi, G., & Alvani, S. M., ZareiMatin, H., & FakheriKozekanan, S. (2015). Cyberloafing management in organizations. *Iranian Journal of Management Studies*, *8*(3), 335–349.

Jia, H., Jia, R., & Karau, S. (2013). Cyberloafing and personality: The impact of the Big Five traits and workplace situational factors. *Journal of Leadership & Organizational Studies*, *20*(3), 358–365. doi:10.1177/1548051813488208

Joyce, W. F., McGee, V. E., & Slocum, J. W. Jr. (1997). Designing lateral organizations: An analysis of the benefits, costs, and enablers of nonhierarchical organizational forms. *Decision Sciences*, *28*(1), 1–25. doi:10.1111/j.1540-5915.1997.tb01300.x

Junglas, I., Abraham, C., & Watson, R. T. (2008). Task-technology fit for mobile locatable information systems. *Decision Support Systems*, *45*(4), 1046–1057. doi:10.1016/j.dss.2008.02.007

Karadağ, E., Tosuntaş, Ş. B., Erzen, E., Duru, P., Bostan, N., Şahin, B. M., & Babadağ, B. (2015). Determinants of phubbing, which is the sum of many virtual addictions: A structural equation model. *Journal of Behavioral Addictions*, *4*(2), 60–74. doi:10.1556/2006.4.2015.005 PMID:26014669

Kay, A. (1984). Computer software. Scientific American, 251(3), 52-59. Kay, A. (1990). User interface: A personal view. In B. Laurel (Ed.), *The art of human computer interface design* (pp. 191–207). Addison-Wesley.

Koay, K. Y., & Soh, P. C. H. (2018, August). Does Cyberloafing Really Harm Employees' Work Performance?: An Overview. In *International Conference on Management Science and Engineering Management* (pp. 901-912). Springer.

Kostova, T., & Roth, K. (2003). Social capital in multinational corporations and a micro-macro model of its formation. *Academy of Management Review, 29*(2), 297–317. doi:10.5465/amr.2003.9416356

Kramer, R. M. (1991). Intergroup relations and organizational dilemmas: The role of categorization processes. In L. L. Cummings & B. M. Staw (Eds.), *Research in Organizational Behavior* (Vol. 13, pp. 191–228). JAI Press.

Kryukova, T. L., & Ekimchik, O. A. (2019). Phubbing as a Possible Threat to Close Relationships' Welfare. *Counseling Psychology and Psychotherapy, 27*(3), 61–76. doi:10.17759/cpp.2019270305

Kurzweil, R. (2004). The law of accelerating returns. In *Alan Turing: Life and legacy of a great thinker* (pp. 381–416). Springer. doi:10.1007/978-3-662-05642-4_16

Kwak, H. (2012). Self-disclosure in online media: An active audience perspective. *International Journal of Advertising, 31*(3), 485–510. doi:10.2501/IJA-31-3-485-510

Lam, C. (2016). Improving technical communication group projects: An experimental study of media synchronicity theory training on communication outcomes. *Journal of Business and Technical Communication, 30*(1), 85–112. doi:10.1177/1050651915602293

Ledbetter, A. M. (2014). The past and future of technology in interpersonal communication theory and research. *Communication Studies, 65*(4), 456–459. doi :10.1080/10510974.2014.927298

Liden, R. C., Wayne, S. J., & Sparrowe, R. T. (2000). An examination of the mediating role of psychological empowerment on the relations between the job, interpersonal relationships, and work outcomes. *The Journal of Applied Psychology, 85*(3), 407–416. doi:10.1037/0021-9010.85.3.407 PMID:10900815

Lim, V. K. (2002). The IT way of loafing on the job: Cyberloafing, neutralizing and organizational justice. *Journal of Organizational Behavior: The International Journal of Industrial, Occupational and Organizational Psychology and Behavior, 23*(5), 675-694.

Lim, V. K., & Chen, D. J. (2012). Cyberloafing at the workplace: Gain or drain on work? *Behaviour & Information Technology, 31*(4), 343–353. doi:10.1080/01449290903353054

Lim, V. K., & Teo, T. S. (2005). Prevalence, perceived seriousness, justification and regulation of cyberloafing in Singapore: An exploratory study. *Information & Management, 42*(8), 1081–1093. doi:10.1016/j.im.2004.12.002

Lim, V. K., Teo, T. S., & Loo, G. L. (2002). How do I loaf here? Let me count the ways. *Communications of the ACM, 45*(1), 66–70. doi:10.1145/502269.502300

Lim, V. K. G., & Chen, D. J. Q. (2009). Impact of cyberloafing on affect, work depletion, facilitation and engagement. In *Conference Paper SIOP* (*Vol. 2009*, pp. 1-20). Academic Press.

Liu, D., & Yang, C. (2016). Media niche of electronic communication channels in friendship: A meta-analysis. *Journal of Computer-Mediated Communication, 21*(6), 451–466. doi:10.1111/jcc4.12175

MacMillian Dictionary. (2013, May 21). *Cyberloafing*. Retrieved from: https://www.macmillandictionary.com/buzzword/entries/cyberloafing.html

Madianou, M., & Miller, M. (2012). Polymedia: Towards a new theory of digital media in interpersonal communication. *International Journal of Cultural Studies, 16*(2), 169–187. doi:10.1177/1367877912452486

Mähler, V., & Westergren, U. H. (2018, September). Working with IoT–A Case Study Detailing Workplace Digitalization ThroughIoT System Adoption. In *IFIP International Internet of Things Conference* (pp. 178-193). Springer.

Mainiero, L. A. (1989). *Office romance: Love, power, and sex in the workplace.* Rawson Associates.

Maity, M., Dass, M., & Kumar, P. (2018). The impact of media richness on consumer information search and choice. *Journal of Business Research, 87*, 36–45. doi:10.1016/j.jbusres.2018.02.003

Mantovani, G. (1996b). Social context in HCI: A new framework for mental models, cooperation and communication. *Cognitive Science, 20*(2), 237–296. doi:10.120715516709cog2002_3

Marsh, E. (2019, January 10). *Is your organisation's digital workplace causing technostress?* Retrieved from: https://www.linkedin.com/pulse/your-organisations-digital-workplace-causing-elizabeth-marsh

Mastrangelo, P. M., Everton, W., & Jolton, J. A. (2006). Personal use of work computers: Distraction versus destruction. *Cyberpsychology & Behavior, 9*(6), 730–741. doi:10.1089/cpb.2006.9.730 PMID:17201599

Mayo, E. (1933). *The Human Problems of an Industrial Civilization*. Macmillan.

McGregor, R. (2018, April 10). *The pros and cons of a digitized work culture*. Retrieved from: https://www.thedigitalenterprise.com/articles/hr/the-pros-and-cons-of-a-digitized-work-culture

McLuhan, H. M. (1966). Marshall McLuhan. *Information Theory*, 234.

Muro, M., Liu, S., Whiton, J., &Kulkarni, S. (2017). *Digitalization and the American workforce*. Academic Press.

Naidoo, V. (2018). Impact of Digitization on Learning and Opportunities in the Workplace. In *Radical Reorganization of Existing Work Structures Through Digitalization* (pp. 156–171). IGI Global. doi:10.4018/978-1-5225-3191-3.ch009

Niinimäki, T., Piri, A., Lassenius, C., & Paasivaara, M. (2012). Reflecting the choice and usage of communication tools in global software development projects with media synchronicity theory. *Journal of Software: Evolution and Process*, *24*(6), 677–692.

Oberst, U., Wegmann, E., Stodt, B., Brand, M., & Chamarro, A. (2017). Negative consequences from heavy social networking in adolescents: The mediating role of fear of missing out. *Journal of Adolescence*, *55*, 51–60. doi:10.1016/j.adolescence.2016.12.008 PMID:28033503

Ozler, D. E., &Polat, G. (2012). Cyberloafing phenomenon in organizations: Determinants and impacts. *International Journal of eBusiness and eGovernment Studies, 4*(2), 1-15.

Pathak, S. (2013, October 7). *McCann Melbourne made up a word to sell a print dictionary: New campaign for Macquarie birthed 'phubbing'*. Retrieved from https://adage.com/article/news/mccann-melbourne-made-a-word-sell-a-dictionary/244595/

Pettegrew, L. S., & Day, C. (2015). Smart phones and mediated relationships: The changing face of relational communication. *The Review of Communication, 15*(2), 122–139. doi:10.1080/15358593.2015.1044018

Pot, F. D. (2017). Workplace innovation and wellbeing at work. In *Workplace Innovation* (pp. 95–110). Springer. doi:10.1007/978-3-319-56333-6_7

Prasad, A. (2018, October 8). *10 ways technology has reshaped the modern workplace*. Retrieved from: https://www.quickfms.com/blog/6-ways-technology-has-reshaped-the-workplace

Riach, K., & Wilson, F. (2007). Don't screw the crew: Exploring the rules of engagement in organizational romance. *British Journal of Management, 18*(1), 79–92. doi:10.1111/j.1467-8551.2006.00503.x

Rintala, N., & Suolanen, S. (2005). The implications of digitalization for job descriptions, competencies and the quality of working life. *Nordicom Review, 26*(2), 53–67. doi:10.1515/nor-2017-0258 PMID:17290637

Riordan, C. M., & Griffeth, R. W. (1995). The opportunity for friendship in the workplace: An underexplored construct. *Journal of Business and Psychology, 10*(2), 141–154. doi:10.1007/BF02249575

Roberts, J. A., & David, M. E. (2017). Put down your phone and listen to me: How boss phubbing undermines the psychological conditions necessary for employee engagement. *Computers in Human Behavior, 75*, 206–217. doi:10.1016/j.chb.2017.05.021

Roethlisberger, F.J., & Dickson, W. (1939). Management and the Worker. Harvard University Press.

Ryoo, S. Y., & Koo, C. (2010). The moderating effect of media synchronicity in the communication media use and knowledge creation. *Asia Pacific Journal of Information Systems, 20*(2), 103-124.

Saat, R. M., & Selamat, M. H. (2014). An examination of consumer's attitude towards corporate social responsibility (CSR) web communication using media richness theory. *Procedia: Social and Behavioral Sciences, 155*(C), 392–397. doi:10.1016/j.sbspro.2014.10.311

Safeer, R., & Allen, J. (2019). Defining a Culture of Health in the Workplace. *Journal of Occupational and Environmental Medicine, 61*(11), 863–867. doi:10.1097/JOM.0000000000001684 PMID:31348414

Schroeder, R. (1996). *Possible worlds: The social dynamic of virtual reality technology*. Boulder, CO: Westview Press.

Sheer, V. C. (2010). Hong Kong adolescents' use of MSN vs. ICQ for developing friendships online: Considering media richness and presentational control. *Chinese Journal of Communication, 3*(2), 223–240. doi:10.1080/17544751003740409

Sheer, V. C. (2011). Teenagers' use of MSN features, discussion topics, and online friendship development: The impact of media richness and communication control. *Communication Quarterly, 59*(1), 82–103. doi:10.1080/01463373.2010.525702

Shrivastava, A., Sharma, M. K., & Marimuthu, P. (2016). Internet use at workplaces and its effects on working style in indian context: An exploration. *Indian Journal of Occupational and Environmental Medicine*, *20*(2), 88. doi:10.4103/0019-5278.197531 PMID:28194082

Smith, D. C. (1977). *Pygmalion. A computer program to model and stimulate creative thought*. BirkhaüserVerlag.

Smollan, R. K., & Sayers, J. G. (2009). Organizational culture, change and emotions: A qualitative study. *Journal of Change Management*, *9*(4), 435–457. doi:10.1080/14697010903360632

Stephens, K., Barrett, A. K., & Mahometa, M. J. (2013). Organizational communication in emergencies: Using multiple channels and sources to combat noise and capture attention. *Human Communication Research*, *39*(2), 230–251. doi:10.1111/hcre.12002

Steuer, J. S. (1992). Defining virtual reality: Dimensions determining telepresence. *Journal of Communication*, *42*(4), 73–93. doi:10.1111/j.1460-2466.1992.tb00812.x

Thomas, E. (2013). Supplier integration in new product development: Computer mediated communication, knowledge exchange and buyer performance. *Industrial Marketing Management*, *42*(6), 890–899. doi:10.1016/j.indmarman.2013.05.018

Timonen, H., & Vuori, J. (2018, January). Visibility of Work: How Digitalization Changes the Workplace. *Proceedings of the 51st Hawaii International Conference on System Sciences*. 10.24251/HICSS.2018.634

Ugrin, J. C., & Pearson, J. M. (2013). The effects of sanctions and stigmas on cyberloafing. *Computers in Human Behavior*, *29*(3), 812–820. doi:10.1016/j.chb.2012.11.005

Venkatraman, S. M. K., Cheung, C., Lee, Z. W. D., Davis, F., & Venkatesh, V. (2018). The "Darth" side of technology use: An inductively derived typology of cyberdeviance. *Journal of Management Information Systems*, *35*(4), 1060–1091. doi:10.1080/07421222.2018.1523531

Vitak, J., Crouse, J., & LaRose, R. (2011). Personal Internet use at work: Understanding cyberslacking. *Computers in Human Behavior*, *27*(5), 1751–1759. doi:10.1016/j.chb.2011.03.002

Vlahovic, T., Roberts, S., & Dunbar, R. (2012). Effects of duration and laughter on subjective happiness within different modes of communication. *Journal of Computer-Mediated Communication*, *17*(4), 436–450. doi:10.1111/j.1083-6101.2012.01584.x

Walther, J. B., & Parks, M. R. (2002). Cues filtered out, cues filtered in Computers-mediated communications add relationships. In Handbook of interpersonal communication. Academic Press.

Weedmark, D. (2019, May 16). *What are some positive & negative technology training impacts on an employee?* Retrieved from: https://smallbusiness.chron.com/positive-negative-technology-training-impacts-employee-37082.html

Williams, K. D. (2001). *Ostracism: The power of silence*. Guilford Press.

Williams, K. D. (2001). *Ostracism: The power of silence*. The Guilford Press.

Winstead, B. A., Derlega, V. J., Montgomery, M. J., & Pilkington, C. (1995). The quality of friendships at work and job satisfaction. *Journal of Social and Personal Relationships*, *12*(2), 199–215. doi:10.1177/0265407595122003

Wyatt, K., & Phillips, J. G. (2005). Internet Use and Misuse in the Workplace. *Proceedings of the 17th Australian Conference on Computer-Human Interaction*.

Zhou, Z., Su, C., Zhou, N., & Zhang, N. (2016). Becoming friends in online brand communities: Evidence from China. *Journal of Computer-Mediated Communication*, *21*(1), 69–86. doi:10.1111/jcc4.12147

Chapter 11
The Change in Nature of an Organization and Its Work

Ashwini Yogendra Sonawane
Vishwakarma University, India

ABSTRACT

It's obvious. Deviations are entirely around us. As the situation is promptly fluctuating, in today's sphere of globalization the structure, pattern, and process of work are changing drastically, and working for an organization is likely to be very different due to competitive pressures and technological breakthroughs. Now the organizational work is more focused on technological competence, workforce diversity, teamwork, leadership, social-based skills, strategic planning, cross-culture training, and effective communication, which holds the keys to the growth of the organization. As the nature of the work environment continues to change, new trends have emerged at the individual, team, and organizational levels too. Basically, when we talk about the change, there is a close relationship between culture and change. Culture generally talks about existing values, practices, set of procedures, norms, and various beliefs by the member of an organization, and these are highly resistant to change.

INTRODUCTION

Concept of Organization

We survive and work in a world of organizations. The family into which we born, the school or college in which we do our education, the religious place where we go for worship and the retail store from which we buy our daily requirements are

DOI: 10.4018/978-1-7998-3515-8.ch011

all organizations. Principally organizations are classified to business as well as non-business organizations. However, they have countless relevance for business organizations since they operate in an extremely dynamic environment. It can be further categorized as economic, educational, administrative, cultural, social, religious, political, professional and military organizations.

"When men or materials are organized to perform in stationary connections that can be boundlessly continual, an organization is born and is at work". "An office is such an organization."

Organization diverge in composition-

1. Workforces, resources, instructions, proceedings, the effort can synchronize to develop an organization.
2. Organizations are operated from end to end through rulebooks.
3. The organization is made likely by the conjoining approach of menfolk.
4. The human race itself is at its base an organization of species and hence it crafts numerous organizations for its persistence and progression.
5. Organizations are innate in a society that is cognizant. Consequently, it can be said: lifespan developments by mindfulness and consciousness progress are by the organization.''
6. Organizations can comprise predominantly of individuals, powers, procedures, structures or assertiveness.
7. Nevertheless, there is a core element, it cannot arise into animation

We can rightly say that in every organization, management is the most imperative ingredient to give unique flavor in the modern world. It is a dreadful job to achieve anything single-handedly. This wakefulness has directed to the realization, "The modern age is the age of organizations".

To an inexpert eye, every organization seems to be identical, but this is not true at all. Every organization is unique, have their own taste and flavors, different strategies and style and varieties in working combinations which distinguish it from all other organizations. This makes cataloging of organizations into exact styles challenging. Blau and Scot classify organizations into four categories using the criterion of cui bono- who benefits:

1. Organizations that benefit their owners. All business organizations fall into this category.
2. Organizations that benefit their members. A wide class of unions, cooperatives, and the club come under this category.
3. Organizations that benefit their clients. Examples are Insurance companies, private schools, etc.

4. Organizations that benefit the whole society such as government departments.

Organizations, to deal with worldwide struggle and the fluctuating corporate atmosphere, visualizing an "ultramodern situation" with a new-fangled purpose and goalmouths to be accomplished.

Definition of Organization-

"The term organization may be defined as a collective entity of people who consciously engage in some activity on a sustained basis for achieving an objective or set of objectives."

-Allen

An organization is "a consciously coordinated social entity, with a relatively identifiable boundary, which functions on a relatively continuous basis to achieve a common goal or a set of goals"

-Robbins, 2001, p. 704

Organizational Change

Change is an endless process, a yarn knitted into the material of our individual and proficient breaths. Change happens inside our biosphere, in addition, beyond in nationwide and global events, in the corporeal surroundings, in the means, establishments are organized and demeanour their commercial, in political and socioeconomic glitches and keys, and in social standards and morals. By way of, the world is converting into extra multifaceted and progressively interconnected, variations seemingly far away affect us. Hence, change may occasionally seem to happen often and haphazardly. We are gradually becoming conscious of in what way we are connected to each other and to our whole sphere. Organizations must also be conscious of their all-inclusive characteristics and of the habits their followers affect each other. The unbelievable volume of variation has forced personalities and Organizations to see "the giant depiction" and to be conscious in what way proceedings move them and vice versa.

Organizational change is mutually the course in which an organization changes its arrangement, plans, policies, functioning devices, skills, or organizational culture to affect change inside the organization and the effects of these changes on the organization. Organizational change can be incessant or happen for separate epochs of the period.

Organizational change emphases on how individuals and groups are affected by a structural transition. It contracts with numerous diverse disciplines, from behavioral and societal arts to information technology and commercial keys. In a project management context, organizational change may refer to the change regulator progress wherein variations to the scope of a project are officially presented and accepted.

It is symbiotically commanding that on behalf of one to entirely comprehend the significance, the concept of organizational change and development there is a necessity to increase in value what an organization is in expressions of its physiognomies as an exposed system. It is definitely the decent information and holds of the features that will cover the method for a healthier investigation and understanding of organizational change and development, with exceptional importance on policies for handling organizational change.

The fractional or entire adjustment of fresh knowledge thought or behavior by organizational followers is denote d to as organizational change (Burnes, 2004). Slight miracle contends that varying the idea and task declarations, organizational policy, organizational values, organizational arrangement, method, procedures of manufacture and direction style are around of the marks of organizational change. It ascends as an outcome of forces from the exterior surroundings and it is essential for inner orientation of fundamental shortcomings.

The impact of organizational culture on individual behavior towards organizational change is reverberating. Diverse categories of organizational culture have different stages of reception of behavior towards organizational change. This means that a few types of organizational culture could ease the suitability of change, whereas other kinds of culture

Organizational Change Management– A Paradigm Shift

Organisational Change Management has been well-defined as 'the method of frequently reintroducing an organization's path, structure, Values and ethics, technology and many more and competences to assist the dynamic desires of exterior and interior clients (Moran & Brightman 2000). Kanter (1992) contends that we all survive in a persistently fluctuating world, and change has an influence on the individual personalities and the organization as an entire. In this situation, organizations devise to gaze into the forthcoming to discover different and new benefits. Different Innovative technologies, a wide range of products, smart entrants, new protocols, and confident publics with new standards, knowledge, and experience in the direction of the contemporary organization. However, models and methods to organizational change management are so often contradictory, missing in observed evidence and built on unobstructed assumptions about the nature of

Figure 1. Diagrammatic representation of organisational change management

Diagrammatic Representation of Organisational Change Management

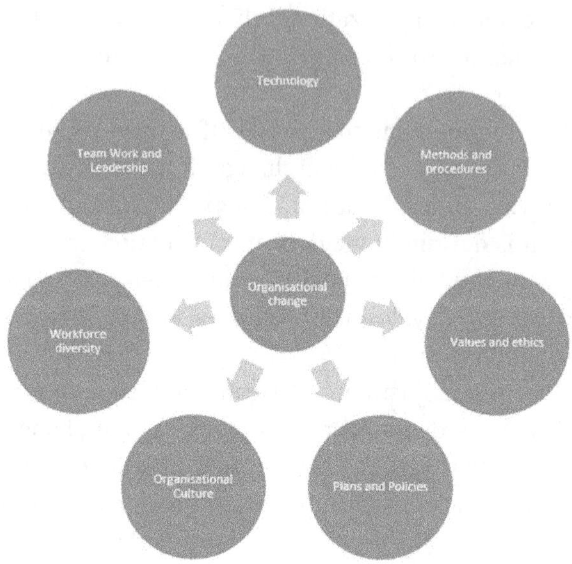

modern organizational change management. This heading "Organizational Change Management– A Paradigm Shift" stares at some of the main variables and styles to organizational change management as a vital first step in the direction of creating a different background for handling change.

Following are the few variables to look into in Organisational Change Management-

1. Technology
2. Workforce Diversity
3. Methods and Procedures
4. Values and Ethics
5. Plans and Policies
6. Organisational Culture
7. Teamwork and Leadership

In this chapter, basically, we are going to brief about the two most important variable namely Technology and Workforce diversity and also their relationship.

TECHNOLOGY

In this contemporary era of reckless strode technological expansions, the progression in technology will not stop to accelerate the upcoming events. In this respect, technology is not only set to alter the biosphere, but also influence organizations, their strategies as well as their policies (Hampel & Martinsons, 2009). The wild strode commercial world also comes to influence organizations and how they function. In fact, the indispensable workforce dynamics of an elderly peers of Baby Boomers, continuous technological evolutions, the effect of universal competition have transformed the means specialists go by training and developing their workforce in order to articulate them to turn into high end performers. Being able to take a pre-emptive method distinguishes among prosperous and non-successful businesses. Technology is one major element of the 21st century changes; it is clear that the fast technological advancements have shifted the workplace and improved the method we function and acquire. Accordingly, organizations are not only presented with opposition encounters, but also with certifying they keep up-to-date when it comes to progressive technology to confirm their sustained progress and achievement (Johnston & Packer, 1987).

Assuming the speedy developments and the improved dependence on expertise and technology, the query in what way it is varying effort and service or employment is extremely noticeable for intellectuals of organizational psychology and organizational behavior. We animate in a universe where technology, specifically data and communication technology, is altering the methods in which big business generates and seizure significance, just how and where we work, and in what way we interact and communicate. Ponder five technologies that are renovating the very nitty-gritty of universal business and the establishments that drive it: cloud and mobile computing, big data and machine learning, sensors and intelligent manufacturing, advanced robotics and drones, and clean-energy technologies. These technologies are not just assisting individuals to do stuff superior and sooner, nonetheless, they are empowering deep variations in the behaviors that effort is completed in organizations. As Murray (2015, p. 6) contends, "Organized these revolutions are tearing us in the direction of a new-fangled developed rebellion. Savvy business leaders recognize they have to moreover point out how these technologies will alter their dealings or face distraction by others who point it out initially."

To illustrate technology's impact on work, work systems, and organizations, we present two popular technologies: electronic monitoring systems and robots. Let's study in detail and know what the expert opinions are -

Electronic Monitoring Systems

Monitoring denotes structures, individuals, and procedures cast-off to assemble, accumulation, analyze, and account the activities or performance of personalities or groups on the work (Alge 2001, Ball 2010). Our emphasis now is going on electronic monitoring and surveillance systems (Riedy & Wen 2010). Monitoring nowadays might shoulder a diversity of methods: telephone, video, Internet, and GPS. In the historical, benches have commonly sided with companies who many times preferred to monitor their personnel, disagreeing that since monitoring receipts throughout work by means of managerial resources (e.g. commercial computer systems, electronic mail), monitoring is acceptable (Kidwell & Sprague 2009).

Several establishments are setting new machinery, consignments, set-up, devices, and even personnel with networked sensors and actuators that empower them to monitor their atmosphere, account their grade, obtain directions, and take movements built on the data they have collected. So we can say the big phrase "the Internet of Things" is very true. By nursing these managerial assets in real-time, firms can well switch the movement of processes and evade disturbances by captivating instant movements and attractive in defensive resolutions when glitches arise. Groups are similarly emerging strategies around by means of blogs and social networks such as Facebook outside of work, and this can shake employees' insights of conviction and forfeiture of individual control (McNall & Stanton 2011). Though social media have profoundly altered the habits of persons cooperate with information, it is significant to focus that the word social media does not denote to an exact technology, nonetheless slightly to a family of technologies with a mutual agreed of principles at the center of their project (Landers & Goldberg 2014). Such principles comprise the following: Operators must be capable to create their specific content to segment by way of their desire, statistics ought to be delivered at liberty and decently, individual thoughts from impartial individuals can be reliable, and the mob is astute. Perceptibly not entirely of these concepts are encountered in rehearsal.

Robots

Robots have remained on plant levels for eras. Centuries before they were generally immense, costly equipment that had to be bounded by enclosed to retain them since smashing hooked on creatures. Additionally, they might accomplish only a solitary assignment (e.g., spot welding) over and over, although enormously wild and exactly. They remained neither reasonable nor applied for minor industries. Nowadays, nevertheless, so-called collaborative technologies are planned to effort, combined with individuals in adjacent situations (Davenport & Kirby 2015). They charge as diminutive as $23,000 and propose minor industries enticements to systematize in order to surge the whole efficiency and to inferior employee charges (Aeppel 2014). Additionally, improvements in artificial intelligence, pooled with enhanced sensors, are creation it likely for robots to make additional composite verdicts and to attain how to accomplish responsibilities on their own, empowering them to achieve the sound in ambiguous and runny circumstances. Not only robots are becoming entrenched into managerial societal schemes, but they are also charming societal performers in those schemes. As renowned by Coovert & Thompson (2014b), ponder the terms co-worker and colleague. Factually, they indirect new individuals, nonetheless this might no longer be the case as cobots (co-worker robots) arrive at the workstation as crew associates. As robots progress, they are probable to develop additional flexible to the work full atmosphere, with multimodal borders empowering them to interconnect more professionally and efficiently with anthropological colleagues, receiving as well as diffusing data (Redden et al. 2014).

A significant experiment to anthropological issues, specialists are to design and develop human-robot regulator interfaces that are artless and stress-free to use, yet robust, as the networks that permit isolated robots to take stroke deprived of a human machinist could be topic to hacking. As Redden et al. (2014) have expressed in their complete evaluation of human issues and ergonomic issues related to the policy and application of robots in an organization, communal recognition is serious. If robots are actually to develop crew associates, people essentially admit them, interconnect excellently with them, grow shared mental models with them, and perhaps most importantly, trust them. As robots execute extra and new independent responsibilities, in theory, a machinist's job should reduce, freeing him or her to perform other tasks. However, the allocation of functions between humans and robots is an area that needs considerable research attention because automation has been shown to create its own set of problems. These comprised reduced state consciousness; a disbelief of automation; abuse, exploitation, and neglect; satisfaction; decrements in alertness; and undesirable special effects on additional sides of anthropological enactment (Redden et al. 2014). Exploration and principle in areas such as work analysis, groups, recruitment, training and development, selection, leadership, motivation, and performance management can assist the successful architecture and amalgamation of robots into workgroups and establishments (Coovert & Thompson 2014b, Miles & Hollenbeck 2014).

The best example of this is the Kiva robot, an architect by Amazon, is designed and planned to scurry through huge warehouses, appealing racks of well-arranged products and supplying the products to people who set the orders. A warehouse equipped with Kiva robots can handgrip up to four times as many orders as a similar unautomated warehouse, where employees might spend as much as 70% of their time walking about to retrieve goods

Workforce Diversity

The notion of diversity was primarily instigated from the U.S in the late 1980s (Shen et al., 2009; Meena & Vanka, 2013). Though, the previous two eras have perceived the expansion of diversity as a commercial policy across the sphere. Indian trade has also in full swing of leveraging diversity (Meena & Vanka, 2013) in order to have communal, financial and radical gains (Wambui et al., 2013). There are numerous explanations why diversity has to develop such persistent anxiety nowadays such as globalization, shifting employee markets, teamwork policies, the change from engineering to service frugality, mergers, and associations, etc. (Cascio, 1998). Diversity inventiveness improves inspiration, revolution, global empathy, elasticity, and output in the organization and harvests modest benefits. (Kundu, 2003; Wambui et al., 2013). Procter & Gamble, Avon, Xerox, FedEx, etc. are the few cases of businesses that hold diversity as an advantage (Cascio, 1998; Gomez-Mejia, 2010), to improve their managerial efficiency and performance. (Henry & Evans, 2007).

Fluctuating demographics are an influential push to state diversity in the work. Workforce diversity has been driven by many extra aspects as well. As organizations spread geologically and the allow movement of workers diagonally through nationwide, confines strengthen, the necessity to interrelate efficiently with wider electorates becomes grave. For example, as facility develops a more share of countries' financial prudence along with advanced stages of international and national service sector and growing competition, capabilities in cross-cultural management become vital if organizations are to recognize how to assist and recollect a client base that is abundant in varied and challenging than the earlier (Bergesen & Sonnett, 2001). The capability to comprehend numerous perceptions (e.g., cultural) in communications can donate to competence, while the absence of this skill can diminish from it. Technological improvements to propose the opportunity of employed with people one might not ever encounter and after diverse cultural upbringings (Kasper-Fuehrer & Ashkanasy, 2001).

However, in the view of Farrer (2004), the simple appearance of variety or accepting multiplicity as a thought unaided does not assurance achievement; establishments want to efficiently achieve diversity by rejoicing, appreciating, and vigorously inspiring the diversity of the workforce. Management of diversity has thus developed the highest importance for chief managers of organizations everywhere in the world (Wikina, 2011)

In yet another study of federal agencies in the USA, Brewer (2005) revealed that efforts to improve employee perceptions of fairness and equity through various diversity initiatives significantly improved employee perceptions of the firm performance. Furthermore, a recent report by Deloitte (2013) discovered that when employees perceived that their organization was committed to and supportive of diversity, they reported better business performance and were more likely to agree that they work in a high performing organization. Thus, employee perceptions of diversity practices like equal representation and developmental opportunities, hiring and retaining diverse employees, and promotion of gender diversity employed to support organizational diversity are likely to influence perceptions of organizational performance.

To elaborate furthermore on Indian Context, to safeguard equivalent prospects, the constitution forbids discernment on estates of faith, sex, class, or domicile of birth (Kundu, 2003). Supplementary, to restitution and remedy prevailing for social hierarchies, Indian constitution holds confirmatory act similarly all over the states in favour of disadvantaged strata and conserves "reservation" (quotas) in the civic zone to defend its traditionally discriminated strata: SCs, STs, and OBCs (Haynes and Alagaraja, 2016; Haq, 2012). Nevertheless, the lawful and organizational structure for diversity in India is not entirely inclusive and is faintly imposed, as these philosophies do not spread to the private or isolated or agricultural segments which incorporate approximately 80 percent of the workforce (Woodard and Saini, 2006).

Varying Workforce Diversity Paradigms

The existing revision talk over four paradigms (perceptions) on Workforce diversity:

1. Resistance
2. discernment and equality
3. legality
4. Knowledge and efficiency.

The subsequent units concisely converse the simple creeds of these paradigms and tactical replies to individual paradigms.

The table below will describe the complete scenario of paradigms of workforce diversity-

In the framework of diversity management, aspiring executives are fortified to possess ethnic diversity abilities. In addition to the demand being completed by globalization in the trade, there are core demands for diversity management. One of these demands is the best use of the unique features of workforces by smearing specific policies. Workforce diversity is inclined by countless features, comprising demographic changes, kinds of diversity, the grade of the burden for diversity, or mergers and acquisitions, the worldwide marketplace, government rules, rivalry, workers' self-esteem, and personnel harmonizing. It is, hence, necessary to integrate exterior and interior forces into corporate aims so that the organization understands diversity broadly. These paradigms, discussed, can be employed by organizations

Table 1. Diversity paradigms and planned reactions for any organization

Diversity Paradigm	Attention/Instruction	Problem Statement	Tactical Reaction
Resistance Paradigms	1.Unique variances among cultural and racial clusters/rare burdens for workforce diversity 2.Recommendation: Endure similarity	Variety as nonissue or risk	Reactive Evasion/renunciation/ Disobedience
Discernment Paradigms	1.Confirmatory Act: equivalent prospect/ behavior/ employment 2.Recommendation: Integrate personalities	Variance causes problem	Defensive • Negotiating with diverse concern crowds
Legality	1.Appreciating all alterations between individuals 2. Recommendation: Rejoice alterations	Variances generate prospects	Accommodative •Encouraging diversity in the place of work
Knowledge and efficiency	1. Allowing for variances and resemblances 2.Pre-emptive reply to matters of competition, civilization, and gender 3.Recommendation: Acculturate/Diversity	Variances and resemblances proposed prospects	Proactive • Integrating diversity matters hooked on additional happenings of the association

Source: Adapted from Dass and Parker (1999)

in scheduling and forecasting diversity evolution. An expressive method to support an organization in its struggle to achieve diversity accomplishment is to design its own band for forecasting its evolution.

Technology and Workforce Performance

Current technologies procedure entails involving and identifying new-fangled awareness, which in shot needs the inner improvement of social abilities and information. Any technological improvement is said to influence the recital of organizations in an optimistic way, which consequently marks the employees' efficiency and enactment (Mudford, 2000). Conversely, the better-quality enactment and efficiency levels can only ensue if the appropriate means are operated in an operative and well-organized style (Dauda, 2009). The appropriate use of skills in the workstation can support employees to be extra operative in their job performing, which recovers the organizational enactment. Nevertheless, it is imperative to identify that the contemporary successes are based on past-improved performances; and in order to maintain a long-lasting organizational accomplishment, organizations have to endure cultivating their personnel with the wanted abilities and understanding to superlative address the upcoming requirements and demands of the company's presentation.

The "Workforce performance is meticulously associated to technical variations and insurgency. Technological variation could magnificently be coped up through the human resource combined approach" (Dauda, 2009, p. 16), which provokes fellowship, connotation and liberalism. According to the resource-based theory, organizational resources are tremendously significantly for the business's expansion, and that human capital is a vital source of an organisation. The role of this source be contingent on the employees' capability and interest, and on well-organized human resource management (Mumford, 2000). With the endless want to recover presentation and attain novel facts and capabilities, workers are provided with numerous opportunities to do so, which comprises training, instruction, tutoring, mentoring, etc. Additionally, employee presentation and organizational competence request that a leader with a tactical decisional control sees the necessity to present the invention and generate the alteration, in this concern, Dauda and Akingbade (2011, p.34) discussed that organizational variation and modernism can only take place when the wants encompass the following:

1. Variation in executive plan and policy;
2. Make establishments extra reliable with mutually separable requirements and the situation;
3. Change in the overall constitution, formation, and roles;
4. Change the impetus of the personnel;
5. Marked and improved development;
6. Advanced inter-groups associations; and
7. Adaptation to the new-fangled atmosphere.

With the perceptible influence and technical progressions have on employee enactment, the focus on initiatives that foster employee performance is very important. Likewise, organizations competing in a tough market should utilize proper management programs that guarantee a collaborative continuous organizational improvement between management and individual employees. Various studies have recurrently revealed a positive relationship between a company's technological evolution and performance and determined that modern technology is significant to employee performance (Foster, 1986).

So, lastly, technology and workforce diversity are explained in detail to explain the concept of Organizational Change Management– A Paradigm Shift. These two are the utmost imperative variables.

CONCLUSION

In today's sphere, varied personnel is flattering the norm. No organization or association in this world of globalization would endure without the changes for upbringing. Exploiting on the possible welfares of changes, organizations may achieve a modest benefit in inventiveness, modernization, worldwide thoughts, problem-solving, and flexibility.

REFERENCES

Aeppel, T. (2014). Robots work their way into small factories. *The Wall Street Journal*, pp. B1-2.

Aladwani, A. M. (2001). Change management strategies for successful ERP implementation. *Business Process Management Journal*, *7*(3), 266–275. doi:10.1108/14637150110392764

Alge, B. J. (2001). Effects of computer surveillance on perceptions of privacy and procedural justice. *The Journal of Applied Psychology*, *86*(4), 797–804. doi:10.1037/0021-9010.86.4.797 PMID:11519663

Amusan, L., Adeyeye, A. I., & Oyewole, S. (2019). Women as Agents of Terror: Women Resources and Gender Discourse in Terrorism and Insurgency. *Politikon*, *46*(3), 345–359. doi:10.1080/02589346.2019.1642681

Ansoff, H. I. (1991). Critique of Henry Mintzberg's 'The design school: Reconsidering the basic premises of strategic management'. *Strategic Management Journal*, *12*(6), 449–461. doi:10.1002mj.4250120605

Anyieni, A. G. (2013). *Effect of strategic planning on the performance of small and medium enterprises in Kenya: A summary review of the literature*. Academic Press.

Appelbaum, S. H., St-Pierre, N., & Glavas, W. (1998). Strategic organizational change: The role of leadership, learning, motivation and productivity. *Management Decision*, *36*(5), 289–301. doi:10.1108/00251749810220496

Ball, R. D., Del Debbio, L., Forte, S., Guffanti, A., Latorre, J. I., Rojo, J., & Ubiali, M.Nnpdf Collaboration. (2010). A first unbiased global NLO determination of parton distributions and their uncertainties. *Nuclear Physics B*, *838*(1-2), 136–206. doi:10.1016/j.nuclphysb.2010.05.008

Bergesen, A. J., & Sonnett, J. (2001). The global 500: Mapping the world economy at century's end. *The American Behavioral Scientist*, *44*(10), 1602–1615. doi:10.1177/00027640121958078

Bersin by Deloitte. (2013). *Predictions for 2014*. Bersin by Deloitte.

Brewer, M. B., & Pierce, K. P. (2005). Social identity complexity and outgroup tolerance. *Personality and Social Psychology Bulletin*, *31*(3), 428–437. doi:10.1177/0146167204271710 PMID:15657457

Burnes, B. (2004). *Managing change: A strategic approach to organisational dynamics*. Pearson Education.

Burton, R. M., Obel, B., & Håkonsson, D. D. (2015). *Organizational design: A step-by-step approach*. Cambridge University Press. doi:10.1017/CBO9781316160787

Cascio, W. F., & Montealegre, R. (2016). How technology is changing work and organizations. *Annual Review of Organizational Psychology and Organizational Behavior*, *3*(1), 349–375. doi:10.1146/annurev-orgpsych-041015-062352

Chawla, S., & Sharma, R. R. (2016). How women traverse an upward journey in Indian industry: Multiple case studies. *Gender in Management*, *31*(3), 181–206. doi:10.1108/GM-06-2015-0050

Cnaan, R. A., & Cascio, T. A. (1998). Performance and commitment: Issues in management of volunteers in human service organizations. *Journal of Social Service Research*, *24*(3-4), 1–37. doi:10.1300/J079v24n03_01

Cnaan, R. A., & Cascio, T. A. (1998). Performance and commitment: Issues in management of volunteers in human service organizations. *Journal of Social Service Research*, *24*(3-4), 1–37. doi:10.1300/J079v24n03_01

Cox, T. H., & Blake, S. (1991). Managing cultural diversity: Implications for organizational competitiveness. *The Academy of Management Perspectives*, *5*(3), 45–56. doi:10.5465/ame.1991.4274465

Dale, J., & Foster, P. (1986). *Feminists and state welfare* (Vol. 86). Routledge & Kegan Paul.

Dass, P., & Parker, B. (1999). Strategies for managing human resource diversity: From resistance to learning. *The Academy of Management Perspectives*, *13*(2), 68–80. doi:10.5465/ame.1999.1899550

Dobson, I. R. (2018). Salary diversity: Australian universities and their general staff. *Australian Universities' Review. The*, *60*(2), 77.

Edwards, P., & Redden, M. H. (2014). *Brony Study.* Academic Press.

Farrer, J. (2004). A practical approach to diversity. *Industrial and Commercial Training*, *36*(4), 175–177. doi:10.1108/00197850410542437

Gomez-Mejia, L. R., Makri, M., & Kintana, M. L. (2010). Diversification decisions in family-controlled firms. *Journal of Management Studies*, *47*(2), 223–252. doi:10.1111/j.1467-6486.2009.00889.x

Hinds, P., & Kiesler, S. (1995). Communication across boundaries: Work, structure, and use of communication technologies in a large organization. *Organization Science*, *6*(4), 373–393. doi:10.1287/orsc.6.4.373

Johnsen, C. G. (2018). Who's afraid of organization? Concepts, process and identity thinking. *Philosophy of Management*, *17*(3), 303–319. doi:10.100740926-017-0079-5

Johnston, W. B., & Packer, A. E. (1987). *Workforce 2000: Work and workers for the 21st century*. Hudson Institute.

Kasper-Fuehrera, E. C., & Ashkanasy, N. M. (2001). Communicating trustworthiness and building trust in inter-organizational virtual organizations. *Journal of Management*, *27*(3), 235–254. doi:10.1177/014920630102700302

Kidwell, R. E., & Sprague, R. (2009). Electronic surveillance in the global workplace: Laws, ethics, research, and practice. *New Technology, Work and Employment*, *24*(2), 194–208. doi:10.1111/j.1468-005X.2009.00228.x

Kundu, S. C., Bansal, J., & Chawla, A. S. (2015). Managing Workforce Diversity through HR Practices: A Review. *Emerging Horizons in Business Management*, 115-124.

Kundu, S. C., & Mor, A. (2017). Workforce diversity and organizational performance: A study of the IT industry in India. *Employee Relations*, *39*(2), 160–183. doi:10.1108/ER-06-2015-0114

Kundu, S. K., & Katz, J. A. (2003). Born-international SMEs: BI-level impacts of resources and intentions. *Small Business Economics*, *20*(1), 25–47. doi:10.1023/A:1020292320170

Landers, R. N., & Goldberg, A. S. (2014). Online social media in the workplace: A conversation with employees. *Psychology of workplace technology*, 284-306.

McNall, L. A., & Stanton, J. M. (2011). Private eyes are watching you: Reactions to location sensing technologies. *Journal of Business and Psychology*, *26*(3), 299–309. doi:10.100710869-010-9189-y

Moran, J. W., & Brightman, B. K. (2000). Leading organizational change. *Journal of Workplace Learning*, *12*(2), 66–74. doi:10.1108/13665620010316226

Mrass, V., Peters, C., & Leimeister, J. M. (2016). *New Work Organization through Crowdworking Platforms-A Case Study*. Academic Press.

Murray, E., Cho, J. H., Goodwin, D., Ku, T., Swaney, J., Kim, S. Y., & McCue, M. (2015). Simple, scalable proteomic imaging for high-dimensional profiling of intact systems. *Cell*, *163*(6), 1500–1514. doi:10.1016/j.cell.2015.11.025 PMID:26638076

Omisore, S. (2019). *Corporate Entrepreneurship, Strategy Formulation, and the Performance of the Nigerian Manufacturing Sector* (Doctoral dissertation). University of East London.

Parker, D., Charlton, J., Ribeiro, A., & Pathak, D., R. (. (2013). Integration of project-based management and change management: Intervention methodology. *International Journal of Productivity and Performance Management*, *62*(5), 534–544. doi:10.1108/IJPPM-10-2012-0108

Price, K. (2011). E-books for free: finding, creating and managing freely available texts. *E-books in libraries: a practical guide*, 53-67.

Riedy, M. K., & Wen, J. H. (2010). Electronic surveillance of Internet access in the American workplace: Implications for management. *Information & Communications Technology Law*, *19*(1), 87–99. doi:10.1080/13600831003726374

Shah, N., & Ghulam Sarwar Shah, S. (2010). Relationships between employee readiness for organisational change, supervisor and peer relations and demography. *Journal of Enterprise Information Management*, *23*(5), 640–652. doi:10.1108/17410391011083074

Tuan, L. T. (2019). Can managing employee diversity be a pathway to creativity for tour companies? *International Journal of Contemporary Hospitality Management*.

Wikina, S. B. (2015). *Diversity and inclusion in the information technology industry: relating perceptions and expectations to demographic dimensions* (Doctoral dissertation).

Witte, N. I. E. L. S. (2014). *Technology Acceptance of Business Meetings in a 3D Virtual Environment Supported by a Content Management System* (Master's thesis). University of Twente.

Woodard, N., & Saini, D. S. (2006). *Diversity management issues in USA and India: Some emerging perspectives*. Academic Press.

Chapter 12
Promoting Road Freight Industry to Women:
Motivations and Challenges of Female Truck Drivers in the UK

Autumn Mabel Fitzpatrick
University of Huddersfield, UK

Gökcay Balci
University of Huddersfield, UK

ABSTRACT

Distribution and freight transportation play a significant role in the development of a region, but the sector is usually a male-dominated one. Considering the shortage of drivers in some countries such as the UK and lack of studies investigating the challenges female drivers face, it is crucial to identify motivations and challenges. Identifying challenges would help promoting the industry to more female drivers. Thus, the chapter aims to discover the main motivations and challenges as well as discover if females feel they are treated equally to males within this industry. Accordingly, a qualitative study is designed, and a total of 16 interviews have been conducted with female truck drivers in the UK. The results indicate that the main motivation for female truck drivers is the freedom that the job allows. The study also found a number of challenges faced by female truck drivers in their day-to-day working life. The biggest challenge for female truck drivers is clearly shown to be a lack of facilities.

DOI: 10.4018/978-1-7998-3515-8.ch012

INTRODUCTION

Within the UK there is a deficit of around 59,000 Truck drivers (FTA, 2019), and this is an aging workforce. This means that the majority of drivers are of an older age with few younger people joining the industry. This is a concern as truck drivers are essential workers in the movement of goods, which is the key in distribution of value (Kotler & Armstrong, 2012). Truck drivers are necessary in the movement of all things ranging from animal feeds and raw materials to road maintenance and delivering to supermarkets and so are vital to ensuring that the country remains operative. There is a very small number of females within this profession, the Road Haulage Association (RHA) claims that only between 1 and 2% of drivers are female. By encouraging more females to consider or become truck drivers, this deficit could be reduced. Therefore, knowing what motivates and challenges female truck drivers plays a vital role.

Encouraging more females joining the industry is also a large step for equality in workforces, the more normalised female truck drivers become the more it will be seen as an option for women to join this industry as currently it is saturated with males. There is also a great gap of literature focusing on female truck drivers. The lack of information surrounding this aspect highlights that there is a need to study what motivates and challenges female truck drivers. Furthermore, the literature surrounding truck drivers generally is lacking surrounding their motivations and challenges also. There is some information in previous literature but it is limited. For instance, Reed & Cronin (2003) investigated the health issues faced by female truck drivers. Naysmith & Rubincam (2012) studied the perceptions and experiences of female truck drivers and their employees in South Africa. The existing literature covers the health of truck drivers and therefore does not have the detail surrounding what encourages them within their profession. This is again important as with the current deficit of drivers more information needs to be collected in order to see what policies and motivators can be put in place to make truck driving a more desirable career.

The literature is also lacking a focus directly on female truck drivers particularly within the UK. This gap in knowledge shows a need to focus on females working in the industry in order to better understand what motivates and challenges them. This leads to the purpose of this study in taking a direct approach in finding the challenges and motivations. Accordingly, the aim of this book chapter is to discover the main motivations and challenges of being a female truck driver in the UK. Main objectives of this book chapter are to discover if females feel they are treated equally to males within this industry; if females feel accepted and included within their roles; how females find working in such a male dominated industry and also; how female truck drivers decided to be a truck driver. It will also be important to discover how female truck drivers manage with other issues such as keeping safe and managing their personal lives.

The second part of the study continue with literature review, which will focus on female truck drivers and then which will consider females working in other male dominated industries as some of the issues they face will be similar. The literature review will look at previous research and publications about these things in order to later determine whether the results from interviewees selected for this project relate to previous studies. It is also important to discover whether the results link to females in other male dominated industries to see if there is a broader gender issue with these industries or whether the results link directly to female truck drivers. The third part explains the methodology section in which the procedure of semi-structured interviews is described. The fourth part in this chapter presents the findings of our qualitative interviews with a critical discussion. The chapter is ended with the discussion and conclusion part.

LITERATURE REVIEW

Women in Male Dominated Industries

Rubin et al. (2019) conducted a study on females working in highly male dominated industries and the effect of sexism on their mental health and job satisfaction. Although the main focus of this study is not on the haulage profession itself, key links can be made with the industry being heavily male dominated. It was found that there was a relation between sexism and lack of belonging in the industry. This relation was justified with poorer mental health and job satisfaction (Rubin et al., 2019). As the findings of this study show, females facing sexism within the workplace will have a lower level of job satisfaction. With there being such a limited number of females in this profession compared to males, it could suggest that sexism is occurring as previously noted in other studies such as Naysmith and Rubincam (2012)'s, meaning that there is an issue that needs to be addressed further in order to remove this as a challenge for females and encourage more females to join these industries. However, it was also found in the study of Rubin et al. (2019) that there was no relation between perceived self-reported femininity and greater level of sexism. This is important to note as it highlights that sexism as a challenge does not just affect females who feel they are more feminine. This shows that it is a challenge that is faced in general by all women within male dominated industries and that females who may express themselves with more stereotypically masculine characteristics, are not exempt from being discriminated against.

Wright (2016) believes that the subject choices made at school might explain why women are underrepresented in those male dominated jobs. This could indicate that one challenge that females face in working in male dominated industries, for example as a truck driver, is influenced by a lack of encouragement. During a child's more formative years when they are more impressionable, if various career paths are painted to be inappropriate, it is highly unlikely they will pursue this venture. This is a challenge that can also affect females that already do the job, as if colleagues and others working around them have also grown up believing that females do not belong within the haulage industry or have little place working in male dominated industries, then they are more likely to outcast female colleagues. In the case of female truck driver's, a motoring school aimed at recruiting females into the industry was launched. They held their first 'taster day' in 2014 and it was hoped that 'the taster days will allow potential drivers to experience driving a modem HGV and speak to female mentors and local operators about the reality of life behind the wheel, what will be expected of them as a driver and the positives of a career in logistics' (Pink, 2014, p:8). This is important as it brings awareness to truck driving for females, something which could help bridge the deficit of drivers in the UK. This again highlights how education and career advice at a young age can encourage or deter females from joining certain industries or lines of work. If in their younger influential year's females were taught that careers such as truck driving where viable options for them there may be a higher chance of them choosing that career when the time comes.

The ergonomics of trucks and other transport vehicles are also considered to be an issue as they are usually designed according to physical characteristics of men. A research paper focussed on female pilots found that cockpits of planes are not designed according to women's stature (Tim et al., 2019). The study also indicates that the schools do not employ sufficient female instructor who can be role model. This is similar to Wright's (2016) findings about careers advice, the lack of role models in the industry means that there is limited career advice available to young females wanting to join these industries as there is limited people to look up to or gain this advice from. It was further suggested that more mentoring programs should be created to enable women to connect with each other (Germain et al., 2012). These link directly to female truck drivers. As truck driving is still a largely male dominated industry, cabs of trucks are not made with female stature in mind such as high sun visors and high steps on the trucks for accessing and exiting the cab. Furthermore, mentoring programmes and efforts to recruit females to the industry are limited. The Road Haulage Association (RHA) have a branch called 'She's RHA,' however, there would need to be more advertisement of these schemes in order to encourage more females into these roles.

Studies Related to Female Truck Drivers

One study on truck drivers in USA found that in order to attract new drivers to the industry the most positive aspects should be stressed and decided from interviews conducted that these where: seeing new things meaning days were always different; it is possible to make a good wage; the job allows for independence without being micro-managed constantly; the trucks are designed to be comfortable and face less breakdowns than older vehicles used to; and that most units now have 'sophisticated communication gear' from televisions to satellite navigation systems (Johnson et al., 2011). This is important to note as this is an international issue whereby destinations will be different each day and independence is key due to spending long hours driving alone. Furthermore, internationally many trucks are now of a higher specification particularly for those expected to stay away from home in them. These positive aspects could be seen as motivators for truck drivers and therefore a reason why they continue doing this job. This can also be seen with Beilock (2003) who conducted a survey and found that while the long hours and time away from home could be seen as a negative factor; truck driver's tend to see it as 'offering freedom, adventure, and variety (Beilock, 2003, p. 157). Freedom and passion for the independence available can be seen as key motivator within the industry, with independence also being noted within the studies of Prockl et al. (2017).

Greenfield et al. (2016) reviewed the health risks that LGV drivers are exposed to, with this highlighting that truck drivers can be more prone to health complications due to the nature of their work. The particular problems mentioned are drivers being obese due to unhealthy foods, working overtime, and suffering lack of sleep. This is indicative to the line of work that they do, as this can involve working for extended periods of time behind the wheel, meaning little exercise is possible, as well the working hours which can cause a severe lack of choice in food establishments to maintain a balanced diet. Boeijinga (2016) also found that rest and stopping places truck drivers stop at are detrimental to their health as they 'negatively affects their eating patterns because of a lack of healthy food options' (Boijinga, 2016, p.386). This again is expected to be a challenge of the female truck drivers interviewed. The lack of healthy eating facilities is a challenge to truck drivers as it is important to maintain a healthy balanced diet that is not possible when on the road. The lack of these facilities are likely to put off potential truck drivers as there are jobs available where it is easier to maintain a healthy lifestyle. It has been further found that although regulations set restriction on certain amount of driving, drivers usually work over time in the practice (Greenfield et al., 2016). This means that despite the regulations in place drivers face extra work, which they carry out, in their job than what is permitted, thus leading to them putting more strain on themselves than the regulations dictate. This overwork and excess stress is also liable to increase the chance of health issues in drivers.

Prockl et al. (2017: p.184-196) stated 'that money cannot buy job satisfaction but may help an employer remain attractive to a truck'. This indicates that although money is not a priority in retaining truck drivers there is some influence from the rate of pay. This study however, was conducted with participants who all already drove trucks as a job and therefore, it can still be speculated that to attract more drivers to the industry money could still be an incentive, but this isn't necessarily a means for retaining existing drivers.

This study further found that one major influence on job satisfaction and retention proneness is the relationship held between drivers and those at management level (Prockl et al., 2017). This indicates that if the relationship and the expectations from management are reasonable to the driver, they are more likely to be satisfied in their work. Fournier et al. (2012) similarly found that Driver job satisfaction is negatively impacted if their voice is not considered and unreasonable demands are requested. Therefore, it seems plausible to believe that those involved at management level need to maintain a good relationship and open communication with drivers in order to ensure drivers are content with their work. If relationships are good between dispatchers and driver efficiency is improved (Fournier et al., 2012). Depending on the nature of the relationship between these party's a driver could either view the management of the company as a motivator of the job or a challenge.

Cherry & Adelakun (2012) conducted a study on drivers and discovered that 'aggressive drivers, lane changing behaviour, congestion, and merging cars are the biggest threat to their productivity and safety'. The habits of car drivers can pose threat to the safety not only of the truck drivers but also to the car drivers themselves. This is again another issue that would require policy change either through the development of infrastructure (Cherry and Adelakun, 2012) or through education. Despite this study being based in the US it is likely that urban and other built up areas globally will see similar challenges. Therefore, it is likely that this affects truck drivers in the UK as well.

Naysmith and Rubincam (2012) conducted a study on female truck drivers and their employers in South Africa. They found that most females who already did the job faced very little issues from colleagues. However, when interviewing employers of haulage firms one stated that 'we don't hire female drivers because they would just confuse our male drivers about where they have to go' (Naysmith and Rubincam, 2012, pp. 579-599). This highlights that there may be an issue with equality from further up the chain of command rather than by direct colleagues that female truck drivers would be in contact with. The comparison between the two statements could also suggest that once established within the truck driving profession the matter of equality is not an issue, however, during job applications gender will be taken into account when deciding an applicant's 'worthiness' of employment. It was further found that 'while female drivers seemed to feel that their relationships with co-workers were productive, they did express a certain sense of unease about another aspect of the job, namely safety' (Naysmith and Rubincam, 2012 pp. 579-599).

One article published in the Commercial Motor discussed the challenges female truck drivers face and different ways in which females could be attracted to work as LGV drivers. Pink (2013) found that 'the hours involved in LGV driving, especially long-distance trunking, can also be problematic for females with young families to consider, as is the lack of decent, secure truckstop facilities for women.' (Pink, 2013, pp. 20-21) This is seen to be problematic and a deterrent for female truck drivers as if they do not have somewhere safe to stay and to meet their basic needs, they are likely not to do such a job when there are jobs available where they would be able to go home each night. Therefore, if these facilities are not to a good enough standard females will not be inclined to become truck drivers.

'Despite the barriers, Waters, who gained her LGV licence at the age of 50, says she would definitely recommend a driving job to women considering a lifetime career.

"I loved the open road, being your own boss, more or less. It was a great life, and I wish I had got my licence earlier. I miss the fact I was doing a professional job; proud to be a truck driver."

Waters is, however, concerned that women drivers may experience prejudice, which needs to be addressed. "There are a lot of companies who do not take on women drivers and, if they do, the women always have to prove they are as good as the male drivers."' (Pink, 2013, pp. 20-21)

This citation gives several points to consider on how to increase the appeal for women to pursue a career in driving large goods vehicles. There is a motivating aspect for female truck drivers clearly highlighted as it is observable that the independence gained from the profession and the need for one's own initiative brings an element of complexity to the job that is inviting. However, it also shows a large challenge faced by women in the industry in the fact that they need to prove themselves rather than their driving qualifications being accepted to the same degree as their male counterparts. This is an issue in that if women are to be encouraged to become truck drivers it is important that they should be treated equally to males with the same driving qualifications.

METHODOLOGY

This study aims to identify motivations and challenges of female truck drivers working in the UK. The paper adopts a qualitative approach because a deeper understanding on the topic is required. The paper required a more insightful response from participants which the interview allows for meaning that instead of interviewees just giving straight answers they were allowed to detail anecdotes, and the motivations and challenges that they face in-depth. In other words, as Bryman (2012)also suggests, the paper should adopt a qualitative approach because more insightful data is required on the topic. Semi-structured interviews were conducted with industry experts for data collection since this method is ideal to understand attitudes and preferences of customers with a deeper perspective (Bryman, 2012)).

The interviewees were selected based on the non-probabilistic judgmental sampling (Malhotra, 2007). The study consisted of 16 participants, who were selected from a range of female truck drivers. The drivers were found by posting on a range of social media pages and chosen from people who volunteered to take part as well as personal industry connections. All of the interviewees were both female and truck drivers. They varied in age from 20 to 58 years old, these ladies had held their licenses for varying amounts of time; between 7 months and 35 years. The interviews conducted varied in length with the shortest being around 10 minutes and the longest taking around 45 minutes. These interviews took place from the 16th-23rd April 2020.

This study was conducted from home using over the phone interviews. This is because the nature of the work the interviewees perform means that their time at home is very valuable. Furthermore, participants were based nationwide from the Scottish Highlands, to the South of England. Another reason why over the phone interviews were important was due to the study starting at the beginning of the Covid-19 pandemic. This meant that social distancing and self-isolation was being carried out by all people in the UK and most businesses were closed except those that were essential. Most haulage firms continued with business as it is a vital way of distributing necessary goods making the time of these drivers even more valuable as they are key workers. However, Saunders et al (2019) have studied research that has discovered that 'telephone interviews were on average shorter than face-to-face ones' (Saunders et al, 2019, p.472).

Apart from the demographic questions, major questions asked in the interviews are listed here: What made you decide to become a driver? To what extent do you feel you are treated equally to the males in your line of work ? How included and accepted do you feel in your line of work How do you find working in such a male dominated industry? How do you feel about your safety while doing your job? How do you find balancing your personal life with your work life? What are your main motivations to do your job? What are the main challenges you face in your job? What would you say needs to be done in order to improve your working conditions?

RESULTS

Motivations and Career Decision of Female Truck Drivers

There were several common answers that were given in response to this topic ranging from family involvement and being at a 'loose end' in previous employment. 37.5% of respondents had some involvement due to family. One interviewee was married to a contract haulier and was at a loose end in her old job and decided to follow a driving career. Two other interviewees 'followed in their father's footsteps.' They both had a father who drove/drives trucks and decided to follow the same path. This is important as these interviewees all had a family involvement which meant that they had a direct link to somebody already involved in the industry and likely would not have chosen this career path was it not for people directly related already following this career.

A further 5 interviewees were at a 'loose end' in their current careers before choosing to become truck drivers. These females worked in a variety of industries with one originally being a sports therapist. Her choice to change her career to truck driving was that she 'wanted a change.' This led to her going away and thinking about what she enjoyed finally deciding on a career in driving trucks. This is also similar to another interviewee who chose to leave her career in the bank due to lack of progression. She too decided to take a plunge and went on to obtain her Category C (Class 2) license.

One less common answer however, that came up twice was through involvement with horses. One interviewee saw friends driving HGV horseboxes and 'wanted to one up them' and so gained her category C+E (Class 1) license. This is important also as it implies that some females become involved as truck drivers from an element of competition. The other interviewee who became a truck driver due to involvement with horses was originally working on a stable yard and moved onto horse transportation where she was put through her Category C+E (Class 1) test, from there she moved onto general haulage. The horse transportation is a higher skilled form of haulage, involving more responsibility and increased pressure whereas she found general haulage to be less demanding and an easier form of driving both physically and mentally, encouraging the change. This relates to the earlier point of these females finding the jobs requiring the 'lower skill set' more appealing.

Finally, 3 of the interviewees had always wanted to drive trucks. The first participant had watched the 1977 BBC documentary 'Destination Doha' when she was a young girl and decided then that was what she wanted to do. The 'sense of adventure and freedom shown' was a factor that made her want to follow a career in truck driving. Another participant had always wanted to drive however, due to the cost of obtaining a HGV license could only afford to do so a few years back. The starting prices of obtaining a category C (class 2) license can range from £1000-2000, dependent on experience, if the training price includes tests (theory and practical), the medical, and/or the Driver Certificate of Professional Competence (DCPC) which is required to drive professionally. These prices are differing dependent on the company you train with as well as if you pass the tests first time and what the package includes. The final interviewee who gave this same reason had always wanted to drive but when at school was told 'women could not drive unless they joined the army' and so she 'forgot' about following that career. This is important because as previously discussed in the literature review Wright (2016) criticised the lack of careers advice for young women wanting to join male dominated industries. This point was further backed in the literature review by Pink (2014) and Struthers and Stratchan (2019). The lack of education and support given to females wanting to join industries that are predominantly male means that these jobs are avoided even by females who want to be involved.

The interviewees were also directly asked what the main motivations of their job were. There were several reasons why females were motivated to drive trucks but, the main reason being that they 'loved' the job. 13 out of 16 interviewees spoke about how they enjoyed the job. This was due largely to the sense of adventure and freedom that they receive. Two interviewees both spoke of seeing different things with one saying, 'even the same roads are always different.' This is important as this freedom is something that could be used to advertise truck driving as a desirable career which is something noted in studies by Beilock (2003), Prockl et al. (2017), Johnson et al. (2011), and Pink (2013). For this study to align with other studies focussed on truck drivers implies this freedom is one of the largest motivators to encourage people to join the industry and more focus should be drawn to truck driving as a career that allows freedom and adventure.

Two answers that were slightly against the other 11 but held similarities was a link to family. These interviewees continue driving and their largest motivation is to make their families proud. One interviewee who followed her father into the truck driving career remains motivated as she believes it makes him proud. This is important as this could be a way that more truck drivers could be recruited into the industry. If current drivers encouraged or educated their children or young people that they know about truck driving, then perhaps this could increase the number joining the industry.

There was however one answer that was a completely different motivation. This interviewee worked with her husband and for his business. Her main motivation was to grow and expand the business. Money was a further motivator that was mentioned by 5 interviewees as a further point but as discovered in previous studies by Prockl et al. (2017). However, similarly to that study it was found that the main motivation was centred on enjoying the freedom and adventure the job brings rather than just the money.

Challenges of Female Truck Drivers: Safety and Personal Life

Two questions were asked linking directly to the challenges faced by female truck drivers. These challenges are imperative to know in order to understand changes that may be required in order to make truck driving a desirable career choice for females. The two questions are as follows: What are the main challenges you face in your job? What would you say needs to be done in order to improve your working conditions?

The main challenges and what these drivers would like to change had some variation, but all gave answers that either regarded: facilities; the physical characteristics of the work (including but not limited to the layout of the cab); other road users; management; and food options. Some responses regarding the challenges had varying amounts of interviewees with these responses.

The largest challenge for female truck drivers which a majority wished to change was the access to facilities. The lack of suitable toilets was broached by eleven of the sixteen interviewees. This highlights that this is clearly a great difficulty. Many spoke of how when on the road the facilities available to them were limited and to a low standard. Of the 11 respondents who spoke of this 6 said how the only facilities available on many sites were either only directed to men or 'portaloos.' Two interviewees found this to be a problem as it meant that they had issues finding somewhere suitable to deal with personal hygiene during their menstrual cycle. This is likely to be an issue that faces many other female truck drivers as they require somewhere clean and hygienic when they are faced with this. Furthermore, facilities such as showers were also discussed by several interviewees who were required to sleep out with one interviewee describing service stations as 'expensive, stinky, horrible and ill-equipped.' This is a problem that requires changing as without suitable facilities for females on the road it is unlikely more females will choose to join the truck driving industry as there are jobs were separate and clean facilities will be readily available to them.

A further issue raised by 2 interviewees about these facilities was the lack of availability of healthy food. This is something that Greenfield et al. (2016) who found that most truck drivers are obese. Greenfield et al. (2016) finding this could be linked to the lack of establishments offering healthy food at affordable prices as these interviewees have discussed.

Several difficulties with the physical aspect of truck driving was raised by some interviewees. Aspects about the cab were mentioned by three drivers. The lack of storage space and cooking facilities in cabs that are required to be slept out in were discussed by one driver. If drivers are expected to essentially live in these vehicles throughout the week it is important that the vehicles have the necessary things in order for them to do so, if they cannot they are unlikely to choose this side of truck driving as a career and will instead opt for a job where they are able to go home. Furthermore, one participant discussed how she felt 'sun visors were made for taller people' the implementation of the sun-visors links to the findings of Germain et al (2012) who found that cockpits on planes where not created with the female stature in mind highlighting how this too is the case with trucks. It was also suggested by another interviewee that the steps to access the cab could be lowered. This again suggests the lack of consideration to the stature of the average female compared to the average male.

Further physical difficulties that were discussed was more to do with the actual work needing to be carried out such as moving heavy and large objects. One participant explained how sometimes opening and closing container doors could be a challenge which sometimes required 3-4 large men. This is problematic as if female truck drivers cannot carry out the physical demands of their job, they are again unlikely to choose truck driving as a career. With the advancement of technology there is likely to be some methods which could be implemented which could be the focus of further research in order to discover methods by which the physical demands of truck driving could be reduced.

Other road users were a further challenge that 6 interviewees discussed. One participant explained how she felt many road users were 'not considerate to lorry drivers' and another furthered this by saying, they 'cut you up; pull out on you; and block you' and then went on to say how car drivers 'automatically blame the lorry driver.' Problems arise when attracting new truck drivers into the industry if they feel that they so not get respect from other road users. The stopping distances and time for a loaded truck are longer than those for a car. When travelling if a car moves in front of a truck without leaving enough space for the truck to stop when the car stops is likely to cause accidents. When asked what would improve their working conditions, all interviewees who claimed that other road users were a challenge to their working life believed that education of others was one thing that would improve things. A change to policy regarding driving tests would be one way to educate others meaning that if when learning to drive car users were taught more clearly about the dangers and differences of trucks, they would be more aware. Further to this, policies could be put in place whereby schools teach about the dangers of trucks while they are impressionable. Other road users being a challenge is similar to previous findings and a further policy change that could be suggested would be in the development of infrastructure (Cherry and Adelakun, 2012) as discussed previously within the literature review.

A final challenge that was discussed by 2 interviewees was management. One explained how she felt that management wanted them 'to work miracles' meaning that when she was asked to practise safety, she felt that what they actually wanted speed. A further felt that management did not respect drivers. This is similar to the findings of Fournier et al. (2012) who found the relationship between management and drivers impacts on truck driver's satisfaction within their job. These interviewees highlight this point as they feel that one of the largest challenges in their job is the management.

Overall, it is clear that the largest challenges faced by females in this industry is the lack of suitable facilities available to them and that this is the main thing that they would change in order to improve their working conditions.

One question focussed on the personal challenges and balancing work with life of female truck drivers. This question was as follows: How do you find balancing your personal life with your work life? Over half of the participants stated they did not find balancing work and life particularly difficult. Out of the 9 interviewees that found balancing work and personal life easy, only two did 'nights out;' the rest claimed that being able to go home every night was one of the reasons why they had a good balance with one saying 'tramping wouldn't work' for her. This means that they believe if they had to work away, they would not have the same work life balance as they currently do. Two participants who did not have issues with balance did stay out. One believes that due to her partner working as a driver the balance is easier to find as he understands. This implies that if it was not for him also being a driver there may not be a good balance between her work life and her personal life; another also mentioned working with family being one of the reasons why she has a work life balance further highlighting this point.

However, as stated above, 7 out of 16 interviewees did have issues balancing their personal life with one even asking, 'what's a personal life?' when this question was posed. All interviewees held the view that the long hours that the job demands are the main reason for them struggling to find a balance. The demanding nature of the job is clearly the largest reason why these drivers face issues with balancing their work and home life, meaning that in order to make truck driving more attractive for females (or anybody wishing to join the industry) it needs to be ensured that the time demands of the job allow for sufficient time off where they can live a life away from work. This is similar to the findings of Greenfield et al who found that health complications are common in truck drivers due to the number of hours they work.

A further participant said that she found balancing her personal and work life 'horrendous' and said, 'it's terrible for relationships.' This was a statement that was mentioned several times with one participant who did not find balance a struggle even saying, 'I can understand how it could put a strain on a new relationship.' This combined with the interviewee who found it easier to balance her life as her partner also drove and understood makes it appear as though those who are female driving trucks may have an issue with balancing relationships with those outside the truck driving industry. This could make truck driving appear unappealing to aspiring truck drivers as it implies that if they take up this profession, they will not be able to maintain their relationships.

Due to the split between those who do not have a problem balancing their personal and work life and those that do being so minimal more research into this aspect could be done in order to reach a theoretical saturation. Due to the limited difference in answers it is unclear how much effect the impact of truck driving is on female truck driver's personal lives. The interviewees were asked about how they felt about their safety at work with the following

This question prompted again a mostly positive response with the majority of interviewees saying they felt mostly safe in their work. However, when it came to 'sleeping out' some did have concerns, and several had experienced some issue where they felt unsafe.

In regard to sleeping out in the trucks many described themselves as feeling vulnerable and those who felt like this were cautious about where they chose to park for the night. One interviewee claimed she would not like to 'night out' and feels as though she receives a lot of looks and attention when taking breaks at services or on lorry parks. Another interviewee who does sleep out chooses not to stay overnight at services for this reason opting to try and stay on well-lit industrial estates where there are some other trucks present. This is due to her being concerned about there being lots of different drivers present and feeling that all eyes are on her. However, two other interviewees both make a conscious effort to try and stay at service stations or truck-stops that are well lit. The common factor here is that all of these drivers choose somewhere that is lit implying that there is a lot of consideration about their safety when choosing where to stay.

A further interviewee chooses not to stay out however, when she has to another driver is usually sent in convoy (multiple trucks running together) so that she has somebody nearby. This implies that her employer feels as though there is some lack of safety for female truck drivers. Despite this, one interviewee did claim that she felt it was 'no different to a fella sleeping out' this is important as it implies that while there is an element of feeling vulnerable this feeling may not just be limited to females.

However, safety does not just affect those who have to sleep out. One participant explained how she once 'pulled out' onto a roundabout due to another truck driver not indicating and was then chased by this driver. She explained how when she pulled over, he was shouting at her and although he did not seem violent, she felt that the chase was aggressive. Another driver also felt that in certain places there were people she did not want to be around due to not feeling safe. These issues need to be dealt with and changed in order to attract more female truck drivers into the industry as if they feel as though they are going to be met with hostility, they will not follow truck driving as a career. These findings have some relation to Naysmith and Rubincam's (2012) study where they found that females could be more vulnerable to attack however, not quite as severely. There is little severity from any tales from the interviewees in this study compared to those noted in their research, only an element of extra consideration. On the other hand, other than the few instances explained the female truck drivers interviewed largely felt that their safety was important to their employers and fundamentally felt safe while carrying out their jobs.

Equality in the Workplace

There were three questions asked surrounding how equally female truck drivers felt in relation to their male counterparts. One was directly about the equality and the other centred around inclusion and acceptance from others. The third question focussed on working in a male dominated industry. These questions when asked faced some overlap in the answers, the first two questions were as follows: To what extent do you feel you are treated equally to the males in your line of work? How included and accepted do you feel in your line of work?

All interviewees gave very similar answers to these questions. All stated that their pay was no different to that of their male counterparts. Furthermore, all believed that they were largely included and accepted within their roles however, the majority also stated that they had faced some form of issue where they had felt as though they were looked down upon due to their gender.

One interviewee explained an anecdote of how at one site she delivered to in an artic she had reversed onto a bay and had not lined the trailer up precisely. She then heard one of the men from the distribution centre say, 'oh it's because it's a woman driving.' Additionally, another interviewee believes that there is sometimes 'mansplaining and disregard.' These are factors that can negatively influence a female's experience as a truck driver. These females have the same driving qualifications as the males in the job and therefore, this differing treatment of their ability would be unfair and inappropriate which could possibly lead to females choosing to leave the industry. If they feel as though they are being treated as inferior to males, they are likely to move to a career where they are treated with the same regard.

This point was furthered when one interviewee explained how at a job interview the interviewer told her, 'I wouldn't take you on as a driver but, I would train you up to be a transport manager.' It is apparent that the interviewer holds the belief that as a female she should be in an office and not driving a truck, an issue that has previously been highlighted by Naysmith and Rubincam (2012). Their study found that it appeared to be largely employers that have an issue with female truck drivers rather than direct colleagues a point which is again noted in this study. Attracting females into an industry where they cannot gain access to employment due to sexism at a managerial level means that encouraging females to gain their LGV (Large Goods Vehicle) license is futile. In order to see any positive change to the deficit of drivers through encouraging more females' employers need to be willing to employ females as drivers and not dismiss them due to their sex.

A further point that was raised by several interviewees was that they feel they have to prove themselves to be as good as the males. One stated that she 'feels like to be treated equally you have to prove you're as good as the guys.' Another interviewee remarked that she sometimes 'feels watched' with another commenting that it feels as though some men are waiting for her to 'make a mistake' in order to blame the fact that she is female. This is directly relatable to the findings of Pink (2013) where she found that when women are taken on as truck drivers, they have to prove they are as good as the male drivers. Despite the article written by Pink being written 7 years prior to this study these issues still remain a factor in the everyday life of female truck drivers indicating that very little is being done to tackle the issue and that there are implications in policy that need to be amended in order to make a permanent change.

A further question regarding equality in the workplace was as follows: How do you find working in such a male dominated industry? There was an overwhelming consensus surrounding the answers to this question, the vast majority of interviewees, 15/16, said that they enjoyed working with men and that they thought that there was more 'banter' meaning that there is good friendly exchange of good-humoured teasing between colleagues. The number of women who enjoy working with males and the humour they share, again indicates that it perhaps is not colleagues that pose an issue. Although for the most part in the previous two questions females felt that there were some issues occasionally surrounding acceptance and inclusion; it is worth noting that many believed that customers and the employees at the delivery locations, tended to be the people who had more of an issue with female drivers. This view is also shown from Naysmith and Rubincam's (2012) study, discussed in the literature review, as they found that many female driver's that they interviewed found very little issue when interacting with colleagues.

Three interviewees who held the same view as previously mentioned also stated that they believe being a female in a male dominated industry allows them access to more help where needed. One interviewee she does not 'think they'd help as much if she was a man' with another stating 'men in the job tend to have your back.' This is important as it again highlights how colleagues are not an issue and how the majority of other drivers accept females in the industry. However, one interviewee who held this view also stated she believes she is 'treated a bit better than a lad' but furthered this by saying she believes it is 'maybe a bit of an ego thing.' This, however, could highlight some underlying sexism as it follows the traditional thought that men need to look after women and that without a male to help, these females would struggle with their job.

However, there also needs to be a focus on the one interviewee who had issues with the fact that truck driving is such a male dominated industry. This interviewee while not believing she faces many issues with males does believe that while trying to carry out her work 'feels watched.' This is problematic as it appears that some of the attention received from working in a male dominated industry is highly unwanted and has a negative impact on some female drivers.

DISCUSSION AND CONCLUSION

The research overall did answer the main research question and meet the objectives set. The main motivations and challenges of female truck drivers were largely discovered and the questions relating to equality, inclusion, and acceptance; issues faced by female truck drivers; how they felt about working in a male dominated industry; and how they became truck drivers mostly reached a theoretical saturation from the answers.

There were several reasons behind why many chose to become truck drivers with most having always wanted to; being at a 'loose end' in previous jobs with little room for growth; or family connections. Despite most having encountered some degree of sexism during their time as truck drivers, the majority of females included in this study had little issue with equality, inclusion and acceptance. It was also clear that a vast number had little issue with working in a male dominated industry. Most drivers who participated felt largely safe while doing their jobs however, there does appear to be some imbalance when it comes to managing personal and work life. Policies could be created surrounding this as before becoming a LGV driver a car license must be obtained. Policies to 'follow up' with people who pass driving tests could be done to look into whether they would go on to consider a career in driving after having their license for a certain period of time.

The main focus of this research project was to focus on the main motivations and challenges of female truck drivers in the UK, this too was largely answered. The main motivation for female truck drivers appears to be no different to that found from other studies focussed on female truck drivers and truck drivers of either sex, this being the freedom that the job allows (Beilock, 2003; Prockl et al., 2017). It is clear from the results found from these interviews and the information found from secondary sources that the greatest motivator to drive is the sense of adventure and freedom offered. The ability to be able to go about the work set with little interference is one of the greatest positives that has been found from this study. However, it is important to note that due to a lack of previous research in this area these results are not conclusive. Although from the literature found and the results of this study it does appear that freedom and independence are a large motivator more research is required to ensure the full validity of this result.

However, the study did find a number of challenges faced by female truck drivers in their day-to-day working life. The biggest challenge for female truck drivers is clearly shown to be a lack of facilities, which is parallel to findings in previous reports (Pink, 2013). In order to attract more females into this profession there needs to be changes in the availability and suitability of facilities available. Policies would likely have to be put in place to ensure clean and suitable options for truck drivers to make the industry appear more appealing. Furthermore, the lack of education to other road users is also an issue highlighted by several involved in this study. This again would require policy changes in order to ensure others on the road are aware of the dangers of trucks. However, again due to the lack of research done previously on this subject it is difficult to determine the overall validity. It is important again that more research is done in this area to gather more information on what challenges female truck drivers.

Due to a lack of literature available regarding female truck drivers it would be suggested that more research into this topic would be beneficial. There should be a particular focus on balancing work and personal life as this study did not reach a theoretical saturation in this area as the results between the participants was split relatively equally. It is also important that more research on truck drivers generally is conducted in this area. The implications of a work life balance could affect both sexes of truck driver and therefore, it is important to understand whether this is an issue affecting them. The literature also lacks of government's role to improve women's employability as truck drivers in the UK or in other countries. Challenges and motivations found in this study can be considered as a starting point to investigate the role of governments in promoting females to trucking industry. The government in the UK may organize marketing campaigns and social events with related stakeholders to increase awareness. More attention should also be paid by governments on those challenges such as adverse conditions of restroom on highways.

Only a very small portion (less than 1%) of registered HGV drivers are women in the UK. One of the issues mentioned by interviewees was the difficulty of getting an HGV licence due to its costs. It is also essential to apply more promotion campaigns encouraging women by eradicating stereotypes. Her-GV campaign in the UK was a good example in recent years but there is a need for more similar campaigns. In addition to promotions, necessary financial incentives should be provided for women to have HGV training and licence.

There is a severe lack of focus on the motivations and challenges of truck drivers meaning that there is no definitive way to know how the deficit of drivers could be bridged. However, from this study it appears that truck drivers require better facilities and increased education of others. The results from this study show that female truck drivers are largely motivated by a love of driving however, the challenges they face need to be rectified in order to encourage more into the industry. Policies and education are vital in ensuring that these challenges are reduced or eradicated hopefully leading to an increase in female truck drivers and the driver deficit being bridged.

REFERENCES

Beilock, R. (2003). The elusive sweatshop. *Transportation Quarterly*, *57*(3).

Bryman, A. (2012). *Social research methods* (4th ed.). Oxford University Press. doi:10.1017/CBO9781107415324.004

Cherry, C. R., & Adelakun, A. A. (2012). Truck driver perceptions and preferences: Congestion and conflict, managed lanes, and tolls. *Transport Policy*, *24*, 1–9. doi:10.1016/j.tranpol.2012.07.012

Fournier, P.-S., Lamontagne, S., & Gagnon, J. (2012). Interactions between Dispatchers and Truck Drivers in a High Turnover Context. *Relations Industrielles*, *67*(2), 263–282. doi:10.7202/1009087ar

Germain, M. L., Herzog, M. J. R., & Hamilton, P. R. (2012). Women employed in male-dominated industries: Lessons learned from female aircraft pilots, pilots-in-training and mixed-gender flight instructors. *Human Resource Development International*, *15*(4), 435–453. doi:10.1080/13678868.2012.707528

Greenfield, R., Busink, E., Wong, C. P., Riboli-Sasco, E., Greenfield, G., Majeed, A., Car, J., & Wark, P. A. (2016). Truck drivers' perceptions on wearable devices and health promotion: A qualitative study. *BMC Public Health*, *16*(1), 677. Advance online publication. doi:10.118612889-016-3323-3 PMID:27475984

Johnson, J., Bristow, D., McClure, D., & Schneider, K. (2011). Determinants of Job Satisfaction among Long-Distance Truck Drivers: An Interview Study in the United States. *International Journal of Management*, *28*(1).

Kotler, P., & Armstrong, G. (2012). *Principles Of Marketing*. Pearson Prentice Hall.

Malhotra, N. K. (2007). Marketing Research: An Applied Orientation (5th ed.). Prentice-Hall, Inc.

Naysmith, S., & Rubincam, C. (2012). Women in the driver's seat: An exploratory study of perceptions and experiences of female truck drivers and their employers in South Africa. *Journal of Southern African Studies*, *38*(3), 570–599. doi:10.1080/03057070.2012.708997

Pink, H. (2014). Training firm aims to bring women to sector. *Commercial Motor, 222*(5605).

Prockl, G., Teller, C., Kotzab, H., & Angell, R. (2017). Antecedents of Truck Drivers' Job Satisfaction and Retention Proneness. *Journal of Business Logistics*, *38*(3), 184–196. doi:10.1111/jbl.12156

Reed, D. B., & Cronin, J. S. (2003). Health on the road: Issues faced by female truck drivers. *AAOHN Journal : Official Journal of the American Association of Occupational Health Nurses*, *51*(3), 120–125. doi:10.1177/216507990305100305 PMID:12670099

Rubin, M., Paolini, S., Subašić, E., & Giacomini, A. (2019). A confirmatory study of the relations between workplace sexism, sense of belonging, mental health, and job satisfaction among women in male-dominated industries. *Journal of Applied Social Psychology*, *49*(5), 267–282. doi:10.1111/jasp.12577

Tim, G., Stefan, S., & Kristina, P. (2019). Assessing the role of dynamic capabilities in local food distribution: A theory-elaboration study. *Supply Chain Management*, *24*(6), 767–783. doi:10.1108/SCM-02-2019-0073

Wright, T. (2016). Women's Experience of Workplace Interactions in Male-Dominated Work: The Intersections of Gender, Sexuality and Occupational Group. In Gender, Work and Organization (1st ed.). Palgrave Macmillan UK. doi:10.1111/gwao.12074

Chapter 13
A Neuroimaging Study Protocol on the Motivational Structures of Physicians Belonging to Private and Public Health:
Neuroeconomics in Healthcare

Luis-Alberto Casado-Aranda
University of Granada, Spain

Carmen Fernández-Aguilar
University of Granada, Spain

Juan Sánchez-Fernández
University of Granada, Spain

José Jesús Martín Martín
University of Granada, Spain

Sergio Minué-Lorenzo
Escuela Andaluza de Salud Pública, Spain

ABSTRACT

Health economics literature has demonstrated that physician motivation is related with three reasons—extrinsic motivation, intrinsic motivation, and prosocial motivation—and that this motivational structure is influenced by the type of organization in which they work. Yet this research proves insufficient to identify the origin of the physician's

DOI: 10.4018/978-1-7998-3515-8.ch013

psychological motivations. To shed light on this gap, this chapter aims to outline a neuroimaging methodology which would prove useful to identify the neurocognitive motivational structures of hospital physicians with the proposes the design of several intrasubject laboratory experiments, using the functional neuroimaging technique magnetic resonance imaging (fMRI). Identifying the neuronal origin of doctors' motivational framework belonging to private or public health organizations would be a step forward in defining the most appropriate motivational plan for a medical profile working in different hospital environments.

INTRODUCTION

Health economics literature has demonstrated that physician motivation is related with three reasons: extrinsic motivation, intrinsic motivation, and prosocial motivation and that this motivational structure is influenced by the type of organization in which they work. Most of the research on the structure of physicians' motivations has been conducted either through changes in remuneration systems or through surveys. Yet this research proves insufficient to identify the origin of the physician's psychological motivations. To shed light on this gap, this article aims to outline a neuroimaging methodology which would prove useful to identify the neurocognitive motivational structures of hospital physicians.

This study proposes the design of several intrasubject laboratory experiments based on exposing 60 doctors to extrinsic, intrinsic and prosocial motivational environments and recording the brain activity caused by these stimuli, using the functional neuroimaging technique Magnetic Resonance Imaging (fMRI).

Identifying the neural origin of doctors' motivational framework belonging to private or public health organizations would be a step forward in defining the most appropriate motivational plan for a medical profile working in different hospital environments. The results may be useful to explain the interaction between motivational structure and type of health care organization as well as being able to suggest more efficient cognitive and more affective motivation structures. So, the current research constitutes the first protocol in health organization and management that proposes a neuroimaging methodology as a means of the neuronal origin of doctors' motivational framework belonging to private or public health organizations, where the main objective of this article is to propose a neuroimaging methodology which would prove to be a useful way to identify the neurocognitive motivational structures of hospital physicians belonging to both private and public health organizations. This would allow an analysis methodology of evaluation, based on neuroimaging tools, which would permit the assessment of differences in the psycho-motivational patterns in physicians belonging to public, for-profit and non-profit organizations. This study protocol constitutes the first step in proposing an effective guide in the design of incentive plans for medical personnel belonging to for-profit, non-profit and public organizations, based on the different types of motivations experienced through unconscious mechanisms.

BACKGROUND

The motivation with which a person performs their work is the "energy" or set of forces originating both internally and externally which drives them to initiate work-related behaviour, in a certain way, direction, intensity and duration (Herzberg, 2017). Organizations around the world are currently investing huge amounts of resources in the promotion of worker motivation, as it has become evident that staff motivation and satisfaction are directly related to the quality and performance of the work (Kovacs, 2018). This motivation is especially key for physicians in health care organizations given the sensitivity and the effects of their work on patients and health systems. It has been demonstrated, in fact, that the motivation and satisfaction of physicians affects the accuracy of the medical services provided (Avery and Schultz, 2017).

Health economics literature has traditionally debated the mechanisms of motivation for physicians which improve their performance and quality, and it assumed that the main work motivation is financial reward (Russell, 2015). However, over the past few decades, the development of behavioural economics (Kahneman, 2012) and neuroeconomics (Lee & Reeve, 2019) have expanded this analytical framework by incorporating the capabilities of other non-monetary motivators such as intrinsic motivation (Fine, 2018) and altruistic or prosocial physician behaviour (Böckler, et al. 2018).

The empirical evidence shows that the lack of work motivation affects the performance of health workers, the provision of services and the performance of the health system, (Kjellström et al, 2017). That is why the present study protocol aims to respond or support the problem of work motivation in the health sector. In this regard, it is important to identify and characterize the type of work motivators to which physicians respond and their relationship with the type of organization in which they work in order to increase job satisfaction and improve patient outcomes.

TYPES OF MOTIVATORS IN THE HEALTH SECTOR

Extrinsic Motivation

The extrinsic motivation of doctors depends on remuneration structures and financial incentives. In recent decades, financial rewards have experienced an extraordinary boom with the roll out of Pay for Performance (P4P) systems, an incentive method that rewards not only the quantity but also the quality of services provided (OECD, 2018). In a recent systematic review of the analyses of the effectiveness of P4P programmes, P4P was shown to have no consistent effect on intermediate health outcomes and there was insufficient evidence to characterise any effect on patient health outcomes. Despite the numerous studies conducted, the evidence available on outcomes is modest at best, or proves to be negative (Bonfrer, Figueroa, & Zheng, 2018).

Intrinsic Motivation

Health economics has considered other motivators in addition to economic incentives by way of the physician's role of usefulness, given the idiosyncratic nature of the physician-patient relationship. The classic works of Evans (1984) posits that physicians not only wish to maximize their income, but also incorporate the maximization of patient health, prestige, and ethical concern into their utility function. More recently, Doublas (2015) argues that the work of the physician involves a trade-off between the ethical and the selfish objectives in the function of their utility. Intrinsic motivation is linked to curiosity, competence, increased physician autonomy and job satisfaction (Nantha, 2013).

Prosocial Motivation

Prosocial motivation is seen as an inherent part of medical ethics which encompasses empathy, compassion and altruism (Hein and Singer, 2008). Empathy is defined as the ability to share the emotional states of others; compassion emphasizes concern for care, but not necessarily sharing feelings (with the patient). Finally, altruistic behaviours are those that intentionally benefit the patient, do not incur personal gain, and sometimes come at a personal cost (Böckler, A; et al. 2018).

HEALTH MOTIVATORS IN PUBLIC AND PRIVATE HEALTH ORGANIZATIONS

Different studies have emphasized the relevance of the interaction between the type of organization and the motivational structure of the employees, although results are ambiguous and fairly inconclusive (Bonfrer, Figueroa, & Zheng, 2018). Intrinsic and altruistic motivation are shown to have some relevance in public employees. This is evident through the notion of "ethics of the common good" in French-speaking countries and through the notion of a public service "ethos" used in the British context as well as in private organizations providing public services (Ritz, Brewer & Neumann, 2016). Akerlof and Kranton (2005) have expanded on this by adding that the concept of identity and belonging to the organization influences the motivational structure of workers within it.

This interaction is especially relevant in healthcare, where motivations such as altruism and compassion in the doctor-patient relationship are basic elements of the social contract. Where there is also a predominance of public and non-profit organizations over for-profit ones (Oppel et al., 2019). Physicians belonging to healthcare entities with different foundational values and different working conditions are presented with different psycho-professional schemes, given the differences in their mission and values (Serra, Serneels, and Barr, 2011). In the health sector, the for-profit private sector aims to maximize profits by offering health care to those who can afford it. Private non-profit health care entities, on the other hand, aim to improve the lives of the most vulnerable and disadvantaged and to combat the root causes of poverty. The goal of the public sector is to provide free and universal health care to all patients (Serra, Serneels, and Barr, 2011).

In a review of 149 studies, Rosenau and Linder (2003) conclude that physicians in the non-profit sector are better able to perform their tasks and achieve more goals than those in the for-profit sector who, contrary to expectations, are not more cost-efficient. Comparing professionals in the three types of health care entities (i.e., public, private for-profit and non-profit), Horwitz (2005) conducted a similar review in which he concludes that physicians in the for-profit sector are more sensitive to ethical-social decisions than the rest. Jelstad (2007) found no significant differences between the two professionals. However, Ben-Ner et al. (2012) in a qualitative questionnaire-based study, found that non-profit and public sector physicians are inherently more motivated than for-profit physicians. Along the same lines, Barigozzi and Burani (2016), based on a study carried out in two hospitals (for-profit and non-profit), state that despite the fact doctors from non-profit entities earn less salary, they provide more patient care and feel that their work is more attractive. Similarly, Lázaro et al. (2005) through a descriptive questionnaire study of 2,262 doctors in the Principality of Asturias, concluded that Spanish doctors in the public sector respond more intensely to intrinsic motivation than their colleagues in the private sector, who are more influenced by economic incentives, the main component of extrinsic motivation. Serra and colleagues (2011) conducted similar questionnaires, this time through 90 medical students, and concluded that staff in the non-profit and public sectors are more enthusiastic, bring more compassion to and put more effort into their tasks. The authors added that the greater the identification of physicians with their philanthropic entities and values the greater the reason for their enthusiasm.

All things considered, the available evidence on the interaction between medical professional motivation and nature of the organization (profit or non-profit) is limited, with ambiguous and contradictory results. In addition, most of the research on the structure of physicians' motivations has been conducted either by way of analysis of the results of experiments in modifying remuneration systems or through different types of surveys of medical professionals. Although these measures are capable of capturing preferences, behaviours and the conscious decisions of physicians related to their motivation system, they are insufficient in capturing the effects of motivational factors such as empathy, compassion or autonomy on physician satisfaction and performance, whose origin and manifestation in everyday life is rapid, involuntary and often unconscious (Berdud, Cabases, Nieto, 2016).

NEUROECONOMICS AND MOTIVATION OF HEALTH PERSONNEL

Neuroeconomics is the branch of economics that studies the neuropsychological origin of economic decision-making. Recent developments in neuroeconomics have allowed progress to be made in the analysis of the interaction between doctors' motivations and the type of health organisation in which they work. Recording the neuro reactions that take place while medical practitioners belonging to different organizations visualize information and make decisions about their motivation, in real time, could prove a very useful methodology (Figure 1). These brain activations can be taken as direct measurements of the value, reward, control, empathy, compassion, or satisfaction experienced by physicians (Lee & Reeve, 2012; Decety, Yang, & Cheng, 2010).

In the case of intrinsic motivation, studies by Lee & Reeve (2012) find that the area of the brain associated with the presence of spontaneous self-satisfactions (interest, enjoyment) the insula, is activated. Extrinsic motivation, on the other hand, is related to the posterior cingulate cortex, an area involved in weighing socially acquired values, such as financial values. Some neuroscientific studies have begun to examine intrinsic motivation and intrinsic motivational processes (e.g., curiosity and competence), (Gruber, Gelman, & Ranganath, 2014; Murayamaa, Matsumotob,

Izumab, & Matsumoto, 2010; Sicsic, Le Vaillant, & Franc, 2014). In these studies, striatum activity was observed when participants were intrinsically motivated during task performance phases. Striatum activity is known to be associated with reward processing and has been observed to play a crucial role in extrinsic motivation (Haber & Knutson, 2010).

Figure 1. Figure of the added value of Neuroeconomics to the study of physicians' motivations belonging to profit, non-profit and public organizations

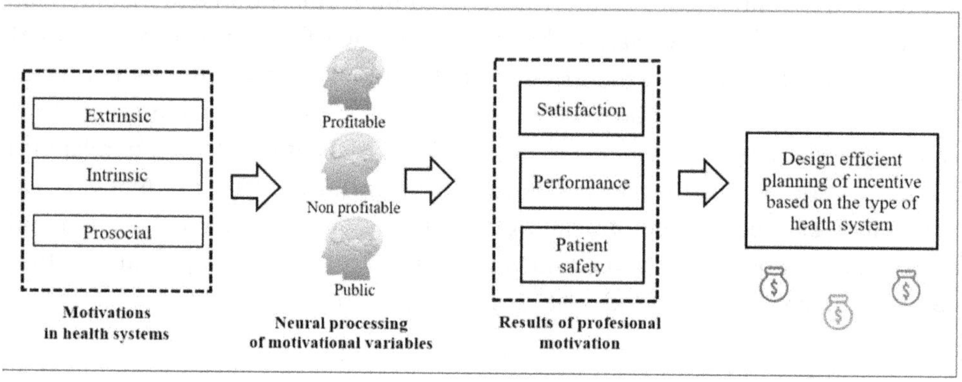

Finally, in the case of the study of the conditions under which people behave prosocially, (Dovidio, 2006; Penner, Piliavin, Schroeder, & Dovidio, 2005), recent fMRI research in social neuroscience has begun to identify the brain networks involved in empathy and its modulation (Decety, Yang, & Cheng, 2010; Hein & Singer, 2008). Most of these studies have focused on measuring the brain signals which are triggered when participants observe other people in pain. Empathetic responses to witnessing another in pain are often experienced as aversive (Lamm, Decety, & Singer, 2011). This can be especially problematic for people working in professions where pain is commonly encountered, such as medicine. Research indicates that perceiving or even imagining other people to be in pain is associated with activations in a neural circuit involved in pain processing, including the somatosensory cortex, anterior insula, and anterior cingulate cortex (ACC), (Akitsuki & Decety, 2009). These results suggest that caring for people in pain triggers a kind of empathic mimicry response in the observer. Hein (2008) and Decety (2010) identified the neural mechanisms associated with empathy, which are present when medical practitioners processed images of patients experiencing pain. Their data reveals that, unlike non-medical participants, the brain areas related to self-regulation (dorsal lateral cortex) and executive attention (pre-central and superior parietal gyrus) were observed to be activated more strongly by images of patients in pain. Some fMRI studies show that observing images of another person's emotional state triggers the brain reactions involved with processing that same state, whether it is disgust, pain, or social emotion (Ruby & Decety, 2004). Klimecki et al. (2013) conducted an experiment to dissociate empathy and compassion. The results indicate the existence of different neuronal networks. Empathy is related to the crucial brain networks in empathy for pain, while compassion produces greater activation in brain networks related to reward.

Figure 2. Brain areas involved with the typologies of motivation: (A) intrinsic, (B) extrinsic, and (C) prosocial

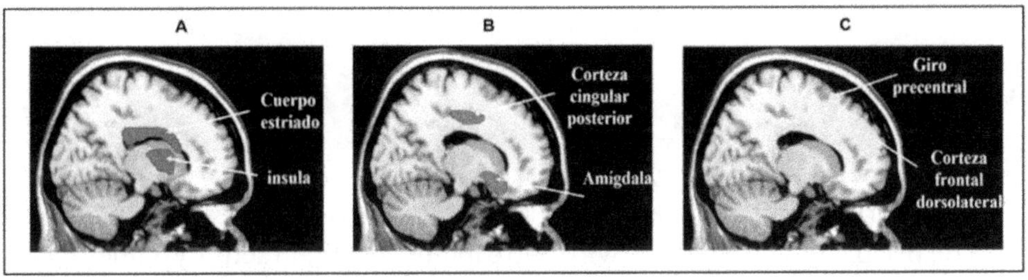

MAIN FOCUS OF THE CHAPTER

A Neuroimaging Tool: fMRI

Our study proposes the use of functional Magnetic Resonance Imaging (fMRI: functional Magnetic Resonance Imaging). The fMRI is a non-invasive tool that detects changes in the level of blood oxygenation in the brain (called the fMRI's BOLD signal), derived from the metabolic changes in blood flow produced by neural activity. This is done with an MRI scanner, which measures the contrasts in the activity levels in different regions of the brain that are associated with particular mental functions, while also allowing visual representation and localization of results by way of MR brain images (Solnais et al. 2013). The fMRI is exquisite in assessing specific brain areas in high resolution (1 mm3) and provides an acceptable temporal resolution (2-5 seconds). The fMRI will provide an indirect measurement of neural activity experienced by physicians while subjected to motivational stimuli, thus allowing the assessment of the neural origin of motivational decision-making processes.

Selection of Centers and Study Participants

Three health care organizations in Spain will be selected, one for each type of healthcare entity (public, private for-profit and private non-profit), and these will provide the study participants. The identification of the sample size required to obtain results which it would be possible to extrapolate is acquired by the statistical procedure using the fMRIPower tool (Mumford & Nichols, 2008). According to its operating paradigm, 20 subjects belonging to each organization are required to obtain an 85% statistical power, i.e. a total of 60 physicians (20 in each type of organization). Given that the aim is to shed light on the differences in the brain of doctors with extensive experience in the organization, doctors who have worked in hospitals belonging to the for-profit, public and non-profit sectors for more than 5 years will be selected.

STUDY DESIGN

Three experiments will be implemented.

The 60 participants will take part in a functional magnetic resonance imaging (fMRI) experiment. The objective will be to capture their brain activity while reading sentences showing the three types of motivators and for them indicate to what extent these motivations are reasons for their work.

In order to achieve the proposed objectives, a three-phase time planning is proposed, one for each type of motivator (Figure 2):

First Phase: Extrinsic Motivation in Health Professionals

Based on the definitions of extrinsic motivation, the first phase aims to present sentences familiar to health professionals which describe situations that motivate them according to the external incentives and rewards which they receive for carrying out their work. Examples of extrinsic motivation sentences are performing a job for the "Good salary I get" or for "Good reputation outside the workplace". Based on sentences included in research analyzing extrinsic motivation in tangential environments (such as Lee, Reeve, Xue, & Xiong, 2012), 50 sentences will be written. A pilot test will permit the selection of 30 sentences after homogenizing message structure, word count and manipulation of extrinsic motivation. Another 30 sentences will be designed to serve as a control (e.g., "Right click").

During the scan process, the 30 sentences which express the previously designed extrinsic motivations will be shown and another 30 neutral ones that will serve as control. After each motivation sentence, the participants will indicate through two controls (two buttons on each) to what extent this motivation is key to carrying out their work (1 = not important; 4 = very important). Inter-stimulus intervals of random duration will be inserted between the trials. The paradigm appearance order will be random, and the total duration will be approximately 16 minutes.

Second Phase: Intrinsic Motivation in Health Professionals

Following a similar structure to Phase One, this section aims to present sentences familiar to health professionals that describe situations that motivate them due to the anticipation of spontaneously experiencing self-satisfaction during a task (Lee et al. 2012). This concerns performing a task because it is inherently interesting and enjoyable. Examples of intrinsic motivation sentences are performing a task because "I feel personal satisfaction in doing my job" or because of "The moments of pleasure my job brings". Based on sentences included in the research analyzing intrinsic motivation in different environments (such as Serra, Serneels, and Barr (2011)) 50 sentences will be written. As in the previous phase, a pre-test will allow the selection of 30 intrinsic motivation sentences and 30 neutral ones after homogenizing the structure of the message, word count and manipulation of intrinsic motivation.

Third Phase: Prosocial Motivation in Health Professionals

Three experiments will be implemented:

Empathy

In cognitive neuroscience, perceiving or imagining others experiencing pain has been associated with activating the brain circuit involved with empathy. Based on this research, this experiment aims to compare the neuronal responses in physicians from for-profit, public and non-profit organizations when exposed to images of people experiencing pain. In short, images of different parts of the body experiencing pain when pricked with a sharp object will be presented (15 of the mouth, 15 of the hand and 15 of the foot). Control images of body parts that do not experience pain when rubbed with cotton will also be designed (15 mouth, 15 hand, and 15 foot). A pre-test will corroborate that valence and arousal are homogeneous for images of painful conditions and those that do not involve pain. This methodology is similar to that followed by Decety, Yang, & Cheng (2010). In order to correlate brain responses with some individual variables, 10 days before the scan session, participants will respond to several scales to measure the susceptibility of their emotions of others (Doherty, 1997) and empathy through the index of interpersonal reactivity (Davis, 2018).

Figure 3. Structure of the experimental task that evaluates empathy

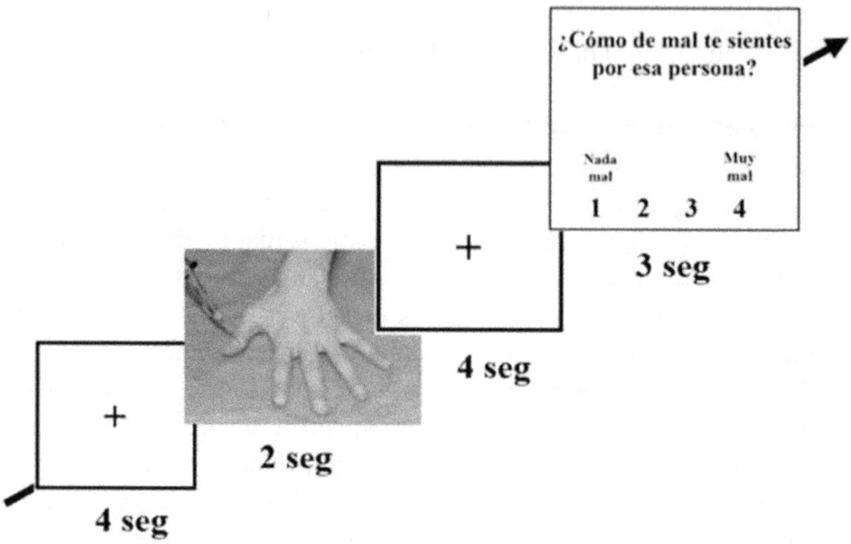

Then during the scan 90 images of body parts will be shown (45 in pain and 45 not in pain). To minimize any possible habituation effect, different locations on each body part of two human actors will be used. After each image, the participants will indicate through two controls (two buttons on each) to what extent they feel for that person (1 = no discomfort; 4 = a lot of discomfort), with a maximum duration of 5 seconds response time. The order of appearance of the trials will be random and the total duration of the paradigm will be approximately 16 minutes. After scanning, participants will be presented with the same set of images, previously viewed, and asked to indicate the intensity of pain and displeasure experienced through a scale (1 = no pain/non-displeasure, 10 = extreme pain/displeasure).

Compassion

Developing a scale for measuring compassion during health care professional performance has been a difficult task, given the divergent definitions of the construct itself. However, in the last five years, some very interesting scales have been posited in the field of health, such as The Schwartz Center Compassionate Care ScaleTM (Lown et al., 2015) and the Compassion Competence Scale (Lee & Seomun, 2016). For simplicity (indispensable in fMRI studies) and analogy to the objectives of this research proposal, the Compassion Competence Scale will be used. In short, the 17 items included in this scale will be used as a measurement of the neuronal compassion experienced by healthcare professionals in different organisations during the performance of their tasks. Phrases such as "When talking to patients, I show a good sense of humour in order to project a good mood", "I always pay attention to what patients say" or "I respond as quickly as possible to patients who require my attention" will be used. Another 17 phrases will be designed to serve as controls (e.g. "I work in the health sector" or "I press the right button").

Given the importance of also correlating brain responses with some individual variables of interest, 10 days before the scan session, participants will also respond to the scales specified in the previous experiment. Then during the scan, the 17 phrases of the Compassion Competence Scale, 7 seconds each, will be shown. After each item, the participants will indicate through two controls (two buttons each) to what extent they implement these actions in their daily life (1 = never; 4 = always), with a maximum duration of 5 seconds. The remaining 17 neutral phrases will also be included to serve as controls. Order appearance will be random, and the total duration of the paradigm will be 8 minutes.

Altruism

The Self-reporting Scale of Altruism (Philippe Rushton, Chrisjohn, and Cynthia Fekken, 1981) has traditionally been used to assess the behaviour of individuals that benefit other agencies, do not involve personal benefit and sometimes incur personal cost. This scale includes items such as "I have donated money to a non-profit organization". Given the specificity of altruistic behaviour in the health care setting, which is paramount in the decisions that befall the patient, the above scale is insufficient. To date there is no research that has cited a scale of altruism in healthcare, although studies such as Burks, Youll, and Durtschi, (2012) define altruistic behaviour in healthcare as behaviour that extends beyond typical professional tasks, such as "I provide informal medical advice outside working hours.

In order to use circumstances that objectively describe altruistic behaviour in Spain from the perspective of the physicians themselves, a focus group of 8 physicians will be convened initially. All behaviour resulting from the session will be subjected to a pre-test that will allow the altruistic nature of the identified behaviours to be corroborated. The 30 circumstances deemed to be most altruistic will be selected and another 30 sentences will be designed to serve as a control (for example: "I work in the health sector"). The 30 altruistic circumstances, 7 seconds each, will then be shown during the scan. After each item, the participants will indicate through two controls (two buttons on each) to what extent they fulfil these actions in their daily life (1 = never; 4 = always), for a maximum duration of 5 seconds. The remaining 30 neutral 7-second sentences will also be included to serve as controls. Order appearance will be random, and the total duration of the paradigm will be 14 minutes.

After the scan, participants will be presented with images of body parts experiencing pain (based on Decety, Yang, & Cheng, 2010) and asked how much money (0 = $0; 7 = >$150) and time (0 = 0 hours; 7 = >10 hours) they would spend on helping the person. The goal of this task is to predict measurements of altruistic behaviour in practitioners (such as money or time spent) by means of the neural activations previously experienced during the fMRI session when visualizing situations of altruism.

Figure 4. Structure of the study protocol

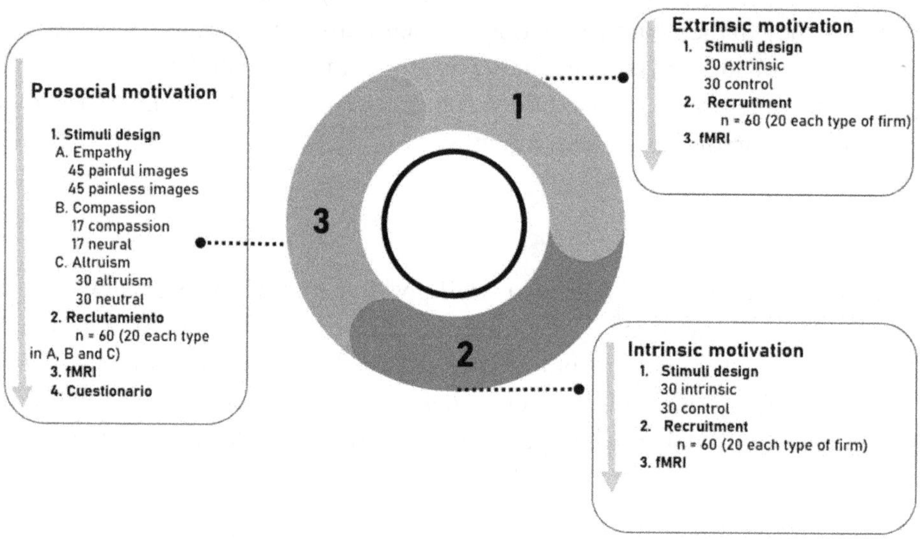

SOLUTIONS AND RECOMMENDATIONS

Research in health economics, as seen through specialized literature, is advancing in the understanding of the unconscious decisions of the physician's trough the motivation. Nevertheless, resorting to neuroscience can trigger several predicaments and concerns.

The Reverse Inference Problem

Functional neuroimaging techniques measure local brain activity in response to cognitive tasks, such as viewing persuasive messages. The data collected from these experiments allow the neuroscientist to infer the role of brain regions during cognitive functions (Casado-Aranda et al., 2020; Poldrack, 2006). However, there is an increase of the use of neuroimaging data to infer the engagement of cognitive functions (the empathic and emotional burden of the physician involved with the patient's pain) based on activation brain regions, resulting in the opposite inferences. These results can, thus, be misleading as brain region X could be activated by a cognitive process P, as well as other processes L, M, N. Similarly, a cognitive process P could trigger not only region X, but also regions W, Y and Z (Weber et al., 2015). In other words, activation of a region does not necessarily equate with a specific cognitive process. This type of bias is known as the "reverse inference problem" and neurological studies try to deter it by complementing brain imaging data with traditional observations or self-reports. The use of two measurement tools for the same task (e.g., a displayed imagen) therefore helps 'triangulate' the findings and reveal the active psychological processes. This is the tendency of recent fMRI experiments to gain clearer insight into the real effects of a media feature.

Researchers also show a great deal of interest in exploring whether a specific neural activation (through changes in activations of a specific area, the so-called parameter estimate) can be correlated with self-report responses (i.e., attitude toward a case) (Casado-Aranda et al., 2020).

Consistency Fallacy

It is also common in fMRI studies to conclude that the consistency between theoretical propositions and fMRI data demonstrates the validity of the theory. In many cases, this conclusion is overstated, a drawback known as the consistency fallacy (Weber et al., 2015). Consistency of fMRI data with a theory cannot solely serve as evidence to confirm the theory. On the contrary, researchers should not rule out alternative explanations as their findings could yield other sets of brain activations that are inconsistent with the predictions of the patterns of known results (Coltheart, 2013).

Ethical Issues

Ethical problems in neuroscience research have spawned a new field called neuroethics concerned with legal, moral, and social implications. To avoid falling into these quandaries, traditional neuroscience research has resorted to measures such as the protection of participants and the full disclosure of goals, risks and benefits. Applying neuroscience to the field of human behavior, due to the large quantity of sensitive information, implies not only observing ethical measures, but also protecting vulnerable segments of society from information exploitation, and accurate media and data representations.

In this case, All experimental procedures in this study protocol have been supervised and approved by the Committee on Ethics in Human Research of the University of Granada and will closely follow the Protocol of the Declaration of Helsinki by the World Medical Association. The participation of study subjects is voluntary.

The idea that the goal of human neuroscience is to open a "black box" (i.e., the brain) without considering ethical issues appears to be exaggerated. There are no real reasons why such a field as health decision making should not profit from neuroscience as do other disciplines, such as engineering and biology. On the contrary, human neuroscience should be viewed as a new and promising field of research that aims to reveal signs about decision-making processes and behaviors. Although neuroscience can help reveal the underlying mechanisms by which medical decision making, laboral motivation, as well as doctors' cognitive and affective states. It does not highlight "the perfect way" to makes decisions.Therefore, health managers and professionals in the health organizations still should be able to use and incorporate neuroscience information to the formulation of decision plans and strategies. With those purposes in mind, the creation of interdisciplinary professional groups, in which a psychologist interchanges data with a neurologist and business workers, should be key in edge-cutting health organizations of today.

FUTURE RESEARCH DIRECTIONS

Based on the finding of health economics research using neurological techniques and taking into consideration the drawbacks and solution that could emerge from this research, the current paper advances the following future lines of study:

1. Define the most suitable incentive plan for a medical profile that works in the public or private sphere, based on the determination of the type of motivation that is most effective in capturing their attention and reward, and provoking emotional responses and efficient cognitive skills, which result in their intrinsic personal and professional satisfaction.
2. Advise a universal guide to financial and intrinsic remuneration, as well as the expected standards of altruism, compassion and empathy among medical personnel belonging to for-profit, non-profit and public entities.
3. Provide new methodologies for analyzing the effectiveness of incentive plans, emphasizing the most relevant type of motivation for each profile of medical practitioner.
4. Seek how to provide new methodologies for analyzing incentive plans, tangentially applicable not only to the main public and private medical

organizations, but also to other sectors in which the professional-user relationship is very intense, such as the scope of nursing or education.

fMRI Analysis and Procedural Issues

When carrying out future neuroscience health economics research, investigators should be very careful when deducing cognitive processes based on brain activations. When they infer cognitive processes, they must cite them in the discussion section of their papers and consider them as secondary to avoid large problems in data-sharing and replication. To alleviate these types of challenges, subsequent studies in this field should link a specific mental process involved in a communication task to a set of brain regions. Weber et al. (2015) offer a clear example: if communication researchers are able to demonstrate that attitude change selectively engages specific brain systems, then it is clear that the mind contains a specialized and dissociable mechanism for attitude change and that brain activity in this system can be used to predict attitude change. Future work could also extrapolate certain conclusions found at the psychological level to the communication field.

Simultaneously, researchers in this field must strictly follow general ethical procedures, specifically those related to human neuroscience. They are advised, therefore, to provide all the pertinent information on their research, to obtain informed consent of participants, to use the data only for scientific aims and, finally, to certify that their findings reflect reality.

CONCLUSION

The empirical evidence gathered over recent decades on the motivational structure and identity within organizations has not yet been successfully implemented in the world of physicians and health care organizations. In fact, there are great differences of opinion about the role of different motivators and their implications on behaviour and work motivation in physicians. Although the literature on health economics has identified certain differences between the motivational framework of physicians belonging to public and private entities, no study has evaluated the neuronal origin of these motivations. This is especially necessary given the rapid, involuntary and unconscious manifestation of extrinsic, intrinsic and prosocial motivations in medical personnel.

The use of neuroimaging techniques allows, an innovative way to evaluate of the interaction of the motivational structure of physicians and the type of organization, and could help to draw interesting conclusions which will help to provide an understanding of the origin of the physicians' motivation with respect to the type of hospital in which they work. This is crucial for organizational efficiency, since physician motivation and satisfaction are directly related to the quality, performance and accuracy of medical services provided (Avery and Schultz, 2017; Greenfield, Pawsey, & Braithwaite, 2011).

This study protocol aims to evaluate for the first time the usefulness of fMRI in detecting the differences in brain activation patterns involved with different types of motivations present in medical practitioners belonging to for-profit, non-profit and public health entities.

However, the implementation of this study protocol may face some challenges. The first is that the application of neuroimaging techniques in health economics is relatively recent. This means that the development of neuronal research hypotheses should be based on the conclusions of studies pertaining to the fields of psychology and social neuroscience, and not to a strictly medical one. Second, neuroimaging tools also require a great financial expense (between 100 € and 600 € per scanning hour) given the need to source technicians with specialized knowledge. Thirdly, the experimental context of neuroimaging tools gives rise to an artificial environment that can restrain the external validity of consumer neuroscience research. Moreover, certain neurophysiological tools differ in their level of artificiality. For example, fMRI requires participants not to move more than 3 millimeters within the full-body tube during the experiment (Dimoka et al., 2010). Forth, data derived from the application of neuroscientific tools requires an intense process of analysis that includes movement correction (fMRI or eye tracking), preparation for proper recordings (EKG electrode placing), manual data extraction (observation in eye tracking studies), and large volumes of imaging data (fMRI). The preparation of fMRI data, for example, requires slice timing correction, realignment, co-registration, segmentation, normalization, and smoothing. Finally, ethical problems in neuroscience research have spawned a new field called neuroethics concerned with the discipline's legal, moral, and social implications. Applying neuroscience to the field of health economics, due to the large quantity of sensitive information, means not only observing ethical norms, but also protecting vulnerable segments of society from government exploitation (Sebastian, 2014).

Despite the proven effects that professional motivation has on the performance of the medical practitioner, it is surprising how most studies fail to analyze the neuronal origin of different types of motivation of the doctor. This study protocol advances for the first time a methodology of analysis that, based on neuroimaging tools, allows an objective evaluation of neuronal differences in the psycho-motivational patterns of physicians belonging to public or private organizations.

SUGGESTIONS

The scarce research that analyses the differences between personnel belonging to these entities, together with the potential for neuroscience to detect the psychological origin of motivations and decision making in health, calls for the use of neuroeconomics as a tool which would permit a better doctor-patient relationship, selection of the medical profile to best suit organizations and an efficient allocation of health resources.

FUTURE SCOPE

Researchers using this study protocol, or its derivatives are encouraged to report and publish their findings. The results derived from the application of this study protocol will allow the definition of the idiosyncratic motivational structure of hospital doctors working in different hospitals with different values and missions (public, for-profit and non-profit). These results can serve as a guide to structure the set of monetary and non-monetary incentives that are most effective in attracting their attention, and provoking efficient emotional and cognitive responses, resulting in their intrinsic personal and professional satisfaction.

ACKNOWLEDGMENT

The authors thank the Unit of Excellence at the University of Granada for funding this research. The project is funded by the Unit of Excellence at the University of Granada.

This research was supported by the University of Granada

REFERENCES

Akerlof, G., & Kranton, R. (2005). Identity and the economics of organizations. *The Journal of Economic Perspectives*, *19*(1), 9–32. doi:10.1257/0895330053147930

Akitsuki, Y., & Decety, J. (2009). Social context and perceived agency affects empathy for pain: An event-related fMRI investigation. *NeuroImage*, *47*(2), 722–734. doi:10.1016/j.neuroimage.2009.04.091 PMID:19439183

Avery, G., & Schultz, J. (2017). Regulation, Financial Incentives, and the Production of Quality. *American Journal of Medical Quality*. PMID:17656731

Barigozzi, F., & Burani, N. (2016). Screening workers for ability and motivation. *Oxford Economic Papers*, *68*(2), 627–650. doi:10.1093/oep/gpw005

Ben-Ner, A., & Putterman, L. (2012). *Economics, Values, and Organization*. University of Minnesota: Cambridge University Press.

Berdud, M., Cabasés, J., & Nieto, J. (2016). Incentives and intrinsic motivation in healthcare. *Gaceta Sanitaria*, *30*(6), 408–414. doi:10.1016/j.gaceta.2016.04.013 PMID:27321370

Böckler, A., Tusche, A., Schmidt, P., & Singer, T. (2018). Distinct mental trainings differentially affect altruistically motivated, norm motivated, and self-reported prosocial behaviour. *Scientific Reports*, *8*(1), 13560. doi:10.103841598-018-31813-8 PMID:30202029

Bonfrer, I., Figueroa, J., Zheng, J., Orav, E. J., & Jha, A. K. (2018). Impact of Financial Incentives on Early and Late Adopters among US Hospitals: Observational study. *BMJ (Clinical Research Ed.)*, *360*, j5622. doi:10.1136/bmj.j5622 PMID:29298765

Burks, D., & Kobus, A. (2012). The legacy of altruism in health care: The promotion of empathy, prosociality and humanism. *Medical Education*, *46*(3), 317–325. doi:10.1111/j.1365-2923.2011.04159.x PMID:22324531

Casado-Aranda, L.-A., Sánchez-Fernández, J., & Ibáñez-Zapata, J.-Á. (2020). Evaluating Communication Effectiveness Through Eye Tracking: Benefits, State of the Art, and Unresolved Questions. *International Journal of Business Communication*. Advance online publication. doi:10.1177/2329488419893746

Casado-Aranda, L.-A., Sánchez-Fernández, J., Ibáñez-Zapata, J.-Á., & Liébana-Cabanillas, F. J. (2020). How consumer ethnocentrism modulates neural processing of domestic and foreign products: A neuroimaging study. *Journal of Retailing and Consumer Services*, *53*, 101961. doi:10.1016/j.jretconser.2019.101961

Davis, L., Stewart, A., Stanwoodd, G., Raajaram, G., Randy, D., & Blakely, K. (2018). Functional coding variation in the presynaptic dopamine transporter associated with neuropsychiatric disorders drives enhanced motivation and context-dependent impulsivity in mice. *Behavioural Brain Research*, *337*(30), 61–69. doi:10.1016/j.bbr.2017.09.043 PMID:28964912

Decety, J., Yang, C., & Cheng, Y. (2010). Physicians down-regulate their pain empathy response: An event-related brain potential study. *NeuroImage*, *50*(4), 1676–1682. doi:10.1016/j.neuroimage.2010.01.025 PMID:20080194

Dimoka, A. (2010). What Does the Brain Tell Us About Trust and Distrust? Evidence from a Functional Neuroimaging Study. *Management Information Systems Quarterly*, *2*(34), 373–396. doi:10.2307/20721433

Doherty, J., & Hampton, A. (2008). Decoding the neural substrates of reward-related decision making with functional MRI. *Proc Natl Acad Sci*, *104*(4), 1377-82.

Dovidio, J. (2006). The social psychology of prosocial behavior. London: Lawrence Erlbaum Publishers.

Evans, J. (1984). Heuristic and analytic processes in reasoning. *British Journal of Psychology*, *75*(4), 451–468. doi:10.1111/j.2044-8295.1984.tb01915.x

Faber, S., Douglas, T., Heise, F., & Hewstone, M. (2015). Cognitive Enhancement and Motivation Enhancement: An Empirical Comparison of Intuitive Judgments. *AJOB Neuroscience*, *6*(6), 1. doi:10.1080/21507740.2014.991847

Fine, M. (2018). *Health care revolt: How to organize, build a health care system, and resuscitate democracy: all at the same time*. PM Press.

Graber, M., Kissam, S., Payne, V., Meyer, A. N. D., Sorensen, A., Lenfestey, N., Tant, E., Henriksen, K., LaBresh, K., & Singh, H. (2012). Cognitive intervention to reduce diagnostic error: A narrative review. *BMJ Quality & Safety*, *21*(7), 535–537. doi:10.1136/bmjqs-2011-000149 PMID:22543420

Greenfield, D., Pawsey, M., & Braithwaite, J. (2011). What motivates professionals to engage in the accreditation of healthcare organizations? *International Journal for Quality in Health Care*, *23*(1), 8–14. doi:10.1093/intqhc/mzq069 PMID:21084322

Gruber, M., Gelman, B., & Ranganath, C. (2014). States of curiosity modulate hippocampus-dependent learning via the dopaminergic circuit. *Neuron*, *84*(2), 486-96.

Haber, S., & Knutson, B. (2010). The reward circuit: Linking primate anatomy and human imaging. *Neuropsychopharmacology*, *35*(1), 4–26. doi:10.1038/npp.2009.129 PMID:19812543

Hein, G., & Singer, T. (2008). I feel how you feel but not always: The empathic brain and its modulation. *Current Opinion in Neurobiology*, *18*(2), 153–158. doi:10.1016/j.conb.2008.07.012 PMID:18692571

Herzberg, F. (2017). *Motivation to work*. Routledge. doi:10.4324/9781315124827

Horwitz, S. (2005). The Compositional Impact of Team Diversity on Performance: Theoretical Considerations. *Human Resource Development Review*, *4*(2), 219–245. doi:10.1177/1534484305275847

Jelstad, B. (2007). *Beyond Money: Intrinsic work motivation in profit and nonprofit organizations* (Doctoral thesis). Norwegian School of Economics and Business Administration.

Kahneman, D. (2012). *Pensar rápido, Pensar despacio*. Debate.

Kjellström, S., Avby, G., Areskoug-Josefsson, K., Gäre, B. A., & Bäck, M. A. (2017). Work motivation among healthcare professionals. *Journal of Health Organization and Management*, *31*(4), 487–502. doi:10.1108/JHOM-04-2017-0074 PMID:28877624

Klimecki, O., Leiberg, S., Lamm, C., & Singer, T. (2013). Functional Neural Plasticity and Associated Changes in Positive Affect. *Cerebral Cortex (New York, N.Y.)*, *23*(7), 1552–1561. doi:10.1093/cercor/bhs142 PMID:22661409

Kovacs, C., Stiglbauer, B., Batinic, B., & Gnambs, T. (2018). Exploring Different Forms of Job (Dis)Satisfaction and Their Relationship with Well-Being, Motivation and Performance. *Applied Psychology*, *67*(3), 523–556. doi:10.1111/apps.12128

Lamm, C., Decety, J., & Singer, T. (2011). Meta-analytic evidence for common and distinct neural networks associated with directly experienced pain and empathy for pain. *NeuroImage*, *54*(3), 2492–2502. doi:10.1016/j.neuroimage.2010.10.014 PMID:20946964

Lázaro, P., Palma, M., Azcona, B., Cardona, P., & Chinchilla, N. (2005). From individual motivation to organizational compensation: The physician's perspective. *Annual Meeting of the International Society of Technology Assessment in Health Care (ISTAHC)*.

Lee, W., & Reeve, J. (2012). Motivational neuroscience. The Oxford handbook of human motivation.

Lee, Y., & Seomun, G. (2016). Development and validation of an instrument to measure nurses' compassion competence. *Applied Nursing Research*, *30*, 76–82. doi:10.1016/j.apnr.2015.09.007 PMID:27091258

Lown, B. A. (2016). A social neuroscience-informed model for teaching and practising compassion in health care. *Medical Education*, *50*(3), 332–342. doi:10.1111/medu.12926 PMID:26896018

Mumford, J., & Nichols, T. (2008). Power calculation for group fMRI studies accounting for arbitrary design and temporal autocorrelation. *Neuroimage*, *39*(1), 261-8.

Murayamaa, K., Matsumotob, M., Izumab, K., & Matsumoto, K. (2010). Neural basis of the undermining effect of monetary reward on intrinsic motivation. *Proceedings of the National Academy of Sciences of the United States of America, 107*(49), 20911–20916. doi:10.1073/pnas.1013305107 PMID:21078974

Nantha, S. (2013). Intrinsic motivation: How can it play a pivotal role in changing clinician behaviour? *Journal of Health Organization and Management*. PMID:23802402

Oppel, E., Winter, V., & Schreyögg, J. (2019). Examining the relationship between strategic HRM and hospital employees' work attitudes: An analysis across occupational groups in public and private hospitals. *International Journal of Human Resource Management, 30*(5), 5. doi:10.1080/09585192.2016.1254104

Ouchi, W. (1981). Efficient Boundaries. *Interim technical rept*, (1), 42.

Penner, A., Piliavin, J., Schroeder, D., & Dovidio, J. (2005). Prosocial Behavior: Multilevel Perspectives. *Annual Review of Psychology, 56*(1), 365–392. doi:10.1146/annurev.psych.56.091103.070141 PMID:15709940

Philippe, R. R., & Fekken, G. (1981). The altruistic personality and the self-report altruism scale. *Personality and Individual Differences, 2*(4), 293–302. doi:10.1016/0191-8869(81)90084-2

Ritz, A., Brewer, G., & Neumann, O. (2016). Public Service Motivation: A Systematic Literature Review and Outlook. *Public Administration Review, 76*(3), 414–426. doi:10.1111/puar.12505

Rosenau, P., & Linder, S. (2003). Two Decades of Research Comparing For-Profit and Nonprofit Health Provider Performance in the United States. *Social Science Quarterly, 84*(2), 219–241. doi:10.1111/1540-6237.8402001

Ruby, P., & Decety, J. (2004). How Would You Feel versus How Do You Think She Would Feel? A Neuroimaging Study of Perspective-Taking with Social Emotions. *Journal of Cognitive Neuroscience, 16*(6), 988–999. doi:10.1162/0898929041502661 PMID:15298786

Russell, G. (2015). Does paying for performance in primary care save. *BMJ (Clinical Research Ed.), 350*(mar02 5), h1051. doi:10.1136/bmj.h1051 PMID:25731697

Sebastian, V. (2014). Neuromarketing and Neuroethics. *Procedia: Social and Behavioral Sciences, 127*, 763–768. doi:10.1016/j.sbspro.2014.03.351

Serra, D., Serneels, P., & Barr, A. (2011). Intrisic motivations and the non-profit health sector: Evidence from Ethiopia. *Personality and Individual Differences, 51*(3), 309–314. doi:10.1016/j.paid.2010.04.018

Sicsic, J., Le Vaillant, M., & Franc, C. (2014). Building a composite score of general practitioners' intrinsic motivation: A comparison of methods. *International Journal for Quality in Health Care, 26*(2), 167–173. doi:10.1093/intqhc/mzu007 PMID:24521704

Solnais, C. A.-P.-F.-A., Andreu-Perez, J., Sánchez-Fernández, J., & Andréu-Abela, J. (2013). The contribution of neuroscience to consumer research: A conceptual framework and empirical review. *Journal of Economic Psychology, 36*, 68–81. doi:10.1016/j.joep.2013.02.011

ADDITIONAL READING

García-Mochón, L., Martín-Martín, J. J., Aranda-Regules, J. M., Rivas-Ruiz, F., & Vas, J. (2015). Cost effectiveness of using moxibustion to correct non-vertex presentation. Acupuncture in Medicine. *Journal of the British Medical Acupuncture Society, 33*(2), 136–141. doi:10.1136/acupmed-2014-010696 PMID:25669428

Herrero Tabanera, L., Martín Martín, J. J., & López del Amo González, M. del P. (2015). Eficiencia técnica de los hospitales públicos y de las empresas públicas hospitalarias de Andalucía. Gaceta Sanitaria, 29(4), 274-281. Q3, JCR.

Mumford, J. A., & Nichols, T. E. (2008). Power calculation for group fMRI studies accounting for arbitrary design and temporal autocorrelation. *NeuroImage, 39*(1), 261–268. doi:10.1016/j.neuroimage.2007.07.061 PMID:17919925

Pérez-Romero, C., Ortega-Díaz, M. I., Ocaña-Riola, R., Martín-Martín, J. J., Pérez-Romero, C., Ortega-Díaz, M. I., … Martín-Martín, J. J. (2017). Análisis de la eficiencia técnica en los hospitales del Sistema Nacional de Salud español. Gaceta Sanitaria, 31(2), 108-115. Q3, JCR

Philippe Rushton, J., Chrisjohn, R. D., & Cynthia Fekken, G. (1981). The altruistic personality and the self-report altruism scale. *Personality and Individual Differences, 2*(4), 293–302. doi:10.1016/0191-8869(81)90084-2

Stanton, S. J., Sinnott-Armstrong, W., & Huettel, S. A. (2017). Neuromarketing: Ethical implications of its use and potential misuse. *Journal of Business Ethics, 144*(4), 799–811. doi:10.100710551-016-3059-0

Thomas, A. R., Pop, N. A., Lorga, A. M., & Ducu, C. (2017). *Ethics and Neuromarketing. Implications for Market Research and Business Practice* (1st ed.). Springer. doi:10.1007/978-3-319-45609-6

KEY TERMS AND DEFINITIONS

Clinical Decision Making: Is the process the process used by healthcare professionals and which affects their patients, an enormously broad and diverse concept that ranges from diagnosis to treatment, through many other aspects related to healthcare activity.

Electroencephalography: Neurological tool that measures the electrical changes produced by brain activity.

Functional Magnetic Resonance Imaging: Neurological technique that measures the magnetic changes produced by neural activity.

Health Economics: It is a field of research whose object of study is the optimal use of resources for disease care and health promotion. Their task is to estimate the organizational efficiency of health services and suggest ways to improve this organization.

Incentives System: Is the program offered by a business organization to workers in order to stimulate the performance of their work activity and increase production.

Work Motivation: Is the ability of organizations to maintain the positive stimulus of their employees in relation to all the activities they carry out to carry out its objects, that is, in relation to work.

Compilation of References

Acquaah, M. (2012). Social networking relationships, firm-specific managerial experience and firm performance in a transition economy: A comparative analysis of family owned and nonfamily firms. *Strategic Management Journal, 33*(10), 1215–1228. doi:10.1002mj.1973

Aeppel, T. (2014). Robots work their way into small factories. *The Wall Street Journal*, pp. B1-2.

Agnihotri, R., Kothandaraman, P., Kashyap, R., & Singh, R. (2012). Bringing "social" into sales: The impact of salespeople's social media use on service behaviors and value creation. *Journal of Personal Selling & Sales Management, 22*(3), 333–348. doi:10.2753/PSS0885-3134320304

Agrawal, P., & Gautam, O. (2019). The Effects of Leaders' Behavior on Job Satisfaction, Organizational Citizenship Behavior, Deviant Behavior, and Job Performance of Employees. In Analyzing Workplace Deviance in Modern Organizations (pp. 100-113). IGI Global.

Agrawal, P., & Gautam, O. (2018). Truancy and Job Satisfaction towards Sponsored Child-Care Facility in India. *Prabandhan: Indian Journal of Management, 11*(7), 23–35. doi:10.17010/pijom/2018/v11i7/129937

Agrawal, P., & Gautam, O. (2019). The Effects of Leaders' Behavior on Job Satisfaction, Organizational Citizenship Behavior, Deviant Behavior, and Job Performance of Employees. In *Analyzing Workplace Deviance in Modern Organizations* (pp. 100–113). IGI Global.

Aguilera, R. V., & Jackson, G. (2003). The Cross-national Diversity of Corporate Governance Dimensions and Determinants. *Academy of Management Review, 28*(3), 447–465. doi:10.5465/amr.2003.10196772

Agustiawan, K. (2015). *Transforming the BUMN into an Indonesian State Holding Company.* Ash Center Harvard Kennedy School.

Agwa. (2018). *Workplace Deviance Behaviors, Leadership, Suleyman Davut Göker.* IntechOpen. Available from: https://www.intechopen.com/books/leadership/workplace-deviance-behaviors doi:10.5772/intechopen.75941

Ahmad, A., & Omar, Z. (2016). Workplace spirituality among Malaysian community service employees in the public sector. *Asian Social Science, 12*(9), 193–201. doi:10.5539/ass.v12n9p193

Aichhorn, N., & Puck, J. (2017). Bridging the language gap in multinational companies: Language strategies and the notion of company-speak. *Journal of World Business*, *52*(3), 386–403. doi:10.1016/j.jwb.2017.01.002

Aiello, J. R., & Kolb, K. J. (1995). Electronic performance monitoring and social context: Impact on productivity and stress. *The Journal of Applied Psychology*, *80*(3), 339–353. doi:10.1037/0021-9010.80.3.339 PMID:7797458

Akca, M. (2020). An Investigation of the Relationship Between Favoritism and Workplace Deviance: Meditation Role of Negative Emotions. In *Analyzing Workplace Deviance in Modern Organizations* (pp. 114–138). IGI Global. doi:10.4018/978-1-5225-9996-8.ch007

Akdoğan, A., & Demirtaş, Ö. (2014). Etik Liderlik Davranişlarinin Etik İklim Üzerindeki Etkisi: Örgütsel Politik Algilamalarin Araci Rolü. *Afyon Kocatepe Üniversitesi İktisadi ve İdari Bilimler Fakültesi Dergisi*, *16*(1), 107–124.

Akerlof, G., & Kranton, R. (2005). Identity and the economics of organizations. *The Journal of Economic Perspectives*, *19*(1), 9–32. doi:10.1257/0895330053147930

Akitsuki, Y., & Decety, J. (2009). Social context and perceived agency affects empathy for pain: An event-related fMRI investigation. *NeuroImage*, *47*(2), 722–734. doi:10.1016/j.neuroimage.2009.04.091 PMID:19439183

Akkoç, İ. (2012). Gelişim Kültürü ve Etik İklimin Yenilikçiliğe Etkisinde Dağıtım Adaletinin Rolü. *Journal of Alanya Faculty of Business*, *4*(3), 45–60.

Aladwani, A. M. (2001). Change management strategies for successful ERP implementation. *Business Process Management Journal*, *7*(3), 266–275. doi:10.1108/14637150110392764

Alder, G. S. (2001). Employee reactions to electronic performance monitoring: A consequence of organizational culture. *The Journal of High Technology Management Research*, *12*(2), 323–342. doi:10.1016/S1047-8310(01)00042-6

Alder, G. S., & Ambrose, M. L. (2005a). An examination of the effect of computerized task specific monitoring feedback on monitoring fairness, performance and satisfaction. *Organizational Behavior and Human Decision Processes*, *97*(2), 161–177. doi:10.1016/j.obhdp.2005.03.003

Alder, G. S., & Ambrose, M. L. (2005b). Towards understanding fairness judgments associated with computer task-specific monitoring: An integration of the feedback, justice, and monitoring research. *Human Resource Management Review*, *15*(1), 43–67. doi:10.1016/j.hrmr.2005.01.001

Aldrich, H., & Auster, E. R. (1986). Even dwarfs started small: Liabilities of age and size and their strategic implications. *Research in Organizational Behavior*.

Alge, B. J. (2001). Effects of computer surveillance on perceptions of privacy and procedural justice. *The Journal of Applied Psychology*, *86*(4), 797–804. doi:10.1037/0021-9010.86.4.797 PMID:11519663

Algesheimer, R., Dholakia, U. M., & Gurău, C. (2011). Virtual team performance in a highly competitive environment. *Group & Organization Management, 36*(2), 161–190. doi:10.1177/1059601110391251

Alias, M., & Rasdi, R. M. (2015). Organizational predictors of workplace deviance among support staff. *Procedia: Social and Behavioral Sciences, 172*, 126–133. doi:10.1016/j.sbspro.2015.01.345

Ali, M., Lei, S., & Wei, X.-Y. (2018). The mediating role of the employee relations climate in the relationship between strategic HRM and organizational performance in Chinese banks. *Journal of Innovation & Knowledge, 3*(3), 115–122. doi:10.1016/j.jik.2016.12.003

Alkhalifah, A., & D'Ambra, J. (2011). Applying task-technology fit to the adoption of identity management systems. *Proceedings of the 22nd Australasian Conference on Information Systems.*

Allen, T. D., Eby, L. T., Poteet, M. L., Lima, L., & Lentz, E. (2004). Mentoring benefits: A meta-analysis. *The Journal of Applied Psychology, 89*, 127–136. doi:10.1037/0021-9010.89.1.127 PMID:14769125

Allison, M. T. (n.d.). Organizational Barriers to Diversity in the Workplace: Benefits, Challenges, and the Required Managerial Tools. *Journal of Insure Research, 31*(1), 78-101.

Alvesson, M., & Sveningsson, S. (2003). Managers doing leadership: The extra-ordinarization of the mundane. *Human Relations, 56*(12), 1435–1459. doi:10.1177/00187267035612001

Amble, B. (2004). *Does cyberloafing undermine productivity?* Management-Issues Ltd. Retrieved from: http://www.managementissues.com /2006/8/24/research/does cyberloafing-undermining-productivity. asp

Ambrose, M. L., Seabright, M. A., & Schminke, M. (2002). Sabotage in the workplace: The role of organizational injustice. *Organizational Behavior and Human Decision Processes, 89*(1), 947–965. doi:10.1016/S0749-5978(02)00037-7

Ambrosini, V., & Bowman, C. (2009). What are dynamic capabilities and are they a useful construct in strategic management? *International Journal of Management Reviews, 11*(1), 29–49. doi:10.1111/j.1468-2370.2008.00251.x

American Management Association. (2007). *The Latest on Workplace Monitoring and Surveillance.* American Management Association of USA. Available from: http://press.amanet.org/pressreleases/177/2007electronicmonitoringsurveillancesurvey/

Amusan, L., Adeyeye, A. I., & Oyewole, S. (2019). Women as Agents of Terror: Women Resources and Gender Discourse in Terrorism and Insurgency. *Politikon, 46*(3), 345–359. doi:10.1080/02589346.2019.1642681

Anandarajan, M., Simmers, C. A., & D'Ovidio, R. (2011). Exploring the underlying structure of personal web usage in the workplace. *Cyberpsychology, Behavior, and Social Networking, 14*(10), 577–583. doi:10.1089/cyber.2010.0136 PMID:21728817

Andreassen, C. S., Torsheim, T., & Pallesen, S. (2014). Predictors of Use of Social Network Sites at Work - A Specific Type of Cyberloafing. *Journal of Computer-Mediated Communication, 19*(4), 906–921. doi:10.1111/jcc4.12085

Andreoli, N., & Lefkowitz, J. (2009). Individual and organizational antecedents of misconduct in organizations. *Journal of Business Ethics, 85*(3), 309–332. doi:10.100710551-008-9772-6

Anitha, J. (2014). Determinants of employee engagement and their impact on employee performance. *International Journal of Productivity and Performance Management, 63*(3), 308–323. doi:10.1108/IJPPM-01-2013-0008

Ansoff, H. I. (1991). Critique of Henry Mintzberg's 'The design school: Reconsidering the basic premises of strategic management'. *Strategic Management Journal, 12*(6), 449–461. doi:10.1002mj.4250120605

Anyieni, A. G. (2013). *Effect of strategic planning on the performance of small and medium enterprises in Kenya: A summary review of the literature*. Academic Press.

Apers, C., & Derous, E. (2017). Are they accurate? Recruiters' personality judgments in paper versus video resumes. *Computers in Human Behavior, 73*, 9–19. doi:10.1016/j.chb.2017.02.063

Appelbaum, S. H., Deguire, K. J., & Lay, M. (2005). The relationship of ethical climate to deviant workplace behaviour. *Corporate Governance: The International Journal of Business in Society,5*(4), 43-55.

Appelbaum, S. H., Iaconi, G. D., & Matousek, A. (2007). Positive and negative deviant workplace behaviors: causes, impacts, and solutions. *Corporate Governance: The International Journal of Business in Society, 7*(5), 586-598.

Appelbaum, S. H., Deguire, K. J., & Lay, M. (2005). The relationship of ethical climate to deviant workplace behaviour. *Corporate Governance, 5*(4), 43–55. doi:10.1108/14720700510616587

Appelbaum, S. H., St-Pierre, N., & Glavas, W. (1998). Strategic organizational change: The role of leadership, learning, motivation and productivity. *Management Decision, 36*(5), 289–301. doi:10.1108/00251749810220496

Armengol, X., Fernandez, V., Simo, P., & Sallan, J. M. (2017). An examination of the effects of self-regulatory focus on the perception of the media richness: The case of E-mail. *International Journal of Business Communication, 54*(4), 394–407. doi:10.1177/2329488415572780

Arnaud, A. (2010). Conceptualizing and measuring ethical work climate: Development and validation of the ethical climate index. *Business & Society, 49*(2), 345–358. doi:10.1177/0007650310362865

Arokiasamy, A. R. A. (2013). Literature review on workforce diversity, employee performance and organizational goals: A concept paper. Journal of Arts. *Science & Commerce, 4*(4), 58–63.

Aryati, A. S., Sudiro, A., Hadiwidjaja, D., & Noermijati, N. (2018). The influence of ethical leadership to deviant workplace behavior mediated by ethical climate and organizational commitment. *International Journal of Law and Management, 60*(2), 233–249. doi:10.1108/IJLMA-03-2017-0053

Asadullah, M. N., Xiao, S., & Yeoh, E. (2015). Subjective well-being in China, 2005–2010: The role of relative income, gender, and location. *China Economic Review.*

Ashford, S. J., Lee, C., & Bobko, P. (1989). Content, cause, and consequences of job insecurity: A theory- based measure and substantive test. *Academy of Management Journal, 32*(4), 803–828. doi:10.2307/256569

Ashforth, B. E. (1997). Petty tyranny in organizations: A preliminary examination of antecedents and consequences. *Canadian Journal of Administrative Sciences, 14*(2), 126–140. doi:10.1111/j.1936-4490.1997.tb00124.x

Au, Y., & Marks, A. (2012). Virtual teams are literally and metaphorically invisible": Forging identity in culturally diverse virtual teams. *Employee Relations, 34*(3), 271–287. doi:10.1108/01425451211217707

Avery, G., & Schultz, J. (2017). Regulation, Financial Incentives, and the Production of Quality. *American Journal of Medical Quality*. PMID:17656731

Bacong, C.I.M., & Encio, H.A. (2017). Effect of employee relation to job performance in engineering, construction and manufacturing company. *Asia Pacific Journal of Educational, Arts and Sciences, 42*(2), 103-110.

Badea, M. (2014). Social Media and Organizational Communication. *Social and Behavioral Sciences, 149*, 70–75.

Badger, J. M., Kaminsky, S. E., & Behrend, T. S. (2014). Media richness and information acquisition in internet recruitment. *Journal of Managerial Psychology, 29*(7), 866–883. doi:10.1108/JMP-05-2012-0155

Bajaj, R. (2013). Suggestions to implement human relations and its determinants in public sector. *American Journal of Engineering Research, 2*(12), 91–97.

Bakker, A., & Demerouti, E. (2007). The Job Demands-Resources model: State of the art. *Journal of Managerial Psychology, 22*(3), 309–328. doi:10.1108/02683940710733115

Balamurugan, G., & Abinaya, R. (2016). A study on employee retention strategies in leading IT companies at Trichy. *Intercontinental Journal of Human Resource Research Reviews, 4*(3), 42-47.

Ballinger, G., Craig, E., Cross, R., & Gray, P. (2011). A stitch in time saves nine: Leveraging networks to reduce the costs of turnover. *California Management Review, 53*(4), 111–133. doi:10.1525/cmr.2011.53.4.111

Ball, K. (2010). Workplace surveillance: An overview. *Labor History, 51*(1), 87106. doi:10.1080/00236561003654776

Ball, R. D., Del Debbio, L., Forte, S., Guffanti, A., Latorre, J. I., Rojo, J., & Ubiali, M.Nnpdf Collaboration. (2010). A first unbiased global NLO determination of parton distributions and their uncertainties. *Nuclear Physics B*, *838*(1-2), 136–206. doi:10.1016/j.nuclphysb.2010.05.008

Banai, M., & Reisel, W. D. (1993). Expatriate managers' loyalty to the MNC: Myth or reality? An exploratory study. *Journal of International Business Studies*, *24*(2), 233–248. doi:10.1057/palgrave.jibs.8490231

Bandura, A. (1973). *Aggression: A social learning analysis*. Prentice-hall.

Bardoel, E. A. (2016). Work–life management tensions in multinational enterprises (MNEs). *International Journal of Human Resource Management*, *27*(15), 1681–1709. doi:10.1080/09585192.2015.1074089

Barigozzi, F., & Burani, N. (2016). Screening workers for ability and motivation. *Oxford Economic Papers*, *68*(2), 627–650. doi:10.1093/oep/gpw005

Barkema, H. G., & Vermeulen, F. (1998). International expansion through start-up or acquisition: A learning perspective. *Academy of Management Journal*, *41*(1), 7–26.

Barley, S. R., & Bechky, B. A. (2017). From the editor: The changing nature of work: Careers, identities, and work lives in the 21st century. Academy of Management Discoveries, 3(2), 111-115.

Barnett, T., & Vaicys, C. (2000). The moderating effect of individuals' perceptions of ethical work climate on ethical judgments and behavioral intentions. *Journal of Business Ethics*, *27*(4), 351–362. doi:10.1023/A:1006382407821

Barney, J. (1991). Firms resources and sustained competitive advantage. *Journal of Management*, *17*(1), 99–117. doi:10.1177/014920639101700108

Baron, R. A., & Neuman, J. H. (1996). Workplace violence and workplace aggression: Evidence on their relative frequency and potential causes. *Aggressive Behavior: Official Journal of the International Society for Research on Aggression*, *22*(3), 161–173. doi:10.1002/(SICI)1098-2337(1996)22:3<161::AID-AB1>3.0.CO;2-Q

Barrett, M., & McCallum, C. (1996). Globalization and the employment relationship: towards an explanatory framework. Research papers in international business, 4-95.

Barrett, B., Grabow, M., Middlecamp, C., Mooney, M., Checovich, M. M., Converse, A. K., Gillespie, B., & Yates, J. (2016). Mindful climate action: Health and environmental co-benefits from mindfulness-based behavioral training. *Sustainability*, *8*(10), 1040. doi:10.3390u8101040 PMID:28008371

Bartlett, C. A., & Ghoshal, S. (1989). *Managing across boarders*. Harvard Business School Press.

Bartlett, C. A., & Ghoshal, S. (2002). Building Competitive Advantage Through People. *MIT Sloan Management Review*, *43*(2).

Bates, S. (2004). Getting engaged. *HRMagazine*, *49*(2), 44–51.

Baucus, M. S., & Near, J. P. (1991). Can illegal corporate behavior be predicted? An event history analysis. *Academy of Management Journal, 34*(1), 9–36.

Baumeister, R. M., & Leary, M. R. (1995). The need to belong: Desire for interpersonal attachments as a fundamental human motivation. *Psychological Bulletin, 117*(3), 497–529. doi:10.1037/0033-2909.117.3.497 PMID:7777651

Baumruk, R. (2004). The missing link: The role of employee engagement in business success. *Workspan, 47*, 48–52.

BBC. (2019, June 26). *Robots 'to replace up to 20 million factory jobs' by 2030.* Retrieved from: https://www.bbc.com/news/business-48760799

Behringer, N., & Sassenberg, K. (2015). Introducing social media for knowledge management: Determinants of employees' intentions to adopt new tools. *Computers in Human Behavior, 48*, 290–296. doi:10.1016/j.chb.2015.01.069

Beilock, R. (2003). The elusive sweatshop. *Transportation Quarterly, 57*(3).

Belizón, M. J. (2019). Employee voice in Spanish subsidiaries of multinational firms. *European Journal of Industrial Relations, 25*(1), 75–90. doi:10.1177/0959680118776076

Ben-Ner, A., & Putterman, L. (2012). *Economics, Values, and Organization.* University of Minnesota: Cambridge University Press.

Bennett, R. J., & Robinson, S. L. (2000). Development of a measure of workplace deviance. *The Journal of Applied Psychology, 85*(3), 349–360. doi:10.1037/0021-9010.85.3.349 PMID:10900810

Berdud, M., Cabasés, J., & Nieto, J. (2016). Incentives and intrinsic motivation in healthcare. *Gaceta Sanitaria, 30*(6), 408–414. doi:10.1016/j.gaceta.2016.04.013 PMID:27321370

Bergesen, A. J., & Sonnett, J. (2001). The global 500: Mapping the world economy at century's end. *The American Behavioral Scientist, 44*(10), 1602–1615. doi:10.1177/00027640121958078

Berman, A., & Dorrier, J. (2016). Technology feels like it's accelerating—because it actually is. *Singularity Hub.* Retrieved from: https://singularityhub.com/2016/03/22/technology-feels-like-its-accelerating-because-it-actually-is

Berman, E. M., West, J. P., & Richter, M. N. Jr. (2002). Workplace relations: Friendship patterns and consequences (according to managers). *Public Administration Review, 62*(2), 217–230. doi:10.1111/0033-3352.00172

Bersin by Deloitte. (2013). *Predictions for 2014.* Bersin by Deloitte.

Berthon, P. R., Pitt, L. F., Plangger, K., & Shapiro, D. (2012). Marketing meets Web 2.0, social media, and creative consumers: Implications for international marketing strategy. *Business Horizons, 55*(3), 261–271. doi:10.1016/j.bushor.2012.01.007

Bharadwaj, A. S. (2000). A resource-based perspective on information technology capability and firm performance: An empirical investigation. *Management Information Systems Quarterly, 24*(1), 169–196. doi:10.2307/3250983

Biazin, C., Solano-Charris, E. L., & Quintero, J. A. (2017). Supply Chain and Operations Strategies for Problem-Solving in Latin American Countries: An Introduction. *Journal of Operations and Supply Chain Management*, 1-5.

Bilkey, W. J., & Tesar, G. (1977). The export behavior of smaller-sized Wisconsin manufacturing firms. *Journal of International Business Studies, 8*(1), 93–98. doi:10.1057/palgrave.jibs.8490783

Biocca, F., & Delaney, B. (1995). Immersive virtual reality technology. In F. Biocca & M. R. Levy (Eds.), *Communication in the age of virtual reality* (pp. 57–124). Lawrence Erlbaum Associates.

Biocca, F., & Levy, M. R. (1995). Virtual reality as a communication system. In F. Biocca & M. R. Levy (Eds.), *Communication in the age of virtual reality* (pp. 15–31). Lawrence Erlbaum Associates.

Bishop, S. R., Lau, M., Shapiro, S., Carlson, L., Anderson, N. D., Carmody, J., Segal, Z. V., Abbey, S., Speca, M., Velting, D., & Devins, G. (2004). Mindfulness: A proposed operational definition. *Clinical Psychology: Science and Practice, 11*(3), 230–241. doi:10.1093/clipsy.bph077

Bizzi, L. (2018). The hidden problem of Facebook and social media at work: What if employees start searching for other jobs? *Business Horizons, 61*(1), 23–33. doi:10.1016/j.bushor.2017.09.002

Blanchard, A. L., & Henle, C. A. (2008). Correlates of different forms of cyberloafing: The role of norms and external locus of control. *Computers in Human Behavior, 24*(3), 1067–1084. doi:10.1016/j.chb.2007.03.008

Blyton, P., & Turnbull, P. (2004). *The dynamics of employee relations (3rd ed.)*. Palgrave Macmillan.

Böckler, A., Tusche, A., Schmidt, P., & Singer, T. (2018). Distinct mental trainings differentially affect altruistically motivated, norm motivated, and self-reported prosocial behaviour. *Scientific Reports, 8*(1), 13560. doi:10.103841598-018-31813-8 PMID:30202029

Bonache, J., Brewster, C., & Suutari, V. (2001). Expatriation: A developing research agenda. *Thunderbird International Business Review, 43*(1), 3–20. doi:10.1002/1520-6874(200101/02)43:1<3::AID-TIE2>3.0.CO;2-4

Bonfrer, I., Figueroa, J., Zheng, J., Orav, E. J., & Jha, A. K. (2018). Impact of Financial Incentives on Early and Late Adopters among US Hospitals: Observational study. *BMJ (Clinical Research Ed.), 360*, j5622. doi:10.1136/bmj.j5622 PMID:29298765

Bowden, J. L. H. (2009). The process of customer engagement: A conceptual framework. *Journal of Marketing Theory and Practice, 17*(1), 63–74. doi:10.2753/MTP1069-6679170105

Bowling, N. A., & Beehr, T. A. (2006). Workplace harassment from the victim's perspective: A theoretical model and meta-analysis. *The Journal of Applied Psychology, 91*(5), 998–1012. doi:10.1037/0021-9010.91.5.998 PMID:16953764

Brannen, M. Y. (2004). When Mickey loses face: Recontextualization, semantic fit, and the semiotics of foreignness. *Academy of Management Review, 29*(4), 593–616. doi:10.5465/amr.2004.14497613

Braun, S., Hernandez Bark, A., Kirchner, A., Stegmann, S., & van Dick, R. (2019). Emails from the boss—Curse or blessing? Relations between communication channels, leader evaluation, and employees' attitudes. *International Journal of Business Communication, 56*(1), 50–81. doi:10.1177/2329488415597516

Bretz, R. D., Boudreau, J. W., & Judge, T. A. (1994). Job search behavior of employed managers. *Personnel Psychology, 47*(2), 275–301. doi:10.1111/j.1744-6570.1994.tb01725.x

Brewer, M. B., & Pierce, K. P. (2005). Social identity complexity and outgroup tolerance. *Personality and Social Psychology Bulletin, 31*(3), 428–437. doi:10.1177/0146167204271710 PMID:15657457

Brewster, C., Bonache, J., Cerdin, J.-L., & Suutari, V. (2014). *Exploring expatriate outcomes.* Taylor & Francis. doi:10.1080/09585192.2013.870284

Brewster, C., Sparrow, P., & Harris, H. (2005). Towards a new model of globalizing HRM. *The International Journal of Human Resource Management Group, 16*(6), 949–970. doi:10.1080/09585190500120590

Bricken, W. (1990). *Virtual reality: Directions of growth* (HITL Technical Report R90-1). Seattle, WA: University of Washington.

Brivot, M., Gendron, Y., & Guenin, H. (2017). Reinventing organizational control: Meaning contest surrounding reputational risk controllability in the social media area. *Accounting, Auditing & Accountability Journal, 30*(4), 795–820. doi:10.1108/AAAJ-06-2015-2111

Brown, K. W., Ryan, R. M., & Creswell, J. D. (2007). Mindfulness: Theoretical foundations and evidence for its salutary effects. *Psychological Inquiry, 18*(4), 211–237. doi:10.1080/10478400701598298

Bryant, P. C., & Allen, D. G. (2013). Compensation, benefits and employee turnover: HR strategies for retaining top talent. *Compensation and Benefits Review, 45*(3), 171–175. doi:10.1177/0886368713494342

Bryman, A. (2012). *Social research methods* (4th ed.). Oxford University Press. doi:10.1017/CBO9781107415324.004

Brynjolfsson, E., & McAfee, A. (2014). *The second machine age. Work, progress, and prosperity in a time of brilliant technologies.* W.W. Norton.

Buckley, P. J., & Casson, M. (1976). A long-run theory of the multinational enterprise. In *The future of the multinational enterprise* (pp. 32–65). Springer. doi:10.1007/978-1-349-02899-3_2

Buckley, P. J., & Casson, M. (2016). *The future of the multinational enterprise.* Springer.

Buitron, V. (2019, January 23). *The Role of Diversity in Innovation.* Retrieved from https://tangocode.com/2019/01/the-role-of-diversity-in-innovation/

Burks, D., & Kobus, A. (2012). The legacy of altruism in health care: The promotion of empathy, prosociality and humanism. *Medical Education, 46*(3), 317–325. doi:10.1111/j.1365-2923.2011.04159.x PMID:22324531

Burma, A. Z. (2014). Human Resource Management and Its Important for Today's Organizations. *International Journal of Education and Social Science*, 85–94.

Burnes, B. (2004). *Managing change: A strategic approach to organisational dynamics.* Pearson Education.

Burton, R. M., Obel, B., & Håkonsson, D. D. (2015). *Organizational design: A step-by-step approach.* Cambridge University Press. doi:10.1017/CBO9781316160787

Carlson, J. B., Zivnuska, S., Harris, R. B., Harris, K. J., & Carlson, D. S. (2016). Social Media Use in the Workplace: A Study of Dual Effects. *Journal of Organizational and End User Computing, 28*(1), 15–31. doi:10.4018/JOEUC.2016010102

Casado-Aranda, L.-A., Sánchez-Fernández, J., & Ibáñez-Zapata, J.-Á. (2020). Evaluating Communication Effectiveness Through Eye Tracking: Benefits, State of the Art, and Unresolved Questions. *International Journal of Business Communication.* Advance online publication. doi:10.1177/2329488419893746

Casado-Aranda, L.-A., Sánchez-Fernández, J., Ibáñez-Zapata, J.-Á., & Liébana-Cabanillas, F. J. (2020). How consumer ethnocentrism modulates neural processing of domestic and foreign products: A neuroimaging study. *Journal of Retailing and Consumer Services, 53*, 101961. doi:10.1016/j.jretconser.2019.101961

Cascio, W. F., & Montealegre, R. (2016). How technology is changing work and organizations. *Annual Review of Organizational Psychology and Organizational Behavior, 3*(1), 349–375. doi:10.1146/annurev-orgpsych-041015-062352

Castillo, C., Mendoza, M., & Poblete, B. (2011). Information credibility on twitter. In *Proceedings of the 20th International Conference on the World Wide Web.* Association for Computing Machinery.

Castrechini, M., Helgeson, H., & Malko, M. (2014). *U.S. Patent Application No. 14/363,765.* US Patent Office.

Chaffey, D. (2003). E-Business and E-Commerce Management. Academic Press.

Chakraborty, T., & Ganguly, M. (2019). Crafting Engaged Employees Through Positive Work Environment: Perspectives of Employee Engagement. In Management Techniques for Employee Engagement in Contemporary Organizations (pp. 180-198). IGI Global.

Chang, J. (2007). International Expansion Path, Speed, Product Diversification and Performance Among Emerging-Market MNEs: Evidence from Asia-Pacific Multinational Companies. *Asian Business & Management, 6*(4), 331–353. doi:10.1057/palgrave.abm.9200228

Chawla, S., & Sharma, R. R. (2016). How women traverse an upward journey in Indian industry: Multiple case studies. *Gender in Management, 31*(3), 181–206. doi:10.1108/GM-06-2015-0050

Cherry, C. R., & Adelakun, A. A. (2012). Truck driver perceptions and preferences: Congestion and conflict, managed lanes, and tolls. *Transport Policy, 24*, 1–9. doi:10.1016/j.tranpol.2012.07.012

Chi, C., & Gursoy, D. (2009). Employee satisfaction, customer satisfaction, and financial performance: An empirical examination. *International Journal of Hospitality Management, 28*(2), 245–253. doi:10.1016/j.ijhm.2008.08.003

Cho, D. Y., Koon, H. J., & Lee, H. Y. (2007). Analysis of trust in internet and mobile commerce adoption. In *Proceedings of the 40th Hawaii International Conference on System Science* (p. 50). IEEE. 10.1109/HICSS.2007.76

Chotpitayasunondh, V., & Douglas, K. M. (2016). How "phubbing" becomes the norm: The antecedents and consequences of snubbing via smartphone. *Computers in Human Behavior, 63*, 9–18. doi:10.1016/j.chb.2016.05.018

Chotpitayasunondh, V., & Douglas, K. M. (2018). The effects of "phubbing" on social interaction. *Journal of Applied Social Psychology, 48*(6), 304–316. doi:10.1111/jasp.12506

Christensen-Salem, A., Walumbwa, F. O., Babalola, M. T., Guo, L., & Misati, E. (2020). A Multilevel Analysis of the Relationship Between Ethical Leadership and Ostracism: The Roles of Relational Climate, Employee Mindfulness, and Work Unit Structure. *Journal of Business Ethics*, 1–20. doi:10.100710551-020-04424-5

Chrobot-Mason, D., & Aramovich, N. P. (2013). The Psychological Benefits of Creating an Affirming Climate for Workplace Diversity. *Group & Organization Management, 38*(6), 659–689. doi:10.1177/1059601113509835

CIPD. (2019). *Research Report on 'Diversity Management that Works - An Evidence-based View*. Author.

Cliff, O. (2014). Discourses of Diversity, Equality and Inclusion: Trenchant Formulations or Transient Fashions? *British Journal of Management, 25*(1), 23–39. doi:10.1111/j.1467-8551.2012.00830.x

Cnaan, R. A., & Cascio, T. A. (1998). Performance and commitment: Issues in management of volunteers in human service organizations. *Journal of Social Service Research, 24*(3-4), 1–37. doi:10.1300/J079v24n03_01

Cohen, S., & Wills, T. A. (1985). Stress, social support, and the buffering hypothesis. *Psychological Bulletin, 98*(2), 310–357. doi:10.1037/0033-2909.98.2.310 PMID:3901065

Cole, M. S., Bruch, H., & Vogel, B. (2006). Emotion as mediators of the relations between perceived supervisor support and psychological hardiness on employee criticism. *Journal of Organizational Behavior, 27*(4), 463–484. doi:10.1002/job.381

Cortina, L. M., & Magley, V. J. (2003). Raising voice, risking retaliation: Events following interpersonal mistreatment in the workplace. *Journal of Occupational Health Psychology*, *8*(4), 247–265. doi:10.1037/1076-8998.8.4.247 PMID:14570522

Costa. (n.d.). *Customer engagement improves brand profits*. Retrieved from https://www.marketingweek.com/customer-engagement-improves-brand-profits/

Cox, T. H., & Blake, S. (1991). Managing cultural diversity: Implications for organizational competitiveness. *The Academy of Management Perspectives*, *5*(3), 45–56. doi:10.5465/ame.1991.4274465

Cox, T., & Beale, R. L. (1997). *Developing competency to manage diversity: readings, cases & activities*. Berrett-Koehler.

Cox, T. Jr, & Beale, R. L. (1997). *Developing Competency to Manage Diversity- Readings, Cases and Activities*. Berrett Koehler Publishers Inc.

Creswell, J. D. (2017). Mindfulness interventions. *Annual Review of Psychology*, *68*(1), 491–516. doi:10.1146/annurev-psych-042716-051139 PMID:27687118

Crouch, C. (2012). Beyond the Flexibility/Security Trade-Off: Reconciling Confident Consumers with Insecure Workers. *British Journal of Industrial Relations*, *50*(1), 1–22. doi:10.1111/j.1467-8543.2010.00825.x

Cullen, J. B., Parboteeah, K. P., & Victor, B. (2003). The effects of ethical climates on organizational commitment: A two-study analysis. *Journal of Business Ethics*, *46*(2), 127–141. doi:10.1023/A:1025089819456

D'Ambra, J., Wilson, C. S., & Akter, S. (2013). Application of the task-technology fit model to structure and evaluate the adoption of E-books by A cademics. *Journal of the American Society for Information Science and Technology*, *64*(1), 48–64. doi:10.1002/asi.22757

Daft, R. L., & Lengel, R. H. (1986). Organizational information requirements, media richness, and structural design. *Management Science*, *32*(5), 554–571. doi:10.1287/mnsc.32.5.554

Daft, R. L., Lengel, R. H., & Trevino, L. K. (1987). Message equivocality, media selection and manager performance: Implications for information systems. *Management Information Systems Quarterly*, *11*(3), 355–366. doi:10.2307/248682

Daft, R., & Lengel, R. (1984). Information richness: A new approach to managerial behavior and organization design. In B. M. Staw & L. L. Cummings (Eds.), *Research in organizational behavior* (Vol. 6, pp. 191–233). JAI Press.

Dailey, S. L. (2016). What happens before full-time employment? Internships as a mechanism of anticipatory socialization. *Western Journal of Communication*, *80*(4), 453–480. doi:10.1080/10570314.2016.1159727

Dale, J., & Foster, P. (1986). *Feminists and state welfare* (Vol. 86). Routledge & Kegan Paul.

Daniel, T. A. (2003). *Tools for Building a Positive Employee Relations Environment.* Wiley Periodicals, Inc. www.interscience.wiley.com doi:10.1002/ert.10086

Daniels, K., & Macdonald, L. (2005). *Equality, Diversity and Discrimination - A student Text.* The Chartered Institute of Personnel and Development.

Das, B. L., & Baruah, M. (2013). Employee retention: A review of literature. *IOSR Journal of Business and Management, 14*(2), 8–14. doi:10.9790/487X-1420816

Dass, P., & Parker, B. (1999). Strategies for managing human resource diversity: From resistance to learning. *The Academy of Management Perspectives, 13*(2), 68–80. doi:10.5465/ame.1999.1899550

Davey, S., Davey, A., Raghav, S. K., Singh, J. V., Singh, N., Blachnio, A., & Przepiórkaa, A. (2018). Predictors and consequences of "Phubbing" among adolescents and youth in India: An impact evaluation study. *Journal of Family & Community Medicine, 25*(1), 35. doi:10.4103/jfcm.JFCM_71_17 PMID:29386960

David, F. R. (2011). *Strategic Management: Concepts and Cases* (13th ed.). Prentice Hall.

Davis, F. D. (1989). Perceived usefulness, perceived ease of use and user acceptance of information technology. *Management Information Systems Quarterly, 13*(3), 319–340. doi:10.2307/249008

Davis, L., Stewart, A., Stanwoodd, G., Raajaram, G., Randy, D., & Blakely, K. (2018). Functional coding variation in the presynaptic dopamine transporter associated with neuropsychiatric disorders drives enhanced motivation and context-dependent impulsivity in mice. *Behavioural Brain Research, 337*(30), 61–69. doi:10.1016/j.bbr.2017.09.043 PMID:28964912

De Vos, A., & Meganck, A. (2009). What HR Managers do versus What Employees Value: Exploring Both Parties' Views on Retention Management from a Psychological Contract Perspective. *Personnel Review, 38*(1), 45–60. doi:10.1108/00483480910920705

Decety, J., Yang, C., & Cheng, Y. (2010). Physicians down-regulate their pain empathy response: An event-related brain potential study. *NeuroImage, 50*(4), 1676–1682. doi:10.1016/j.neuroimage.2010.01.025 PMID:20080194

DeLone, W.H., & McLean, E.R. (1992). Information Systems Success: The Guest for the Dependent Variable. *Infonvation Systems Research, 3*(1), 60-95.

Demangeot, C., & Broderick, A. J. (2016). Engaging customers during a website visit: A model of website customer engagement. *International Journal of Retail & Distribution Management, 44*(8), 814–839. doi:10.1108/IJRDM-08-2015-0124

Demek, K. C., Raschke, R. L., Janvrin, D. J., & Dilla, W. N. (2018). Do organizations use a formalized risk management process to address social media risk? *International Journal of Accounting Information Systems, 28*, 31–34. doi:10.1016/j.accinf.2017.12.004

Demir, S. (2018). Etik iklim ve okuldan ayrılma niyeti arasındaki ilişki: Örgütsel bağlılığın aracılık rolü. *Hacettepe Üniversitesi Eğitim Fakültesi Dergisi, 34*(3), 824–838.

Dennis, A. R., Fuller, R. M., & Valacich, J. S. (2008). Media, tasks, and communication processes: A theory of media synchronicity. *Management Information Systems Quarterly*, *32*(3), 575–600. doi:10.2307/25148857

Deshpande, S. P. (1996). Ethical Climate and the Link between Success and Ethical Behavior: An Empirical Investigation of a Non-Profit Organization. *Journal of Business Ethics*, *15*(3), 315–320. doi:10.1007/BF00382957

Deshpande, S. P., & Joseph, J. (2009). Impact of emotional intelligence, ethical climate, and behavior of peers on ethical behavior of nurses. *Journal of Business Ethics*, *85*(3), 403–410. doi:10.100710551-008-9779-z

Devereux, L., Melewar, T., & Foroudi, P. (2017). Corporate Identity and Social Media: Existence and Extension of the Organization. *International Studies of Management & Organization*, *47*(2), 110–134. doi:10.1080/00208825.2017.1256161

Di Lauro, S., Tursunbayeva, A., Antonelli, G. & Martinez, M. (2018). Measuring organizational identity via LinkedIn: The role played by employees' tenure, type of employment contract and age. *Studi Organizzativi,* (2), 114–129.

Di Virgilio, F., Valderrama Santomé, M., & Toural, C. (2019). The roles of job satisfaction and motivation on employees' intentions to use social media for businesses: towards a multilevel and integrative organizational model. In Advances In Global Business And Economics, ANAHEI Publishing, LLC.

Di Virgilio, F. (2018b). Exploring determinants of knowledge sharing: the role of social media in business organizations. Overview and new direction. In F. Di Virgilio (Ed.), *Social Media for Knowledge Management Applications in Modern Organizations* (pp. 1–30). IGI Global. doi:10.4018/978-1-5225-2897-5.ch001

Di Virgilio, F. (Ed.). (2018a). *Social Media for Knowledge Management Applications in Modern Organizations*. IGI Global. doi:10.4018/978-1-5225-2897-5

Di Virgilio, F., & Antonelli, G. (2018). Consumer behavior, trust and electronic word-of-mouth communication: toward a model of understanding of consumer's purchase intentions online. In F. Di Virgilio (Ed.), *Social Media for Knowledge Management Applications in Modern Organizations* (pp. 58–80). IGI Global. doi:10.4018/978-1-5225-2897-5.ch003

Di Virgilio, F., Valderrama Santomé, M., & López Bolás, A. (2018). Social media strategy within organizational communication: major open issues and challenges. In F. Cantoni & G. Mangia (Eds.), *Human Resource management and digitalization* (pp. 205–225). Giappichelli Routledge.

Dicken, P. (1992). *Global shift: The internationalization of economic activity*. Paul Chapman.

Dictionary, B. (n.d.). *Information Technology (IT)*. Retrieved from: http://www.businessdictionary.com/definition/information-technology-IT.html

Dimoka, A. (2010). What Does the Brain Tell Us About Trust and Distrust? Evidence from a Functional Neuroimaging Study. *Management Information Systems Quarterly*, *2*(34), 373–396. doi:10.2307/20721433

Direnzo, M. S., & Greenhaus, J. H. (2011). Job search and voluntary turnover in a boundaryless world: A control theory perspective. *Academy of Management Review*, *36*(3), 567–589.

Dobson, I. R. (2018). Salary diversity: Australian universities and their general staff. *Australian Universities' Review. The*, *60*(2), 77.

Dogan, B. (2016). The effects of globalization on employment: Bounds test approach in Turkey sample. *Asian Economic and Financial Review*, *6*. doi:18488/journal.aefr/2016.6.10/102.10.620.633

Doherty, J., & Hampton, A. (2008). Decoding the neural substrates of reward-related decision making with functional MRI. *Proc Natl Acad Sci*, *104*(4), 1377-82.

Dolan, E. W. (2018, May 19). *Study finds cyberloafing can help employees cope with workplace boredom.* Retrieved from: https://www.psypost.org/2018/05/study-finds-cyberloafing-can-help-employees-cope-workplace-boredom-51278

Dougherty, D. (1992). Interpretive barriers to successful product innovation in large firms. *Organization Science*, *3*(2), 179–202. doi:10.1287/orsc.3.2.179

Dovidio, J. (2006). The social psychology of prosocial behavior. London: Lawrence Erlbaum Publishers.

Dreher, G. F., & Ash, R. A. (1990). A comparative study of mentoring among men and women in managerial, professional, and technical positions. *The Journal of Applied Psychology*, *75*(5), 539–546. doi:10.1037/0021-9010.75.5.539

Dreo, H., Kunkel, P., & Mitchell, T. (2003). *Virtual teams guidebook for managers*. Quality Press.

Du, Y., Zhang, L., & Tekleab, A.G. (2018). Job strains, job control, and POS on employee performance: an interactionist perspective. *Journal of Business Research*, 213-216. doi:10.1016/j.jbusres.2017.09.040

Dunning, J. H. (2001). The Eclectic (OLI) Paradigm of International Production: Past, Present and Future. *International Journal of the Economics of Business*, *8*(2), 173–190. doi:10.1080/13571510110051441

Earnest, D. R., Allen, D. G., & Landis, R. S. (2011). Mechanisms linking realistic job previews with turnover: A meta-analytic path analysis. *Personnel Psychology*, *64*(4), 865–897. doi:10.1111/j.1744-6570.2011.01230.x

Edwards, P., & Redden, M. H. (2014). *Brony Study.* Academic Press.

Effron, M., Gandossy, R., & Goldsmith, M. (2003). Human Resources in the 21st Century. John Wiley & Sons.

Eisenhardt, K. M. (1989). Making fast strategic decisions in high- velocity environments. *Academy of Management Journal, 32*(3), 543–576.

Elçi, M., & Alpkan, L. (2006). The influences of ethical climate on organizational citizenship behaviors. *Hacettepe University Journal of Economics and Administrative Sciences, 24*(1), 141–170.

Elçi, M., & Alpkan, L. (2009). The impact of perceived organizational ethical climate on work satisfaction. *Journal of Business Ethics, 84*(3), 297–311. doi:10.100710551-008-9709-0

Ellis, S. R. (1991). Nature and origins of virtual environments: A bibliographical essay. *Computing Systems in Engineering, 2*(4), 321–347. doi:10.1016/0956-0521(91)90001-L

Enders, A., Hungenberg, H., Denker, H. P., & Mauch, S. (2008). The long tail of socialnetworking: Revenue models of social networking sites. *European Management Journal, 26*(3), 199–211. doi:10.1016/j.emj.2008.02.002

Epstein, M. J. (2018). Adapting For Digital Survival. *Strategic Finance, 99*(8), 26–33.

Ericson, R. V., Ericson, R. V., & Haggerty, K. D. (1997). *Policing the risk society*. Clarendon Studies in Criminolo. doi:10.3138/9781442678590

Eschenbrenner, B., Nah, F. F. H., & Telaprolu, V. R. (2015). Efficacy of social media utilization by public accounting firms: Findings and directions for future research. *Journal of Information Systems, 29*(2), 5–21. doi:10.2308/isys-50894

Evans, J. (1984). Heuristic and analytic processes in reasoning. *British Journal of Psychology, 75*(4), 451–468. doi:10.1111/j.2044-8295.1984.tb01915.x

ExnerR. (2012, December 12). *MNP*. Retrieved from MNP: https://www.mnp.ca/en/posts/do-i-need-a-holding-company

Faber, S., Douglas, T., Heise, F., & Hewstone, M. (2015). Cognitive Enhancement and Motivation Enhancement: An Empirical Comparison of Intuitive Judgments. *AJOB Neuroscience, 6*(6), 1. doi:10.1080/21507740.2014.991847

Farrer, J. (2004). A practical approach to diversity. *Industrial and Commercial Training, 36*(4), 175–177. doi:10.1108/00197850410542437

Feeley, T. H., Hwang, J., & Barnett, G. A. (2008). Predicting employee turnover from friendship networks. *Journal of Applied Communication Research, 36*(1), 56–73. doi:10.1080/00909880701799790

Ferdman, B., M., & Sagiv, L. (2012). Diversity in Organizations and Cross-Cultural WorkPsychology: What If They Were More Connected? *Industrial and Organizational Psychology: Perspectives on Science and Practice, 5*(3).

Ferdman, B. M., & Sagiv, L. (2012). Diversity in Organizations and Cross-Cultural Work Psychology: What If They Were More Connected? *Industrial and Organizational Psychology: Perspectives on Science and Practice, 5*(3), 323–345. doi:10.1111/j.1754-9434.2012.01455.x

Ferrell, O. C., & Ferrell, L. (2008). A macromarketing ethics framework: Stakeholder orientation and distributive justice. *Journal of Macromarketing*, *28*(1), 24–32. doi:10.1177/0276146707311290

Festing, M., & Schäfer, L. (2014). Generational challenges to talent management: A framework for talent retention based on the psychological-contract perspective. *Journal of World Business*, *49*(2), 262–271. doi:10.1016/j.jwb.2013.11.010

Field, J., & Chelliah, J. (2012). Social-media misuse a ticking time-bomb for employers: Robust policies and procedures needed to reduce the risks. *Human Resource Management International Digest*, *20*(7), 36–38. doi:10.1108/09670731211270301

Fine, M. (2018). *Health care revolt: How to organize, build a health care system, and resuscitate democracy: all at the same time*. PM Press.

Fisher, C. D., Locke, E. A., & Henne, D. L. (1992). The new look in job satisfaction theory and research. In *Job satisfaction: Advances in research and applications* (pp. 165–194). The Free Press.

Flanagan, J. A. (1994). Restricting electronic monitoring in the private workplace. *Duke Law Journal*, *43*(6), 1256–1281. doi:10.2307/1372857

Fleming, J. H., Coffman, C., & Harter, J. K. (2005). Manage your Human Sigma. *Harvard Business Review*, *83*(7), 106–114. https://hbr.org/2005/07/manage-your-human-sigma PMID:16028821

Fornell, C., & Larcker, D. F. (1981). Evaluating structural equation models with unobservable variables and measurement error. *JMR, Journal of Marketing Research*, *18*(1), 39–50. doi:10.1177/002224378101800104

Fournier, P.-S., Lamontagne, S., & Gagnon, J. (2012). Interactions between Dispatchers and Truck Drivers in a High Turnover Context. *Relations Industrielles*, *67*(2), 263–282. doi:10.7202/1009087ar

Fox, A. (2007). Caught in the Web: Internet surfing takes on addictive qualities for some employees who may be hiding their abuse at work-at a cost to both themselves and their employers. *HRMagazine*, *52*(12), 34.

Fox, S., Leicht, R. M., & Messner, J. I. (2010). Assessing the relevance of media synchronicity theory to the use of communication media in the AECO industry. *Journal of Architectural Engineering*, *16*(2), 54–62. doi:10.1061/(ASCE)AE.1943-5568.0000012

Fox, S., Spector, P. E., & Miles, D. (2001). Counterproductive work behavior (CWB) in response to job stressors and organizational justice: Some mediator and moderator tests for autonomy and emotions. *Journal of Vocational Behavior*, *59*(3), 291–309. doi:10.1006/jvbe.2001.1803

Frankel, J. A. (2000). *Globalization of the economy*. National Bureau of Economic Research. https://www.nber.org/papers/w7858

Franko, L. G. (1989). Global corporate competition: Who's winning, who's losing, and the R&D factor as one reason why. *Strategic Management Journal*, *10*(5), 449–474. doi:10.1002mj.4250100505

Freimark, M. (2012). *The role of organizational citizenship behavior and organizational justice on intention to cyberloaf through a general deterrence theory lens.* Southern Illinois University at Carbondale.

Fulk, J. (1993). Social construction of communication technology. *Academy of Management Journal, 36*, 921–951.

Futrell, C.M., & Parasuraman, A. (1984). The Relationship of Satisfaction and Performance to Salesforce Turnover. *Journal of Marketing.*

Gallup, Inc. (2017). *State of the American Workplace.* Retrieved from https://news.gallup.com/reports/199961/7.aspx

Gallup. (2013). *State of the Global Workplace: Employee Engagement Insights for Business Leaders.* Gallup Inc.

Gavino, M. C., Wayne, S. J., & Erdogan, B. (2012). Discretionary and transactional human resource practices and employee outcomes: The role of perceived organizational support. *Human Resource Management, 51*(5), 665–686. doi:10.1002/hrm.21493

Gebauer, J., Shaw, M. J., & Gribbins, M. L. (2010). Task-technology fit for mobile information systems. *Journal of Information Technology, 25*(3), 259–272. doi:10.1057/jit.2010.10

Geissler, C., & Krys, C. (2013). The Challenges of Strategic Management in the Twenty-first Century. *@Springer Fachmedien Wiesbaden.*

George, A. (2012). Business environment factors- a conceptual frame work. Academic Press.

Gephart, R. P. Jr. (2002). Introduction to the brave new workplace: Organizational behavior in the electronic age. *Journal of Organizational Behavior: The International Journal of Industrial. Occupational and Organizational Psychology and Behavior, 23*(4), 327–344. doi:10.1002/job.143

Germain, M. L., Herzog, M. J. R., & Hamilton, P. R. (2012). Women employed in male-dominated industries: Lessons learned from female aircraft pilots, pilots-in-training and mixed-gender flight instructors. *Human Resource Development International, 15*(4), 435–453. doi:10.1080/13678868.2012.707528

Ghansah, E. (2011). *The role of employee retention on job performance* (Unpublished dissertation). Kwame Nikrumah University of Science and Technology.

Ghezzi, A., Gastaldi, L., Lettieri, E., Martini, A., & Corso, M. (2016). A role for startups in unleashing the disruptive power of social media. *International Journal of Information Management, 36*(6), 1152–1159. doi:10.1016/j.ijinfomgt.2016.04.007

Giacalone, R. A., & Greenberg, J. (1997). Antisocial behavior in organizations. *Sage (Atlanta, Ga.).*

Glassop, L. I. (2002). The organizational benefits of teams. *Human Relations, 55*(2), 225–247. doi:10.1177/0018726702055002184

Global Diversity and Inclusion: Fostering Innovation Through a Diverse Workforce. (2011). *Forbes Insights*. Retrieved from https://www.forbes.com/forbesinsights/innovation_diversity/

Gökoğlu, S. K., & Öztürk, E. B. (2020). A Cross-Cultural Review of Workplace Deviance Research. In *Analyzing Workplace Deviance in Modern Organizations* (pp. 23–46). IGI Global. doi:10.4018/978-1-5225-9996-8.ch002

Goldman, A., & Tabak, N. (2010). Perception of ethical climate and its relationship to nurses' demographic characteristics and job satisfaction. *Nursing Ethics*, *17*(2), 233–246. doi:10.1177/0969733009352048 PMID:20185447

Goldsmith, M., & Thomas, R. R. (2003). *Understanding Referent Groups and Diversity: A Key Challenge for Human Resource Leaders. In Human Resources in the 21st Century*. John Wiley & Sons.

Gomez-Mejia, L. R., Makri, M., & Kintana, M. L. (2010). Diversification decisions in family-controlled firms. *Journal of Management Studies*, *47*(2), 223–252. doi:10.1111/j.1467-6486.2009.00889.x

Gong, Y. (2003). Toward a dynamic process model of staffing composition and subsidiary outcomes in multinational enterprises. *Journal of Management*, *29*(2), 259–280. doi:10.1177/014920630302900207

Goodhue, D. L., & Thompson, R. L. (1995). Task-technology fit and individual performance. *Management Information Systems Quarterly*, *19*(2), 213–236. doi:10.2307/249689

Gossett, L. M. (2001). The long-term impact of short-term workers. *Management Communication Quarterly*, *15*(1), 115–120. doi:10.1177/0893318901151007

Govaerts, N., Kyndt, E., Dochy, F., & Baert, H. (2011). Influence of learning and working climate on the retention of talented employees. *Journal of Workplace Learning*, *23*(1), 35–55. doi:10.1108/13665621111097245

Govendo, A. J. (2005). Workforce, diversity and corporate creativity. Handbook of Business Strategy, 6(1), 213-218. doi:10.1108/08944310510557495

Govindappa. (2017). Impact of employee engagement on organizational success: A study in TATA Advanced Materials. *International Journal of Academic Research and Development*, 1202-1207.

Graber, M., Kissam, S., Payne, V., Meyer, A. N. D., Sorensen, A., Lenfestey, N., Tant, E., Henriksen, K., LaBresh, K., & Singh, H. (2012). Cognitive intervention to reduce diagnostic error: A narrative review. *BMJ Quality & Safety*, *21*(7), 535–537. doi:10.1136/bmjqs-2011-000149 PMID:22543420

Granovetter, M. S. (1995). *Getting a job: A study of contacts and careers*. University of Chicago Press. doi:10.7208/chicago/9780226518404.001.0001

Greenfield, D., Pawsey, M., & Braithwaite, J. (2011). What motivates professionals to engage in the accreditation of healthcare organizations? *International Journal for Quality in Health Care*, *23*(1), 8–14. doi:10.1093/intqhc/mzq069 PMID:21084322

Greenfield, R., Busink, E., Wong, C. P., Riboli-Sasco, E., Greenfield, G., Majeed, A., Car, J., & Wark, P. A. (2016). Truck drivers' perceptions on wearable devices and health promotion: A qualitative study. *BMC Public Health, 16*(1), 677. Advance online publication. doi:10.118612889-016-3323-3 PMID:27475984

Green, K. A., López, M., Wysocki, A., & Kepner, K. (2012). *Diversity in the Workplace: Benefits, Challenges, and the Required Managerial Tools, University of Florida IFAS Extension. This document is HR022, one of a series of the Food and Resource Economics Department, Florida Cooperative Extension Service*. Institute of Foodand Agricultural Sciences, University of Florida.

Griffin, R. W., O'Leary-Kelly, A., & Collins, J. (1998). Dysfunctional work behaviors in organizations. *Journal of Organizational Behavior, 5*, 65–82.

Gruber, M., Gelman, B., & Ranganath, C. (2014). States of curiosity modulate hippocampus-dependent learning via the dopaminergic circuit. *Neuron, 84*(2), 486-96.

Gunnigle, P., Lavelle, J., & Monaghan, S. (2019). Multinational companies and human resource management in Ireland during recession: A retrospective from a highly globalized economy. *Thunderbird International Business Review, 61*(3), 481–489. doi:10.1002/tie.21978

Gupta, R. (2013). *Workforce diversity and Organizational performance*. Academic Press.

Guzzo, R. A., Noonan, K. A., & Elron, E. (1994). Expatriate managers and the psychological contract. *The Journal of Applied Psychology, 79*(4), 617–626. doi:10.1037/0021-9010.79.4.617

Haber, S., & Knutson, B. (2010). The reward circuit: Linking primate anatomy and human imaging. *Neuropsychopharmacology, 35*(1), 4–26. doi:10.1038/npp.2009.129 PMID:19812543

HaighA. (n.d.). *Stop phubbing*. Retrieved from http://stopphubbing.com

Haimes, Y. Y. (2012). Systems-based guiding principles for risk modeling, planning, assessment, management, and communication. *Risk Analysis, 32*(9), 1451–1467. doi:10.1111/j.1539-6924.2012.01809.x PMID:22548671

Hair, J. F., Ringle, C. M., & Sarstedt, M. (2011). PLS_SEM: Indeed a silver bullet. *Journal of Marketing Theory and Practice, 19*(2), 139–150. doi:10.2753/MTP1069-6679190202

Hallett, T. (2002). *Christmas cyberloafing cost UK businesses£ 154 million*. Academic Press.

Hanna, R., Rohm, A., & Crittenden, V. L. (2011). We're all connected: The power of the social media ecosystem. *Business Horizons, 54*(3), 265–273. doi:10.1016/j.bushor.2011.01.007

Han, S. J., & Beyerlein, M. (2016). Framing the Effects of Multinational Cultural Diversity on Virtual Team Processes. *Small Group Research, 47*(4), 351–383. doi:10.1177/1046496416653480

Hansen, J. M., & Levin, M. L. (2016). The effect of apathetic motivation on employees' intentions to use social media for businesses. *Journal of Business Research, 69*(12), 6058–6066. doi:10.1016/j.jbusres.2016.06.009

Harder, T. (2019). *Antecedents of Workplace Deviance*. Celebration of Student Scholarship.

Harikrishnan, G. (2014). Study on Labour Welfare Measures - With Special Reference to Rubber Board of India. *Global Journal of Commerce & Management Perspective*, 82-85.

Harmeling, C. M., Moffett, J. W., Arnold, M. J., & Carlson, B. D. (2017). Toward a theory of customer engagement marketing. *Journal of the Academy of Marketing Science*, *45*(3), 312–335. doi:10.100711747-016-0509-2

Harper, D. (1990). Spotlight abuse-Save profits. *Industrial Distribution*, *79*, 47–51.

Harter, J. K., Schmidt, F. L., & Hayes, T. L. (2002). Business-unit-level relationship between employee satisfaction, employee engagement, and business outcomes: A meta-analysis. *The Journal of Applied Psychology*, *87*(2), 268–279. doi:10.1037/0021-9010.87.2.268 PMID:12002955

Harzing, A.-W., & Feely, A. J. (2008). The language barrier and its implications for HQ-subsidiary relationships. *Cross Cultural Management*, *15*(1), 49–61. doi:10.1108/13527600810848827

Haythornthwaite, C. (2000). Online personal networks: Size, composition and media use among distance learners. *New Media & Society*, *2*(2), 195–226. doi:10.1177/14614440022225779

Heaphy, E. D., & Dutton, J. E. (2008). Positive social interactions and the human body at work: Linking organizations and physiology. *Academy of Management Review*, *33*(1), 137–162. doi:10.5465/amr.2008.27749365

Heavey, A. L., Holwerda, J. A., & Hausknecht, J. P. (2013). Causes and consequences of collective turnover: A meta-analytic review. *The Journal of Applied Psychology*, *98*(3), 412–453. doi:10.1037/a0032380 PMID:23668597

Hein, C. (2005). *Reconciling work and family responsibilities: Practical ideas from global experience*. International Labour Organization.

Hein, G., & Singer, T. (2008). I feel how you feel but not always: The empathic brain and its modulation. *Current Opinion in Neurobiology*, *18*(2), 153–158. doi:10.1016/j.conb.2008.07.012 PMID:18692571

Hemmasi, M. (1983). Competitive environment, business strategy, and organizational structure, an analysis of firm performance. LSU Historical Dissertations and Theses, 5-30.

Henle, C. A., & Blanchard, A. L. (2008). The interaction of work stressors and organizational sanctions on cyberloafing. *Journal of Managerial Issues*, 383–400.

Henle, C. A., Giacalone, R. A., & Jurkiewicz, C. L. (2005). The role of ethical ideology in workplace deviance. *Journal of Business Ethics*, *56*(3), 219–230. doi:10.100710551-004-2779-8

Henseler, J., Ringle, C. M., & Sinkovics, R. R. (2009). The use of partial least squares path modeling in international marketing. In *New challenges to international marketing* (pp. 277–319). Emerald Group Publishing Limited. doi:10.1108/S1474-7979(2009)0000020014

Herrera, F. (n.d.). *The digital workplace: Think, share, do. Transform your employee experience*. Deloitte. Retrieved from: https://www2.deloitte.com/content/dam/Deloitte/mx/Documents/human-capital/The_digital_workplace.pdf

Herzberg, F. (2017). *Motivation to work*. Routledge. doi:10.4324/9781315124827

He, W., Zha, S., & Ling, L. (2013). Social media competitive analysis and text mining: A case study in the pizza industry. *International Journal of Information Management*, *33*(3), 464–472. doi:10.1016/j.ijinfomgt.2013.01.001

Hewlett, S. A., Marshall, M., & Sherbin, L. (2013). How diversity can drive innovation. *Harvard Business Review- Innovation*. Retrieved from https://hbr.org/2013/12/how-diversity-can-drive-innovation

Hilmersson, M. (2014). Small and medium-sized enterprise internationalisation strategy and performance in times of market turbulence. *International Small Business Journal: Researching Entrepreneurship*, *32*(4), 386–400. doi:10.1177/0266242613497744

Hinds, P., & Kiesler, S. (1995). Communication across boundaries: Work, structure, and use of communication technologies in a large organization. *Organization Science*, *6*(4), 373–393. doi:10.1287/orsc.6.4.373

Hoehle, H., & Huff, S. (2012). Advancing task-technology fit theory: a formative measurement approach to determining task-channel fit for electronic banking channels. *Information Systems Foundations: Theory Building in Information Systems*, 133-170.

Hogan, J., & Hogan, R. (1989). How to measure employee reliability. *The Journal of Applied Psychology*, *74*(2), 273–279. doi:10.1037/0021-9010.74.2.273

Hollingworth, D., & Valentine, S. (2014). Corporate social responsibility, continuous process improvement orientation, organizational commitment and turnover intentions. *International Journal of Quality & Reliability Management*, *31*(6), 629–651. doi:10.1108/IJQRM-09-2012-0131

Hong, S. J., Thong, J. Y., Moon, J. Y., & Tam, K. Y. (2008). Understanding the behaviour of mobile data services consumers. *Information Systems Frontiers*, *10*(4), 431–445. doi:10.100710796-008-9096-1

Horwitz, F. (2017). International HRM in South African multinational companies. *Journal of International Management*, *23*(2), 208–222. doi:10.1016/j.intman.2017.01.005

Horwitz, F., & Budhwar, P. (2015). *Handbook of Human Resource Management in Emerging Markets*. Edward Elgar Publishing. doi:10.4337/9781781955017

Horwitz, S. (2005). The Compositional Impact of Team Diversity on Performance: Theoretical Considerations. *Human Resource Development Review*, *4*(2), 219–245. doi:10.1177/1534484305275847

How Many Phones Are in the World. (n.d.). Retrieved from https://www.bankmycell.com/blog/how-many-phones-are-in-the-world

Howald, N., Lortie, B., Gallagher, C., & Albert, M. A. (2018). *Preventing and Deterring Organizational Deviance. Society for Industrial and Organizational Psychology.* White Paper Series.

Huang, C. C., You, C. S., & Tsai, M. T. (2012). A multidimensional analysis of ethical climate, job satisfaction, organizational commitment, and organizational citizenship behaviors. *Nursing Ethics*, *19*(4), 513–529. doi:10.1177/0969733011433923 PMID:22753457

Hudson, S. (2019). *Hearst*. Retrieved from Chron: https://smallbusiness.chron.com/disadvantages-holding-company-form-organization-22665.html

Hülsheger, U. R., Alberts, H. J., Feinholdt, A., & Lang, J. W. (2012). Benefits of mindfulness at work: The role of mindfulness in emotion regulation, emotional exhaustion, and job satisfaction. *The Journal of Applied Psychology*, *98*(2), 310–325. doi:10.1037/a0031313 PMID:23276118

Hunt, D. M., & Michael, C. (1983). Mentorship: A career training and development tool. *Academy of Management Review*, *8*(3), 475–485. doi:10.5465/amr.1983.4284603

Hyman, R. (1999). National industrial relations systems and transnational challenges: An essay in review. *European Journal of Industrial Relations*, *5*(1), 89–110. doi:10.1177/095968019951006

Hymer, S. (1970). The efficiency (contradictions) of multinational corporations. *The American Economic Review*, *60*(2), 441–448.

Hymer, S. H. (1976). *The international operations of national firms: A study of foreign direct investment*. Mit Press.

Irani, F. N. H. A., & Noruzi, M. R. (2011). Globalization and challenges; what are the globalization's contemporary issues? *International Journal of Humanities and Social Science*, *1*(6), 216–217.

Irick, M. L. (2008). Task-technology fit and information systems effectiveness. *Journal of Knowledge Management Practice*, *9*(3), 1–5.

Isaac, R. G. (1993). Organizational culture: Some new perspectives. Handbook of organizational behavior, 99.

Ismail, S., & Yuhanis, N. (2018). Determinants of ethical work behaviour of Malaysian public sector auditors. *Asia-Pacific Journal of Business Administration*, *10*(1), 21–34. doi:10.1108/APJBA-07-2017-0068

Jackson, S. E., Joshi, A., & Erhardt, N. L. (2003). Recent Research on Team and Organizational Diversity: SWOT Analysis and Implications. *Journal of Management*, *29*(6), 801–830. doi:10.1016/S0149-2063(03)00080-1

James, H., & Watt, S. A. (1995). *Research Methods for Communication Science*. Allyn and Bacon.

Jandaghi, G., & Alvani, S. M., ZareiMatin, H., & FakheriKozekanan, S. (2015). Cyberloafing management in organizations. *Iranian Journal of Management Studies*, *8*(3), 335–349.

Jaramillo, F., Mulki, J. P., & Solomon, P. (2006). The role of ethical climate on salesperson's role stress, job attitudes, turnover intention, and job performance. *Journal of Personal Selling & Sales Management*, *26*(3), 271–282. doi:10.2753/PSS0885-3134260302

Jassim, R. K. (1998). *Competitive advantage through the employee* (Unpublished doctoral dissertation). Reg. Eng. College of Technology at Jeddah.

Jehanzeb, K., & Bashir, N. A. (2013). Training and development program and its benefits to employee and organization: A conceptual study. *European Journal of Business and Management*, *5*(2), 243–250.

Jelstad, B. (2007). *Beyond Money: Intrinsic work motivation in profit and nonprofit organizations* (Doctoral thesis). Norwegian School of Economics and Business Administration.

Jenkins, R. (2006). Globalization, foreign investment and employment in Vietnam. *Transactional Corporations, 15*(1), 115-142.

Jensen, J. M., & Raver, J. L. (2012). When self-management and surveillance collide: Consequences for employees' organizational citizenship and counterproductive work behaviors. *Group & Organization Management*, *37*(3), 308–346. doi:10.1177/1059601112445804

Jha, J. K., & Varkkey, B. (2017). Convergence or divergence: The impacts of globalization on employee relations in India and China. *IJES*, *25*(2), 44–57.

Jia, H., Jia, R., & Karau, S. (2013). Cyberloafing and personality: The impact of the Big Five traits and workplace situational factors. *Journal of Leadership & Organizational Studies*, *20*(3), 358–365. doi:10.1177/1548051813488208

Jiang, X. (2009). Strategic Management for Main Functional Areas in an Organization. *International Journal of Business and Management*, *4*(2). Advance online publication. doi:10.5539/ijbm.v4n2p153

Jin, L., Wen, M., Fan, J. X., & Wang, G. (2012). Tans-local ties, local ties and psychological well-being among rural-to-urban migrants in Shanghai. *Social Science & Medicine*, *75*(2), 288–296. doi:10.1016/j.socscimed.2012.03.014 PMID:22546316

Johanson, J., & Vahlne, J.-E. (1977). The internationalization process of the firm—A model of knowledge development and increasing foreign market commitments. *Journal of International Business Studies*, *8*(1), 23–32. doi:10.1057/palgrave.jibs.8490676

John, G., & Graham, J. (2005). *Employee Relations* (4th ed.). Published by Chartered Institute of Personnel and Development.

Johnsen, C. G. (2018). Who's afraid of organization? Concepts, process and identity thinking. *Philosophy of Management*, *17*(3), 303–319. doi:10.100740926-017-0079-5

Johnson, J., Bristow, D., McClure, D., & Schneider, K. (2011). Determinants of Job Satisfaction among Long-Distance Truck Drivers: An Interview Study in the United States. *International Journal of Management*, *28*(1).

Johnston, W. B., & Packer, A. E. (1987). *Workforce 2000: Work and workers for the 21st century*. Hudson Institute.

Johnston, W., & Packer, A. (1987). *Workforce 2000*. Hudson Institute.

Joyce, W. F., McGee, V. E., & Slocum, J. W. Jr. (1997). Designing lateral organizations: An analysis of the benefits, costs, and enablers of nonhierarchical organizational forms. *Decision Sciences*, *28*(1), 1–25. doi:10.1111/j.1540-5915.1997.tb01300.x

Judge, W. Q., & Miller, A. (1991). Antecedents and outcomes of decision speed in different environmental contexts. *Academy of Management Journal*, *34*(2), 449–463. PMID:10111313

Junglas, I., Abraham, C., & Watson, R. T. (2008). Task-technology fit for mobile locatable information systems. *Decision Support Systems*, *45*(4), 1046–1057. doi:10.1016/j.dss.2008.02.007

Kabat-Zinn, J. (1994). *Wherever you go, there you are*. Hyperion.

Kahneman, D. (2012). *Pensar rápido, Pensar despacio*. Debate.

Kahn, K., & Mentzer, J. (1994). The impact of team-based forecasting. *Journal of Business Forecasting*, *13*(2), 18–21.

Kalev, A., Dobbin, A. F., & Kelly, E. (2006). Best Practices or Best Guesses? Assessing the Efficacy of Corporate Affirmative Action and Diversity Policies. American Sociological Review, 71, 589–617. doi:10.1177/000312240607100404

Kaplan, A. M., & Haenlein, M. (2010). Users of the world, unite! The challenges and opportunities of social media. *Business Horizons*, *53*(1), 59–68. doi:10.1016/j.bushor.2009.09.003

Karadağ, E., Tosuntaş, Ş. B., Erzen, E., Duru, P., Bostan, N., Şahin, B. M., & Babadağ, B. (2015). Determinants of phubbing, which is the sum of many virtual addictions: A structural equation model. *Journal of Behavioral Addictions*, *4*(2), 60–74. doi:10.1556/2006.4.2015.005 PMID:26014669

Karagözoğlu, Ş., Özden, D., & Yildirim, G. (2014). Yoğun bakım hemşirelerinin hastane etik iklim algısı. *Turkish Journal of Research & Development in Nursing*, *16*(1), 34–45.

Kasper-Fuehrera, E. C., & Ashkanasy, N. M. (2001). Communicating trustworthiness and building trust in inter-organizational virtual organizations. *Journal of Management*, *27*(3), 235–254. doi:10.1177/014920630102700302

Kaur, J. (2017). Exploring relationships among ethical climate types and organizational commitment: A case of Indian banking sector. *Journal of Indian Business Research*, *9*(1), 20–40. doi:10.1108/JIBR-02-2015-0022

Kay, A. (1984). Computer software. Scientific American, 251(3), 52-59. Kay, A. (1990). User interface: A personal view. In B. Laurel (Ed.), *The art of human computer interface design* (pp. 191–207). Addison-Wesley.

Kaye, B., & Jordan-Evans, S. (2008). *2003, Love 'Em or Lose'Em – Getting Good People to Stay*. Berett Koehler Publishers Inc.

Kelly, E., & Dobbin, F. (1998). *How Affirmative Action Became Diversity Management- Employer Response to Antidiscrimination Law, 1961 to 1996. Princeton University - American Behavioral Scientist*. Sage Publications.

Kelly, J. (1992). Does job re-design theory explain job re-design outcomes? *Human Relations*, *45*(8), 753–774. doi:10.1177/001872679204500801

Kennon, J. (2018, October 29). *The Balance*. Retrieved from The Balance: https://www.thebalance.com/understanding-a-holding-company-357341

Khalifa, M., & Shen, K. N. (2008). Drivers for transactional B2C m-commerce adoption: Extended theory of planned behavior. *Journal of Computer Information Systems*, *48*(3), 111–117.

Khanna, T., & Rivkin, J. W. (2001). Estimating the performance effects of business groups in emerging markets. *Strategic Management Journal*, *22*(1), 45–74. doi:10.1002/1097-0266(200101)22:1<45::AID-SMJ147>3.0.CO;2-F

Khansa, L., Kuem, J., Siponen, M., & Kim, S. S. (2017). To cyberloaf or not to cyberloaf: The impact of the announcement of formal organizational controls. *Journal of Management Information Systems*, *34*(1), 141–176. doi:10.1080/07421222.2017.1297173

Kidwell, R. E., & Martin, C. L. (2005). The prevalence (and ambiguity) of deviant behavior at work. *Managing Organizational Deviance*, 1-21.

Kidwell, R. E., & Sprague, R. (2009). Electronic surveillance in the global workplace: Laws, ethics, research, and practice. *New Technology, Work and Employment*, *24*(2), 194–208. doi:10.1111/j.1468-005X.2009.00228.x

Kietzman, J. H., Hermkens, K., McCarthy, I. P., & Silvestre, B. S. (2011). Social media? Get serious! Understanding the functional building blocks of social media. *Business Horizons*, *54*(3), 241–251. doi:10.1016/j.bushor.2011.01.005

Kılıç, S. (2013). *Algılanan örgütsel etik iklim ile üretkenlik karşıtı iş davranışları arasındaki ilişkiler*. Niğde Üniversitesi Sosyal Bilimler Enstitüsü Yayınlanmamış Doktora Tezi.

Kim, J., & Lee, J. E. R. (2011). The Facebook paths to happiness: Effects of the number of Facebook friends and self-presentation on subjective well-being. *Cyberpsychology, Behavior, and Social Networking*, *14*(6), 359–364. doi:10.1089/cyber.2010.0374 PMID:21117983

Kingsford, R. T., & Biggs, H. C. (2012). Strategic Adaptive Management. Academic Press.

Kish-Gephart, J. J., Harrison, D. A., & Treviño, L. K. (2010). Bad apples, bad cases, and bad barrels: Meta-analytic evidence about sources of unethical decisions at work. *The Journal of Applied Psychology*, *95*(1), 1–31. doi:10.1037/a0017103 PMID:20085404

Kitchenham, B., Brereton, O. P., Bugden, D., Turner, M., Bailey, J., & Linkman, S. (2009). Systematic literature reviews in software engineering–a systematic literature review. *Information and Software Technology*, *51*(1), 7–15. doi:10.1016/j.infsof.2008.09.009

Kjellström, S., Avby, G., Areskoug-Josefsson, K., Gäre, B. A., & Bäck, M. A. (2017). Work motivation among healthcare professionals. *Journal of Health Organization and Management*, *31*(4), 487–502. doi:10.1108/JHOM-04-2017-0074 PMID:28877624

Kleinberg, J. (2008). The Convergence of Social and Technological Networks. *Communications of the ACM*, *51*(11), 66–72. doi:10.1145/1400214.1400232

Klimecki, O., Leiberg, S., Lamm, C., & Singer, T. (2013). Functional Neural Plasticity and Associated Changes in Positive Affect. *Cerebral Cortex (New York, N.Y.)*, *23*(7), 1552–1561. doi:10.1093/cercor/bhs142 PMID:22661409

Klotz, A. C., & Buckley, M. R. (2013). A historical perspective of counterproductive work behavior targeting the organization. *Journal of Management History*, *19*(1), 114–132. doi:10.1108/17511341311286222

Koay, K. Y., & Soh, P. C. H. (2018, August). Does Cyberloafing Really Harm Employees' Work Performance?: An Overview. In *International Conference on Management Science and Engineering Management* (pp. 901-912). Springer.

Kobrin, S. J. (1991). An empirical analysis of the determinants of global integration. *Strategic Management Journal*, *12*(S1), 17–31. doi:10.1002mj.4250120904

Kogut, B., & Zander, U. (1992). Knowledge of the Firm, Combinative Capabilities, and the Replication of Technology. *Organization Science*, *3*(3), 383–397. doi:10.1287/orsc.3.3.383

Kohlberg, L. (1967). Moral and religious education and the public schools: A developmental view. *Religion and Public Education,* 164-183.

Kohlberg, L. (1984). *The psychology of moral development.* Essays on moral development. Harper & Row.

Kohli, C., Suri, R., & Kapoor, A. (2015). Will social media kill branding? *Business Horizons*, *58*(1), 35–44. doi:10.1016/j.bushor.2014.08.004

Kor, Y., & Mesko, A. (2013). Dynamic managerial capabilities: Configuration and orchestration of top executives' capabilities and the firm's dominant logic. *Strategic Management Journal*, *34*(2), 233–244. doi:10.1002mj.2000

Kossek, E. E., & Lobel, S. A. (1995). *Managing Diversity Human Resource Strategies for Transforming the Workplace. Introduction: Transforming Human Resource Systems to Manage Diversity - an Introduction and Orienting Framework.* Blackwell Publishers Ltd.

Kostova, T., & Roth, K. (2003). Social capital in multinational corporations and a micro-macro model of its formation. *Academy of Management Review*, *29*(2), 297–317. doi:10.5465/amr.2003.9416356

Kotler, P., & Armstrong, G. (2012). *Principles Of Marketing*. Pearson Prentice Hall.

Kovacs, C., Stiglbauer, B., Batinic, B., & Gnambs, T. (2018). Exploring Different Forms of Job (Dis)Satisfaction and Their Relationship with Well-Being, Motivation and Performance. *Applied Psychology*, *67*(3), 523–556. doi:10.1111/apps.12128

Kramer, R. M. (1991). Intergroup relations and organizational dilemmas: The role of categorization processes. In L. L. Cummings & B. M. Staw (Eds.), *Research in Organizational Behavior* (Vol. 13, pp. 191–228). JAI Press.

Kreitz, P. A. (2007). Best Practices for Managing Organizational Diversity. *SLAC-PUB-12499*.

Kreitz, P. A. (2007). *Best Practices for Managing Organizational Diversity*. SLAC-PUB-12874.

Kryukova, T. L., & Ekimchik, O. A. (2019). Phubbing as a Possible Threat to Close Relationships' Welfare. *Counseling Psychology and Psychotherapy*, *27*(3), 61–76. doi:10.17759/cpp.2019270305

Kuenzi, M., & Schminke, M. (2009). Assembling fragments into a lens: A review, critique, and proposed research agenda for the organizational work climate literature. *Journal of Management*, *35*(3), 634–717. doi:10.1177/0149206308330559

Kumar, K. V., & Devi, V. R. (2014). Social media in financial services a theoretical perspective. *Procedia Economics and Finance*, *11*, 306–313. doi:10.1016/S2212-5671(14)00198-1

Kundu, S. C., Bansal, J., & Chawla, A. S. (2015). Managing Workforce Diversity through HR Practices: A Review. *Emerging Horizons in Business Management*, 115-124.

Kundu, S. C., & Mor, A. (2017). Workforce diversity and organizational performance: A study of the IT industry in India. *Employee Relations*, *39*(2), 160–183. doi:10.1108/ER-06-2015-0114

Kundu, S. K., & Katz, J. A. (2003). Born-international SMEs: BI-level impacts of resources and intentions. *Small Business Economics*, *20*(1), 25–47. doi:10.1023/A:1020292320170

Kurzweil, R. (2004). The law of accelerating returns. In *Alan Turing: Life and legacy of a great thinker* (pp. 381–416). Springer. doi:10.1007/978-3-662-05642-4_16

Kwak, H. (2012). Self-disclosure in online media: An active audience perspective. *International Journal of Advertising*, *31*(3), 485–510. doi:10.2501/IJA-31-3-485-510

Kwok, C. K., Au, W. T., & Ho, J. M. (2005). Normative controls and self-reported counterproductive behaviors in the workplace in China. *Applied Psychology*, *54*(4), 456–475. doi:10.1111/j.1464-0597.2005.00220.x

Lam, C. (2016). Improving technical communication group projects: An experimental study of media synchronicity theory training on communication outcomes. *Journal of Business and Technical Communication*, *30*(1), 85–112. doi:10.1177/1050651915602293

Lamm, C., Decety, J., & Singer, T. (2011). Meta-analytic evidence for common and distinct neural networks associated with directly experienced pain and empathy for pain. *NeuroImage*, *54*(3), 2492–2502. doi:10.1016/j.neuroimage.2010.10.014 PMID:20946964

Landers, R. N., & Goldberg, A. S. (2014). Online social media in the workplace: A conversation with employees. *Psychology of workplace technology*, 284-306.

Langton, N., & Robbins, S. (2006). *Organizational behaviour*. Toronto: Pearson Prentice Canada.

Lansiluoto, A. (2004). *Economic and competitive environment analysis in the formation of strategy*. Publications of the Turku School of Economics and Business Administration.

Lázaro, P., Palma, M., Azcona, B., Cardona, P., & Chinchilla, N. (2005). From individual motivation to organizational compensation: The physician's perspective. *Annual Meeting of the International Society of Technology Assessment in Health Care (ISTAHC)*.

Ledbetter, A. M. (2014). The past and future of technology in interpersonal communication theory and research. *Communication Studies*, *65*(4), 456–459. doi:10.1080/10510974.2014.927298

Lee, W., & Reeve, J. (2012). Motivational neuroscience. The Oxford handbook of human motivation.

Lee, S., & Kleiner, B. H. (2003). Electronic surveillance in the workplace. *Journal of Management Research News*, *26*(2/3/4), 72–81. doi:10.1108/01409170310784014

Lee, Y., & Seomun, G. (2016). Development and validation of an instrument to measure nurses' compassion competence. *Applied Nursing Research*, *30*, 76–82. doi:10.1016/j.apnr.2015.09.007 PMID:27091258

Leftheriotis, I., & Giannakos, M. N. (2014). Using social media for work: Losing your time or improving your work? *Computers in Human Behavior*, *31*, 134–142. doi:10.1016/j.chb.2013.10.016

Levin, M. A., Hansen, J. M., & Laverie, D. (2012). Toward understanding new sales employees' participation in marketing-related technology: Motivation, voluntariness, and past performance. *Journal of Personal Selling & Sales Management*, *32*(3), 379–393. doi:10.2753/PSS0885-3134320307

Lewis, P., Thornhill, A., & Saunders, M. (2003). Employee Relations: Understanding the Employment Relationship Harlow. *Financial Times*.

Liden, R. C., Wayne, S. J., & Sparrowe, R. T. (2000). An examination of the mediating role of psychological empowerment on the relations between the job, interpersonal relationships, and work outcomes. *The Journal of Applied Psychology*, *85*(3), 407–416. doi:10.1037/0021-9010.85.3.407 PMID:10900815

Lim, V. K. (2002). The IT way of loafing on the job: Cyberloafing, neutralizing and organizational justice. *Journal of Organizational Behavior: The International Journal of Industrial, Occupational and Organizational Psychology and Behavior*, *23*(5), 675-694.

Lim, V. K. G., & Chen, D. J. Q. (2009). Impact of cyberloafing on affect, work depletion, facilitation and engagement. In *Conference Paper SIOP* (*Vol. 2009*, pp. 1-20). Academic Press.

Lim, V. K., & Chen, D. J. (2012). Cyberloafing at the workplace: Gain or drain on work? *Behaviour & Information Technology*, *31*(4), 343–353. doi:10.1080/01449290903353054

Lim, V. K., & Teo, T. S. (2005). Prevalence, perceived seriousness, justification and regulation of cyberloafing in Singapore: An exploratory study. *Information & Management*, *42*(8), 1081–1093. doi:10.1016/j.im.2004.12.002

Lim, V. K., Teo, T. S., & Loo, G. L. (2002). How do I loaf here? Let me count the ways. *Communications of the ACM*, *45*(1), 66–70. doi:10.1145/502269.502300

Litzky, B. E., Eddleston, K. A., & Kidder, D. L. (2006). The good, the bad, and the misguided: How managers inadvertently encourage deviant behaviors. *The Academy of Management Perspectives*, *20*(1), 91–103. doi:10.5465/amp.2006.19873411

Liu, J. J., & Chlamtac, I. (2004). Mobile Ad-Hoc Networking with a View of 4G Wireless: Imperatives and Challenges. In S. Basagni, M. Conti, S. Giordano, & I. Stojmenovic (Eds.), Mobile Ad Hoc Networking (pp. 1-46). John Wiley & Sons, Inc.

Liu, C. M., & Chiu, C. K. (2020). Modeling turnover intention and job performance: The moderation of perceived benevolent climate. *Review of Managerial Science*, *14*(3), 611–631. doi:10.100711846-018-0302-3

Liu, D., Brass, D., Lu, Y., & Chen, D. (2015). Friendships in online peer-to-peer lending: Pipes, prisms, and relational herding. *Management Information Systems Quarterly*, *39*(3), 729–742. doi:10.25300/MISQ/2015/39.3.11

Liu, D., & Yang, C. (2016). Media niche of electronic communication channels in friendship: A meta-analysis. *Journal of Computer-Mediated Communication*, *21*(6), 451–466. doi:10.1111/jcc4.12175

Lobel, S. A., & Faught, L. (1996). Four Methods for Proving the Value of Work/Life interventions: Here is advice on choosing the most appropriate business methods for demonstrating that work/life interventions add value to the organization. *Compensation and Benefits Review*, *28*(6), 50–57. doi:10.1177/088636879602800609

Locke, E. A. (1976). The nature and causes of job satisfaction. In M. D. Dunnette (Ed.), *Handbook of industrial and organizational psychology*. Rand McNally College.

Lopez, T. B., Babin, B. J., & Chung, C. (2009). Perceptions of ethical work climate and person–organization fit among retail employees in Japan and the US: A cross-cultural scale validation. *Journal of Business Research*, *62*(6), 594–600. doi:10.1016/j.jbusres.2008.05.018

Lorenzo, R., & Voigt, N. (2017, April 26). *The Mix That Matters: Innovation Through Diversity*. Retrieved from https://www.bcg.com/en-au/publications/2017/people-organization-leadership-talent-innovation-through-diversity-mix-that-matters.aspx

Lown, B. A. (2016). A social neuroscience-informed model for teaching and practising compassion in health care. *Medical Education*, *50*(3), 332–342. doi:10.1111/medu.12926 PMID:26896018

Luo, Y., & Shenkar, O. (2006). The multinational corporation as a multilingual community: Language and organization in a global context. *Journal of International Business Studies*, *37*(3), 321–339. doi:10.1057/palgrave.jibs.8400197

Luo, Y., & Tung, R. L. (2007). International expansion of emerging market enterprises: A springboard perspective. *Journal of International Business Studies, 38*(4), 481–498. doi:10.1057/palgrave.jibs.8400275

Luthans, F., Luthans, K. W., & Luthans, B. C. (2004). Positive psychological capital: Beyond human and social capital. *Business Horizons, 47*(1), 45–50. doi:10.1016/j.bushor.2003.11.007

MacMillian Dictionary. (2013, May 21). *Cyberloafing*. Retrieved from: https://www.macmillandictionary.com/buzzword/entries/cyberloafing.html

Madianou, M., & Miller, M. (2012). Polymedia: Towards a new theory of digital media in interpersonal communication. *International Journal of Cultural Studies, 16*(2), 169–187. doi:10.1177/1367877912452486

Mähler, V., & Westergren, U. H. (2018, September). Working with IoT–A Case Study Detailing Workplace Digitalization ThroughIoT System Adoption. In *IFIP International Internet of Things Conference* (pp. 178-193). Springer.

Maier, C., Laumer, S., Eckhardt, A., & Weitzel, T. (2015). Giving too much social support: Social overload on social networking sites. *European Journal of Information Systems, 24*(5), 447–464. doi:10.1057/ejis.2014.3

Mainiero, L. A. (1989). *Office romance: Love, power, and sex in the workplace*. Rawson Associates.

Maity, M., Dass, M., & Kumar, P. (2018). The impact of media richness on consumer information search and choice. *Journal of Business Research, 87*, 36–45. doi:10.1016/j.jbusres.2018.02.003

Malhotra, N. K. (2007). Marketing Research: An Applied Orientation (5th ed.). Prentice-Hall, Inc.

Maloof, A. D. (2018). *The Moderating Effects of Ethical Leadership and Ethical Climate on the Relationship Between Employee Integrity and Workplace Deviance* (Doctoral dissertation). Alliant International University.

Mannix, E., & Neale, M. A. (2005). What differences make a difference? The promise and reality of diverse teams in organizations. *Psychological Science in the Public Interest, 6*(2), 31–55. doi:10.1111/j.1529-1006.2005.00022.x PMID:26158478

Mantovani, G. (1996b). Social context in HCI: A new framework for mental models, cooperation and communication. *Cognitive Science, 20*(2), 237–296. doi:10.120715516709cog2002_3

Marcus, B., Schuler, H., Quell, P., & Hümpfner, G. (2002). Measuring counterproductivity: Development and initial validation of a German self-report questionnaire. *International Journal of Selection and Assessment, 10*(1-2), 18–35. doi:10.1111/1468-2389.00191

Marsh, E. (2019, January 10). *Is your organisation's digital workplace causing technostress?* Retrieved from: https://www.linkedin.com/pulse/your-organisations-digital-workplace-causing-elizabeth-marsh

Martin, C. (2011). *The third screen: Marketing to your customers in a world gone mobile*. Academic Press.

Martini, A., Massa, S., & Testa, S. (2013). The Firm, the platform and the customer: A'double mangle' interpretation of social media for innovation. *Information and Organization*, *23*(3), 198–213. doi:10.1016/j.infoandorg.2013.07.001

Martin, K. D., & Cullen, J. B. (2006). Continuities and extensions of ethical climate theory: A meta-analytic review. *Journal of Business Ethics*, *69*(2), 175–194. doi:10.100710551-006-9084-7

Mastrangelo, P. M., Everton, W., & Jolton, J. A. (2006). Personal use of work computers: Distraction versus destruction. *Cyberpsychology & Behavior*, *9*(6), 730–741. doi:10.1089/cpb.2006.9.730 PMID:17201599

Mathews, J. A. (2006). Dragon multinationals: New players in 21 st century globalization. *Asia Pacific Journal of Management*, *23*(1), 5–27. doi:10.100710490-006-6113-0

Mathews, J. A. (2017). Dragon multinationals powered by linkage, leverage and learning: A review and development. *Asia Pacific Journal of Management*, *34*(4), 769–775. doi:10.100710490-017-9543-y

Mathimaran, K.B., & Kumar, A.A. (2017). Employee retention strategies-An empirical research. *Global Journal of Management and Business Research: E Marketing, 17*(1), 17-21.

Mayer, D. M., Aquino, K., Greenbaum, R. L., & Kuenzi, M. (2012). Who displays ethical leadership? An examination of antecedents and consequences of ethical leadership. *Academy of Management Journal*, *55*(1), 151–171. doi:10.5465/amj.2008.0276

Mayer, D. M., Kuenzi, M., & Greenbaum, R. L. (2010). Examining the link between ethical leadership and employee misconduct: The mediating role of ethical climate. *Journal of Business Ethics*, *95*(1), 7–16. doi:10.100710551-011-0794-0

Mayo, E. (1933). *The Human Problems of an Industrial Civilization*. Macmillan.

McCabe, D. L., Treviño, L. K., & Butterfield, K. D. (2001). Cheating in academic institutions: A decade of research. *Ethics & Behavior*, *11*(3), 219–232. doi:10.1207/S15327019EB1103_2

McCarthy, A., Darcy, C., & Grady, G. (2010). Work-life balance policy and practice: Understanding line manager attitudes and behaviors. *Human Resource Management Review*, *20*(2), 158–167. doi:10.1016/j.hrmr.2009.12.001

McDonald, P., & Thompson, P. (2016). Social media(tion) and the reshaping of public/private boundaries in employment relations. *International Journal of Management Reviews*, *18*(1), 69–84. doi:10.1111/ijmr.12061

McGregor, R. (2018, April 10). *The pros and cons of a digitized work culture*. Retrieved from: https://www.thedigitalenterprise.com/articles/hr/the-pros-and-cons-of-a-digitized-work-culture

McLuhan, H. M. (1966). Marshall McLuhan. *Information Theory*, 234.

McNall, L. A., & Stanton, J. M. (2011). Private eyes are watching you: Reactions to location sensing technologies. *Journal of Business and Psychology*, *26*(3), 299–309. doi:10.100710869-010-9189-y

Mehra, S. (2020). Organizational Culture, Climate, and Workplace Deviance. In *Analyzing Workplace Deviance in Modern Organizations* (pp. 66–78). IGI Global. doi:10.4018/978-1-5225-9996-8.ch004

Mellahi, K., & Collings, D. G. (2010). The barriers to effective global talent management: The example of corporate elites in MNEs. *Journal of World Business*, *45*(2), 143–149. doi:10.1016/j.jwb.2009.09.018

Menguc, B., Auh, S., Fisher, M., & Haddad, A. (2013). To be engaged or not to be engaged: The antecedents and consequences of service employee engagement. *Journal of Business Research*, *66*(11), 2163–2170. doi:10.1016/j.jbusres.2012.01.007

Meyers, M. C., & Van Woerkom, M. (2014). The influence of underlying philosophies on talent management: Theory, implications for practice, and research agenda. *Journal of World Business*, *49*(2), 192–203. doi:10.1016/j.jwb.2013.11.003

Meyers, N. (2003). *Employee Privacy in the Electronic Workplace: Current Issues for IT Professionals*. In *14th Australasian Conference on Information Systems*, Perth, Western Australia.

Miao, C. F., Evans, K. R., & Zou, S. (2007). The role of salesperson motivation in sales control systems Intrinsic and extrinsic motivation revisited. *Journal of Business Research*, *60*(5), 417–425. doi:10.1016/j.jbusres.2006.12.005

Michailova, S., Mustaffa, Z., & Barner-Rasmussen, W. (2016). Subsidiaries of Multinational Corporations: A Framework for Analyzing Employee Allegiances. *Journal of Leadership & Organizational Studies*, *23*(2), 116–127. doi:10.1177/1548051816633071

MillerR. (2018, May 2). Retrieved from https://www.salesforce.com/blog/2018/05/diversity-drives-innovation-for-small-businesses.html

Mitchell, M. S., & Ambrose, M. L. (2007). Abusive supervision and workplace deviance and the moderating effects of negative reciprocity beliefs. *The Journal of Applied Psychology*, *92*(4), 1159–1168. doi:10.1037/0021-9010.92.4.1159 PMID:17638473

Mitschein, M. (2018). *Why Diversity and Inclusion Matters – From an Innovation Perspective.* Retrieved from https://www.digitalistmag.com/future-of-work/2018/08/22/why-diversity-inclusion-matters-from-innovation-perspective-06183094

Moberg, D. J. (1997). On employee vice. *Business Ethics Quarterly*, *7*(4), 41–60. doi:10.2307/3857208

Moen, P., & Roehling, P. (2005). *The career mystique: Cracks in the American dream.* Rowman & Littlefield.

Mohammadi, A., Broström, A., & Franzoni, C. (2017). Workforce Composition and Innovation: How Diversity in Employees' Ethnic and Educational Backgrounds Facilitates Firm-Level Innovativeness. *Journal of Product Innovation Management, 34*(4), 406–426. doi:10.1111/jpim.12388

Mohr, D. C., Young, G. J., & Burgess, J. F. Jr. (2012). Employee turnover and operational performance: The moderating effect of group-oriented organisational culture. *Human Resource Management Journal, 22*(2), 216–233. doi:10.1111/j.1748-8583.2010.00159.x

Moran, J. W., & Brightman, B. K. (2000). Leading organizational change. *Journal of Workplace Learning, 12*(2), 66–74. doi:10.1108/13665620010316226

Mrass, V., Peters, C., & Leimeister, J. M. (2016). *New Work Organization through Crowdworking Platforms-A Case Study*. Academic Press.

Mulki, J. P., Jaramillo, J. F., & Locander, W. B. (2009). Critical role of leadership on ethical climate and salesperson behaviors. *Journal of Business Ethics, 86*(2), 125–141. doi:10.100710551-008-9839-4

Mumford, J., & Nichols, T. (2008). Power calculation for group fMRI studies accounting for arbitrary design and temporal autocorrelation. *Neuroimage, 39*(1), 261-8.

Murali, S., Poddar, A., & Seema, A. (2017). Employee loyalty, organizational performance and performance evaluation- a critical survey. *IOSR Journal of Business and Management, 19*(8), 62–73. doi:10.9790/487X-1908036274

Murayamaa, K., Matsumotob, M., Izumab, K., & Matsumoto, K. (2010). Neural basis of the undermining effect of monetary reward on intrinsic motivation. *Proceedings of the National Academy of Sciences of the United States of America, 107*(49), 20911–20916. doi:10.1073/pnas.1013305107 PMID:21078974

Muro, M., Liu, S., Whiton, J., &Kulkarni, S. (2017). *Digitalization and the American workforce*. Academic Press.

Murray, E., Cho, J. H., Goodwin, D., Ku, T., Swaney, J., Kim, S. Y., & McCue, M. (2015). Simple, scalable proteomic imaging for high-dimensional profiling of intact systems. *Cell, 163*(6), 1500–1514. doi:10.1016/j.cell.2015.11.025 PMID:26638076

Nagendra, A. (2014). Paradigm shift in hr practices on employee life cycle due to influence of social media. *Procedia Economics and Finance, 11*, 197–207. doi:10.1016/S2212-5671(14)00188-9

Naidoo, V. (2018). Impact of Digitization on Learning and Opportunities in the Workplace. In *Radical Reorganization of Existing Work Structures Through Digitalization* (pp. 156–171). IGI Global. doi:10.4018/978-1-5225-3191-3.ch009

Nantha, S. (2013). Intrinsic motivation: How can it play a pivotal role in changing clinician behaviour? *Journal of Health Organization and Management*. PMID:23802402

Nassuora, A. B. (2013). Understanding Factors Affecting the Adoption of M-commerce by Consumers. *Journal of Applied Sciences*, *13*(6), 913–918. doi:10.3923/jas.2013.913.918

Naware, M., A. (2016). M-Commerce in India. *International Journal of Advanced Research in Computer and Communication Engineering*, 913–915.

Naysmith, S., & Rubincam, C. (2012). Women in the driver's seat: An exploratory study of perceptions and experiences of female truck drivers and their employers in South Africa. *Journal of Southern African Studies*, *38*(3), 570–599. doi:10.1080/03057070.2012.708997

Ngai, E. W., Tao, S. S., & Moon, K. K. (2015). Social media research: Theories, constructs, and conceptual frameworks. *International Journal of Information Management*, *35*(1), 33–44. doi:10.1016/j.ijinfomgt.2014.09.004

Nickols, F. (2016). *Strategy, Strategic Management, Strategic Planning and Strategic Thinking*. Distance Consulting.

Niinimäki, T., Piri, A., Lassenius, C., & Paasivaara, M. (2012). Reflecting the choice and usage of communication tools in global software development projects with media synchronicity theory. *Journal of Software: Evolution and Process*, *24*(6), 677–692.

Nikoloski, K., Dimitrova, J., Koleva, B., & Kacarski, E.M. (2014). From industrial relations to employment relations with focus on employee relations. *International Journal of Sciences: Basic and Applied Research, 18*(2), 117-122.

Nishii, L. H., & Mayer, D. M. (2009). Do Inclusive Leaders Help Reduce Turnover in Diverse Groups? The Moderating Role of Leader-Member Exchange in the Diversity to Turnover Relationship. *The Journal of Applied Psychology*, *94*(6), 1412–1426. doi:10.1037/a0017190 PMID:19916652

Nwokocha, I., & Iheriohanma, E. B. J. (2012). Emerging Trends in Employee Retention Strategies in a Globalizing Economy: Nigeria in Focus. *Asian Social Science*, *8*(10), 198–202. doi:10.5539/ass.v8n10p198

O'Connor, K. W., Schmidt, G. B., & Drouin, M. (2016). Helping workers understand and follow social media policies. *Business Horizons*, *59*(2), 205–211. doi:10.1016/j.bushor.2015.11.005

O'Leary, D. E. (2011a). Blog mining-review and extensions: From each according to his opinion. *Decision Support Systems*, *51*(4), 821–830. doi:10.1016/j.dss.2011.01.016

O'Leary, D. E. (2011b). The use of social media in the supply chain: Survey and extensions. *Intelligent Systems in Accounting, Finance & Management*, *18*(2-3), 121–144. doi:10.1002/isaf.327

Obalade, G. O., & Arogundade, K. K. (2019). Ethical climate and deviant behavior among employees of selected public and private universities: The case of the emerging country. *Corporate Governance and Organizational Behavior Review*, *3*(2), 30–39. doi:10.22495/cgobr_v3_i2_p3

Oberst, U., Wegmann, E., Stodt, B., Brand, M., & Chamarro, A. (2017). Negative consequences from heavy social networking in adolescents: The mediating role of fear of missing out. *Journal of Adolescence, 55*, 51–60. doi:10.1016/j.adolescence.2016.12.008 PMID:28033503

Ohmae, K. (1990). The borderless world. *The McKinsey Quarterly, 3*, 3–19.

Ollier-Malaterre, A., Rothbard, N. P., & Berg, J. (2013). When worlds collide in cyberspace: How boundary work in online social networks impacts professional relationships. *Academy of Management Review, 38*(4), 645–669. doi:10.5465/amr.2011.0235

Omisore, S. (2019). *Corporate Entrepreneurship, Strategy Formulation, and the Performance of the Nigerian Manufacturing Sector* (Doctoral dissertation). University of East London.

Oppel, E., Winter, V., & Schreyögg, J. (2019). Examining the relationship between strategic HRM and hospital employees' work attitudes: An analysis across occupational groups in public and private hospitals. *International Journal of Human Resource Management, 30*(5), 5. doi:10.1080/09585192.2016.1254104

Ouchi, W. (1981). Efficient Boundaries. *Interim technical rept*, (1), 42.

Oviatt, B. M., & McDougall, P. P. (1994). Toward a theory of international new ventures. *Journal of International Business Studies, 25*(1), 45–64. doi:10.1057/palgrave.jibs.8490193

Oviatt, B. M., & McDougall, P. P. (2005). Defining International Entrepreneurship and Modeling the Speed of Internationalization. *Entrepreneurship Theory and Practice, 29*(5), 537–554. doi:10.1111/j.1540-6520.2005.00097.x

Oz, E., Glass, R., & Behling, R. (1999). Electronic Workplace Monitoring: What Employees Think. *International Journal of Management Sciences, 27*, 167–177.

Ozler, D. E., &Polat, G. (2012). Cyberloafing phenomenon in organizations: Determinants and impacts. *International Journal of eBusiness and eGovernment Studies, 4*(2), 1-15.

Pagliaro, S., Lo Presti, A., Barattucci, M., Giannella, V. A., & Barreto, M. (2018). On the effects of ethical climate (s) on employees' behavior: A social identity approach. *Frontiers in Psychology, 9*, 1–10. doi:10.3389/fpsyg.2018.00960 PMID:29951022

Pahuja, S., & Dalal, R.C. (2016). *Study of human resource system, competitive advantage status and their relation in Indian public sector banks*. doi:10.5958/0976-173X.2013.00027.0

Paillé, P., Boiral, O., & Chen, Y. (2013). Linking environmental management practices and organizational citizenship behaviour for the environment: A social exchange perspective. *International Journal of Human Resource Management, 24*(18), 3552–3575. doi:10.1080/09585192.2013.777934

Paniagua, J., & Sapena, J. (2014). Business performance and social media: Love or hate? *Business Horizons, 57*(6), 719–728. doi:10.1016/j.bushor.2014.07.005

Panno, A., Giacomantonio, M., Carrus, G., Maricchiolo, F., Pirchio, S., & Mannetti, L. (2018). Mindfulness, pro-environmental behavior, and belief in climate change: The mediating role of social dominance. *Environment and Behavior, 50*(8), 864–888. doi:10.1177/0013916517718887

Pan, Y., & David, K. T. (2000). The hierarchical model of market entry modes. *Journal of International Business Studies, 31*(4), 535–554. doi:10.1057/palgrave.jibs.8490921

Papadakis, V. M., Lioukas, S., & Chambers, D. (1998). Strategic Decision-Making Processes: The Role of Management and Context. *Strategic Management Journal, 19*(2), 115–147. doi:10.1002/(SICI)1097-0266(199802)19:2<115::AID-SMJ941>3.0.CO;2-5

Parboteeah, K. P., Chen, H. C., Lin, Y. T., Chen, I. H., Lee, A. Y., & Chung, A. (2010). Establishing organizational ethical climates: How do managerial practices work? *Journal of Business Ethics, 97*(4), 599–611. doi:10.100710551-010-0527-9

Parker, D., Charlton, J., Ribeiro, A., & Pathak, D., R. (. (2013). Integration of project-based management and change management: Intervention methodology. *International Journal of Productivity and Performance Management, 62*(5), 534–544. doi:10.1108/IJPPM-10-2012-0108

Parrotta, P., Pozzoli, D., & Pytlikova, M. (2013). The nexus between labor diversity and firm's innovation. *Journal of Population Economics, 27*(2), 303–364. doi:10.100700148-013-0491-7

Pathak, S. (2013, October 7). *McCann Melbourne made up a word to sell a print dictionary: New campaign for Macquarie birthed 'phubbing'.* Retrieved from https://adage.com/article/news/mccann-melbourne-made-a-word-sell-a-dictionary/244595/

Pauleen, D. (2004). *Virtual teams: Projects, protocols and processes*. IGI Global. doi:10.4018/978-1-59140-166-7

Penner, A., Piliavin, J., Schroeder, D., & Dovidio, J. (2005). Prosocial Behavior: Multilevel Perspectives. *Annual Review of Psychology, 56*(1), 365–392. doi:10.1146/annurev.psych.56.091103.070141 PMID:15709940

Peterson, D. K. (2002). Deviant workplace behavior and the organization's ethical climate. *Journal of Business and Psychology, 17*(1), 47–61. doi:10.1023/A:1016296116093

Petrov, C. (2019). *50 M-Commerce Statistics For 2020.* Retrieved from https://techjury.net/stats-about/mcommerce/#gref

Pettegrew, L. S., & Day, C. (2015). Smart phones and mediated relationships: The changing face of relational communication. *The Review of Communication, 15*(2), 122–139. doi:10.1080/15358593.2015.1044018

Pfeffer, J., & Leblelici, H. (1973). The effects of competition on some dimensions of organization structure. Social forces, 52, 268-279.

Philippe, R. R., & Fekken, G. (1981). The altruistic personality and the self-report altruism scale. *Personality and Individual Differences, 2*(4), 293–302. doi:10.1016/0191-8869(81)90084-2

Phillips, K. W. (2014, October 1). *How Diversity Makes Us Smarter*. Retrieved from https://www.scientificamerican.com/article/how-diversity-makes-us-smarter/

Pink, H. (2014). Training firm aims to bring women to sector. *Commercial Motor, 222*(5605).

Pless, N. M., & Maak, T. (2004). Building an Inclusive Diversity Culture: Principles, Processes and Practice. *Journal of Business Ethics*, *54*(2), 129–147. doi:10.100710551-004-9465-8

Pophal, L. G. (2018). *How to handle five generations in the workplace*. Retrieved from: https://hrdailyadvisor.blr.com/2018/02/26/handle-5-generations-workplace/

Porter, M. (1986). *Competition in global industries*. Harvard University Press.

Pot, F. D. (2017). Workplace innovation and wellbeing at work. In *Workplace Innovation* (pp. 95–110). Springer. doi:10.1007/978-3-319-56333-6_7

Prasad, A. (2018, October 8). *10 ways technology has reshaped the modern workplace*. Retrieved from: https://www.quickfms.com/blog/6-ways-technology-has-reshaped-the-workplace

Prasad, P., Pringle, J. K., & Konrad, A. M. (2006). *Examining the Contours of Workplace Diversity - Concepts, Contexts and Challenges. In Handbook of Workplace Diversity*. Sage Publications.

Price, K. (2011). E-books for free: finding, creating and managing freely available texts. *E-books in libraries: a practical guide*, 53-67.

PricewaterhouseCoopers. (2005). *PricewaterHuman Resources Management Strategies to Support Organizational Changes*. Luxembourg: PwC.

Prockl, G., Teller, C., Kotzab, H., & Angell, R. (2017). Antecedents of Truck Drivers' Job Satisfaction and Retention Proneness. *Journal of Business Logistics*, *38*(3), 184–196. doi:10.1111/jbl.12156

Puffer, S. M. (1987). Prosocial behavior, noncompliant behavior, and work performance among commission salespeople. *The Journal of Applied Psychology*, *72*(4), 615–621. doi:10.1037/0021-9010.72.4.615

Pulignano, V., Tregaskis, O., Doerflinger, N., & Bélanger, J. (2018). The distinctiveness of employment relations within multinationals: Political games and social compromises within multinationals' subsidiaries in Germany and Belgium. *The Journal of Industrial Relations*, *60*(4), 465–491. doi:10.1177/0022185618769963

Puritty, C., Strickland, R., Alia, E., Blonder, B., Klein, E., Kohl, M. T., McGee, E., Quintana, M., Ridley, R. E., Tellman, B., & Gerber, L. (2017). Diversity in Science - Without Inclusion, Diversity Initiatives May Not Be Enough - Focus on minority experiences in STEM, not just numbers. *Science*, *357*(6356), 1101–1102. doi:10.1126cience.aai9054 PMID:28912234

Qin, X., Hom, P., Xu, M., & Ju, D. (2013). Applying the job demands resourcesmodel to migrant workers: Exploring how and when geographical distance increase quit propensity. *Journal of Occupational and Organizational Psychology*, *87*(2), 303–328. doi:10.1111/joop.12047

Rahman, M.S., & Taniya, R.K. (2017). Effect of employee relationship management (ERM) on employee performance: a study on private commercial banks in Bangladesh. *Human Resource Management Research, 7*(2), 90-95. doi:10.5923/j.hrmr.20170702.03

Rana, S., Agrawal, P., & Jha, N. (2013). CRM vs. HR Issues: An Extensive. Literature Review. *Global Journal of Business Management, 7*(2), 35–44.

Rao-Nicholson, R., Khan, Z., & Stokes, P. (2016). Making great minds think alike: Emerging market multinational firms' leadership effects on targets' employee psychological safety after cross-border mergers and acquisitions. *International Business Review, 25*(1), 103–113. doi:10.1016/j.ibusrev.2015.09.007

Reed, D. B., & Cronin, J. S. (2003). Health on the road: Issues faced by female truck drivers. *AAOHN Journal : Official Journal of the American Association of Occupational Health Nurses, 51*(3), 120–125. doi:10.1177/216507990305100305 PMID:12670099

Reeves, T. C., McKinney, A. P., & Azam, L. (2013). Muslim women's workplace experiences: Implications for Strategic Diversity Initiatives. Equality, Diversity and Inclusion: An International Journal, 32(1), 49-67.

Reichers, A. E., & Schneider, B. (1990). Climate and culture: An evolution of constructs. *Organizational Climate and Culture, 1*, 5-39.

Riach, K., & Wilson, F. (2007). Don't screw the crew: Exploring the rules of engagement in organizational romance. *British Journal of Management, 18*(1), 79–92. doi:10.1111/j.1467-8551.2006.00503.x

Richardson, J., & McKenna, S. (2006). Exploring Relationships with home and host countries. *Cross Cultural Management, 13*(1), 6–22. doi:10.1108/13527600610643448

Riedy, M. K., & Wen, J. H. (2010). Electronic surveillance of Internet access in the American workplace: Implications for management. *Information & Communications Technology Law, 19*(1), 87–99. doi:10.1080/13600831003726374

Riggle, R. J. (2007). *The impact of organizational climate variables of perceived organizational support, workplace isolation, and ethical climate on salesperson psychological and behavioral work outcomes.* University of South Florida, Graduation Thesis.

Rintala, N., & Suolanen, S. (2005). The implications of digitalization for job descriptions, competencies and the quality of working life. *Nordicom Review, 26*(2), 53–67. doi:10.1515/nor-2017-0258 PMID:17290637

Riordan, C. M., & Griffeth, R. W. (1995). The opportunity for friendship in the workplace: An underexplored construct. *Journal of Business and Psychology, 10*(2), 141–154. doi:10.1007/BF02249575

Ritz, A., Brewer, G., & Neumann, O. (2016). Public Service Motivation: A Systematic Literature Review and Outlook. *Public Administration Review, 76*(3), 414–426. doi:10.1111/puar.12505

Robbins, S. P., Coulter, M., & Fernandez, A. (2018). *Management* (14th ed.). Pearson India Education Services Pvt. Ltd.

Roberts, J. A., & David, M. E. (2017). Put down your phone and listen to me: How boss phubbing undermines the psychological conditions necessary for employee engagement. *Computers in Human Behavior, 75*, 206–217. doi:10.1016/j.chb.2017.05.021

Robertson, B. W., & Kee, K. F. (2017). Social media at work: The roles of job satisfaction, employment status, and Facebook use with co-workers. *Computers in Human Behavior, 70*, 191–196. doi:10.1016/j.chb.2016.12.080

Robinson, D., Perryman, S., & Hayday, S. (2004). *The Drivers of Employee Engagement. Report 408*. Institute for Employment Studies.

Robinson, S. L., & O'Leary-Kelly, A. M. (1998). Monkey see, monkey do: The influence of work groups on the antisocial behavior of employees. *Academy of Management Journal, 41*(6), 658–672.

Robinson, S., & Bennett, R. (1995). A typology of deviant workplace behaviors: A multi-dimensional scaling study. *Academy of Management Journal, 38*, 555–572.

Robinson, S., & Bennett, R. (1997). Workplace deviance: Its definition, its manifestations, and its causes. *Research on Negotiations in Organizations, 6*, 3–27.

Robinson, S., & Greenberg, J. (1999). Employees behaving badly: Dimensions, determinants and dilemmas in the study of workplace deviance. In D. M. Rousseau & C. Cooper (Eds.), *Trends in organizational behavior* (Vol. 5, pp. 1–23). Wiley.

Roethlisberger, F.J., & Dickson, W. (1939). Management and the Worker. Harvard University Press.

Rogerson-Revell, P. (2007). Using English for international business: A European case study. *English for Specific Purposes, 26*(1), 103–120. doi:10.1016/j.esp.2005.12.004

Rosenau, P., & Linder, S. (2003). Two Decades of Research Comparing For-Profit and Nonprofit Health Provider Performance in the United States. *Social Science Quarterly, 84*(2), 219–241. doi:10.1111/1540-6237.8402001

Rosen, L., & Samuel, A. (2015). Conquering digital distraction. *Harvard Business Review, 93*(6), 110–113.

Rothwell, G. R., & Baldwin, J. N. (2006). Ethical climates and contextual predictors of whistle-blowing. *Review of Public Personnel Administration, 26*(3), 216–244. doi:10.1177/0734371X05278114

Rubin, M., Paolini, S., Subašić, E., & Giacomini, A. (2019). A confirmatory study of the relations between workplace sexism, sense of belonging, mental health, and job satisfaction among women in male-dominated industries. *Journal of Applied Social Psychology, 49*(5), 267–282. doi:10.1111/jasp.12577

Ruby, P., & Decety, J. (2004). How Would You Feel versus How Do You Think She Would Feel? A Neuroimaging Study of Perspective-Taking with Social Emotions. *Journal of Cognitive Neuroscience, 16*(6), 988–999. doi:10.1162/0898929041502661 PMID:15298786

Rugman, A. M. (1979). *International diversification and the multinational enterprise*. Academic Press.

Rui, H., Zhang, M., & Shipman, A. (2017). Chinese expatriate management in emerging markets: A competitive advantage perspective. *Journal of International Management, 23*(2), 124–138. doi:10.1016/j.intman.2017.01.002

Russell, G. (2015). Does paying for performance in primary care save. *BMJ (Clinical Research Ed.), 350*(mar02 5), h1051. doi:10.1136/bmj.h1051 PMID:25731697

Ryan, A. M., & Kossek, E. E. (2008). Work-life policy implementation: Breaking down or creating barriers to inclusiveness? *Human Resource Management, 47*(2), 295–310.

Ryoo, S. Y., & Koo, C. (2010). The moderating effect of media synchronicity in the communication media use and knowledge creation. *Asia Pacific Journal of Information Systems, 20*(2), 103-124.

Saat, R. M., & Selamat, M. H. (2014). An examination of consumer's attitude towards corporate social responsibility (CSR) web communication using media richness theory. *Procedia: Social and Behavioral Sciences, 155*(C), 392–397. doi:10.1016/j.sbspro.2014.10.311

Sackett, P. R., & DeVore, C. J. (2002). Counterproductive behaviors at work. In N. Anderson, D. S. Ones, H. K. Sinangil, & C. Viswesvaran (Eds.), Handbook of industrial, work and organizational psychology, Vol. 1. Personnel psychology (p. 145–164). Sage Publications Ltd.

Sadi, S. A., & Noordin, M. F. (2011). Factors influencing the adoption of M-commerce: An exploratory Analysis. *Proceeding of the 2011 International Conference on Industrial Engineering and Operations Management.*

Safeer, R., & Allen, J. (2019). Defining a Culture of Health in the Workplace. *Journal of Occupational and Environmental Medicine, 61*(11), 863–867. doi:10.1097/JOM.0000000000001684 PMID:31348414

Şahin, B., & Dündar, T. (2011). Sağlık sektöründe etik iklim ve yildirma (mobbing) davranişlari arasindaki ilişkinin incelenmesi. *Ankara Üniversitesi SBF Dergisi, 66*(01), 129–159. doi:10.1501/SBFder_0000002198

Salancik, G. R., & Pfeffer, J. (1978). A social information processing approach to job attitudes and task design. *Administrative Science Quarterly, 23*(2), 224–253. doi:10.2307/2392563 PMID:10307892

Salanova, M., Agut, S., & Peiró, J. M. (2005). Linking Organizational Resources and Work Engagement to Employee Performance and Customer Loyalty: The Mediation of Service Climate. *The Journal of Applied Psychology, 90*(6), 1217–1227.

Salomon, M. F., & Schork, J. M. (2003). Turn Diversity to Your Advantage. *Research Technology Management*, *46*(4), 37–44. doi:10.1080/08956308.2003.11671575

Samaranayake, V., & Gamage, C. (2011). Employee Perception towards Electronic Monitoring at Work Place and Its Impact on Job Satisfaction of Software Professionals in Sri Lanka. *Telematics and Informatics*, *29*(2), 233–244. doi:10.1016/j.tele.2011.08.003

Samwell, J.O. (2018). Effects of employee relations on employee performance and organizational performance- study of small organizations in Tanzania. *Global Journal of Management and Research: Administration and Management, 18*(8).

Sánchez Abril, P., Levin, A., & Del Riego, A. (2012). Blurred boundaries: Social media privacy and the twenty-first-century employee. *American Business Law Journal*, *49*(1), 63–124. doi:10.1111/j.1744-1714.2011.01127.x

Sanyal, S., & Hisam, M. W. (2018). The impact of teamwork on work performance of employees: A study of faculty members in Dhofar University. *IOSR Journal of Business and Management*, *20*(3), 15–21. doi:10.9790/487X-2003011522

Sapienza, H. J., Autio, E., George, G., & Zahra, S. A. (2006). A capabilities perspective on the effects of early internationalization on firm survival and growth. *Academy of Management Review*, *31*(4), 914–933. doi:10.5465/amr.2006.22527465

Sarangi, D. (2016). *Employee Engagement and Its Impact on Organizational Success – A Study in Manufacturing Company* (pp. 52–57). India: IOSR Journal of Business and Management.

Sashi, C. M. (2012). Customer engagement, buyer-seller relationships, and social media. *Management Decision*, *50*(2), 253–272.

Sawhney, M., Verona, G., & Prandelli, E. (2005). Collaborating to create: The Internet as a platform for customer engagement in product innovation. *Journal of Interactive Marketing*, *19*(4), 4–17.

Saxena, A. (2014). Workforce Diversity: A Key to Improve Productivity. *Procedia Economics and Finance*, *11*, 76–85. doi:10.1016/S2212-5671(14)00178-6

Schaupp, L. C., & Bélanger, F. (2014). The value of social media for small businesses. *Information Systems*, *28*(1), 187–2. doi:10.2308/isys-50674

Scherer, F. M. (1980). *Industrial market structure and economic performance*. Rand McNally.

Schiemann, F., & Guenther, T. (2013). Earnings predictability, value relevance, and employee expenses. *The International Journal of Accounting*, *48*(2), 149–172. doi:10.1016/j.intacc.2013.04.001

Schminke, M., Ambrose, M. L., & Neubaum, D. O. (2005). The effect of leader moral development on ethical climate and employee attitudes. *Organizational Behavior and Human Decision Processes*, *97*(2), 135–151. doi:10.1016/j.obhdp.2005.03.006

Schneider, B., & Rentsch, J. (1988). Managing Climates and Cultures: A Futures Perspective. In J. Hage (Ed.), *Futures of Organizations*. San Francisco: New Lexington Press.

Schroeder, R. (1996). *Possible worlds: The social dynamic of virtual reality technology*. Boulder, CO: Westview Press.

Scott, C. R., & Stephens, K. K. (2009). It depends on who you're talking to: Predictors and outcomes of situated measures of organizational identification. *Western Journal of Communication*, *73*(4), 370–394. doi:10.1080/10570310903279075

Scott, P. R., & Jacka, J. M. (2011). *Auditing Social Media: A Governance and Risk Guide*. John Wiley & Sons.

Sebastian, V. (2014). Neuromarketing and Neuroethics. *Procedia: Social and Behavioral Sciences*, *127*, 763–768. doi:10.1016/j.sbspro.2014.03.351

Segal, Z., Williams, M. R., & Teasdale, J. (2002). *Mindfulness-based cognitive therapy for depression: A new approach to preventing relapse*. Guilford Press.

Senevirathna, G.A.B.E. (2017). *Factors affecting employee retention*. Academic Press.

Sequeira, A.H., & Dhriti, A. (2015). *Employee relations and its impacts on employee performance: a case study*. doi:10.13140/RG.2.1.3942.5446

Serra, D., Serneels, P., & Barr, A. (2011). Intrisic motivations and the non-profit health sector: Evidence from Ethiopia. *Personality and Individual Differences*, *51*(3), 309–314. doi:10.1016/j.paid.2010.04.018

Shachaf, P. (2008). Cultural diversity and information and communication technology impacts on global virtual teams: An exploratory study. *Information & Management*, *45*(2), 131–142. doi:10.1016/j.im.2007.12.003

Shaheen & Naseem. (2015). A Review of Customer Satisfaction, Employee Satisfaction and their impact on Firm Performance. *International Journal of Management & Organizational Studies*, *4*(1).

Shah, N., & Ghulam Sarwar Shah, S. (2010). Relationships between employee readiness for organisational change, supervisor and peer relations and demography. *Journal of Enterprise Information Management*, *23*(5), 640–652. doi:10.1108/17410391011083074

Shani, A., & Lau, J. (2005). *Behavior in organizations: an experiential approach*. McGraw-Hill.

Sharma, N., & Singh, V. K. (2018). Psychological empowerment and employee engagement: Testing the mediating effects of constructive deviance in Indian IT Sector. *International Journal of Human Capital and Information Technology Professionals*, *9*(4), 44–55. doi:10.4018/IJHCITP.2018100103

Sharma, S., & Gautam, O. (2014). An Empirical Analysis on Office Politics in Indian Organisations. *Human Resource Reflection*, *1*(3), 86–92.

Sharma, S., & Gautam, O. (2014). An empirical analysis on office politics in Indian organizations. *Human Resource Reflection*, *1*(3), 86–92.

Sharma, V. (2016). Exploring employee retention in IT industry in India: Study based on multi response analysis. *IJCEM*, *2*(12), 86–97.

Sheer, V. C. (2010). Hong Kong adolescents' use of MSN vs. ICQ for developing friendships online: Considering media richness and presentational control. *Chinese Journal of Communication*, *3*(2), 223–240. doi:10.1080/17544751003740409

Sheer, V. C. (2011). Teenagers' use of MSN features, discussion topics, and online friendship development: The impact of media richness and communication control. *Communication Quarterly*, *59*(1), 82–103. doi:10.1080/01463373.2010.525702

Sheridan, J. E. (1992). Organizational culture and employee retention. *Academy of Management Journal*, *35*(5), 1036–1049.

Shore, L. M., & Wayne, S. J. (1993). Commitment and employee behavior: Comparison of affective commitment and continuance commitment with perceived organizational support. *The Journal of Applied Psychology*, *78*(5), 774–780. doi:10.1037/0021-9010.78.5.774 PMID:8253631

Shrivastava, A., Sharma, M. K., & Marimuthu, P. (2016). Internet use at workplaces and its effects on working style in indian context: An exploration. *Indian Journal of Occupational and Environmental Medicine*, *20*(2), 88. doi:10.4103/0019-5278.197531 PMID:28194082

Sicsic, J., Le Vaillant, M., & Franc, C. (2014). Building a composite score of general practitioners' intrinsic motivation: A comparison of methods. *International Journal for Quality in Health Care*, *26*(2), 167–173. doi:10.1093/intqhc/mzu007 PMID:24521704

Simha, A., & Cullen, J. B. (2012). Ethical climates and their effects on organizational outcomes: Implications from the past and prophecies for the future. *The Academy of Management Perspectives*, *26*(4), 20–34. doi:10.5465/amp.2011.0156

Simonetti, J. L., & Boseman, F. G. (1975). The impact of market competition on organization structure and effectiveness: A cross- cultural study. *Academy of Management Journal*, *18*(3), 631–638.

Simons, T., & Roberson, Q. (2003). Why managers should care about fairness: The effects of aggregate justice perceptions on organizational outcomes. *The Journal of Applied Psychology*, *88*(3), 432–443. doi:10.1037/0021-9010.88.3.432 PMID:12814293

Sims, R. L., & Keon, T. L. (1997). Ethical work climate as a factor in the development of person-organization fit. *Journal of Business Ethics*, *16*(11), 1095–1105. doi:10.1023/A:1017914502117

Singh, D. (2019). A Literature Review on Employee Retention with Focus on Recent Trends. *International Journal of Scientific Research in Science, Engineering and Technology*, 425–431. doi:10.32628/IJSRST195463

Singh, Y. (2020). Workplace Deviance: A Conceptual Framework. In *Analyzing Workplace Deviance in Modern Organizations* (pp. 1–22). IGI Global. doi:10.4018/978-1-5225-9996-8.ch001

Sluijs, E., & Kluytmans, F. (2017). *Business Strategy and Human Resource Management: Setting the Scene*. Academic Press.

Smith, D. C. (1977). *Pygmalion. A computer program to model and stimulate creative thought*. BirkhaüserVerlag.

Smith, H. J., Thompson, R., & Iacovou, C. (2009). The impact of ethical climate on project status misreporting. *Journal of Business Ethics, 90*(4), 577–591. doi:10.100710551-009-0062-8

Smollan, R. K., & Sayers, J. G. (2009). Organizational culture, change and emotions: A qualitative study. *Journal of Change Management, 9*(4), 435–457. doi:10.1080/14697010903360632

Sollner, R. (2010). *Human Capital Diversity and Product Innovation: A Micro-Level Analysis*. JENA Economic Research Papers.

Solnais, C. A.-P.-F.-A., Andreu-Perez, J., Sánchez-Fernández, J., & Andréu-Abela, J. (2013). The contribution of neuroscience to consumer research: A conceptual framework and empirical review. *Journal of Economic Psychology, 36*, 68–81. doi:10.1016/j.joep.2013.02.011

Song, X. (2017). *The Impact of Regulatory Focus and Perceived Organizational Benevolent Climate on Innovative Behaviors of Knowledge Workers*. Academic Press.

Spanos, Y. E., & Lioukas, S. (2001). An examination into the causal logic of rent generation: Contrasting Porter's competitive strategy framework and the resource-based perspective. *Strategic Management Journal, 22*(10), 907–934. doi:10.1002mj.174

Stahl, G. K., Maznevski, M. L., Voigt, A., & Jonsen, K. (2010). Unraveling the effects of cultural diversity in teams: A meta-analysis of research on multicultural work groups. *Journal of International Business Studies, 41*(4), 690–709. doi:10.1057/jibs.2009.85

Staw, B. M. (1984). Organizational behavior: A review and reformulation of the field's outcome variables. *Annual Review of Psychology, 35*(1), 627–666. doi:10.1146/annurev.ps.35.020184.003211 PMID:19400627

Steele, R., & Derven, M. (2015). Diversity & Inclusion and innovation: A virtuous cycle. *Industrial and Commercial Training, 47*(1), 1–7. doi:10.1108/ICT-09-2014-0063

Steiner, G. (1969). *Strategic factors in business success*. New York: Financial Executive Research Foundation.

Stephens, K., Barrett, A. K., & Mahometa, M. J. (2013). Organizational communication in emergencies: Using multiple channels and sources to combat noise and capture attention. *Human Communication Research, 39*(2), 230–251. doi:10.1111/hcre.12002

Steuer, J. S. (1992). Defining virtual reality: Dimensions determining telepresence. *Journal of Communication, 42*(4), 73–93. doi:10.1111/j.1460-2466.1992.tb00812.x

Stinchcombe, A. L. (2000). *Social structure and organizations*. Emerald Group Publishing Limited. doi:10.1016/S0742-3322(00)17019-6

Strauss, A., & Corbin, J. M. (1990). *Basics of qualitative research: Grounded theory procedures and techniques*. Sage.

Subiyanto, E. (2019). OBOR: A New Hope for Future Indonesian or a New Trap? Case Study in Indonesia. In *Foreign Business in China and Opportunities for Technological Innovation and Sustainable Economics* (pp. 143–156). IGI Global. doi:10.4018/978-1-5225-8980-8.ch007

Subiyanto, E. (2020). A Failure Innovation Strategy of Acquisition during Excess Capaci-ty: Financial Approach based-on Case Study at the State-owned Cement Holding PT Semen Indonesia (Persero) Tbk. *Journal of Innovation and Entrepreneurship*, *9*(1), 20. Advance online publication. doi:10.118613731-020-00134-4

Subramaniam, K.R. (2017). Employer employee relationship and impact on organization structure and strategy. *International Journal of Innovative Trends in Engineering, 27*(43), 39-44.

Sullivan, D. (1994). Measuring the degree of internationalization of a firm. *Journal of International Business Studies*, *25*(2), 325–342. doi:10.1057/palgrave.jibs.8490203

Sun, Y., & Shang, R. A. (2014). The interplay between users' intraorganizational social media use and social capital. *Computers in Human Behavior*, *37*, 334–341. doi:10.1016/j.chb.2014.03.048

Sutherland, J. (2017). Job control, job demands and job satisfaction in Britain: trends and inter-relationships. In *Scottish centre for employment research* (pp. 1–18). SCER.

Swaminathan, P.S., & Rajkumar, S. (2013). Stress levels in organizations and their impact on employees' behaviour. *BVIMR Management Edge, 6*(1), 79-87.

Tannenbaum, S. I., & Yukl, G. (1992). Training and development in work organizations. *Annual Review of Psychology*, *43*, 399–441.

Tansel, A., & Gazioglu, S. (2013). *Management-Employee Relations, Firm Size and Job Satisfaction. IZA Discussion Papers, No. 7308. Institute for the Study of Labor*. IZA.

Tenzer, H., & Pudelko, M. (2017). The influence of language differences on power dynamics in multinational teams. *Journal of World Business*, *52*(1), 45–61. doi:10.1016/j.jwb.2016.11.002

Tenzer, H., Pudelko, M., & Harzing, A.-W. (2014). The impact of language barriers on trust formation in multinational teams. *Journal of International Business Studies*, *45*(5), 508–535. doi:10.1057/jibs.2013.64

Teo, T. S. (2001). Demographic and motivation variables associated with internet usage activities. *Internet Research*, *11*(2), 125–137.

Thomas, E. (2013). Supplier integration in new product development: Computer mediated communication, knowledge exchange and buyer performance. *Industrial Marketing Management*, *42*(6), 890–899. doi:10.1016/j.indmarman.2013.05.018

Thomas, K. W. (2015). *Making Conflict Management a Strategic Advantage*. CPP Inc.

Thomas, R. R., & Woodruff, M. I. (1999). *Building a house for diversity: how a fable about a giraffe & an elephant offers new strategies for today's workforce*. American Management Association.

Thompson, K. H., & Greene, R. R. (1994). Role theory and social work practice. *Human behavior theory: A diversity framework*, 93-114.

Thompson, K., & Keating, M. (2004). An empirical study of executive nationality staffing practices in foreign-owned MNC subsidiaries in Ireland. *Thunderbird International Business Review*, *46*(6), 771–797. doi:10.1002/tie.20035

Tiago, M. T. P. M. B., & Veríssimo, J. M. C. (2014). Digital marketing and social media: Why bother? *Business Horizons*, *57*(6), 703–708. doi:10.1016/j.bushor.2014.07.002

Tim, G., Stefan, S., & Kristina, P. (2019). Assessing the role of dynamic capabilities in local food distribution: A theory-elaboration study. *Supply Chain Management*, *24*(6), 767–783. doi:10.1108/SCM-02-2019-0073

Timonen, H., & Vuori, J. (2018, January). Visibility of Work: How Digitalization Changes the Workplace. *Proceedings of the 51st Hawaii International Conference on System Sciences*. 10.24251/HICSS.2018.634

Tiwari, D.N., & Tyagi, S. (2014). Impact of globalization on work life balance in IFFCO, AONLA, BAREILLEY. *International Journal of Research in Commerce and Management, 5*(8), 55-57.

Tiwari, B., & Lenka, U. (2015). Building and branding talent hub: An outlook. *Industrial and Commercial Training*, *47*(4), 208–211. doi:10.1108/ICT-11-2014-0077

Tlaiss, H. A., Martin, P., & Hofaidhllaoui, M. (2017). Talent retention: Evidence from a multinational firm in France. *Employee Relations*, *39*(4), 426–445. doi:10.1108/ER-07-2016-0130

Totterdell, P., Wall, T., Holman, D., Diamond, H., & Epitropaki, O. (2004). Affect networks: A structural analysis of the relationship between work ties and job-related affect. *The Journal of Applied Psychology*, *89*(5), 854–867. doi:10.1037/0021-9010.89.5.854 PMID:15506865

Treem, J. W., & Leonardi, P. M. (2012). Social media use in organizations: Exploring the affordances of visibility, editability, persistence, and association. *Communication Yearbook*, *36*, 143–189.

Trevino, L. K. (1986). Ethical decision making in organizations: A person-situation interactionist model. *Academy of Management Review*, *11*(3), 601–617. doi:10.5465/amr.1986.4306235

Trif, A., & Paolucci, V. (2019). Employee Relations in Context: Globalization, Uncertainties, and Dynamics of Change. In K. Koch & P. Manzella (Eds.), International Comparative Employee Relations (pp. 14–38). Edward Elgar Publishing. doi:10.4337/9781788973229.00011

Trinkle, B., Crossler, R., & Bélanger, F. (2015). Voluntary disclosures via social media and the role of comments. *Journal of Information Systems*, *29*(2), 101–122. doi:10.2308/isys-51133

Tsai, M. T., & Huang, C. C. (2008). The relationship among ethical climate types, facets of job satisfaction, and the three components of organizational commitment: A study of nurses in Taiwan. *Journal of Business Ethics*, *80*(3), 565–581. doi:10.100710551-007-9455-8

Tuan, L. T. (2019). Can managing employee diversity be a pathway to creativity for tour companies? *International Journal of Contemporary Hospitality Management*.

Tuna, M., & Yeşiltaş, M. (2014). Etik iklim, işe yabancılaşma ve örgütsel özdeşleşmenin işten ayrılma niyeti üzerindeki etkisi: Otel işletmelerinde bir araştırma. *Anatolia: Turizm Araştırmaları Dergisi*, *25*(1), 105–117.

Turkle, S. (2008). Always-on/Always-on-you: The Tethered Self. In J. E. Katz (Ed.), *Handbook of Mobile Communication Studies*. MIT Press. doi:10.7551/mitpress/9780262113120.003.0010

Turnipseed, D. L. (1988). An integrated, interactive model of organisational climate, culture and effectiveness. *Leadership and Organization Development Journal*, *9*(5), 17–21. doi:10.1108/eb053644

Ugrin, J. C., & Pearson, J. M. (2013). The effects of sanctions and stigmas on cyberloafing. *Computers in Human Behavior*, *29*(3), 812–820. doi:10.1016/j.chb.2012.11.005

Ullah, Z., Khan, M. Z., & Siddique, M. (2017). Analysis of employees' perception of workplace support and level of motivation in public sector healthcare organization. *Business and Economic Review*, *9*(3), 240–256. doi:10.22547/BER/9.3.10

Ulrich, C., O'Donnell, P., Taylor, C., Farrar, A., Danis, M., & Grady, C. (2007). Ethical climate, ethics stress, and the job satisfaction of nurses and social workers in the United States. *Social Science & Medicine*, *65*(8), 1708–1719. doi:10.1016/j.socscimed.2007.05.050 PMID:17619068

Urbancova, H., & Snydrova, M. (2017). Remuneration and employee benefits in organizations in the benefits in organizations in the Czech Republic. *Acta Universitatis agriculturae et Silviculturae mendelianae Brunsis, 65*, 357-363. . doi:10.11118/actaun201765010357

Valentine, S., Godkin, L., & Varca, P. E. (2010). Role conflict, mindfulness, and organizational ethics in an education-based healthcare institution. *Journal of Business Ethics*, *94*(3), 455–469. doi:10.100710551-009-0276-9

Valkenburg, P. M., Peter, J., & Schouten, A. P. (2006). Friend networking sites and their relationship to adolescents' well-being and social self esteem. *Cyberpsychology & Behavior*, *9*(5), 584–590. doi:10.1089/cpb.2006.9.584 PMID:17034326

Van Oudenhoven, J. P., van der Zee, K. I., & Van Kooten, M. (2001). Successful adaptation strategies according expatriates. *International Journal of Intercultural Relations*, *25*(5), 467–482. doi:10.1016/S0147-1767(01)00018-9

Vardi, Y. (2001). The effects of organizational and ethical climates on misconduct at work. *Journal of Business Ethics*, *29*(4), 325–337. doi:10.1023/A:1010710022834

Vardi, Y., & Wiener, Y. (1996). Misbehavior in organizations: A motivational framework. *Organization Science*, *7*(2), 151–165. doi:10.1287/orsc.7.2.151

Venkatraman, S. M. K., Cheung, C., Lee, Z. W. D., Davis, F., & Venkatesh, V. (2018). The "Darth" side of technology use: An inductively derived typology of cyberdeviance. *Journal of Management Information Systems*, *35*(4), 1060–1091. doi:10.1080/07421222.2018.1523531

Victor, B., & Cullen, J. B. (1987). A theory and measure of ethical climate in organizations. In W. C. Frederick (Ed.), *Research in corporate social performance and policy* (pp. 51–71). JAI Press.

Victor, B., & Cullen, J. B. (1988). The organizational bases of ethical work climates. *Administrative Science Quarterly*, *33*(1), 101–125. doi:10.2307/2392857

Vitak, J., Crouse, J., & LaRose, R. (2011). Personal Internet use at work: Understanding cyberslacking. *Computers in Human Behavior*, *27*(5), 1751–1759. doi:10.1016/j.chb.2011.03.002

Vlahovic, T., Roberts, S., & Dunbar, R. (2012). Effects of duration and laughter on subjective happiness within different modes of communication. *Journal of Computer-Mediated Communication*, *17*(4), 436–450. doi:10.1111/j.1083-6101.2012.01584.x

Vorvoreanu, M., & Baton, C. H. (2000). Examining electronic surveillance in the workplace: A review of theoretical perspectives and research findings. Conference of the International Communication Association.

Vu, M. C., & Gill, R. (2018). Is there corporate mindfulness? An exploratory study of Buddhist-enacted spiritual leaders' perspectives and practices. *Journal of Management, Spirituality & Religion*, *15*(2), 155–177. doi:10.1080/14766086.2017.1410491

Vyas, J. H., & Shrivastava, R. (2011). Employee Perception of Corporate Social Responsibility and Job Satisfaction in Large Scale Units. *Prabandhan: Indian Journal of Management*, *4*(12), 23.

Wals, K. (2010). *Key Issues in Strategic Human Resources*. Cornell University.

Walther, J. B., & Parks, M. R. (2002). Cues filtered out, cues filtered in Computers-mediated communications add relationships. In Handbook of interpersonal communication. Academic Press.

Wang, D., Fan, D., Freeman, S., & Zhu, C. J. (2017). Exploring cross-cultural skills for expatriate managers from Chinese multinationals: Congruence and contextualization. *Asia Pacific Journal of Management*, *34*(1), 123–146. doi:10.100710490-016-9474-z

Weedmark, D. (2019, May 16). *What are some positive & negative technology training impacts on an employee?* Retrieved from: https://smallbusiness.chron.com/positive-negative-technology-training-impacts-employee-37082.html

Weick, K. E., & Sutcliffe, K. M. (2006). Mindfulness and the quality of organizational attention. *Organization Science*, *17*(4), 514–524. doi:10.1287/orsc.1060.0196

Wei, T. T., Marthandan, G., Chong, A. Y.-L., Ooi, K. B., & Arumugam, S. (2009). What drives Malayasian m-commerce adoption? An empirical analysis. *Industrial Management & Data Systems*, *109*, 370–388.

Wen, H. J., Schwieger, D., & Gershuny, P. (2007). Internet usage monitoring in the workplace its legal challenges and implementation strategies. *Information Systems Management*, *24*(2), 185–196. doi:10.1080/10580530701221072

WhatI. C. E.WhyI. I. I. (2019). Retrieved from https://blog.smile.io/what-is-customer-engagement-and-why-is-it-important

Why Diversity is the Mother of Creativity. (2019, November 13). Retrieved from https://innovationmanagement.se/imtool-articles/why-diversity-is-the-mother-of-creativity/

Wikina, S. B. (2015). *Diversity and inclusion in the information technology industry: relating perceptions and expectations to demographic dimensions* (Doctoral dissertation).

Williams, J. J., & Seaman, A. E. (2016). The influence of ethical leadership on managerial performance: Mediating effects of mindfulness and corporate social responsibility. *Journal of Applied Business Research*, *32*(3), 815–828. doi:10.19030/jabr.v32i3.9659

Williams, K. D. (2001). *Ostracism: The power of silence*. Guilford Press.

Wimbush, J. C., & Shepard, J. M. (1994). Toward an understanding of ethical climate: Its relationship to ethical behavior and supervisory influence. *Journal of Business Ethics*, *13*(8), 637–647. doi:10.1007/BF00871811

Winstead, B. A., Derlega, V. J., Montgomery, M. J., & Pilkington, C. (1995). The quality of friendships at work and job satisfaction. *Journal of Social and Personal Relationships*, *12*(2), 199–215. doi:10.1177/0265407595122003

Witte, N. I. E. L. S. (2014). *Technology Acceptance of Business Meetings in a 3D Virtual Environment Supported by a Content Management System* (Master's thesis). University of Twente.

Woodard, N., & Saini, D. S. (2006). *Diversity management issues in USA and India: Some emerging perspectives*. Academic Press.

Wright, T. (2016). Women's Experience of Workplace Interactions in Male-Dominated Work: The Intersections of Gender, Sexuality and Occupational Group. In Gender, Work and Organization (1st ed.). Palgrave Macmillan UK. doi:10.1111/gwao.12074

Wright, P. M., Dunford, B. B., & Snell, S. A. (2001). Human resources and the resource based view of the firm. *Journal of Management*, *27*(6), 701–721. doi:10.1177/014920630102700607

Wyatt, K., & Phillips, J. G. (2005). Internet Use and Misuse in the Workplace. *Proceedings of the 17th Australian Conference on Computer-Human Interaction.*

Wyatt-Walter, A. (1995). Globalization, corporate identity and European technology policy1. *Journal of European Public Policy*, *2*(3), 427–446. doi:10.1080/13501769508406996

Xu, D., & Meyer, K. E. (2013). Linking theory and context: 'Strategy research in emerging economies' after Wright et al. (2005). *Journal of Management Studies, 50*(7), 1322–1346.

Yamamoto, H. (2011). The relationship between employee benefit management and employee retention. *International Journal of Human Resource Management, 22*(17), 3550–3564. doi:10.1080/09585192.2011.560871

Yasir, M., & Rasli, A. (2018). Direct and indirect effects of ethical leadership on workplace deviance in public healthcare sector of Pakistan. *Journal of Advances in Management Research, 15*(4), 558–574. doi:10.1108/JAMR-11-2017-0109

Yavuz, M. (2019). *Mindfulness-based interventions for the organisational outcomes: a systematic literature review* (Unpublished master thesis). University of Leicester.

Yavuz, M., Ozbilgin, M. F., & Kamasak, R. (2020). Exploring the Interplay Between Deviance and Loneliness at Work. In *Analyzing Workplace Deviance in Modern Organizations* (pp. 48–65). IGI Global. doi:10.4018/978-1-5225-9996-8.ch003

Yener, M., Yaldıran, M., & Ergun, S. (2012). The effect of ethical climate on work engagement. *Procedia: Social and Behavioral Sciences, 58*, 724–733. doi:10.1016/j.sbspro.2012.09.1050

Yeşil, S., Mavi, Y., & Ceylan, S. (2017). Etik İklim Algisi ve Bireysel Sonuçlar Üzerine Etkileri. *Dumlupınar Üniversitesi Sosyal Bilimler Dergisi*, (51), 19–38.

Yilmaz, A. T., & Yildirim, A. (2019). Bir Üniversite Hastanesinde Çalişan Hemşirelerin Etik İklim Algisi. *Elektronik Sosyal Bilimler Dergisi, 18*(69), 162–176.

Yüksel, S. (2012). *The impact of perceptions of ethical work climates and organizational justice on workplace deviance* (Unpublished Doctoral Dissertation). Ankara: Middle East Technical University.

Yurdakul, M. (2013). *İş ahlakında etik iklim: Bireysel ve kurumsal özellikler açısından etik iklimin bankacılık sektöründe araştırılması*. İstanbul Üniversitesi Sosyal Bilimler Enstitüsü Uluslararası İşletmecilik Anabilim Dalı Yayınlanmamış Yüksek Lisans Tezi.

Zaheer, S. (1995). Overcoming the liability of foreignness. *Academy of Management Journal, 38*(2), 341–363.

Zanoni, P., & Janssens, M. (2007). Minority Employees Engaging with (Diversity) Management: An Analysis of Control, Agency, and Micro-Emancipation. *Journal of Management Studies, 44*(0), 8. doi:10.1111/j.1467-6486.2007.00700.x

Zheng, Y., & Smith, C. (2019). Tiered expatriation: A social relations approach to staffing multinationals. *Human Resource Management, 58*(5), 489–502. doi:10.1002/hrm.21937

Zhong, L., Wayne, S. J., & Liden, R. C. (2016). Job engagement, perceived organizational support, high- performance human resource practices, and cultural value orientations: Across-level investigation. *Journal of Organizational Behavior, 37*(6), 823–844. doi:10.1002/job.2076

Zhou, Z., Su, C., Zhou, N., & Zhang, N. (2016). Becoming friends in online brand communities: Evidence from China. *Journal of Computer-Mediated Communication*, *21*(1), 69–86. doi:10.1111/jcc4.12147

Zoghbi-Manrique-de-Lara, P., & Guerra-Baez, R. (2016). Exploring the influence of ethical climate on employee compassion in the hospitality industry. *Journal of Business Ethics*, *133*(3), 605–617. doi:10.100710551-014-2415-1

Zywica, J., & Danowski, J. (2008). The faces of Facebookers: Investigating social enhancement and social compensation hypotheses; Predicting Facebook and offline popularity from sociability and self-esteem, and mapping the meanings of popularity with semantic networks. *Journal of Computer-Mediated Communication*, *14*(1), 1–34. doi:10.1111/j.1083-6101.2008.01429.x

About the Contributors

Radha Yadav is currently working as an Assistant Professor (HR/OB) at Dayananda Sagar University, Bangalore (India). She completed her doctorate degree from Indian Institute of Technology Roorkee, Uttarakhand (India). She has over 7 years' experience in research and academics. Dr. Yadav has published numerous articles in reputed journals and is also experienced as an Editor in special issue of Scopus & ABDC Category journals, Her research interests include Climate change, Climate anxiety, Climate behavioural action, employee relation, women entrepreneurship, organizational commitment, quality of work life, stress and spirituality. Her research techniques include quantitative and qualitative analysis by a various statistical softwares and tools. She is currently representing India on the International project "Climate change and well-being" with De Montfort University, Leicester, UK.

Priyanka Panday is currently working as Assistant Professor (HR/Marketing) at Doon Business School, India. She has over 7 years of work experience in research and academics. She has submitted her Ph.D. in the area of talent management. She has previously taught at Chandigarh University, Mohali, India. Her teaching pedagogy emphasizes on a 'Learning Mindset' and 'Experiential Learning'. Some of the subjects and courses taught by her are Training and Development, Talent management, Managing Organizational Change and organizational development, her research interest includes workforce bullying, employee relation, and gender diversity'. She has published research papers and articles in reputed international publications.

Naman Sharma is currently affiliated with the Indian Institute of Foreign Trade, Kolkata (India) as an Assistant Professor, and has nearly six years of academic experience. Dr Sharma's field of interest is Human Resource Management, Organizational Behavior, Managerial Communication and Entrepreneurship. In his past endeavours, Dr Sharma has worked with Entrepreneruship Development Institute of India and was fortunate to be a part of Entrepreneurial ecosystem of the country. Dr Sharma also has substantial research experience, and his research has been published in ABDC ranked/Scopus Indexed journals and other reputable publishers such as Springer and Emerald Publishing Group. He has also authored/ edited five books with publishers of international repute such as World Scientific/ IGI-Global and is a serving guest editor for various reputed journals.

* * *

Pooja Agrawal currently working in Vishwakarma University as management faculty. Her area of expertise are competency mapping, leadership and Human resource management.

Deeksha Ahuja is a Ph.D student of Faculty of Management Studies at Gurukula Kangri Vishwavidyalaya, Haridwar. She is MBA with specialisation of Human Resource and Finance from Uttarakhand Technical University and B.Com (CFA) from HNBGU. Her research area is Human Resource Management, Corporate Governance and History of Ancient India.

İhsan Akca is an air traffic controller in Turkey. He works as an ATC more than 11 years. He has a master degree in public management. He has studies in management, international relations and aviation related topics.

Meltem Akca is an assistant professor in Alanya Alaaddin Keykubat University. In addition to management, organizational behaviour, entrepreneurship and strategy related area, she is interested in aviation sector. She has cooperation in the aviation industry with many scholars.

Ashish Arya is the Assistant Professor in Faculty of Management Studies, Gurukula Kangri Vishwavidyalaya, Haridwar. By qualification, he is B.E, MBA, UGC (NET), Ph.D with more than 11 years of experience out of which 9 years is in the field of teaching and research in Faculty of Management Studies, Gurukula Kangri Vishwavidyalaya, Haridwar.

Gökcay Balci has obtained his PhD degree in Maritime Business Administration in 2018. Dr Balci has been working as a lecturer in logistics and freight transport at the University of Huddersfield since July 2019. He has publications in leading logistics and transport journals including International Journal of Physical Distribution and Logistics Management, Transport Policy and Journal of Transport Geography.

Luis Alberto Casado Aranda is a PhD and an Assistant Professor in the Marketing and Market Research Department at University of Granada. His research interest focuses on Decision Neuroscience, Consumer Decision Making, Electronic Commerce, Environmental, Healthy and Political Communication as well as fMRI and self-report methods. He is an expert in exploring the neural mechanisms of consumer decision making, specifically in advertising and e-commerce environments. His work has been presented in International Conferences (NeuropsychoEconomics Conferences, International Marketing Trends or International Marketing Conference AEMARK). His investigation appears in high impact peer reviewed journals such as Political Psychology, Political Behavior, Journal of Environmental Management, Journal of Cleaner Production, Journal of Interactive Marketing, Human Brain Mapping, Journal of Neuroscience, Psychology and Economics, and Cyberpsychology & Behavior.

Tanusree Chakraborty is an Associate Professor in Organizational Behaviour and Human Resource area, with Ph.D in Applied Psychology, M.A. (Applied Psychology), MBA (HR), PGDHRM, B.A. (Psychology). Dr. Chakraborty is a Psychologist and is interested in the area of understanding human behaviour. Dr. Chakraborty has been associated with the academic industry for the past 14 years. Prior to joining Rajalakshmi School of Business, she has worked with Presidency University, Bangalore as an Associate Professor. Previously she was working as a faculty and Dean PGDM programme at Thiagarajar School of Management, Madurai. A University rank holder throughout, Dr. Chakraborty was an ex-research fellow with Indian Council of Medical Research. She has hands on experience in coaching and counseling too. As a Trainer, Dr. Chakraborty has facilitated approx. 100 sessions for both public and private sector organizations in the areas of Behavioural Science and Psychometric Testing. She has a number of publications in leading Scopus and ABDC indexed National and International journals. She has presented around 60 of her research papers in national and international conferences of repute.

Kadiyala Chowdary is a student at Amity School of Business, Amity University, Sector-125, Noida, Uttar Pradesh, India. She is currently pursuing her graduation in BBA (Bachelors of Business Administration) and has been granted scholarship for her academic performance. She had participated and presented her research paper in Globus conducted by Amity University.

Aditya Dhiman is the Research Scholar in the Faculty of Management Studies, Gurukula Kangri Vishwavidyalaya. He is also NET qualified and did MBA.

Francesca Di Virgilio (PhD), is Associate Professor of Organization Theory and Human Resources Management in the Department of Economics at University of Molise (Italy). She's Rector's Delegate for placement and technology transfer activities. She was Visiting scholar at Research Center of Industrial relations & Organizational behavior (IROB), Warwick Business School, Warwick (UK). She is member of the Association of Italian Organization Studies Academics (ASSIOA). She is member of Component Auditors MIUR (Italy) for program evaluation and research products Ministerial on organizational design and human resources. She is Advisor to the International Institute for Academic Research and Development (IIFARD). She is Honorary Member of the Editorial Board IJBST Journal group. She is Editorial Board member in the International Journal of Advance Study and Research Work, International Journal of Research Culture Society (IJRCS), International Journal for Innovative Research in Multidisciplinary Field (IJIRMF). She has been published in national and international academic journals and she has contributed more chapters to various edited books. She is reviewer for many International Journals. Her current research focuses on human resources management, organizational behavior, social media policy implementation at work.

Autumn Mabel Fitzpatrick has obtained her BSc Transport and Logistics from the University of Huddersfield and has worked as a truck driver in the UK.

Omvir Gautam currently working in Vishwakarma University as management faculty. His area of expertise are consumer behaviour, service marketing and business analytics.

Celina Joy is a Chartered Accountant with a PhD in Business Policy & Administration. She has industry experience of 18 years and is now teaching management students for the last eleven years.

Sergio Minué-Lorenzo, MD, PhD. Specialist in Family and Community Medicine. Doctor in Economics. Head of Integrated Health Services based on Primary Health Care WHO Collaborating Centre. Professor. Andalusian School of Public Health.

Sakshi Mittal is a student at Amity School of Business, Amity University, Sector- 125, Noida, Uttar Pradesh, India. She is currently pursuing her graduation in BBA (Bachelors of Business Administration). She had participated and presented her research paper in Globus conducted by Amity University.

Saloni Pahuja is working as Assistant Professor in Amity School of Business, Amity University, Sector- 125, Noida, Uttar Pradesh, India. She is a Computer Engineer and completed her masters in the area of Human Resource Management. She has more than nine years of experience in academics and in corporate. She has published many research papers in National and International journals of high repute. She has supervised more than hundred training and research projects at the graduate and postgraduate level. Her teaching and research interests lies in the area of Human Resource Management, Business Research, Strategic HRM, Industrial Relations, and Human Resource Planning & Acquisition. She is Gold Medalist-Awarded with Late Shri Amitabh Khandelwal Memorial Medal (Gold Medal) for being the Topper in MBA and also awarded for best research paper presentations at International level.

Somrita Saha is a double Masters degree holder pursuing a career in academics. She has done her Masters in Applied Psychology with specialization in Industrial Psychology and an MBA with dual specialization in Human Resource and Marketing Management. She has 3.5 years of experience in academics and 2 years as a freelancer corporate trainer. She has worked as a Faculty for management students as well as corporate executives. Also she has the experience of imparting behavioral training in different reputed organizations. Presently she is associated with Amity University as a Faculty for Behavioral Science. She has keen interest in research in areas of Psychology,Organizational Behaviour and Management and wants to excel in the field of academics and research.

Kirti Sharma is a Research Scholar in the Faculty of Management Studies, Gurukula Kangri Vishwavidyalaya, Haridwar. She obtained her BCom and MCom (Finance) from the HNB Garhwal University and Diploma of PGDBA from the Symbiosis, Pune. She also holds a National Certificate of Business Professional Programmer by doing 'O' level from NIELIT, formerly named as DOEACC Society. Her one Research Paper is also accepted in scopus indexed journal.

Betty Sibil is a PhD in Business Policy and Administration. She is a faculty with Pillai Institute of Management Studies and Research for the last 14 years and teaches subjects like Human Resource Management and Training and Development.

Effnu Subiyanto is a professional in PT Semen Indonesia (Persero) Tbk, one of the biggest State-owned cement corporations in Indonesia for over than 25 years experience. He earned bachelor in electrical engineering, master degree in business strategic and doctoral degree in economics. His area of expertise is logistics and transportation, economics, public policies, infrastructure and various related. He is now serving as a post-graduate lecturer at the Widya Mandala Surabaya Catholic University in Indonesia. This chapter of labor issues is due his obligation as chairman of Semen Indonesia's Union to convey the actual conditions regarding holding in Indonesian SOEs.

Malabika Tripathi is currently teaching as Assistant Professor at Amity University, Kolkata at the Department of Applied Psychology and Management. Pursuing PhD from University of Calcutta, Department of Applied Psychology. Organizational Behaviour and Human Resource Development are the core areas of research interest.

Sandeep Yadav is a PhD student in area of Strategic Management at Indian Institute of Management Kozhikode(IIMK), India. His research area is focused in international business strategy, emerging market firms internationalisation and corporate governance.

Meltem Yavuz has a PhD degree in management and organization. She has also logistigs management and psychology masters. She is founder of Mindcrafting Academy in Turkey that is a center of mindfulness based academic studies.

Index

F

G

H

I

J

L

M

N

O